# ROUSSEAU

For Stephanie

# ROUSSEAU

## An Introduction to his Psychological, Social and Political Theory

*N.J.H. Dent*

Basil Blackwell

First published 1988
First published in USA 1989

Basil Blackwell Ltd
108 Cowley Road, Oxford, OX4 1JF, UK

Basil Blackwell Inc.
432 Park Avenue South, Suite 1503
New York, NY 10016, USA

*British Library Cataloguing in Publication Data*

Dent, N.J.H. (Nicholas John Henry)
Rousseau : an introduction to his psychological, social and political theory.
1. French philosophy. Rousseau. Jean-Jacques—Critical studies
I. Title
194

ISBN 0-631-15882-0
ISBN 0-631-15883-9 pbk

*Library of Congress Cataloging in Publication Data*

Dent, N.J.H., 1945–
Rousseau : an introduction to his psychological, social, and political theory.
Bibliography: p.
Includes index.
1. Rousseau, Jean-Jacques, 1712-1778—Contributions in political
science. 2. Rousseau, Jean-Jacques, 1712-1778—Contributions in
psychology. 3. Rousseau, Jean-Jacques, 1712-1778—Contributions
in sociology.
I. Title.
JC179.R9D36 1989      306'.2      88-19246

ISBN 0-631-15882-0
ISBN 0-631-15883-9 (pbk.)

Typeset in 10 on 11½ pt Plantin
by Colset Pte Ltd, Singapore

Printed in Great Britain by
Billing & Sons Ltd, Worcester

Objects of hate are but our own chimaerae.
They arise from wounds within us.

Father Aloysius

(Henry Williamson: *The Golden Virgin*)

# Contents

# *Preface*

I have tried, throughout, to *argue* Rousseau's case through, not just to describe or narrate his ideas. I have wanted to try to show the power of his insights, to show that these cannot be dismissed or ignored. Rousseau has not, in general, been well served by his critics. It appears to have been thought more important to show how wrong he was than to understand him. I do not share that sense of importance.

Pressures of space have led me to exclude quite a lot that was included in the original project for this book. I hope that what remains is sufficiently wide in scope, and may have gained something in the concentration.

The remote instigator of my interest in Rousseau was Dr J.R.S. Wilson, who discussed with me the additional material included in the new Everyman edition of some of Rousseau's works when it appeared in 1973. I should like to thank him for starting my enthusiasm for these ideas. Another stimulus came from John Charvet's: *The Social Problem in the Philosophy of Rousseau.* I found I disagreed with almost every assessment of Rousseau he made, which provoked my combative instincts. I should like also to thank Jonathan Dancy for some very practical encouragement in getting on with this book, and my colleagues at the University of Birmingham for the great support they have given me during the past few years. Finally, I thank my mother and father for their continuous and unstinting help to me.

Sarah Blowen helped me with some translation, and Celia Charlesworth with the typing.

# *Rousseau's Works Cited in the Text*

Abbreviations, translations used, etc. Where no translation is cited, I have made my own. References, in the text and notes, have been made as follows: where I have used a published translation I have given, first, the page reference in that translation, followed, wherever possible, by the volume number, and page number, in J.-J. Rousseau: *Oeuvres Complètes*, eds B. Gagnebin and M. Raymond (Bibliothèque de la Pléiade, 1959– ). This edition of Rousseau's works is not yet complete, so reference to it has not always been possible. Thus DI 57; III, 169 signifies: *A Discourse on the Origin of Inequality* (in the translation used, by G.D.H. Cole, revised and augmented by J.H. Brumfitt and J.C. Hall) p. 57; Volume 3 of the *Oeuvres Complètes*, p. 169. Where I have made my own translation, I give only the *Oeuvres Complètes* reference. In the case of *The Social Contract* (SC) where there are two numbers they refer to Book and Chapter; a third number is a page reference.

| | |
|---|---|
| *A Discourse on the Arts and Sciences* (DAS) | in Jean-Jacques Rousseau: *The Social Contract and Discourses* tr. G.D.H. Cole; revised and augmented J.H. Brumfitt and J.C. Hall (Dent, London, 1973) |
| *A Discourse on the Origin of Inequality* (DI) | in Cole/Brumfitt/Hall |
| *Emile* (or: On Education) (E) | tr., with introduction and notes, Allan Bloom (Basic Books, New York, 1979) |
| *The Social Contract* (SC) | in Cole/Brumfitt/Hall |

| | |
|---|---|
| *A Discourse on Political Economy* (DPE) | in Cole/Brumfitt/Hall |
| 'The General Society of the Human Race' (from Geneva ms of the *Social Contract*; GSR) | in Cole/Brumfitt/Hall |
| 'Considerations on the Government of Poland' (GP) | in Rousseau: *Political Writings* tr. and ed. F. Watkins (Nelson, Edinburgh, 1953) |
| 'Constitutional Project for Corsica' (CPC) | in Watkins |
| *Reveries of the Solitary Walker* (RSW) | tr., with introduction, P. France (Penguin, London, 1979) |
| *The Confessions* (C) | tr., with introduction, J.M. Cohen (Penguin, London, 1954) |
| 'Essay on the Origin of Languages' (OL) | in Jean-Jacques Rousseau: *The First and Second Discourses and Essay on the Origin of Languages,* tr. with introduction and notes V. Gourevitch (Harper & Row, New York, 1986) |
| *Rousseau juge de Jean-Jacques* (RJ) | in *Oeuvres Complètes* Vol. I |
| *Lettres Ecrites de la Montagne* (LM) | in *Oeuvres Complètes* Vol. III |
| *Lettre à Christophe de Beaumont* (LB) | in *Oeuvres Complètes* Vol. IV |
| *Oeuvres Complètes* (OC) | J.-J. Rousseau: *Oeuvres Complètes,* eds. B. Gagnebin and M. Raymond (Bibliothèque de la Pléiade, Editions Gallimard, 1959–) |

I have also used the following abbreviation in the text:

| | |
|---|---|
| *Nicomachean Ethics* (EN) | Aristotle: *Ethica Nicomachea,* tr. W.D. Ross (*The Works of Aristotle,* Vol. IX, ed. W.D. Ross, Oxford University Press, 1963) |

A more comprehensive list of Rousseau's works, and available translations, is given in the Bibliography at the end of the book.

# Chronological Table

Several good accounts of Rousseau's life have been written (including Rousseau's own account) – see the Bibliography at the end of the book. There seemed no point in giving a discursive precis of these, so I include only a table setting down some of the events of his life that bear on the main content of this book (see also OC, I, pp. CIff).

1712　Rousseau born, in Geneva, 28 June. His mother dies, 7 July.

1728　Rousseau, disaffected, leaves Geneva. Meets Mme. de Warens; converts to Roman Catholicism.

1741　*Project for the Education of M. de Sainte-Marie.*

1742　Rousseau reads, to the Academy of Sciences, his *Project for a New Musical Notation.*

1743　Rousseau becomes secretary to the French Ambassador in Venice. Writes: *A Dissertation on Modern Music.*

1744　Leaves Venice after a quarrel with the Ambassador.

1745　Meets Thérèse Levasseur, with whom he lives as man and wife. Completes his opera: *Les Muses Galantes.*

1747　Writes: *L'Engagement Temeraire.*

1749　Rousseau supplies articles on music for d'Alembert's *Encyclopedia.* He is inspired on seeing the Dijon Academy's prize essay subject on the sciences and arts.

1750　*A Discourse on the Arts and Sciences* (the First Discourse). Rousseau wins the prize.

1751　Rousseau engages in polemical exchanges arising from the First Discourse (see V. Gourevitch (ed.), in Works Cited, above).

1752　Rousseau's opera: *Le Devin de Village,* presented with great success at Fontainebleau. The Théâtre-Français presents Rousseau's *Narcissus.*

1753　*Letter on French Music.*

1754   Rousseau rejoins the Church of Geneva.

1755   *A Discourse on the Origins of Inequality* (the Second Discourse) (Rousseau began work on this in 1753). *Discourse on Political Economy*; in Volume V of Diderot and d'Alembert's *Encyclopedia*.

1756   Rousseau takes up residence, with Thérèse and her mother, at The Hermitage. He makes extracts from, and assessments of, the works of the Abbé de Saint-Pierre (*The Project for Perpetual Peace*; *Polysynodie*). *Letter to Voltaire on Providence*. Begins to form the ideas for *La Nouvelle Héloïse (ou Julie)*.

1757   Writes *Lettres Morales*, for Mme d'Houdetot.

1758   *Letter to d'Alembert on the Theatre* (a reply to d'Alembert's article on *Geneva* in Vol. VII of his *Encyclopedia*).

1760   Rousseau is hard at work on *Émile* and *The Social Contract*.

1761   *La Nouvelle Héloïse* published, with immense success. *Essay on the Origin of Languages* completed (probably begun in the 1750s).

1762   *4 Letters to M. Malesherbes*. *Émile* and *The Social Contract* published. Rousseau persecuted. *Letter to Christopher de Beaumont*.

1763   *Dictionary of Music* prepared.

1764   *Letters from the Mountain*. Rousseau begins work on the first part of the *Confessions*.

1765   *Project for a Constitution for Corsica*; unfinished.

1766   Rousseau comes to England, in the company of 'le bon David' Hume. Quarrels with Hume.

1767   Rousseau returns to France. *Dictionary of Music* on sale. Rousseau suffers acute mental distress.

1768   Rousseau marries Thérèse.

1771   The second part of the *Confessions* completed.

1772   Rousseau begins working on *Rousseau juge de Jean-Jacques*. He works also copying music and botanizing. *Considerations on the Government of Poland*.

1774   *Dictionary of Botanical Terms*.

1776   Rousseau begins the *Reveries of a Solitary Walker*.

1778   Rousseau dies, 2 July.

# Breakdown of Contents

Since a study of Rousseau is, necessarily, a study of his works, it may be useful to have a guide as to which chapters here consider which of Rousseau's works. Since my argument is primarily thematic, however, not book-by-book, the guide is only approximate.

These are the works of Rousseau most extensively examined in the book.

# Introduction

This book principally comprises a close study of the ideas and arguments which are central, in my estimation, to four of Rousseau's works: *A Discourse on the Arts and Sciences; A Discourse on the Origin of Inequality; Emile;* and *The Social Contract*.[1] Among these, I give most attention to the three last; and I lay particular stress on the ideas articulated and defended in *Emile*, since this is, in my view, Rousseau's most completely achieved work, and a still much under-appreciated masterpiece. Rousseau himself assigned particular authority to this one among his books. He writes (RJ, I, 933[2]): . . . 'the Author [Rousseau] working his way back from principle to principle did not reach the first principles until his last writings. It was therefore necessary, to proceed synthetically, to begin with these, and this I did in engaging myself first of all with *Emile*, in which he ended . . .' These words are put into the mouth of another ('a Frenchman') with whom Rousseau is in imagined dialogue; but they meet with his immediate approval.

Even this rather small selection from Rousseau's works yields more than can be discussed in wholly adequate detail here; I shall have to pass rapidly over many significant points in them. There is much else in Rousseau's large output that I shall ignore altogether, or draw on only in so far as it speaks to the topics I am already exploring. It would be almost impossible under any circumstances to do complete justice to everything Rousseau wrote about and illuminated. Here, taking a reduced target – though one which contains the works which I believe express his most enduring concerns – will, I hope, compensate for the reduction in scope by the closeness of the treatment possible. There is also the factor that these of his writings are readily accessible in English translation. Although this should not dictate the approach, it will allow the questioning reader easily to assess the material for himself. The overall purpose can only ever be to try to possess Rousseau's ideas more completely; direct contact with his own words is, of course, essential to that.

Thus I have not attempted any 'comprehensive' guide to and assessment of all the elements in Rousseau's wide-ranging and varied thought. Other approaches could emphasize different themes and afford centrality to different works to valuable effect. The path I have followed is only one of those that are possible. I hope, however, that it traverses interesting ground and reveals some arresting views.

A great many commentaries on Rousseau have appeared before this one. Although they differ very much in the interpretations they offer,[3] there are some fairly widely prevailing presumptions brought to the reading of Rousseau's work which stand obdurately in the way of his being seen clear and plain even on first acquaintance, before the work of the interpretative effort has begun to tie him down. I want to try to dislodge some of these presumptions now, so that an initially unprejudiced hearing may be allowed to him.

Rousseau had the misfortune to make some very memorable, epigrammatic, remarks. For instance 'Man is born free; and everywhere he is in chains' (SC I, I; III, 351); 'Nature made man happy and good, but society depraves him and makes him miserable' (RJ, I, 934[4]). The meaning and implications of these sayings strike people as immediately and luminously clear. They begin at once to form their estimate of Rousseau, favourable and supportive or unfavourable and hostile. A little further inquiry reveals that Rousseau also says other things which, given the presumptive construction placed on the above, sit very ill with them. For instance: 'A new enemy is arising which you have not learned to conquer . . . This enemy is yourself. Nature and fortune left you free . . . In learning to desire, you have made yourself the slave of your desires' (E 5, 443; IV, 815-6). Here Emile seems to be held to be *himself* the author of his own ills. Comparable further instances could be added easily. From this it is concluded that Rousseau did not know his own mind; or that he had no consistent mind to know; or that he had a few brilliant insights which he could not control properly; or that he was a rhapsodic writer following his moods but (for good or ill) indifferent to the constraints of 'mere' logic.

Here are a few comments which bear out what I say. Rousseau's arguments – in general, or on particular themes – have been said to be: 'a farrago of contradictions'.[5] Again: 'The difficulty of interpreting him [Rousseau] arises . . . from the fact that most students insist on crediting him with a degree of logical consistency which is not in fact characteristic of his writings . . . Rousseau had few gifts as a systematic thinker . . . he had . . . extraordinary courage in refusing to sacrifice any part of that [political] insight in the interest of superficial consistency.'[6] Again: 'Rousseau was obscure for a simpler reason: because he failed to make his meaning plain . . . If we take some of Rousseau's more often quoted statements literally, and try to elicit their meanings, we soon find ourselves caught up in a web of absurdity.'[7] Finally, I cite: 'The absurdity and incoherence of Rousseau's theory . . .'.[8]

It is notable that these comments do *not* come from Rousseau's more cavalier and hostile critics, but from those who are working closely with his material. It would seem that the idea is still too rare that Rousseau may, after all, have had a clear, sharp, consistent mind, which he knew well and could control and use with great precision. The 'webs of absurdity', the 'farragoes of contradictions' may be the product of our own incomplete comprehension, for all that we have 'done our best for him'. Rousseau thought he worked throughout with a steady purpose: 'I have written on diverse subjects, but always from the same principles; always the same morality, the same faith, the same maxims, and, if you like, the same opinions' (LB IV, 928). But this is easily put aside as self-deceptive good conceit of himself.

I endorse Rousseau's assessment of himself. This means that, throughout, I have done my best to give Rousseau full credit for knowing what he was about, and for having something serious and challenging that he was engaged upon. Nor do I accept that 'consistency' is a dispensable commodity which the 'higher truth' can do without. So I am not committed to celebrating incoherence as profound paradox; or nonsense as gnomic insight. I have tried to uncover a steady, deep, consistent and rich body of ideas pervading those of Rousseau's works under discussion here. I believe this attempt has been regularly and reliably answered by them. Where difficulties arise, I have tested the idea that it is I, not Rousseau, who is the dupe of an unconsidered assumption. If, finally, some problems still remain, I have tried to show that these arise from intransigent intellectually challenging difficulties, not because Rousseau was blindly carried along on an emotional 'swell', and did not know what he was at. I cannot see that one serves an author well by proceeding in any other way.

This approach does entail, however, that some of the traditionally identified 'cruxes' in Rousseau's thought – for example, his supposed ideas regarding some sort of pristine natural innocence, or of the individual's 'submergence' into the general life of the community, and so on – will not appear in a cut and dried form in my discussion. This is because closer study discloses that the throwing up of these as problems depends on prior mistaken constructions. When these latter are rectified, the emergence of these puzzles in standard normal form is precluded. Of course, the issues to which these 'problems' give distorted expression do not disappear altogether. It is rather that, when these issues are understood more carefully, these particular hurdles do not have to be surmounted in order to see them to a finish.

Two specific instances may be mentioned, in a preliminary way. Commentators unfailingly note that Rousseau passes many critical strictures upon human dependency, upon one person relying on, needing, another to support or assist them in their well-being and self-preservation. From this it is at once concluded that Rousseau envisaged as being the best, indeed really the only suitable, circumstance in which a human could avoid becoming deformed and ruined, that in which any dependence of any kind of one person on another was absent, or as limited as possible. Isolated, separate, self-sufficiency for each of us was, it is said, his vision of the manner and condition of that life in which alone we could hope for wholeness and happiness. However, many other passages explicitly or implicitly contradict this idea of his meaning (with the consequences for the assessment of the value of his work of the kinds noted above). It will be one of the prime contentions of this discussion that Rousseau never had such a vision in view. It was always only certain *quite specific* sorts of dependency that Rousseau was critical of; and this for quite specific, determinate and cogent reasons. Other forms of human dependence he accepted not as unfortunate, but unavoidable, necessities, but as essential to, necessary and good contributing constitutive elements in, the full human development and actualization of each of us, components of the plenitude of our proper and good stature and activity. If this is not seen from very early on, then very much of Rousseau's work must seem to be only barely coherent. He will be seen as struggling to reconcile two conditions held to be radically opposed in character and consequences, separateness from others and community with others. All that Rousseau is doing is making clear, firmly and properly grounded, distinctions between kinds of dependence. This is no confusion or evasion; it is only precise thought – eschewal of sweeping, undiscriminating, condemnation.

Connected with this matter is the almost universal misconception of the nature and role of *amour-propre*, as that phenomenon is appealed to by Rousseau when accounting for man's condition in society.[9] *Amour-propre*, we are informed, is taken by Rousseau to comprise vanity, overweening self-conceit, a self-vaunting estimate of oneself in terms of one's superiority over others and their contemptible inferiority. As such, it is taken to account for the great bulk of human desolation in society. It is said that Rousseau was always and everywhere deeply antipathetic towards it. But yet he appears to allow that it is an ineradicable passion, and one which necessarily attends man's incorporation into social life. So, when he is in the mood to allow that man must live with his kind in society, Rousseau is committed to saying that man is automatically condemned to inward desolation and outward depredation.

But here, too, what Rousseau has always in view is certain determinate and particular forms that *amour-propre* (admittedly very readily) assumes. He is not concerned with a blanket condemnation of the whole. As we shall see, Rousseau assigns to *amour-propre* an essential and wholly beneficial rôle in the full self-completion of each several person, as he comes into possession of his standing as a 'moral being' in transaction with other such beings. He does so for precise and cogent reasons. It is only when *amour-propre* becomes disordered ('inflamed') that Rousseau is critical of it as a harmful personal characteristic and a source of social damage. Indeed, inflamed *amour-propre* includes precisely those perverse forms of human dependency, referred to above, which Rousseau was at such pains to uncover. In relation to *amour-propre*, just as in relation to dependency, Rousseau was seeing and marking crucial differences within overall kinds. This is not to be a slippery or ambiguous writer; only to be an intelligent one.

Another obstacle to the understanding of Rousseau is that it is quite often not appreciated at what level the issues he raises, the arguments he canvasses, cut into the substructure of the sustaining framework of ordinary thinking, apprehension and action. It is characteristic of Rousseau to discern and to speak to the most fundamental, and thus most easily overlooked or presumed upon, elements and structures which comprise the manner of our holding any personal standing, of our engagement in social life, of the viability of society or political community. He usually addresses issues which involve a great deal of effort and attention to bring into view as objects for consideration in the first place. Because this is so, we can sometimes mistake the target he is aiming at, and suppose him to be shooting at another, but wildly. Rousseau had, no doubt, his obsessions, particularly with problems of exclusion and personal 'invalidation' (I shall say more on this below). But his genius in part derives from the fact that these are not the boring, repetitive, obsessions of a mind defeated, but those of someone whose own peculiar susceptibilities made him aware of the deepest conditioning structures which sustain personal and social existence as such for everyone, which more comfortable souls simply rest in and rely upon. He was someone who could harness this awareness to penetrating and sustained critique and constructive endeavour.

I give one outline example of the depth of Rousseau's address, and his preoccupation with achieving categorical 'standing' for persons in social transactions. The role of the 'general will' in Rousseau's discussion of civil society, that accounts for its particular significance, structure and terms of operation, is to establish the absolutely basic principles upon which any, and every, several individual may legitimately be considered to comprise a member of one single social or civil 'body'. It establishes the terms and conditions under which any one person may fitly be comprehended under the scope of a civil body, and acquire obligations and responsibilities consequent thereon. It affords to each several constitutive member of the civil body a level civil 'identity', which comprises their primary (though by no means their only) identity. It designates a specification of their self-constitutive character *qua* citizen, in terms of their inviolable holding of certain powers, titles, immunities and opportunities. These cannot be gainsaid without, in that moment, severing their membership of the one body, and hence relieving them of any responsibilities, liabilities and obligations towards others *qua* citizens that could legitimately be claimed from them. We can figure ourselves as right-holders, and hold status as such, only so far as we afford this same character to others and they in turn afford it to us. In this a social bond, which is present in the constitution of each of us in our own character as moral beings, is necessarily established between us; and this is the general will in us.

It is when, and only when, such terms and conditions are unequivocally met, and stand as the irrevocable bound to all civil action, that issues of the authority of majority decisions, the justness of inequalities in power and wealth, and such-like matters can properly be considered. Yet it is not at all uncommon to find the incorporation of individuals into a social body to be a matter taken as read. It is then supposed that Rousseau is speaking to problems that arise with the possibility and legitimacy of that already taken for granted. Not surprisingly, in that case, some of his views are found wayward and his concerns opaque. But this is not his failure, but the failure to see that he has brought a deep, but urgent, issue to the surface and is considering that as a preliminary to any further questions regarding the internal life of an established civil whole. Unless we, ourselves, try to get in touch with the 'taken for granted' and recognize it as problematic we shall simply not see what Rousseau is arguing over, and will misunderstand him or not understand him at all.

Allied to the presumption that Rousseau is not a consistent, not an intellectually controlled and rigorous, writer is the fact that Rousseau is seldom afforded that minute, questioning scrutiny that is, as a matter of course, afforded to Plato, Descartes, Kant, Hume – and many others. In Rousseau's case, distanced, impressionistic extrapolations and suggestions as to what he 'must' have meant serve as the standard coin of debate. This sustains, of course, the presumption that instigated it: nothing is looked at closely enough for it to challenge the pre-judgment as to its character. I have found, to the contrary, that Rousseau's writing almost unfailingly repays the close thought given to it in its detail. If one presses at every step, and conjectures possibilities or problems that might ensue, etc., Rousseau not only meets almost every expectation and demand but also shows one things that one did not envisage or anticipate. In this book, it will only be possible to proceed with a full close reading once or twice. (Book 4 of *Emile* particularly rewards intensive attention.) But I hope enough will be seen to arise from these instances to show that we do him, and ourselves, disservice by supposing he needs only be skimmed to get the 'gist' of the thing.

So rich and fertile are the ideas Rousseau puts forward that, in tracing them out, one is constantly drawn into the consideration of matters one had no inkling of at the start. Even in the material under consideration here, Rousseau propounds ideas of great significance for individual psychology and psychopathology; social and political theory; law; commerce; education; religion; and sociology. But, governed by the perspectives he has opened to view, one is soon led into issues of 'interaction theory', social and group psychology, anthropology, historical and comparative social studies, and much more. I have tried, as far as possible, to curb the temptation to follow all these paths that branch from the main road; but I could see great value in yielding to it.

Finally, a little more on Rousseau's 'obsessions'. Rousseau, as everyone knows, suffered a terrifying paranoid breakdown in 1767–8. Many of his subsequent writings are distressing in their disclosure of his unhappy spirit. Marked signs of paranoia also preceded his breakdown: his morbid suspicions of plots against him; his accusations of others as full of concealed hatred towards him, concerned to humiliate and discredit him; his fears of emotional 'seduction'; his self-presentation as a violated innocent; and much more. However, for most of his life he was in control of his paranoid predisposition and turned it (not, of course, consciously and deliberately) to effective use in his diagnosis and assessment of the condition of 'social man'. The paranoid temper of mind makes one peculiarly receptive to the currents of anger, cruelty and hatred, the strategies of triumph and humiliation, of domination and subjection, which are present at large in human relations. One of Rousseau's special gifts (or burdens) was to be adept in detecting and tracing the serpentine windings of human hatred and vengefulness in all their masks and concealments. Perhaps, in doing so, he sometimes thought he saw envy and spite in activities and practices which were (are) in truth well-meant and benign. Sometimes, too, he may have secretly wanted to spoil that which he grudged others the enjoyment of, by convincing himself and them that it was really self-deceptive, corrupt and poisonous. But generally it seems to me he did not. He neither scorned the good to assuage his anger at not possessing it (he warns explicitly against this, at E 4, 237; IV, 525–6); nor did he either exaggerate, or deny, the evil. He had, in his finest achievement, an even clarity of undistorting vision which could recognize and name monsters and false idealizations, but also contain and cherish finite real goods that afford intrinsic nurture and sustenance. His constructive impulse was not a longing for an Eden to complement a self-engendered vision of hell, but to delineate a human world fit for human life, where paler grey may, with good fortune, preponderate over darker.

I shall speak quite often of the workings and implications of paranoia in parts of the discussion.[10] It is not, however, Rousseau's own paranoia that is in view, but paranoid structures, relations, processes in the life and institutions that make up the character, dispositions and activities of what Rousseau disparagingly calls 'civilized' man (DI, 104; III, 192). These involve strategies and positions that involve triumph over others, glory in their degradation, self-estimation grounded in vengeful humiliation and devaluation of other people, and the like. The legitimacy of this interpretative procedure must stand or fall by the use I make of it (or which could, in better hands, be made of it). I am not, and I repudiate the idea of, suggesting that anything Rousseau says is to be explained away simply as being the delusion of his own tormented mind. Reasons, quite independent of the conjectured or known state of mind of the author at the time of writing, must be used to establish or confute any claim made. My only proposal is: we shall find some telling reasons for taking some of Rousseau's achieved ideas seriously if we see that they are knit together by the theme of a consistent disposition towards paranoia being embodied in the fabric of social life. For there are good reasons for supposing that disposition goes very deep in human life and experience.

In this, and in other connections (for instance, Rousseau's account of the nature and significance of compassion or pity), I have made some use of Melanie Klein's ideas.[11] Many have drawn on Freud's theories of individual psychology and social processes to assist in the interpretation of Rousseau.[12] Yet I think it clear that Klein offers the richer and more apposite framework of notions to work with here. Not only does she articulate the structures and strategies of paranoia, of which I have just spoken, but also her accounts of reparative and creative processes and activities, and of the 'object-relatedness' of even the most rudimentary psychological structures, have precise and effective power to clarify and reinforce many of Rousseau's central insights. In this context, I shall be only very selective and partial in the use of these notions, which many still find questionable. It is only because I believe them to be powerful and illuminating in uncovering Rousseau's meaning that I have drawn on them. I would not want either to be obscured by the other.

# 1

# *Themes and Issues*

## 1 Political Philosophy, or the Psychology of the Individual?

Rousseau is still principally known and studied as a political philosopher. *The Social Contract* is taken to be his major work and the culmination of his inquiries. Whilst I shall give due prominence to Rousseau's political philosophy, as is of course necessary, I shall contend that that body of ideas does not comprise the focal and final point of his intellectual and moral endeavour. I shall argue this not because I want to place works quite other than *The Social Contract*, and those that very clearly inform it (for instance *A Discourse on the Origin of Inequality*, and *Emile*), as the centre of Rousseau's concern and achievement. I argue this because I believe one misses Rousseau's deepest and most abiding concerns in these works (let alone overall) if one takes them always to be preparatory to or a part of his political philosophy. I think that one should, instead, view his political philosophy as the extension and elaboration of a body of ideas and themes which are not to be understood as essentially arising from questions and problems about the nature and grounds of civil society. No doubt Rousseau always had a clear view of the implications of his ideas for such questions; but engagement with those questions is not the original ground of their devising, nor is the resolution of those questions the sole or dominant objective of their potency. This is not to say that once a political structure is erected this will have no retroactive effect in working some modifications in the character and significance of earlier pre-political dispositions, relations etc. It is not a question of the political order being just more of the same that obtained before. But, in Rousseau's view, the super-ordinate rule of the state must conserve and sustain *some* salient elements from the pre-political order, or else be illegitimate. This will be explained in due course.

I afford primary place to Rousseau's interest in the psychological and moral development and character of the particular individual; and in the prospects for the most ample realization of the potential, the completion and happiness, of every several individual. His political proposals are intended, I believe, only to make sense in the light of the *foundational* claims he argues for with regard to the psychological needs and possibilities of the individual person, which claims are largely made in works other than *The Social Contract* itself. As I have said, these claims are not made with the construction of a particular form of civil society specifically and determiningly in view from the beginning.

This contention, quite vague and general though it at present is, may arouse objection. First, it will be said that every account of the character and workings of a good political community must draw on a conception of individual needs and human good. These can be no other benchmark for the propriety of the political structures proposed than their contribution to the well-being of the individuals constituting the community. That Rousseau should afford central place to an examination and assessment of the character of individual human good is nothing distinctive in his work. To do this does nothing to show that political theory is not, and should not be, the dominant and determining issue.

I acknowledge, as Rousseau does, the first point made in the objection. (The idea, often discussed, that in some theories of the state, and in some actual states, the state itself has (some) 'interests' wholly distinct from, and often antipathetic to, all the interests of all of its members seems to me more of a fantasy than a reality.) But there is a real difference between, on the one hand, starting with the idea that the nature of political community is the original issue, and all questions of individual human needs and human happiness must be interpreted in the immediate context of that; and, on the other, starting with ideas about the life, development, relations of individual persons, in contexts other than that of their standing in political community with others, and approaching the instigation (or legitimation) of the terms and conditions of political life as a problem or issue to be contended with from this prior ground. I suggest that Rousseau's is, very much, the second approach. For him, the form and character of political life is not the omni-governing theme for the rest. I do not say, as remarked above, that political life will not effect marked transformations in what preceded it. Nor do I say that Rousseau regarded political life – life in a *polis* – as 'unnatural' or dispensable. (The notion of what is 'natural' or not is particularly problematic in Rousseau's thought, as we shall see. No hasty conclusions should be drawn about the significance he attaches to it.) What I *am* saying is that, for Rousseau, the determining grounds for judgements about the character and quality of political life come from features of individual human experience obtaining originally outside that context, and not *vice versa*.

The second objection I want to consider cuts deeper. It is crucial to Rousseau's own view, as I shall explain, that the general character and particular content of the motives, desires, attitudes, etc. which make up the constitutive principles of the being and agency of any one individual cannot, in many very central instances, obtain or be made sense of without essential reference to that individual's relations to, or forms of connection with, other individuals. (And the same will be true, of course, of their analogous self-constitutive principles.) In many cases, characterizing the dispositions of any one individual necessarily includes characterization of his assessment of and involvement with others, which are inherent in the nature of those dispositions. For example, it is inherent in compassion that one person assess another as suffering and as needing help. Since this is so, the objector finds room for his criticism. He will contend that such dispositions necessarily incorporate an assessment of the other as a co-citizen with the individual, an involvement with him structured by respective political positions and relations. Furthermore, it may be added that not only is Rousseau committed to holding that the terms of political life are inherent to the constitutive active principles of the individual; he also assigns to the quality of political experience a central *causal* role in forming (or deforming) the developed nature of the individual. So, in at least two ways, Rousseau should assign, if not priority, at least equal place, to the character of political existence in accounting for the nature, dispositions and potential of the individual. No independent account can be given of the latter.

The lead-in to the objection describes, as I have said, something Rousseau is very firmly wedded to. It marks one of his very deep breaks with the 'empiricist' tradition of psychology, epistemology, political theory (represented by such as Hobbes and Locke), for which the structure of the mind and the active principles of man is complete and finished from the beginning, waiting only to be given material content by the particular experiences someone chances to undergo. For those writers the structure and content of the individual's mind and active principles is taken to be comprehensively understandable without any necessary reference to his apprehension of and relation to others. For Rousseau, on the contrary, the structures and configurations of the individual mind undergo several radical transformations in a way that is directly correlated to the manner of the individual's encounter of and engagement with others. No account of the individual's psychological character can be correct or comprehensive without this being taken into full account.

However, the inference drawn from this is invalid. It supposes that either we – impossibly – try to explain the nature of the individual's configurations of mind and dispositions in total disregard of his forms of involvement with others. Or else we are bound to suppose those forms of involvement to be primarily (exclusively?) political in character – as if we 'meet' each other most primitively and most decisively as 'citizens', before all else. This is far from obviously true; indeed, it is pretty clearly false. Between my being present to you as a 'citizen' with you of the same body politic, and our being totally unconnected, there are many other possible modes of mutual 'presence'. We may be friends; of the same family; lovers; co-workers; and so on indefinitely.

Each of these offers a way for us to have presence to another and a footing in their actions and sentiments different from that offered by political terms of relation and standing. For Rousseau, this is a very important fact indeed, and one he would not want to see removed or displaced by an 'invasive' state. He objects explicitly to Plato's exclusion, in the *Republic*, of family life and ties from the experience of guardians and auxiliaries:

> I speak of that subversion of the sweetest sentiments of nature, sacrificed to an artificial sentiment which can only be maintained by them – as though there were no need for a natural base on which to form conventional ties; as though the love of one's nearest were not the principle of the love one owes the state; as though it were not by means of the small fatherland which is the family that the heart attaches itself to the large one; as though it were not the good son, the good husband, and the good father who make the good citizen! (E 5, 363; IV, 699–70)

Burke could not have spoken more plainly. (Rousseau's treatment of the good daughter, wife and mother will be considered later.)

It follows that not all modes of incorporation of the other into my experience, and *vice versa*, are political in character; and that the very possibility of effective development and sustaining of political reciprocity depends on this not being so, but on other ties uniting us beforehand. It might be objected to this that the state could use and regulate family bonds in such a way as to 'train' people optimally towards finding their heart's attachment in the 'large' fatherland. But this is not just impractical, it is incoherent. In so far as family ties, for instance, are allowed their growth in a way that is supposedly only preparatory to the formation of the decisive personal tie to the state, they must form a centre of moral and emotional allegiance alternative to that of the state, or else they would never exist in the first place, and the 'artificial sentiment' could not be maintained by them. Love regulated by the bidding of the state, if the state must draw on an extension of that love to become itself an objective of (predominant) loyalty, is a contradiction in terms. The state could then only prevent love; and by this destroy its own claim to allegiance.

Rousseau might appear, elsewhere, to speak very differently from this:

> Every true republican has drunk in love of country, that is to say love of law and liberty, along with his mother's milk. This love is his whole existence; he sees nothing but the fatherland, he lives for it alone; when he is solitary, he is nothing; when he has ceased to have a fatherland, he no longer exists; and if he is not dead, he is worse than dead. (GP ch. IV; III, 966)

Is this one of Rousseau's famous blatant contradictions? I shall not answer this here but will come to it later on (in chapters 5 and 6). Pending the resolution of this (apparent) difficulty, I shall take the view expressed in *Emile*, as quoted, as decisive. I conclude that it is the self-constitution achieved through relations and ties to others in the 'small fatherlands', of family, friendship, even shared participation in games, that has primacy for Rousseau. This, I think, justifies me in contending that the political, for Rousseau, is an outgrowth and extension of the independently existent and characterizable pre-political; the latter does not from the start require the former for its existence and character (so not really being able to be thought of as pre-political in character after all).

I return to my claim that, for Rousseau, the psychological and moral development and character of the particular individual are both of primary interest and have a primary determining role in relation to the rest. I have now added to this that, for Rousseau, individual development and character must necessarily include assessments of and involvements with others, which are taken into and comprise an essential component part of the form and content of (many of) the individual's own constitutive principles and dispositions. ('When he begins to sense his moral being, he ought to study himself in his relations with men'. E 4, 214; IV, 493). This may occasion surprise. For – as noted in the Introduction – Rousseau is widely taken to have held that individual integrity and happiness was only possible to him who was isolated, independent, uninvolved with others. This implies that the dispositions and mind of the individual can be completely understood atomistically. Such justice as there may be in this assessment of Rousseau's views I shall examine carefully in chapter 3. Rousseau writes: '. . . although I want to form the man of nature, the object is not, for all that, to make him a savage and to relegate him to the depths of the woods'. (E 4, 255; IV, 551) What Emile (representative man) is to be untouched, unshaped, by is not others as such – that would leave him 'uncompleted' (cf. E. 3, 203; IV, 481) – but others in certain very specific ways. We shall see what ways those are, and why they are so significant, primarily in chapters 2 and 4.


## 2 Major Themes

### 2.1 Preamble

I have indicated, in the introduction (p. 1), those of Rousseau's works I place at the centre of this discussion. In this section I want to block in some of the major ideas that pervade these works. By doing this, we may be in a position to see some of the principal governing concerns that drive Rousseau's engagement with the issues that preoccupy him. This presentation is sketchy and preliminary. It is intended only to pick out some of the overall themes which will constantly reappear, and which will receive more detailed and precise examination later on.

Rousseau often disowned the status of being 'a philosopher'. Largely this was because he felt that the motives which informed most of the work of those who in his day passed for philosophers were disreputable. Such 'philosophers' sought only public celebrity and invidious distinction, not caring what they said providing only that it won them acclaim and deference. (In this, Rousseau, echoes – as so often – the opinions of Socrates.) In addition, however, many of the issues which have been, and remain, central to philosophy – concerning the nature of substance, the possible sources of sure knowledge, the basis of meaning in language, and so on – receive only small place in Rousseau's work. He did propound some subtle ideas about the genesis and character of general terms and abstract reasoning, and other matters (see, for instance DI 58 ff; III, 146 ff; E2, 108; IV, 345; and many other places; OL *passim*); but his theories about these do not lie at the heart of his work. His principal interests lay consistently in questions of psychological, moral, social and political theory (and practice), here again matching the concerns of Socrates. Questions about happiness, virtue, duty, freedom, authority, were those around which his work revolved. It is some of the basic terms of his approach to such questions I want to set out now.

### 2.2 The Idea of the 'Natural'

The most prominent theme in Rousseau's work, to which he himself attached greatest weight, may be summarily expressed by saying: man is by nature good, but corrupted by society. Thus, for instance, he writes:

> Let him [Emile] know that man is naturally good; let him feel it; let him judge his neighbour by himself. But let him see that society depraves and perverts men; let him find in their prejudices the source of all their vices . . . (E 4, 237, IV, 525)

Or again,

> The fundamental principle of all morals, on the basis of which I have reasoned in all my writings, and which I have developed in this last one [*Emile*] with as much clarity as I was able, is that man is naturally good, loving justice and order; that there is absolutely no original perversity in the human heart, and that the first movements of nature are always right. (LB IV, 935–6)

As I said in the Introduction, this idea of Rousseau's almost immediately conveys a powerful impression to people, which they readily take for his own meaning. But a moment's reflection will suggest how perplexing an idea it is.

We must not assume, but ask, what Rousseau understands by 'nature' or what is 'natural'. How, if at all, can he justify his conception of this? What does he mean by 'goodness', and especially by 'natural goodness'? Is the meaning he affords to these terms acceptable; is there a coherent conception he has here, which he sustains consistently? What are we to take 'society' to be; how is it supposed to work as the agency of 'perversion' and 'depravity'? What, anyway, does Rousseau consider to be depravity; does he have an acceptable and defensible conception of this? Or is he expressing no more than his own peculiar private distaste?

Some of these questions are easier to answer than others. Rousseau's conception of the corrupt character and circumstances of man is initially easier to grasp and defend than his conception of natural innocence or goodness. A first assessment of the latter might suggest that what Rousseau thought of as 'natural' in man's constitution and circumstances were those characteristics and surroundings people had prior to any settled or stable social life and experience at all, whether on a small or large scale. So nothing in their own character, nor in the circumstances in which they live and act, must bear the traces of the presence of the person or action of anyone else in any way at all. Some things Rousseau says do appear powerfully to suggest this reading of his ideas.

If this were right, however, it would immediately encounter severe difficulties. How could one possibly have sound evidence for claims about the character and circumstances of people (if they would be recognizable 'people' anyway) in such a situation? The bare possession of language is an individual's incorporation into himself of a socially originated and sustained practice. Is it 'natural' to man then to be quite inarticulate and incapable of any linguistically mediated thought? Again, Rousseau himself clearly envisages, in *The Social Contract*, some form of human society which is supposed to be good and to be so because in some way, somehow, it keeps faith with what is 'natural' to men. But if what were 'natural' were that now being conjectured, how could this be? We saw also, in section 1 of this Chapter, that Rousseau held that all forms of social connection transmute the character of the mind and active powers of the individual. How, then, could any form of social connection be 'natural' if by natural is meant that which is quite separated from all such? If what is 'natural' to man is what is altogether pre-social in character, this will be left behind the moment any trace of sociality or social practices has found a footing in the life and feelings of an individual. Finally, we may recall that Rousseau contended that without one's self having taken on some of the attributes and titles which are in their nature only derivable from one's having social situatedness, one is only 'half' finished as a human creature, only an 'uncompleted' being. So is 'natural' man, if that *is* 'presocial' man, only 'half' a person? And is the 'completed' person necessarily perverted?

Unless these, and other, pressing questions can satisfactorily be answered Rousseau's ideas are severely flawed from the start. I shall, of course, be examining these points closely later. But some preliminary remarks are necessary, in order to clear away these major obstacles to any effective movement at all. I contend that pre-sociality never was, for Rousseau, the *essential* mark of what is natural in man's character and circumstances. At best it was an accidental mark; that is, it quite often was present along with the essential marks. But, just as often, it was not, and so could never be used as a decisive guide to whether something was natural or not, let alone be taken to comprise the defining significance of its being 'natural'. That which Rousseau *did* consider to be the most significant defining mark of something's being 'natural' to man is something which *can* continue to be present and operative even although a person is thoroughly 'socialized', has irreversibly taken into himself a great many attributes, dispositions, ideas, values which derive from social encounter and relatedness. What is excluded, that which by taking into oneself one becomes corrupted or perverted, is not *all* traces of sociality of all forms and kinds, but only certain very specific forms and kinds which Rousseau had very precise reasons for believing did comprise a corrupted character and state. Rousseau is therefore quite clearly and cogently able to continue to use the criterion of 'naturalness' as a test and measure of the satisfactoriness or otherwise of various particular social attitudes, relations, institutions. For he did not hold that, under all circumstances and without regard to the particular nature of this case or that, where society was, nature was no more.

What is the most crucial defining mark of what is 'natural' in man's character, dispositions, and in the circumstances of his life and action? A *first* pointer is this: Those elements in man's character, dispositions, etc. and in his surrounding circumstances of life and action, is 'natural' to him and them if, and only if, there are no traces, effects, of any kind in their condition of his being *subjected to or controlled by the will of another*. They are 'natural' if, and only if, there are no marks of his being imposed upon by and ordered to the constraining will of another exerting dominion over and against him. It is clear from this that not all forms of social encounter and relation will be against nature. For not all such (fortunately) involve such personal control and subjugation. Friendship, collaboration, play, do not (though it would be naive to suppose that elements of controlling do not quite often enter into such relations also, as Rousseau was well aware: cf. RSW 6, 97; I, 1053, for instance).

What might fit this first characterization of the 'natural'? Briefly, here are some relevant instances. Being beholden to someone's gratuitous favour in order to enjoy the basic necessities of survival would be an unnatural circumstance of life. More complex is cruelty, as an unnatural disposition. A cruel person is, in his own cruelty, always responding – often in an obscure and roundabout way – to what he feels (realistically or fantastically) to have been vindictive impositions or deprivations that have been inflicted on his person, for which he is now exacting talionic vengance. 'Natural' would be having at one's own sovereign disposal and use the means of one's survival, as the surrounding situation for one's life. 'Natural' would be the free (uncommanded) impulse of compassion, which is neither imposed, nor imposes to effect control (unless used as a weapon – compare E 4, 235; IV, 521: 'Ingratitude would be rarer, if good deeds were less commonly something lent out at interest' – my translation). I shall go into such-like cases, and others, in much more detail later.

It can be seen why what counts as 'natural' in this sense, and what is 'natural' *qua* pre-social, should quite often go together. For whatever else may be absent from man's pre-social constitution and circumstances, subjugated domination by another unquestionably is. We can also see why, with this as a core significance for the idea of what is 'natural', Rousseau need not be encumbered with difficulties about, e.g., the bare possession of any language as such being 'unnatural'. It is not, or not obviously, the case that use of a language in itself involves submission of oneself to the controlling will of another imposed over one. (Rousseau thought some types of language did involve this to some extent, and thus feels able to call them 'unnatural'. But this is perfectly clear and consistent.) We can also see how and why Rousseau so closely associated 'naturalness' with 'freedom', although it must be stressed that this latter idea is also put to very complex and subtle use by Rousseau, and no immediate presumption should be made as to its significance. Thus Rousseau writes:

> Liberty consists less in doing just as you will than in not being submitted [prostituted – *soumis*] to the will of another; it further consists in not submitting the will of another to our own. (LM, 8th Letter; III, 841; *une fille soumise* is a prostitute, which gives some idea of the force of Rousseau's thought)

Of course, subjection, control, imposition and domination can comprehend quite a variety of possibilities. It will be important, in due course, to separate out some of these. This is particularly necessary since it is evident that in *any* coordinated action I may undertake with others, of which I am not myself the sole sovereign non-answerable instigator and director, the force and direction of my will must be circumscribed in various ways and measures by the wills of others. Any genuine social life and action I participate in will involve *some* kind of regulation of my will with reference to others. So we shall still need to know how the regulation of the principles and action of my own will by the requirements of a social order will not count as 'unnatural', though now for reasons quite different from those suggested by the first, mistaken, idea of what 'natural' signified, i.e. the pre-social.

It is Rousseau's notion of the 'general will' which is intended to explain the nature and basis of the coordination of separate several individual wills in a way which will not be unnatural to, or domineeringly imposed upon, any of them. I think that it does so successfully, as I argue in chapter 5. Here, I only note that this does seem to locate Rousseau's own thought fairly precisely, for he contends that it is only by obedience to the general will that we are secured 'against all personal dependence' (SC 1, 7; III, 364); and without this 'civil undertakings . . . would be absurd, tyrannical and liable to the most frightful abuses' (*ibid*). This will be taken up and worked through later.

The suggestion that the idea of what is 'natural' is quite centrally the idea of what is unmarked (untainted) by the workings of a domineering imposed will does, then, appear to have strong *prima facie* evidence in its favour. For all that, it may be felt that the use of the notion of what is 'natural' to signify just *this* is peculiar and under-motivated to a fault. If presented as a bald contention, I would agree. But, as we shall see in detail in chapter 2, Rousseau had a powerful and acute insight into the very wide and deep ramifications of situations and relations which are 'unnatural' in this sense. When we see what these ramifications are we shall find it more straightforward that Rousseau, and we, should use the idea of what is natural, with its ordinary loose associations of what is undistorted, unforced, unmoulded, to speak of persons and situations not marked by the work of domination and control by the will of another. His core notion of what is 'unnatural' points towards an *explanation* of distortions, forcings, mouldings of a perverse kind, destructive to oneself and to others. Something does not count as 'unnatural' simply because of being formed or moulded by absolutely *any* 'social' influence. (This is made quite clear at E 4, 212–3; IV, 491; I shall be discussing this vital passage again later on, and I will also add to this account of what is 'natural'.)

## 2.3 Original Sin

One immediate consequence of being in subjection to the domineering will of another, especially if this subjected condition is 'internalized' by its victim, is that the subjugated person will think himself an inferior being, of no significance, contemptible and lacking in any true value to be considered. This, in Rousseau's eyes, is wholly unnatural; it is, in his view, natural to man to place a value on his own person and to expect, if necessary to demand, that he shall be honoured and respected as a person of significant moment and title in his own independent right. No one is by birth a slave, servant or sinner; nor master, lord or saved. This is one of the reasons why he takes exception to the doctrine of 'original sin' (which he discusses extensively in his *Letter to Christopher de Beaumont*; IV, 937 ff). The Genesis story represents Adam and Eve as bound to obedience to the explicit prohibition of God, in regard to a certain very important matter. (cf. Milton: 'Of Man's first disobedience, and the fruit/Of that forbidden tree, whose mortal taste/Brought death into the world, and all our woe . . .'). They flouted that prohibition, brought sin into the world and Adam's seed was thereafter cursed.

I do not want to, nor could I, debate the proper significance to be placed on this. But here is one possibility. No doubt the controlling will of God over us is a very special case (He *is* The Lord, The Master). But, in relation to any temporal embodiment of this will, our primordial moral and deliberative situation is represented as consisting in our standing under dictates the reason and good of which we are not permitted to assess, or are deemed incapable of assessing. We are, therefore, aboriginally denied the right or power to make our own determination and election over certain matters. Such is the position of original servitude, whereby our deciding on our own judgement is identified at once as rebellion. This, in Rousseau's view, was not to be borne, was paradigmatically unnatural. It is easy to suppose that because Rousseau wished this yoke thrown off, he wished each and every one of us to figure ourselves as originally soverign, Lord and Master in God's place.[1] But nothing could be further from his mind. To reason so is to perpetuate the *structure* of domination and servitude, and only to swap places within it, as if liberation meant the power and opportunity to enslave the enslavers. (Of course this is just what many *do* take it to mean; but Rousseau is not one of them.) Over and over again he denounces the servility inherent to the mind that sees freedom only as the chance to impose chains on others, showing that such a mind has wholly absorbed this mode of construing human relations as if it were the only possible or envisageable one. He writes, for instance:

> I laugh at those debased peoples who, allowing themselves to be stirred up by rebels, dare to speak of liberty without having the slightest idea of its meaning, and who, with their hearts full of all the servile vices, imagine that, in order to be free, it is enough to be insubordinate. (GP. ch. 6; III, 974)

We shall not understand Rousseau if we saddle him with the responsibility for the idea that man's natural freedom comprises his scope and entitlement to behave like an arbitrary despot. His objection was to *all* relations of master and slave, domineeringness and subjection, whether one be the slave *or* the master, is put upon or puts upon. Liberty, for Rousseau, means ordering one's objectives and actions to the inward rule of the integrity of one's own proper being. His great objective is to show how the inward rule of the integrity of one's own being necessarily directs recognition and acknowledgement of others as moral beings standing on the same level and with the same titles as oneself. Free will is not lawless will; it is will informed and ordered by its own proper inherent law and precept, which is not created by our own arbitrary decree.

Someone who thinks he enjoys liberty when, and only when, nothing and no-one of any kind stands in his way must necessarily perceive any other person who crosses his path as a violating intruder. How, if this were Rousseau's conception of what it was to enjoy liberty, could it be supposed that social life could be anything but war to the death, or a grudging and resentful stand-off? It is Rousseau's thought, I suggest, that the doctrine of original sin, so far from discouraging this possibility, enunciates the frame of mind, and disposition of feeling, which renders it more likely. It presents us to ourselves as insubordinate and requiring prohibition. If I am taught to think that thinking for myself and acting accordingly is challenging my master, I shall either be crushed or carry the challenge forward. It will never occur to me that neither he nor I need be master; neither he nor I need be slave; and that we might each gain by this.

So Rousseau's contention that it is 'natural' to man to place a value on his own person, and to expect honour and respect as a person holding rightful title as such, is not the claim that we all of us should arrogate to ourselves the titles of (false) gods. That, as I have said, perpetuates the symbiosis of masterhood and slavery, only with competition for the superior role. In his view, the *whole* framework is unnatural, whatever place in it one occupies. It can, then, serve as a mark of the 'naturalness' of a social order that it omits all traces of such forms of relation; and, more positively, embodies and fosters principles of equal standing and mutual reciprocal honour and regard, living by which will yield to each one of us the fundamental principles for our own integrity of being and action in conjunction with others. How this may be I shall attempt to make plain, in subsequent argumentation.

### 2.4 Amour-de-soi *and* Amour-propre

These comments on the nature and significance of the demand for respect of oneself from others; and on, coordinately, our affording like respect to others (whose honour of us, their being honourable beings in our eyes, is then worth something to us – compare E 4, 339; IV, 671, with its reminiscence of Aristotle, EN 1095b, 25–30), lead on to another major guiding theme in Rousseau's work. I have been looking at the natural/social, good/corrupt contrasts in Rousseau's argument; the contrast now to be reviewed in a preliminary way is that between *amour-de-soi(-meme)* and *amour-propre*. Just as we saw that the natural/social contrast was radically misunderstood if taken to be a matter of mutual exclusion, so we shall now see – and explore in more detail in chapters 2 to 4 – that this last contrast is not a matter of mutual exclusion either, despite the virtually unanimous opinion of commentators that it is.

There are no satisfactory one-word, or short-phrase, equivalents in English for *amour-de-soi* and *amour-propre*; I shall use the French phrases throughout. A rough first indication of their sense would be this. *Amour-de-soi* signifies a concern, a care, to look to, guard, preserve and foster one's own personal well-being, guided by a true and clear sense or idea of what the well-being of oneself comprises and requires. As we shall see, largely in chapter 3, Rousseau thinks that the requirements of one's well-being change as the constitution of one's self changes. Since this is so, *amour-de-soi* will take on several different characters. But the common thread that unites them is the constant care for one's personal good, in relation to whatever constitution one's 'person' might have at a particular time in particular circumstances. In its most developed form, *amour-de-soi* is probably most like Joseph Butler's 'reflective self-love'.[2] Rousseau tends particularly to stress the role of *amour-de-soi* in relation to conserving one's *physical* well-being, as a sentient, active, creature making a life by utilizing the resources of the environment. But this is offered only as a particularly clear *case* of the workings of *amour-de-soi*. It is *not* definitive of it that it should be confined only to this.

*Amour-propre* is, initially, more elusive, just because, paradoxically, its significance seems so plain. Its apparently obvious significance is that of being a cherishing regard for one's self (a love of the 'dear self') in terms of one's superiority over others, one's superb distinction over the common herd. *Amour-propre* portends vainglory, a disdainful conceit and pride in oneself as better than others (the pharasaical sin). Or so it would appear. As such it seems radically distinct from *amour-de-soi* (except in so far as one might consider that one's well-being has come to comprise one's strutting glory in the abjection of others before one). Certainly conserving one's physical well-being will seem of little importance, or indeed an impediment, if one is consumed by *amour-propre*. Thus Rousseau writes: 'They must know but little of mankind who imagine that, after they have been once seduced by luxury, they can ever renounce it: they would a hundred times sooner renounce common necessaries, and had much rather die of hunger than of shame' (DPE, 152; III, 277). Yet no-one ever did die of shame.

Just because, on this construal, *amour-propre* requires one's precedence over others, and their inferiority, the mode of social life obtaining between people filled with *amour-propre* will necessarily involve competition for mastery and dominion. Thus *amour-propre* will be a source of unnatural and corrupt relations, attitudes and practices, given what I have argued already about the meanings of 'natural' and 'unnatural' for Rousseau. That is what Rousseau very often contends. Indeed, he is apt to say that *amour-propre* is *the* paramount source of individual and social perversion, whereas he always says that *amour-de-soi* is good, creative, benign and wholly beneficial in its effects for us. This intensifies the sense that we are dealing here with two sharply distinct, antithetical, principles. As I remarked, so the case is seen by virtually all interpreters of Rousseau.

But it is certain that this is mistaken. There are a number of passages, particularly in *Emile*,[3] where Rousseau says that *amour-propre* may be benign, valuable and good for ourselves and in our dealings with others, for all that he equally insists that it very often comes not to be so. Since I do not hold Rousseau to be an incoherent rhapsode, I take it that we are being presented with a conception of *amour-propre* as not, as such, a perverse and corrupting disposition of the kind outlined above, but one which may *or may not* assume that character, depending on certain influences that act upon, or vicissitudes that befall it. *Amour-propre*, in and of itself, may be benign or may be perverse, and must therefore be connected to capacities, concerns, sentiments that can take on a benign or a perverse character, depending on specific factors which affect these in identifiable and explicable ways.

### 2.5 'Moral' Being

Rousseau offers, I believe, a precise account of this, most clearly in the opening pages of Book 4 of *Emile*, which I shall discuss in detail in the next chapter.

The single most important point about the matter is that we are, at that 'moment' in Emile's self-completion, being invited to consider his finding a place and standing for himself with other people in social activities and trans- actions. Prior to this, the studies of Emile's self-constitutive character, modes of understanding, principles and objectives of acting, have treated him as an all-but isolated and separate being, unconnected with, having no inward self- comprising ties to, others. In Rousseau's fictive narrative, this pertains to Emile's pre-adolescence. But this chronological frame is insignificant. The point is that, up to this moment, Emile's (our) composition, in respect of those elements and aspects of his being and self-activity which are independent of his engagement and involvement with others, has been the topic of study. These components of our self's life continue to obtain throughout our lives, of course. It is simply that Rousseau chooses, largely only for presentational reasons, to consider them separately and as if they were definitive of a period in the passage of our earlier years (the 'latency' period).

Now we are being asked to look at those elements and aspects of our self-constitution that are inherent to our engagement with others in relation and common action, at all levels of elaboration and complexity. (Emile has engaged in material transactions, of his self-*qua*-producer only, engaged with other selves-*qua*-producers only, prior to this time.) Rousseau's fundamental insight is that our engagement with others necessarily involves transforma- tions in our self-constitution and self-characterization. We necessarily take on board, and read and enact ourselves through, terms and conceptions which irrevocably alter the character of our self-constitution. As immediate part and parcel of this, there will be the terms and conceptions in which we represent to ourselves the character and position of others in their standing towards us, and our character and position towards them.

One sketchy case will make this plain. If I am out in the jungle and a tiger stalks across my path, what, in relation to the possibilities of transaction between me and the tiger that are available, is my relevant constitution and character to him, and his to me? It is something like this. I am to him: a possible meal; a danger; a predatory presence; a physically threatening obstacle. I am nothing more than 'physically' present to him, as a piece of mobile, intrusive matter. What is he to me? Putting aside possible aesthetic responses, much the same – a terrifying, animate, force poised to rend me. Compare this from Rousseau, speaking of the scope and manner of apprehension of pre-socially constituted man:

> In a word, each man, regarding his fellows almost as he regarded animals of different species, might seize the prey of a weaker or yield up his own to a stronger, and yet consider these acts of violence as mere natural occurrences, without the slightest notion of insolence or despite, or any other feeling than the joy or grief of success or failure. (DI 66 n. 2; III, 219–20)

Could we so engage in our 'social' life with other men? The idea is absurd: social life, in any recognizable character, would not have begun. What then is necessary to its having begun, for something construable as a 'social' relation to connect one with another? The most basic point is this. I must, in my mere physical existence within the ambit of action of another, constitute to him a *limit* to his action, a bound to what he may properly and legitimately do, perhaps – at first – in no more than that he cannot crush me as if I were an annoying fly. And this not merely in view of my posing a threat or prospect of hurtful return to him – as one might hesitate to squash a bee in case it stung. Rather because my being constitutes a *moral check* to the possibility of his action, such that I am present to him as something not fitly to be abused, manhandled or disposed of heedlessly at whim. This point is very well articulated by Simone Weil:[4]

> The human beings around us exert just by their presence a power which belongs uniquely to themselves to stop, to diminish, or modify, each movement which our bodies design. A person who crosses our path does not turn aside our steps in the same manner as a street sign . . . But this . . . influence of the human presence is not exercised by those men whom a movement of impatience could deprive of their lives even before thought had had the time to condemn them. Before these men others behave as if they were not there . . . [These] miserable beings . . . are not men living harder lives than others, not placed lower socially than others, these are another species, a compromise between a man a corpse.

As Weil makes plain, we are dealing here not with a difference in degree ('lower socially'), but with a difference in kind, a categorical difference, between persons and things, living humans and corpses (and not even, really, the corpses-of-humans, which we still invest with 'presence', at least so long as civilization still exists).

It is this same categorical difference that Rousseau is addressing and articulating. When I enter into life connected with others of my kind, I necessarily wish to enter it (for otherwise I should not truly have become party to it at all) as a 'human presence'; that is, to enter it as a creature inherently vested with that standing and place with others which entails that I constitute to them a 'stop', a diminution, a modification, to their plans and actions. Not to possess this standing is for me to be, for them, a mere 'thing', as a sod of turf – the unconsulted and unheeded object upon which they walk unchecked. In so far as I have any dealings with others I must figure myself as a *morally significant* being, a bearer of certain rightful titles and immunities, which I require to be registered and honoured by others; and which, if neccesary, I shall demand from and enforce upon them. Not to do so is to accept, or be crushed into suffering, having status only as a thing, to be used or abused as the whim or will of the other disposes.

The relevant rights and titles need precise formulation. What these are will vary from one type of transaction to another. My rightful 'presence' to you *qua* colleague in a department is more substantial and forceful than it is if I am merely an acquaintance of yours talking with you about your plans to replant your garden. (We are all familiar, of course, with people very recessive about the former, and very intrusive and domineering in the latter. But these are the standard burdens of living with others.) I shall be studying the varieties of possibilities here in some central cases later. At the moment, the point is only the constitution of one's first entry into and standing in the world of humans as a human oneself.

It is the desire, the need, to come to be to yourself, and for others, a 'human presence' that *amour-propre* expresses. *Amour-propre* is the concern to achieve human presence, significant considerable standing, for yourself as your inviolable title in your transactions and relations with others, whom you likewise construe as humans (as you must, otherwise there is no-one for you to be 'in society' with). *Amour-propre* addresses itself to the magnitude of the claim you make for yourself to be a morally potent presence in the actions, feelings, restraints and observances of others. As I have explained, we must, as a condition of the possession by us in our own constitution of 'humanness', assert some kind and degree of such a claim. To do so is not only proper; it is categorically essential to being a human in relation to others at all.

Thus we see how *amour-propre* may be benign, creative, humanly essential, not to be censured or displaced. However, for reasons not yet gone into, some are impelled to make for themselves prodigious claims, as masterful presences in the arena of human dealings, demanding the subjugation of others. This is the 'inflamed' or excessive *amour-propre* which Rousseau consistently criticizes, but which has nearly always been taken by his interpreters as what he meant by *amour-propre* itself. If we make this mistake it renders unintelligible why Rousseau should make an apparently necessary connection between each of us coming into the character of 'moral beings', vested with moral titles and standing, and the coming into play in our character of *amour-propre*. For this would be to say that we only ever encounter others, as one 'human' to another, as someone to dictate to or be dictated to by, someone to lord it over or to be enslaved to. To believe this, or to believe that Rousseau believed this, borders on the insane. This is no problem for Rousseau; it is an illusion born of not understanding Rousseau.

With this material to hand, we can give brief reconsideration to the relations and differences there might be between *amour-propre* and *amour-de-soi*. Our 'selves' can have more or less elaborate and complex constitutions and components. We may, for instance, be (or consider ourselves only in respect of our being) creatures who need food, shelter, warmth, health, the power of effective action to preserve ourselves. We may instead, or in addition, consider ourselves as 'humans' (in Weil's sense), persons who stand in engagement with others who are also persons, and as such figure ourselves as holders of certain rightful titles and immunities. In each case we necessarily want to see ourselves well, to ensure that we are well-situated, thrive and are content and safe. How should we not? In both cases we are looking to take good care of our 'selves', the character and constitution of the 'self' being different in each case. In the former case we may say it is merely the 'physical self'. In the latter case we may say it is the 'moral self' (or that together with the physical self). Taking good care of *both* of these falls under the province of *amour-de-soi*: that is the overall, comprehensive, principle of having good regard to one's well-being, *whatever* constitution one's 'being' has at any time, in any context. Rousseau *tends* to say (but he does not maintain this without reserve – there should now be no confusion[5]) that, when one's 'physical being' alone is under consideration, there is *amour-de-soi*. But when the good of one's 'moral being' is instead, or also, under consideration, that good care gets labelled *'amour-propre'*. But that is all that ordinary non-inflamed *amour-propre is*: it is *amour-de-soi* directed to one's well-being and thriving in one's character of having moral being, standing as 'human'. The sense in which *amour-de-soi* is 'transformed' into *amour-propre* (E 4, 235; IV, 523) is not that it is replaced by, or displaced by, *amour-propre*. It is simply that *amour-de-soi*, when the self that one 'loves' has now the constitution of a 'moral' being, comes to be counted as *amour-propre*. In *amour-propre* one is claiming one's rightful *own* (one's *proprium*, that which is proper to one) as a 'human being', living and interacting with others. In *amour-de-soi* one preserves and conserves one's being whole and entire; but, as I have noted, Rousseau tends to reserve this term for the preservation and conservation of oneself in one's 'physical' being.

Rightly understood, then, *amour-propre* stands to *amour-de-soi* as what the latter consists in when the '*soi*' (the constitution of oneself) comprises a 'moral' self in addition to a 'physical' self. The problem, as Rousseau sees it, is that the demands and requirements one makes for the assurance of the well-being and standing of oneself in one's moral stature tend to become excessive and tyrannical, and to push aside even sensible care of one's health, safety and physical conservation. But these are the diseases of 'inflamed' *amour-propre*, not inherent to its character as such.

This is fairly well summed up in this short paragraph from *Emile*, part of which I quoted before:

> The study suitable for man is that of his relations. So long as he knows himself only in his physical being, he ought to study himself in his relations with things. This is the job of his childhood. When he begins to sense his moral being, he ought to study himself in his relations with men. This is the job of his whole life, beginning from the point we have now reached. (E 4, 214; IV, 493)

I shall be working this out in detail in chapter 2, principally; but it also forms the basis for the understanding of the whole of Rousseau's moral, social and political theory at large. There are, however, two further points I want to make about this now, in a preliminary fashion.

## 2.6 De-humanization

I have been stressing how, properly understood, *amour-propre* is that which directs us to finding for ourselves a categorical moral standing with others. Such regard for oneself is essential to achieving what Weil called 'human presence'. Without this we are for others mere things, or corpses – or, to use another phrase of Weil's, the 'living dead'. It is absolutely necessary to our own survival and sanity that we are not situated like that. I have mentioned, in passing, that many make excessive demands for domination over and precedence before others as their title; this is 'inflamed' *amour-propre*. We need also to look at the situation of those who are at the 'receiving end', are the victims, of the excesses of others' *amour-propre*. Directly in view of the latter's overweening demands for power and prestige, the former will be caused to suffer a circumscription, amounting even sometimes to total deletion, of their 'human presence'. Their doing so is, of course, inherent to the others' triumphant lordship. Thus they suffer the external imposition on them of diminished or deleted humanity in their own persons; and, in certain circumstances, they can 'internalize' this as their own immediate self-figuration, taking themselves for inferior creatures, those who count-for-nothing. (I have heard of an African girl who was christened 'Count-for-nothing'.) By this they are deprived not only of their birthright, but also their basic knowledge and recognition of what they are in themselves, that is moral persons with ineliminable titles and standing.

Thus the victims of racial prejudice, anti-semitism, and such-like categorical discriminations, suffer not only a fundamental outrage to their proper titles and standing, but also – in a quite clear and literal sense – de-humanization, de-gradation, displacement from the *gradus* of being members of humankind. The surprise is not that such people should resent this in every fibre of their being, but rather that they should still be able to retain, and to demand full recognition of, their sense of themselves as wholly and rightfully 'human' despite centuries of civil and cultural oppression. Rousseau did not speak of these specific forms of the denial of the humanity of others: to this extent he was of his age. But he spoke repeatedly, and centrally, of the non-human situatedness of the peasantry and dispossessed poor; of other persecuted religious minorities, and the like. In so doing, he broached, and gave clear grounding for, those moral and political movements towards 'liberation' which have so marked, and continue to mark, the moral climate of the past two centuries. (As I remarked before, Rousseau would *not* endorse 'liberation' conceived in terms of the replacement of one tyranny by another, the oppressors and oppressed merely swapping places).

In every case, he excogitated the connection between these large-scale civil and political inequities and the fundamental human need, and title, to have and hold categorical standing as a person with persons. Doing so enables him rightly to see, and to stress, the continuity between such very visible and marked cases, and the seemingly more minute and personal devaluation and invalidation which is suffered (and/or may be felt to be suffered) by, for example, an individual whose cooperation is simply presumed on without his ever having been consulted, let alone allowed time or place to comment, in some matter which largely affects him. Or again, the sense of being written out of existence as wholly without signifying presence, which an adolescent may suffer (take himself to suffer) when his right, won by increasing age, to take part in or stand as one ratifier of proposals about the manner of common life of the home, up to now 'managed' exclusively by his parents, is not at all perceived. As Rousseau notes (E 4, 215; IV, 494), adolescents are peculiarly prickly in such matters, standing as they do at the threshold of full adult incorporation as completely titled participants. They are very anxious to demand full recognition for their standing, and will often let nothing that might be construed as the smallest slight to their 'persons' pass unrequited. Thus they are often strident and demanding: their *amour-propre* is very ready to break bounds. Just because it is, Rousseau is very insistent that they earlier be given no delusively inflated idea of their supreme importance, of others' duty to stand obedient before them. To do so is to store up ruin for them. (Compare the fable of the 'two young men', told at E 4, 227ff; IV, 512ff, which is highly pertinent to this.)

As I have suggested in section 1, it is the individual personal significance of such insults to and denials of 'humanity' in one's presence to others to which Rousseau affords central explanatory and moral import. Large-scale, entrenched, civil and political inequalities and degradations are, in his view, to be made sense of as elaborations of those same phenomena of personal invalidation, with its return of self-assertive combativeness, which we see and experience in the minutiae of our lives. Many will, of course, contend that this is the wrong order of priority, philosophically and in terms of moral and political action. Rousseau does not think so; I shall be trying to show the force of his approach explicitly and implicitly throughout.

## 2.7 *The Elementary Forms of* Amour-propre

Stressing that the primary locus of the effort after self-consolidation as a person lies in small-scale human interchanges of many kinds leads on to the second elaboration I want to make at this point. In Rousseau's order of exposition, as I have so far reported this, the self-appropriation and utilization of oneself in one's 'physical being'[6] precedes and is completed before one embarks upon the difficult task of contending for station with others as a 'moral being'. It might then be imagined that this second phase in one's self's development and completion (what Rousseau calls one's 'second birth'; E 4, 211–2; IV, 489–90) somehow emerges 'out of the blue', with all the predicaments and concerns preliminary to it conjured *ad hoc* out of the air. If this were indeed so, Rousseau's project – however fine the points he makes in parts of it – would be broken-backed. For no continuous, intelligible and defensible general programme of account would have been achieved.

But this is not the situation at all. Emile's (everyman's) prior separate development in his 'physical being' is a quite deliberate and carefully managed holding back of an insistent press of himself upon others as a fully titled, demanding and commanding, human presence for them, which is already contained in the primordial movements of the human *psyche* in its effort after taking secure hold on life right from the beginning – as described by Rousseau in *Emile* Book 1, and in the early parts of Book 2. The emergence of Emile's concern to achieve standing for himself as a 'person' in his presence for others does not come inexplicably and unprepared for. It is, rather, the *re*-emergence of patterns of self-articulation, and of conceptions of and modes of address to others, which are contained (in rudimentary forms) in the very first stirrings of our engagement with the world. Emile's upbringing between, roughly, two and sixteen years, comprises his tutor's (Jean-Jacques') deliberate stress on *other* facets of his embodied self's striving for life (his life in his physical being). This is a necessary and desirable foundation if the claims of *amour-propre*, when these *are* voiced and answered, are to be handled and managed in a way that is constructive and creative. Nothing comes unexplained and unprepared for in Rousseau's account: the materials are all present, in germinal and prefiguring form, from the very start.

As I have suggested before, and will argue in more detail in the next section, we do not have to take Rousseau's genetic story of Emile's development with absolute literalness to grasp what is essential in what is being said. Rousseau's principal thought is that we are, potentially and actually, very complex creatures indeed, in the character of our desires, needs, ideas, values, etc. Some of these needs and desires fall into very roughly demarcatable groups: some are primarily addressed to our self-maintenance and survival as intact and viable physical creatures. Others are primarily concerned with our involvement and connection as a 'human presence' with other humans. We may look at these rough groupings more or less independently first; and then study their inter-relations and transformations as they are put together to make up the complete picture of the whole person in full possession and disclosure of all that comprises their life. We may, indeed, have good reason for holding that unless things are pretty well sorted out and stably ordered in relation to one of the approximate groupings of human needs etc., things may go badly awry in relation to other groupings. So it would be best to come to terms with the former first. But none of this is really *a priori* pedagogics. It is rather a carefully structured account of the multiplicity of elements that make up humankind's self-composition, each in their respective significance and in their inter-relation with other elements. All of this is as much applicable to the presently enacted life of an adult as it is to the fictive upbringing of a young man from infancy. This latter form of presentation allows a very clearly ordered treatment of the issues. The trouble is, and the assessment of Rousseau's work has suffered from this, that the manner of presentation may be taken for part of the substance of the matter. Thus Rousseau may be censured for propounding bizarre or unworkable pedagogic procedures. But, as I have said, pedagogy is not really at the heart of his concerns. These lie in the analysis and explanation of the character and interrelations of the multiple facets of the complete character of humans.

Consonant with this, Rousseau does not contend that the infant is some passive *tabula rasa* waiting only to be written on by whatever experiences befall him (cf. very clearly, E I, 65–6; IV, 286–7). If we argue that it is, we shall never be able to explain how the complexities of human forms and human modes of life come about (except by, incoherently, supposing 'culture' to spring up out of nowhere. But how extant blank sheets could enculturate new blank sheets is not clearly comprehensible). Rather, Rousseau holds that, in the neonate, the seeds of all that is to come are already present, and reveal their presence in primitive disclosures of patterns and modes that will later become explicitly articulated and consolidated.

Most significant, in the present context, among these elementary prefigurations are those that pertain to *amour-propre* (to which, indeed, Rousseau makes very early reference,[7] only for the matter to be put on one side as Emile's 'physical' development takes precedence, until his 'second birth' (really, his rebirth) at the start of Book 4). These pertain to the infant's and child's anger, rage and resentment at (what he inchoately apprehends as) frustration, denial or deprivation of that which will foster and answer his needs and demands for sustenance and support. Intrinsic to this is the infant's sub-articulate representation of himself as having an unquestionable title to be well-served (his 'omnipotence' fantasy). This carries a coordinate representation of others as fit only to serve him, and as malign or vengefully derelict if they do not. All of this is a clear, and very penetrating, depiction of elements in what we may properly call the 'paranoid' position, or configuration, in an infant's development, or as an aspect in the psychological dispositions and address of an adult. Certain components within the overall reactivity of the infant, certain components that may remain present in the reactivity of adults, suggest very strongly that the primitive standpoint from which efforts are made to form a construal of what the world contains,[8] how it works, is that of commanding it as the tool of one's imperious will. When the world fails to be immediately subservient, it is both attacked, but also felt to be malign and threatening in its withholding and denial of the satisfaction of the infant's desire. Thus we find the characteristic oscillation between megalomania and a sense of persecution, between demandingness and placatory appeasement.

If it is correct to suppose (and Rousseau makes a convincing case for it; there is much other evidence for this also) that this pattern of reactivity with its incorporated ideational structure is very prominent in human psychological processes and activities, then the materials and attitudes which, on fuller articulation and consolidation, will be clearly recognizable as *amour-propre* (especially in its tendency to take an 'inflamed' form) are present *ab initio*. For the initial 'presence' to the world which is taken up is of oneself as entitled to make masterful and domineering demands upon it to be at one's absolute disposal. This, of course, prefigures the posture of the master over the slave, the exploiter's rejoicing in the dispossession of the exploited. So Rousseau is enabled to produce a continuous, integrated, account here, which introduces no new elements *ad hoc* simply to meet an unanticipated problem.

I am not suggesting that this 'paranoid' structure is the only one present and operative in the activity and reactivity of the elementary mind. This could not be so. Other processes are also going forward, which counter and ameliorate the generally deleterious character of the former. One such is the desire to explore and gain effective hold on the way the world really works, which Emile's tutor places at the forefront to begin with. But, as we shall see later, many other strands are woven into the overall pattern as well.

Quite generally, I shall use the notion of a 'configuration of mind' to refer to the obtaining of various differing three-part structures which comprise various aspects (or phases) in human self-unfolding into action. In every case there is: (a) the form and content of the individual's own self-constitution, his desires, attitudes, beliefs, values etc. This may, but need not, include his own *conscious* construal of his own self-constitution (which could be mistaken). (b) The individual's construal of the self-constitution of the other(s), particularly as they address him, with whom he takes himself to be engaged, related at any time. Such construals are always complementary to the individual's own self-construals. Also, and very importantly, they may often be quite erroneous or very partial in the 'reading' they give to the character and dispositions of the other(s). (c) There is also the individual's construal of the kind and range of possible forms of interchange and relation that may obtain between himself and the other(s). This, again, will be complementary to the constructions placed on his own and the other(s) constitution and dispositions. This may be very partial or erroneous. Using this frame of account[9] as fundamental, we shall be in the best position to interpret the character and force of Rousseau's explanations. For, throughout his work, he insisted that what we are to and for ourselves is strictly coordinated with what we take others to be for us, ourselves to be for them, and with the forms of transaction that are available between us. There can be no question of understanding the character of the individual human soul-in-action by looking at it solipsistically. We know ourselves, we are ourselves, only in interchange with our surroundings. This is what lies at the root of Rousseau saying, in the passage quoted earlier, that 'The study suitable for man is that of his relations'. For, in the manner and content of those transactions is comprised the concrete substantiality of his life as an animate, sensitive, feeling and thinking being.

We find, then, an extraordinary convergence of Rousseau's ideas into a system of great integration and coherence. That which is 'unnatural' is that which is (de)formed by the work on it of a domineering and oppressive will. Such wills are, originally, exhibitions of 'inflamed' *amour-propre*, an excess in self-assertion as an overbearing 'human presence' for others. 'Inflamed' *amour-propre* is the upshot of distortions in one of the primitive modes of human address to the world as the arena in which to make one's way as a living, forceful and potent creature. It is no wonder that Rousseau held that he had always reasoned, at bottom, upon the same principles.

## 2.8 Self-alienation

I have looked so far at such general themes in Rousseau's work as concern contrasts and connections between the natural and the social; between the good and the corrupt; between *amour-de-soi* and *amour-propre*. I have tried to indicate firmly the lines of interpretation I think should be given to these which I shall be following out. Other related ideas – often, as with some of the above, mistakenly taken to comprise exclusive contrasts – are those to do with independence and dependence; freedom and enslavement (both external and 'internal'); power and servitude; integrity and self-alienation or self-estrangement. Some of these have been touched on explicitly already; I do not want to give further description of them at this point, except to say a little more about the last.

Rousseau contends that one whose life and character is dominated by inflamed *amour-propre* suffers self-alienation or self-estrangement.[10] What might this mean? Someone who requires, in order to know and feel his 'weight' as a signifying person to others, that he hold dominating power over them or invidious prestigious precedence before them[11] must at every point order his own life with a view to his continuing to have command over others. It is inherent to the constitution of his own self-construction that he stands over others in these sorts of ways. If we now focus, because this is a particularly clear case, on the way by which we can continue to domineer over others in terms of our exclusive possession of invidious prestige, it becomes clear that, to do so, we need to curry and secure the special acclaim and deference of others for ourselves, drawing it away from other people. This means we must watch and play up to the invidiously discriminating prepossessions of others; we are therefore controlled in the *persona* we adopt, the manners and aspirations we parade, by the judgment and opinion of what we put on display made by *alio*, another. We are therefore under the direction of *alii*, suffer self-subordination to others, self-alienation. Thus Rousseau writes:

> Even domination is servile when it is connected with opinion, for you depend on the prejudices of these you govern by prejudices. To lead them as you please, you must conduct yourself as they please. They have only to change their way of thinking, and you must perforce change your way of acting. (E 2, 83–4; IV, 308–9)

(Another of Rousseau's crucial notions, of the empire of 'opinion' or 'prejudice', comes to the surface here.)

It should not be supposed that this is some knowingly embraced and played 'social game', which you exploit for your own purposes, all the while keeping your true inward self distant from and untouched by it. Sometimes it may be so. Most commonly, however, the objectives of superordinate power and celebrity before others come to be immediately self-constitutive, with the attendant shaping of the self to the pleasure of others being, all unwares, taken into oneself. What the notion of self-estrangement adds to that of self-alienation is that we, by this, have become strangers to who we really are, to our own proper needs, purposes, goods; our being and lives have become unnatural, in just the manner outlined earlier.

The contrast is with someone who knows, owns, and furthers the values and goods which are inherent to the well-being of his own constitution as a human being. As we have seen, some of these values and goods *do* require that we hold and deploy a position in our own person for others. So it is clear that it is not alien to our own proper constitution to need, and to require, some forms of acknowledgement and recognition from others. To require *any* such thing is *not* automatically to have become abandoned, in one's own being, to the control and direction of others. It is, however, essential to be clear which requirements placed on others to receive for oneself recognition from them are compatible with, indeed essential to, one's proper good and whole completion, and why they are. And, on the other hand, to be clear which requirements are either irrelevant to this, or positively inimical to it because involving self-estrangement. It is Rousseau's achievement, not his failure, to be able to show that between total mutual isolation and complete lack of interconnection, on the one side; and, on the other, the loss of one's self under the direct, or indirect, invasive and controlling direction of the other, there lay the possibility and reality of each our own full self-articulation and self-possession in mutual reciprocal recognition.

Rousseau was never encumbered by, so we should not encumber him with, the (obviously bizarre) idea that *all* human encounter entailed self-estrangement. *Some* specific modes of encounter do, and Rousseau sharply diagnosed and criticized these. But he never held that the cure was complete withdrawal. There are modes of human mutuality which are wholly necessary to each our own full constitutive character, and are wholly benign. The project is to identify these, and to explain their significance. It is not to turn aside from anything and everything of this kind.

While arguing that many of Rousseau's themes are articulated in polar terms (dependence/independence; free/enslaved; and so on) I have been very careful to stress that his was no rhetoric of mutually exclusive dichotomies. This is not because he says one thing, but, to our detriment and confusion, means another; but because, to adapt a remark of Wollheim's, he was guilty of no more than intelligence. He knew, and made perfectly clear, that 'dependence' for instance does not signify one and the same thing in every imaginable circumstance. It was not, therefore, to be subject to some indiscriminate criticism. We can depend on others because we are not economically self-sufficient; or not emotionally sufficient to ourselves; or not capable of sustaining a sense of our own personal worth without endless 'stroking'. And so on. Each of these has its distinctive features, distinctive problems, and requires particular treatment, which Rousseau gives. To say, as many have done, that Rousseau sees 'dependence' *tout court* as containing the seed of all our trouble is not to see what he is saying.

It may be objected that if we ascribe to Rousseau specific, detailed theses about *particular* modes of dependence, freedom, naturalness, etc., his argument may gain in coherence but will lose in breadth and scope of explanatory effect. But an idea can be far-reaching, in the end, only because it *is* sharply focused and exactly deployed. So it is with Rousseau's ideas.

### 3  Analysis and Genesis

When discussing aspects of Rousseau's views about the nature and significance of *amour-propre*, in section 2, I noted that he presents nearly all of these views in terms of phases, or stages, in the historical development of Emile's (everyman's) personality and character (or, in the case of the argument in DI, in terms of phases in the history of humankind at large). I suggested that this embedding of his points as parts of the narrative of a psychological development was not essential to their nature and cogency. Further, reading them only in those terms is often apt to mislead, and to give rise to questions and difficulties which mask what is really significant, because they attend the manner of presentation not the content of what is being presented.

Virtually *all* of Rousseau's major works are cast in the form of a narrative of a succession of events. Sometimes, without doubt, this is not a mere presentational manner, but crucial to the content and cogency of what is being claimed, since much is made to depend on what happens at this moment or that. Also, one of Rousseau's major ideas was that actual human history is not a history of progress, liberation, enlightenment and increasing happiness – quite the opposite. That is, of course, specifically a view about the course of successive events, and could not be abstracted from that. But, on many important points, we could and should make such an abstraction, in order to grasp better the material we are being offered.

To take, briefly, the case of *amour-propre* once more. What is really in view here is claims about aspects of human self-constitution, as a bearer of moral significance having a categorical standing for others. Also in view are contentions about the significance of this for the freedom, happiness and fulfilment of each of us. These points are apt to get overlaid, or masked, if it is thought to be crucial that *amour-propre* does or does not precede competent mastery of the environment; is or is not brought on specifically by sexual jealousy;[12] and so on. Such questions are interesting, in their way. Where Rousseau *needs* to rely on some particular claim about the order of genesis of this or that, then this must be defended. But we should not, throughout, feel that we must engage in *a priori*, or empirical, history and pedagogy. We are offered an account of the nature and ramifications of certain patterns of mind, feeling and action. We can look at that account, assess its cogency, examine the reasonableness of the claims made about it, without being concerned how it came into being. Indeed, questions about the latter would be of little interest if that into the coming-into-being of which we were inquiring were of little interest. So the primary emphasis must always fall on the structure and elements of the mind of individuals, the forms of society, as objects for critical examination and interpretation. Once it is clearer what these comprise, then we may consider how they might come to be or pass away. But that is a secondary matter. In fact, of course, unless one is very clear what it is one is addressing, one will not be clear what it is one must account for the rise or demise of, and one will be liable to produce irrelevant genetic stories.

So, for all these reasons, I have separated fairly rigorously throughout questions about the 'what' from questions about the 'how come'; that is, questions which pertain to the analysis of configurations of mind, society, political institutions, from questions about the genesis of these. This is, I believe, an aid to clarity, in seeing the telling points and focusing on the right queries. I do not, however, ignore genetic issues – to do so would be absurd. Not only are there some genetic points that are inseparable from analytic ones; but also so much in Rousseau does revolve round issues of how things came into being (and hence, for instance, give rise to suggestions about how they might be prevented from coming into being) that one would produce a seriously unbalanced account if one did ignore these. Rousseau had many shrewd, and well-grounded, views on these matters too; but for all that I would not want to make this his major achievement. There is just as much that is speculative and insufficiently defended, and it is easy to be dragged down, unnecessarily, by this.

If we free ourselves a little from such impediments, we do not, of course, free ourselves altogether from all empirical checks and constraints. Substantive claims about human needs, the character and possibilities of human feelings and attitudes, the ways various facets of mind may interact, must be made. If this is not so, all the theorizing floats in the air, and does not connect and cohere with ground-level realities. But it could never be otherwise. Theories about individuals, about morality, society, politics, must latch on to real phenomena or be of minimal interest only. Rousseau has no greater, though of course no lesser, responsibility than anyone in this regard. The question is not whether he makes empirical suppositions, but which ones he makes and how defensible they are. Plato divided men's souls into three elements; Hobbes claimed an innate egoism in man. The issue cannot be one of remaining sceptically distanced just because such suggestions are being made at all. It can only be to evaluate, as soundly as one can, the worth of the particular suppositions that this particular theorist makes either in general, or for this or that particular point in his argument. As I shall try to show, Rousseau comes out rather well on this score. He did not, for instance, hold – contrary to common estimation of his views – that we are all at root, before we are damaged by 'society', utterly pure and pristine in angelic goodness and innocence. As I have indicated already, the tendency to domineering control of others is something Rousseau thinks goes rather deep. We need, without preconceptions, to see what he takes for men's actuality and possibility, and to see if it can bear the weight he places on it.

Although I do separate analytic and genetic questions in what follows, I have sometimes still spoken of one configuration of mind as being, analytically understood, a 'development' of another. This is not because I am assuming the one grows out of the other in an empirically traceable way, though in fact it may do so. I speak so because the one contains and displays many like elements and structrues possessed by the other, but in a more elaborated form. It should cause no confusion to regard the one as being a development of the other, in that what is prefigured there is in the other case fully delineated. Where a particular course of chronological development is in view, I shall say so and discharge the attendant commitments accordingly.

## 4 The First Topic

The first substantive issue I want to consider in depth is an *analysis* of *amour-propre* in its normal, and in its 'inflamed', character. I have said a good deal on this in section 2 above, which will facilitate the discussion. So the issue is: what is *amour-propre* composed of? What are its component elements – the values, self-assessments, assessments of others, dispositions etc., it involves? How do these relate to each other, how are they 'knit' together? What larger significance-does it have, for the happiness and personal integrity of the individual? What are its social and political manifestations and implications? Only once the analysis has been completed shall I consider Rousseau's ideas of how 'inflamed' *amour-propre*, in particular, came into being, the genesis of that.

It may seem perverse to begin with what lies so close, in Rousseau's view, to man's depraved and corrupted character and circumstances (though I have contended that *amour-propre* does not, in its very essence, result in this). But I do not think it is. It is only when we understand properly what it is in and about *amour-propre* that Rousseau found good or evil, and why he did, that we shall be in a position to understand what he wanted to argue constructively for, and why he did so. Without this as a guide, it would be very easy to focus on adventitious and irrelevant features in what Rousseau says is 'natural' and 'good' in and for men, and to miss the core of his claims about these, for the lack of an idea of what problematic he is specifically speaking to.

It is also fairly clear that Rousseau's own ideas about man's 'natural' character, and 'natural' circumstances and situation, were not completely whole and clear in his mind from his very first writings. As we shall see, in his early *A Discourse on the Arts and Sciences*, Rousseau's comments on what he takes to be man's intact condition and blessed circumstances are sketchy. It is straightforward that his views about this should deepen and extend as he focussed steadily on the problems 'corrupt' man and society disclosed to him over a long period. I think we grasp the driving intent in Rousseau's own thinking better if we start with the latter.

I shall begin, then, with an examination of Rousseau's first account of social decline and depravity, as put forward in *A Discourse on the Arts and Sciences*.

# 2

# *Self-Estrangement and Subservience to Others*

## 1 Preliminaries

A very prominent feature of Rousseau's work is his criticism of 'society'. The major purpose of this chapter is to consider the nature and basis of his criticisms, and to evaluate them. What precise faults and defects did Rousseau have in view when he called 'social' or 'civilized' man depraved and corrupt? What exactly was it in social life and social structures he took such exception to? These questions relate to the analysis of the elements and structure of the character and circumstances of social man, to the components in their inter-relations that make up his dispositions, beliefs, values, and make up the institutions and practices he participates in and sustains.

I consider here also Rousseau's theories about the genesis of the depravity in society as (in his view) we ordinarily find it, and of the depravity of social man. This will give us an idea of how Rousseau thinks about the 'root-stock' from which these monster growths have sprung, or on to which they have been grafted. This 'root-stock', man's 'natural' condition and situation, will then be considered in detail in chapter 3. Finally, here, I abstract from Rousseau's criticisms a picture of what, in the light of them, he must be committed to seeing as the necessary correctives and ameliorations if men are to thrive and prosper. In effect, a constructive 'agenda' will issue; and I shall show how he does indeed take up and follow through the main heads on that agenda.

It is worth repeating, what I have already stressed in chapter 1, that when Rousseau criticizes 'society' he is *not*, and must not be taken to be, censuring all forms of human connection without distinction or limit. He always had in view *particular* modes of social relation and interaction which, for specific reasons, he held to be damaging and corrupting. It never was his idea that personal salvation or wholeness could be ours in the condition and circum-stances we should be in if we never, in any way, had connection with others. We shall see, in due course, what form 'society' should take, in Rousseau's view, if it is to be benign, creative and enlarging to individuals, as it ought

to be. But he begins by studying forms of sociality which are quite the opposite in their effects (even if not in their intent). This is what I consider now.

I begin with Rousseau's first investigation of 'corrupt' society, as articulated in *A Discourse on the Arts and Sciences*, usually called the First Discourse
(published in 1750). This was not his first publication; he had previously
published poems, and discussions on music. But it is the first in which those
concerns which drive and dominate all his major work find expression.

## 2  A Discourse on the Arts and Sciences

### 2.1  Preamble

The story of how Rousseau came to write this is famous. I give his own
words:

> One day [on his way to visit Diderot, confined at Vincennes] I took the *Mercure
> de France* and, glancing through it as I walked, I came upon this question
> propounded by the Dijon Academy for next year's prize: Has the progress of the
> sciences and arts done more to corrupt morals or improve them?
>   The moment I read this I beheld another universe and became another man
> . . . when I reached Vincennes I was in a state of agitation bordering on delirium
> . . . All my little passions were stifled by an enthusiasm for truth, liberty, and
> virtue . . . (C 8, 327–8; I, 350–1).

### 2.2  Outline of the Argument

The question posed by the Academy is a causal question. The full question
reads: 'Has the restoration of the arts and sciences had a purifying effect upon
morals?' Rousseau's approach to the issues he reviews is shaped by this as an
inquiry into causation.

The essay opens with some remarks whose bearing is at first uncertain; I shall
return to these. Rousseau then cites in The First Part many instances from
history where the arts and sciences were flourishing in a nation but that nation
was in moral decline or decay; and instances where a country was backward in
learning but full of moral vigour and strength. By moral excellence here,
Rousseau understands people 'attentive only to the obligations of humanity
and the necessities of nature . . . serving his country, obliging his friends, and
relieving the unhappy' (DAS, 14; III, 17). Although Rousseau often mentions
military success as the sign of the moral 'health' of a society, he does so only
because he takes it to be indicative of the strength of mutual loyalty and willingness to give service for the protection and good of one's fellows. When Rousseau
berates learning for its 'uselessness' it is routinely its making no contribution
to the general well-being of men, understood in the sense outlined, that he has
in mind. We see already great stress on mutual cooperative endeavour and
common support in shared life in Rousseau's moral ideas.

Even if Rousseau's historical accuracy is not questioned, we can only infer from what he has so far said that moral decadence and a high level of, and value placed upon, learning coincide, not that the latter *causes* the former (or *vice-versa*). Rousseau plainly saw this, as he explains in replies to his critics.[1] We *can* infer that a high level of, or value placed upon, learning is not by itself sufficient to cause or maintain moral vigour; but that it is so would have been an extreme claim to make; and that it is not so is not a very interesting conclusion to reach.

In the Second Part Rousseau tries to substantiate the claim that a high level of, or value placed on, learning has a significant deleterious causal impact on morals. He considers the advancement of the sciences and arts as a complex individual and social phenomenon, which discloses many and various motives, interests and values, linked and contributory to aspects of the social framework, social strategies and processes. He refuses to take the self-presented image of the scientist or artist, as for instance a pure and disinterested seeker after truth untouched by social ambition and personal interests, unquestioningly at face value. Self-deception, conscious or unconscious interested deception of others, may lead to the creation of this image, which affords those who present themselves as made in it certain decided advantages. Rousseau is engaged in the process of unmasking (a favourite image of his), of demystifying, a mode of personal and social activity, trying to expose the (disreputable) intents and strategies which find obscured satisfaction through it.

He contends that much of the 'higher learning' is born of dubious, even immoral, dispositions:

> Astronomy was born of superstition, eloquence of ambition, hatred, falsehood, and flattery; geometry of avarice; physics of an idle curiosity; all, even moral philosophy, of human pride. Thus the arts and sciences owe their birth to our vices; we should be less doubtful of their advantages, if they had sprung from our virtues. (DAS, 14; III, 17)

The higher learning is maintained by luxury and engenders further luxurious indulgence and wastrelism; it is the handmaid of idleness, and encourages people away from responsible and humanely worthwhile activity (ibid). Whilst learning is supposedly devoted to establishing the truth, it engenders disabling doubt (DAS 23; III, 27); it also prides itself on its power to make a mock of common beliefs and social dogmas that sustain ordinary human action. Where learning is highly valued and honoured in a nation people will use the academic calling merely as a path to personal prestige and celebrity, and say whatever they think will capture applause whether or not it is true or they think it is (DAS 16; 17–18; III, 19, 21–2)

If intellectual sophistication and refinement are especially esteemed, basic moral decency, basic literacy, which are essential to the possibility of fundamental human well-being, will be regarded as trifling and insignificant:

The question is no longer whether a man is honest, but whether he is clever. We do not ask whether a book is useful, but whether it is well written. Rewards are lavished on wit and ingenuity, while virtue is left unhonoured. There are a thousand prizes for fine discourses, and none for good actions (DAS 22; III, 25)

Finally, access to the higher learning has become available to, and personally important to, many who have neither the true disposition to it nor the ability for it. They have been then uprooted from that in which they could have excelled, and been any good to themselves and others (DAS 24–5; III, 28–9). However, there are those (Rousseau cites Bacon, Descartes, Newton) whose native genius enabled them to 'raise monuments to the glory of human understanding'. But, he says, they would have done so without the lavish seats of higher education or the distinctive prestige set upon intellectual display. Such men merit true and real honour, and may be allowed to stand as true beneficiaries of mankind. This is not because their work has immediate practical utility, but because their discoveries as such enrich the plentitude of possessed human life and experience. So Rousseau is not extolling low-browed subarticulacy; true understanding merits honest esteem, in his view. It is only when learning is turned by disreputable purposes into a deformed mockery of itself that he is critical of it.

Rousseau concludes that, with such few exceptions, the advancement of learning is both a manifestation of and a further contributory cause towards moral degeneracy, moral irresponsibility and the defeat of virtue and goodness.

### 2.3 A First Appraisal of the Argument

Some of Rousseau's particular points are questionable. Even if scientific inquiries (e.g. geometry – one of his cited cases) were born of vices, this does not show that further commitment to their development was the expression of vice or fostered vice. But Rousseau himself puts this point only moderately. Again, we may be impatient with what looks like Rousseau's *own* self-serving scorn of teachers who stifle genius ('Ordinary masters would only have cramped their intelligence, by confining it within the narrow limits of their own capacity'; DAS 25; III, 29). I want, however, to try to bring out Rousseau's overall thrust in his discussion, rather than pick up this or that small point.

Rousseau is reflecting on the advancement of learning as a general phenomenon bedded in the concerns, objectives and values that shape the lives of individual people and the social climate of a nation. So he considers the motives and advantages that are being fostered and celebrated in making such an 'advance'. His view is not that the constitutive criteria for the cogency of, say, physical inquiry embody class or gender prejudices for instance, though this idea has been, and is, propounded. Rather, he sees that engaging in scientific, literary or artistic work represents a choice, in effect a moral choice, being made by people about how they would do well to comport themselves and use their life's time. So he wants to ask: What values are embraced in making such a choice, and in such a path of life being celebrated and prestigious in the culture and institutions of a country?

It is not implausible to hold that such a choice for one's life's direction would not be widespread – though some might still make it – unless clearly envisageable and striking personal advantages were foreseen from it, advantages which it needed no great refinement to grasp the significance of (for refinement, if it comes at all, comes as a result of the life undertaken after the choice, and does not exist beforehand). Rousseau is suggesting that the most palpable of such advantages is the enjoyment of singular repute and distinction, invidious[2] prestigious superiority over common, ignorant, coarse people. But, evidently, the life of learning would not yield that to any individual unless there was a general social orientation towards paying the tribute of prestige to people for ingenuity and wit of this kind. So his second suggestion is that differential tribute and acclaim would not be given to such effusions unless luxurious indolence and indulgence had become very widespread, causing people to look around them for diversions and trinkets to exercise their restless favour or scorn upon.

Let us consider these suggestions in turn. Rousseau is not saying, in relation to the first, that (most) men choose scientific and artistic endeavour as a sufficient good to make it their life's direction because of its inherent power to give enlargement to the mind, or for its potential use to oblige humanity – and then they find, as an agreeable bonus, that they are well-regarded, esteemed and honoured by others. Here, as elsewhere[3], Rousseau thinks there is nothing at all wrong with this; he *never* held that esteem, repute, and honour should be altogether expelled from all individual and social relations (if ever they possibly could be). He only wanted them to be given to the *right* things, to that which is in truth excellent, estimable and honourable (see the point, made above, about Rousseau's notion, in this argument, of what true moral excellence comprises). His point rather is that the winning of applause, securing a place of disdainful superiority, themselves *comprise* the qualities which make a course of life worth choosing in people's eyes. So this or that life is chosen, and engaged with in this or that manner, only so far as the person judges these primary decisive goals of his will be furthered and secured.

This has several important implications. First, some achievement or accomplishment within that course of life will count as desirable, meritorious, if and only if it is one that wins applause, esteem, invidious singularity for its exponent. Its being 'excellent' signifies *only*: it has the power to (or does) elicit prestige and differential celebrity (for me). What the achievement may in itself be, aside from this, is *immaterial*. It may be the discovery of an important truth. But if it were, that would be altogether incidental. If a falsehood would elicit fawning deference that would do just as well. These pseudo-excellences or merits are what Rousseau at various times and places calls: caprice, artificial, fashionable, prestige, mere opinion, 'merits'. He has a great deal to say about them; here we are noting only their first introduction. (See, especially, DAS, 17–18, 22; III, 21, 25–6).

The idea of a prestige-merit has an immediate corollary. Reputation, enjoyment of singular precedent distincion, are 'possessions' that are embodied in the attitudes held by other people towards one. (I forget who said that the definition of a 'celebrity' was 'someone who was famous for being famous'.) They consist in one's having and holding a certain place in the feelings, regard and activities of others. Acquiring and keeping such possessions then necessarily requires the compliance of others, their willingness (for whatever reason) to hold one up and pay their tribute to one. The retention of reputation, therefore, demands the perpetuation of that compliance. Unless people are unwaveringly besotted with you, you must be constantly mindful to control and direct their wayward favour so that it adheres to you. To do so, you must study, both manipulate but also fit yourself to, the currents and fashions of acclaim and disdain that vacillate this way or that. You must cut a figure which is in consonance with their predelictions, their prejudices, within the limits of your power to sway these (which is usually very limited). If you do not, you will be passed over, scorned and dismissed. By this, you lose the primary good which you were seeking. (Compare this: 'It is true that in France Socrates would not have drunk the hemlock, but he would have drunk a potion infinitely more bitter, of insult, mockery, and contempt a hundred times worse than death'. (DAS, 13; III, 15). This is the fate that awaits the honest man who insists on telling his prestige-craving fellows unpopular truth. This Rousseau came to feel was his fate too.)

Of course, there are opinion-makers, who seem effortlessly to call the tune to which everyone else dances for fear they are left out. But the prestigious glory of those who hold their place only by opinion never lasts long; yesterday's god is today's fallen idol. This is, as much as anything, because the compliant deference and adulation of others can never be reliably counted on. One is not alone in desiring invidious precedent regard for oneself. Others are filled with this desire too, and will use the glory that connection with you reflects on them for personal advancement of the same general kind for themselves only so long as they think it serves them well. Hangers-on are only disappointed and resentful stars. This entails that mutual relations are necessarily those of competition and malice, of efforts to displace, deride and downgrade curbed only by the fear that one may also be dragged down if one too obviously seeks to replace the now dominating presence in the highest prestigious position.

The theme of this correlative malicious, aggressive, desire to humiliate does not bulk large in DAS (but see p. 6; III, 8–9). We shall return to it later. But how it is located in the overall frame of ideas should now be plain enough. The more prominent point is that to do with being required, by the hope of claiming singular distinction, to mould oneself to a form pleasing and admirable according to the predelictions of others. This is the first sighting of Rousseau's claim that power and command that rest in opinion and prejudice are delusory; the master is in fact enslaved to his slave. We see also the immediately related claim that those who stand in command are moulded by the requirements which the need to curry favour of others imposes on them. This explains why the first *Discourse* should open, apparently inexplicably, with Rousseau speaking of the stifling of natural liberty, and of men being caused 'to love their own slavery, and so [be made] what is called a civilized people' (DAS, 4–6; III, 7–9). We can see why these comments are perfectly in order, and how they give voice to Rousseau's deeper concerns.

Rousseau says little in detail in this essay about the 'cost' to the individual of setting as his paramount goal the possession of invidious distinction for himself. He tends to talk more of the price paid by those who still try to keep faith with real excellence. But we can readily imagine what some of these costs would be: and sketching some of these out will be useful preparation for appreciating Rousseau's later extended treatment of these matters. It is evident, for instance, that the prospect of gaining such a prize – if prize it should be called – is rather small. The pursuit of it will be treacherous; retaining it will be perilous. So a life given up to this is unlikely to yield happiness in its course. We shall also have to consider whether the crown, were it won, is inherently apt to yield its wearer reward and happiness. For the path may be painful, *and* the objective empty.

Second, as noted above, the whole tenor of such a life will be coloured by aggression, competition, vindictiveness, humiliation and the like. Third, necessarily only very few can enjoy prominent and palpable distinction (logically, only *one* can enjoy preeminent distinction, but that is *very* unlikely to be instantiated). If everybody is somebody, nobody is anybody. Thus, the majority are bound to feel their dearest desire frustrated. The formation of sub-groups, so that there can be more big fishes because there are lots of little ponds, may ease this frustration a little. But jealousy and spite will still live within the groups; and between them there will be no respect or regard, but hostility or contemptuous indifference. To achieve singular distinctive applause for oneself one will, also as noted, be obliged to cut the cloth of oneself to meet the taste of others. Such attributes or occupations which, in themselves, would answer one's real need will be despised and disregarded by oneself in so far as they are believed to be ridiculous to others. Finally, in so far as someone's sense of his own identity as a person of significance has come to reside in his holding particular prestigious attention and regard, the removal of that will be his annihilation (his becoming no-thing).[4] I think it is quite clear that all of these represent very heavy liabilities which one takes on if one pursues prestigious distinction as one's good.

We could note two further ramifications of the case. To win invidious prestige and celebrity, putting on a *show* of possessing the appropriately remarkable and distinguished qualities will do just as well, sometimes better, than really possessing them. We are thus confronted with a *double* appearance – we are twice removed from reality. Not only, first, are the 'excellences' in view only pseudo-excellences, mere prestige-eliciting attributes regardless of their actual truth, beauty or goodness; but also the show, the pretence, of these (pseudo-) excellences will be on display, not even their real instantiation (which might, ultimately, be a partial salvation from them). This reproduces exactly Plato's double concern in the *Republic* with, first, what *real* justice is, in contrast with its superficial or merely external imitations; and with, second, the benefits of *really possessing* real justice, as opposed to only pretending to possess, or passing for a possessor of, it (or, even, a pretend possessor to superficial justice). This likeness between Rousseau and Plato is no accident. Rousseau was deeply concerned with the man hiding behind the mask; with the show of politeness that veils spite; the pretended generosity which seeks only to chain its recipient (cf. DAS 6–7; III, 8–9).

The second aspect I want to look at is this. I have made it sound as if people very consciously looked at ostentatious reputation as one possible good for themselves, and then elected to make possession of it their goal (however misguidedly). But this was only part of the explanatory strategy, to try to bring out how values and disvalues were being figured in various modes of life. There need be no question of things proceeding so. A child slowly learns to find a footing within the constellation of values and praised accomplishments that are presented to him as the immediate material of his life circumstances. He comes to know as valuable whatever is presented and responded to as such by those around him. He cleaves to these; they become the stuff of his own desire and aspiration. But yet it can be, and often is, that what he learns as constitutive of value, of excellence, what he learns as comprising the substance of this peculiar but important thing ('good'), is mere prestige goods, whose sole meaning consists in their power to enable one to gloat and glory in the destitution of others. So the idol of reputation occupies the child's soul all unawares. He finds himself meeting and interacting with others in the modes of jealousy and suspicion, envy and denigration, triumph and humiliation. This is a much more likely, and straightforward, way in which such-like human forms persist than through conscious choice. But the explanation remains superficial as yet, for the original instigation and prevalence of these modes remains unaccounted for. We shall return to this.

Rousseau's diagnosis of the character, role and ramifications of the craving for invidious repute is fairly potent. It would be easy to dismiss it as the soured spoiling of something undertaken by someone who hated and resented his not enjoying it, as he felt he had supreme right to. But this would be improper. Not only is this supposed ground for dismissal no ground at all; but also the view cannot be easily dismissed. However partial one might eventually conclude Rousseau's assessment to be, it simply cannot be denied that he saw many things which just *are* so.

The second suggestion Rousseau is making is that the higher learning comes to be one of the foci for divisions in precedence because of the prevalence of luxurious indolence and indulgence. Does he make out a convincing case for saying this? Does he successfully explain why competition for singular superior prestige should come to be so prominent a matter; and also why scientific and artistic activity should come to be what this peculiarly revolves around? I do not want to work through the points, but only to say that I do not think he does. This should not lead, however, to indifference to his thesis, for three reasons. First, he does offer, elsewhere, other very powerful and penetrating explanations of the emergence of these and related phenomena. So, if he fails here – as I think he does – it does not follow that he has given up on the issues and makes no other reasonable attempt to come to terms with them. Second, even if his given account here is not convincing, there are very significant connections between indolence, captious censoriousness, and the desire to dominate, which his ideas suggest. Some of these will be looked at later. Finally, we are encountering here for the first time a very general point in Rousseau's scheme of work. He always contends that we, and things, began well, but went bad (to put it crudely). But how, out of what is good, if it really is out-and-out good, can bad issue? By diabolic intervention? That would be a mere trick. Were there then tares among the original seeds? But if this were so, things did not begin 'all good' after all.

Many think this is an explanatory dilemma that Rousseau lands *himself* in and from which he never extricates himself. I shall argue, however, that he never was in this dilemma; but also that he gives a most convincing account of the emergence, and eventual dominance, of competition, the desire to do-down, to glory in the destitution of others, which is compatible with all he meant, and all he need and should have meant, by man's original goodness or intactness. But it is not to be wondered at that he should not have had this complex matter completely clear in his first essay into these issues. There is a hard and challenging point in view here, which will require several attempts to come to grips with firmly.

Before moving on to a second level of appraisal of Rousseau's ideas in the first *Discourse* I shall say a little about what he envisages as an ameloration of the degeneracy he sees, as a better scheme of things. He evinces a fairly unremarkable and undeveloped approval for simple, rustic, vigorous peoples and modes of life. However, he does not impose strictures on all learning. When is it, to him, acceptable, and why is it? It is not, as I said, that he thinks no honour, praise, and good repute should fall on those who do well; the point is only that the 'well' should be genuine and true and the esteem be founded on that, not that the desire for esteem precede it (and negate it). Honour can and should be given to virtue (DAS 22; III, 25); and real virtue is a contribution to the permanent and true interests of mankind. Among such permanent interests is our need to know what we are, what our situation under the heavens is.

It is proper to man to *know* his place in the scheme of things, not just blindly to occupy it, as an octopus or tree does. Men are creatures who have the power of understanding, and that power may properly be used. Thus it is that Bacon, Descartes, Newton by their work as such are benefactors of mankind. Rousseau as ardently believes there are things inherently good to men, enriching and sustaining, as he also believes the craving for reputation, with all its attendants, is not. But most of us are not equipped in Newton's way to bring good to ourselves and to others:

> Why should we build our happiness on the opinions of others, when we can find it in our own hearts? Let us leave to others the task of instructing mankind in their duty, and confine ourselves to the discharge of our own. We have no occasion for greater knowledge than this. (DAS 26; III, 30)

We see easily enough the thrust of this. But the treatment is slight. We are not, for instance, shown how our meeting the obligations of humanity, relieving need etc., is supposed to be beneficial to us ourselves. Very often, of course, it strikes us as very burdensome. If everyone did so, then we ourselves would gain at least as much as we gave out; and we should, too, avoid the desolation wrought by the predominance of competition. But these look like simple trade-offs. They do not yet suggest that there is anything intrinsically beneficial to us in establishing ties of loyalty, support, shared care between ourselves and others. One specific point is worth noting about this, however. The composition of those 'real' excellences Rousseau speaks of in this place (DAS 14; III, 17–18) includes forms of connection and association with others. Service of country, obliging friends, make no sense unless one has, is tied into, a country, is linked with others in affectionate union. Also, receipt of honour and glory, which entails a standing for oneself with others, is accepted by Rousseau, providing it goes on *true* merit. In none of this is there any suggestion that true human well-being and happiness requires total separation from others. So either we must say that Rousseau did not come to that idea until later, or else we may wonder whether he ever did espouse that idea. That the latter is my view I have made quite plain already. Whatever independence from others' 'opinion' Rousseau is arguing for the necessity of, it is *not* a kind and degree of 'independence' that requires one's being, or behaving as if one were, nothing but a solitary in a deserted planet. It is clear enough already, in fact, that the 'opinions' to be eschewed are those, but only those, that have to do with making available in social strategies positions of invidious precedence over others. Other ways by which human character and human relations are informed and ordered by other actions of 'opinion' of other kinds, are not in view. This is always how Rousseau took the matter.

Although I have said – though not here laid out the reasons for saying – that Rousseau does not, in my view, make a sufficient case in the first *Discourse* explaining just how and why the rage of reputation should come to play such a large role in individual motivation and in shaping social relations, it will be worth some reflection to consider whether his general picture of the power and centrality of this concern in human life is at all convincing. Rousseau stresses the significance of this 'rage' in connection with the advance and prestige of learning in particular. But this is because the question he was set singled out the arts and sciences not because he thinks the phenomena he is discussing are peculiarly confined to these areas. It is quite clear that he regards the motivations and processes he is examining to be altogether widespread. So we may ask two questions. First, does the craving for invidious singularity, the rage for distinctive repute, have the implications and corollaries Rousseau claims it has? Second, is it plausible to hold that this craving for (or, more colourlessly, desire for) dominant (domineering) prestige is as pervasive and potently affecting to individual life and social relations and transactions as Rousseau is contending?

In response to the first question, my own judgement is that Rousseau's diagnosis of the immediate and remote ramifications of the rage for distinction is very penetrating. I think he has seen deeply into the concealed perversions of the meanings of ideas, of personality, of relations, that ensue upon the search for invidious position occupying paramount place as the leading goal in people's lives. The picture he sketches in this first consideration of these issues will be sharpened and extended in his subsequent writings. But here already he offers us a decidedly effective account.

The second question is more problematic. Rousseau does not pretend to be speaking solely about the conscious, avowed thoughts and motivations of people. It is part of his view, indeed, that people are quite largely unaware of some of the desires at work in shaping their choices, perspectives on value and on worthwhile opportunities, etc. Theories about people's concealed or even denied motivation, and about the values and achievements that are tacitly incorporated into and displayed in social structures and processes, have a peculiarly problematic status. What form *any* such theory should take – must it, for example, use notions which the people under interpretation could, in principle, understand and themselves employ, or not; what tests are proper to the accreditation of any such theory – are very controversial issues. It is out of the question to take up such problems here,[5] so I shall make only some informal comments.

It seems to me, first, that Rousseau's account is no worse placed as such than any account that does not take at face value people's self-representations. No account in fact can do this, without conceding that people must be very muddled and confused about themselves and their social setting. Almost everyone speaks and acts over time in ways that are discordant and 'internally' incongruous. It is not as such an esoteric, theoretical, activity to try to move beyond the 'surface' disorder, to look for patterns and constellations which make a more lucid, uniform, shape out of ourselves and others. This part of our *ordinary* engagement with ourselves, who are often more strange to ourselves than those we ordinarly think of as 'others' we encounter.[6] So I do not think there is any reason at all in advance to be disdainful of accounts which, on some points, will by-pass a person's own self-accounting. There is no reason to suppose Rousseau's account in particular to be peculiarly weak.

Second, if we try for a while to see ourselves, other people with whom we are engaged in various transactions, and so on, in the terms and structures that Rousseau's interpretative 'grid' provides us with, I do think it makes very compelling, if disturbing, sense. Much by way of the hopes and distresses, glories and humiliations, that people hope for or fear, rejoice in or suffer under, becomes rather palpably intelligible if seen in terms of the desire for prestigious superiority over others being what is in contention. Of course, it is easy (too easy) to put it all down to this, and to feel superiority oneself for having so 'seen through' it. I mentioned this before. But Rousseau never thought – witness, if no more, his comments on Bacon, Descartes and Newton – that the rage for singularity was the only operative motive in people's lives and dealings; some motives were perfectly beneficial and constructive.

Did he, however, think it was the paramount factor accounting for personal desolation and social corruption, of the kinds I have outlined? It obviously does not, in Rousseau's view, operate on its own. It is related to indolence and luxurious indulgence, in ways that have been indicated. These, in turn, are connected with various economic processes, inequalities in wealth and power in society and so on. It would be wrong to think that some one interpretative notion was carrying all the weight. However, it is the phenomenon to which Rousseau affords most conspicious place, and his doing so may seem questionable. I think it is not worth considering its scope and limits as *the* central interpretative – explanatory idea at length, in fact. As I shall go on to show, the 'rage for singularity' will soon be superseded as a central notion. It would, therefore, be better to look at Rousseau's finished conceptions, against the background of which this one appears only as a special case, before assessing this issue. As a step towards identifying these more penetrating conceptions, however, I want to introduce some conjectures about the underlying roots of the rage for singularity, suggested by Rousseau's own connecting of this with indolence and luxury.

## 2.4 Some Underlying Conceptions

At various points Rousseau makes a differentiation between activities and objectives that are inherently good for people and apt for providing sustenance and reward, on the one side; and the objective of gaining invidious prestige and superior domineering precedence over others, on the other. This way of putting it implies that the latter objective is no good at all for people – not merely is it damaging in its personal and social effects, and the thief of alternative more worthwhile endeavours, but it is itself inherently void.

Rousseau wants to claim this, I believe. His doing so raises at least two pressing questions. First, how and why is its pursuit and possession an expense of spirit in a waste of shame? Second, if it is like this, how can it be that it comes to be seen so largely and dominantly attractive, worthwhile, comes to be the major purpose for life for so many, as Rousseau holds it does? If it is, truly reckoned, so nugatory what can account for its having such an arrestingly potent face? Any account which makes out that people's choice of such an end as the principal end for their lives is evidently absurd, for the end in the terms of that theory is evidently trivial, must be mistaken. Some account *must* be given to display the immense attraction of this objective, for all that it may, in the end, be argued that choice of it is a damaging mistake. Many accounts of the foolishness of 'worldly' concerns are not worth serious consideration because they fail on this requirement. Some very central human constituents must be finding expression here, for such concerns are so pervasive, so very hard to cede (even if we think they should be given up, which we may not). No account which does not bring these out can be adequate. Does Rousseau's account do so?

I think Rousseau's penetration is very great when he addresses these questions. What I shall say about them here is preliminary to a more finished account to come, but it will be useful to prepare for that account. The points I am about to bring forward may not be clearly on view in the arguments of the first *Discourse*. But I do suggest they are operative in shaping and directing those arguments.

The possession of singular prestige, of superior standing, is testimony to personal power and force in encounter and contention with other persons. The display of personal power is a proof to oneself of one's possession of real, effective existence as having living presence and forceful hold in and on the world, particularly the world of other humans. We crave, as the condition of having any sense of ourselves as living, vital, existences at all, proofs of our reality; this we secure only by enforcing ourselves upon our surroundings such that we experience a world showing the effects of our presence. This summary statement requires amplification and explanation.

For *anything*, human, animate, inanimate, to have existence, actuality,[7] is for it to have causal potency, for it to be the source of effects which can be peculiarly assigned to it as the (predominant) producer of these. Anything which has no such effects, or the most minimal effects, is, informally, a mere shadow, an effect and not itself a centre or source of its own proper action. In classical metaphysics, 'reality' (actuality) had its 'degrees'. Something was 'more' real than something else if the origin and nature of more phenomena could be traced as issuing from the inherent powers of the former than the latter. Particularly, the latter was 'less real' if certain behaviours of it could be traced to (explained by) dispositions or activities of the former. The 'most' real, or the 'really' real, was that from the inherent constitution and character of which *all* else issued as its manifestation or disclosure. Such was substance, or God, the only Independent, Self-Sufficient, 'thing'.

These remoter metaphysical notions need not detain us. Our ordinary thinking displays such patterns of ideas. Someone may be a 'shadow' of their former selves, in being enfeebled, lacking in effective power or vigour to 'make any mark'. An 'insubstantial contribution' to a discussion is one that generates few potent implications, effects no change to whatever is already under way, and so on. Humans need to know their own actuality (not, or very rarely, under that description, of course). Not to know (feel, sense) this – in whatever ways awareness of it comes or is won – is to feel oneself to be nothing, to be a non-person who might just as well simply cease to exist. And, except in the direst extremities, this cannot be endured: it is to have become of the walking dead.

Something of what we acquire for ourselves in our engagements and negotiations with the world, with other people, is a confirmed sense of our own existence as real, potent, effect-working creatures, along with whatever overt objectives and goods we are addressing ourselves to. Ordinarily, this basic self-possession of ourselves as living actualities is established *ambulando*, as we learn that we can do sums, grow radishes, cause our mother or father to provide ice-cream, upset our siblings by design. These, and a thousand other small things, show us that we are undeniably *there* as an active source of effects.

From time to time, however, our sense of our own vigorous actuality becomes fragile. Perhaps it is systematically disconfirmed by people around us wholly ignoring us. Perhaps we are rendered utterly powerless by illness, unable to move, speak. In such circumstances, a disturbing inchoate sense of non-reality can become apparent; we feel ourselves to be ephemeral trivia, or quite transparent, as everything just proceeds with our representing no solid obstacle or presence that must be negotiated around. Empty idleness, can have the same effect – to pick up on Rousseau's suggestion. There is nothing we do, there is nothing to be done – the world does without us. This establishes to us our non-being, our absence, our inexistence. But we cannot abide this: we need to establish our presence, to show we *are* in having active and potent being. But since there is no *task* to embody our active work, the endeavour to establish our potent presence must find another articulation, another mode of disclosure. This is done by finding a way of exhibiting the potency of our will directly and as such, not through its unfolding in the course of endeavour towards some other objective (e.g. making a garden, holding a job). No other mode for establishing its reality is available. How then is this done?

The form in which this is available to us is through combat and contention with other human wills, as itself the immediate matter for our self's activity.

This captious engagement becomes the objective, the end, itself, for in it is comprised the only material which remains to us in which we can disclose and substantiate our effective existence. To elicit, contend with, triumph over, the assertion of another towards one comes to comprise the whole matter of one's own self's assertion. Thus what is at hazard in competition for invidious prestige, for domineering precedence, is substantiation of one's very existence, which lacks other proofs, in certain circumstances. Where there is significant work to be done, and where people have vivid awareness of their own potent force in moving forward the work, contention for prestige, carping over credit, tends to diminsh. It is not that people do not need still to be 'valued', to be honoured. If this were not done, they should rightly feel that they were being discounted as nothings. But to 'count' at all, it is not necessary, not need it be felt necessary, that everyone else count for nothing in invidious comparison with one.

We have, then, the materials for an understanding of why, first, the quest for and achievement of singular prestige should be empty; of why, second, it should none the less appear of such immense importance; and, third, of why conditions of idle uselessness might cause it to assume a large place. In respect of the first point, the 'emptiness' stems from the subsitution of the mere passage of combative, disquieted, wills as proof of personal actuality in place of the production of some valuable, and valued, change which bears the impress of one's active work. The underside of desolation attaching to this emptiness is due to having secured only fraudulent testimony to the reality of one's being, rather than having found an answer to the real need. Despair of finding solid answer to that remains. In relation to the second point, the apparently undeniable good of this comes from its relation to an absolutely central and imperative human need, the assuaging of a paramount fear of inexistence. In relation to the last point, the removal, or absence, of substantial calls presented by one's life's circumstances, in response to which one can display vigorous potent efficacy, throws one into a personal vacuum in which one dies. The crucial point in this is (to take Rousseau's own account from *Emile* 4, 213: IV, 491) that, in the quest for invidious distinction, our proper and necessary desire to know we have firm place and forceful presence in life has turned 'against its own principle'. In its own disarray, that desire finds a goal which defeats its own possibility of arriving at a satisfactory answer. Triumph over others, glorying in their despite, is only ever an imperfect substitute for achieving a solid sense of personal actuality in good, personally-achieved work; it masks, whilst never actually meeting, the need for that sense. The will proves its reality in effective activity; a will that challenges others in striving after self-confirmation of its power defeats itself.

Quite apart from the possible deficiencies in the particular lines of inquiry opened here, many will feel, I am sure, that no explanations of any kind are really called for to account for the phenomenon of seeking precedence over abjected others. It will be said that this is an original good – for, after all, some goods must be original, or else explanations must go on for ever. Or it may be said that, whilst not an original good, it is very good as means to secure substantial original goods, for example, money, sexual choice, use of work of others, etc. It would be foolish to deny that preeminence before others is very useful as a means, in some matters. But I do dispute that it is very useful in all matters; and I dispute that there are not just as effective means, for example, those that rely on trust, exchange, voluntary cooperation, etc., which avoid the manifold disadvantages that attend seeking and holding on to preeminence. I also dispute that it is an original good. Despair and anger lie in the hearts of those for whom gloating over the subjected humiliation before them of others is seen as their 'good'. Perhaps because it is, fortunately, rather uncommon to find this quite unmixed with other motives and concerns, it is fairly easy to overlook the desolation of the supposed victor. But Rousseau contends that it is unavoidably there, and that makes it not an original good, but a complex personal evil (quite aside from the cost it inflicts on others).[8] This will become clearer when we examine Rousseau's developed account of 'inflamed' *amour-propre*, to which I now turn.

### 3 *Amour-propre* – First Considerations

Many points in the above discussion are unclear and under-defended. It would not be to the point to press further on the same material, for Rousseau's ideas about the issues he was considering in the first *Discourse* underwent considerable change in the years following its publication. It is this final interpretation of the nature and causes of self-aggrandisement and social discord offered by Rousseau that I now want to consider. One point at least from the foregoing should be firmly retained. The 'rage for singularity' Rousseau is so critical of is an offshoot – a distorted offshoot – of a centrally necessary human concern, to know, feel and enact one's actuality as a forceful being. In the rage for singularity we see an essential human need expressing itself in a deformed (and ultimately self-defeating) way. So there is no question of *everything* that relates to the desire for invidious distinction being censured and expelled in Rousseau's account. Underlying that desire are concerns and interests crucial to our survival, integrity and well-being as significant beings. As I shall explain, the same is true in relation to *amour-propre*. Interpreters have virtually always referred to this in what are, in fact, its 'inflamed' or 'perverse' manifestations, taking these erroneously for the thing itself. Rightly seeing that Rousseau is intensely critical of *these* manifestations of *amour-propre*, but wrongly thinking that these constitute the whole substance of the matter, they conclude that he intended to expel *amour-propre* from individual human lives and human relations *altogether* (if this could be done), or to circumscribe it as much as possible. But this is mistaken. As it is with the craving for reputation so it is with 'inflamed' *amour-propre*. Both of these are malign forms that essential, creative and benign human concerns have assumed, under certain untoward circumstances. If this is not appreciated, Rousseau's arguments in these areas will not be understood.

I shall treat the accounts of *amour-propre* given in *A Discourse on the Origin of Inequality* (the second *Discourse*) and in *Emile* together, although seven years separate their publication (the second *Discourse*, 1755; *Emile*, 1762). Differences of view on this point between these, which on the surface may seem to be quite great, will be shown to be insignificant. Following the publication of the first *Discourse*, Rousseau engaged in polemical exchanges regarding it.[9] But he also worked with great energy and success in music and drama. His play *Narcissus* was performed in 1752; and his opera *Le Devin du Village* met with great acclaim when performed at Fontainebleau that same year, before the King and Queen.[10] He also wrote his *Letter on French Music* in 1753, which created an enormous sensation, and is still capable of exciting rage. We cannot, unfortunately, examine these here. In 1753 also, the Dijon Academy proposed a second prize essay, the set topic for which stands as the title of Rousseau's second *Discourse* (he did not win the prize this time). With this topic before him, Rousseau returned to social and political themes, and I now take up these.

The question set was: 'What is the origin of inequality among men, and is it authorized by natural law?' Like the first prize essay question, this addresses a causal issue. But, in consonance with what I stated in chapter 1, section 3, I shall carefully separate analytic and genetic aspects in the points Rousseau makes, and consider the former first. I shall do the same in my treatment of *Emile*, where related issues are presented as moments in the life-history of one (exemplar) individual. I shall also be concentrating here almost exclusively on 'inflamed' *amour-propre*; my treatment of it in its benign and orderly character is given in chapter 4, but it is necessary, to begin with, to say something to enforce this distinction between these modes or forms of *amour-propre*, since this will not be found immediately acceptable.

Where, in the first *Discourse*, the characters of competition, exclusion, domination, are explained by Rousseau by reference to the nature and workings of the rage for distinction, these matters are clarified in his later works by reference to *amour-propre*. Since social and political inequalities exhibit, in Rousseau's view, just such relations of competition, exclusion and domination, etc., he appeals to the notion of *amour-propre* to explain the nature, grounds and origin of inequalities of these kinds among men. By considering *amour-propre* we shall, then, best be placed to understand his account and assessment of the significance of human inequality.

I indicated, in chapter 1, sections 2.4 onwards, the line I intended to follow here; I now propose to consolidate that. I begin with the apparently superficial problem of finding a proper translation for the phrase *amour-propre*. Bloom[11] leaves it untranslated, but remarks that it shoud be 'defined contextually' (484). This cannot be satisfactory, since it leaves in doubt whether there is any unified, coherent conception in use by Rousseau here, and whether it has any viable application to human realities of experience and activity. When Bloom does go on to make some amplifying comments on how *amour-propre* should be taken, it becomes clear that he mistakes its significance. He says: 'in its non-"extended sense", it would be translated vanity or pride'; and he suggests that *amour-propre* stands to *amour-de-soi* as a 'bad' form of self-love stands to a 'good' form. Foxley[12] has 'selfishness' for *amour-propre*, thus automatically implying that it is morally improper and inadmissible.

Will any of this do? The evidence suggests not. Rousseau writes (E 2, 92; IV, 322): 'The sole passion natural to man is *amour-de-soi* or *amour-propre* taken in an extended sense. This *amour-propre* in itself or relative to us is good and useful . . . It becomes good or bad only by the application made of it and the relations given to it.' The precise effect of this passage is, however, doubtful, for here an 'extended sense' is spoken of, without explanation. Not doubtful is the passage at E 4, 235 (IV, 523) where Rousseau is considering 'the point where *amour-de-soi* turns into *amour-propre* and where begin to arise all the passions which depend on this one.' (Which point this is, and why it is so significant, will be explained.) Rousseau goes on:

> But to decide whether among these passions [which are those that arise from and depend on *amour-propre*] the dominant ones in his [Emile's] character will be humane or gentle or cruel and malignant, whether they will be passions of beneficence and commiseration or of envy and covetousness, we must know what position he will feel he has among men, and what kinds of obstacles he may believe he has to overcome to reach the position he wants to occupy (ibid.; see also E 4, 243, 215; IV, 534, 494).

If this is read with attention, we see that Rousseau is claiming that such passions as cruelty, malice, envy and covetousness are *not* inherent to or necessarily attendant upon *amour-propre*. According to Rousseau, the 'secondary' passions (which arise from and depend upon *amour-propre*) may *quite as well* be humanity, gentleness, benevolence and compassion instead. *Amour-propre* as such is, then, something more basic than any of these secondary passions, whether these be agreeable or disagreeable in character. Whether the one kind or the other kind of passion will arise from it will, we are told, revolve round variations in what Emile (everyman) will feel about (what should be) his 'position' among men; and around what he believes are the obstacles that stand (or are put) in the way of his reaching and holding that position. This is nothing more than Rousseau plainly says. Yet it is sufficient on its own to dispose of the idea that it is intrinsic to, or inevitably attendant upon, *amour-propre* as such that we should be cruel, domineering, supercilious, contemptuous, seek to enslave and humiliate others, and so on. If these, which are secondary passions, *do* accrete to *amour-propre*, this is only because some 'problems' have come to attach to holding a certain 'position' among men, and/or to acquiring or retaining that position. It is precisely such 'problems' Rousseau articulates and discusses, showing then on the one hand how *amour-propre* can acquire these disagreeable secondary accretions (and become in my terms, following Rousseau, 'inflamed'); and also, on the other hand, how it can acquire agreeable secondary accretions, and possess a benign and creative character, manifestations and ramifications.

This passage is no isolated instance, going against the whole trend of Rousseau's thought. At E 4, 244 (IV, 536) Rousseau says: '*Amour-propre* is a useful but dangerous instrument . . . it . . . rarely does good without evil.' Although this remark carries a warning, it equally clearly says that *amour-propre* can do good and be useful. Again, soon after this, Rousseau stresses that it is very important, even when chiding Emile for his faults, to leave room and place for Emile's *amour-propre* to live (E 4, 248; IV, 541). This would make barely any sense if it were Rousseau's view that *amour-propre* were inevitably perverse and evil in its consequences. Also, Rousseau specifically distinguishes *amour-propre* from vanity, and singles out the latter for especial strictures (E 4, 245; IV, 537). Translation of *amour-propre* as 'vanity' is, thus, particularly wrong-headed.[13]

One further passage may be cited, which is peculiarly controversial. At E 4, 242 (IV, 547), Rousseau writes : 'Let us extend *amour-propre* to other beings. We shall transform it into a virtue, and there is no man's heart in which this virtue does not have its root.' What *could* this mean if *amour-propre* were supposed to comprehend malice, disdain, overweening dominance? Charvet,[14] sensing this, writes that 'It may be wondered whether Rousseau means *amour-propre* here rather than *amour-de-soi* . . .' And Horowitz[14] quotes this passage starting: 'Extend self-love . . .', and simply inserts without comment the phrase '[amour de soi]' after 'self-love' although the text has '*amour-propre*'. Such are the pressures that an initial mistake about the nature of *amour-propre* can exert. I shall discuss this passage myself in detail in chapter 4.

I take it as certain, then, that *amour-propre* as such may acquire agreeable or disagreeable secondary attachments, but is not in its own nature or by its ineliminable attendants malign. What is it, therefore, in itself? How and why does it acquire the one or the other set of secondary elaborations? And why is it particularly *prone*, as Rousseau undoubtedly holds it is, to acquire evil and exceptionable secondary elaborations? I shall not give a full answer to the first two of these questions directly, since until we have treated of *amour-de-soi* (in chapter 3), *amour-propre* cannot be seen in its overall proper place and significance (in chapter 4). My concern at this point is with 'inflamed' *amour-propre*, with, first, the analysis of its character and implications; and, secondly, with its genetic conditions. It is this that stands as the extension and deepening of the explanatory notions Rousseau employed in diagnosing the individual and social phenomena he looked at in the first *Discourse*. We are examining, at present, man in his 'diseased' state and circumstances, not in his 'healthy' life. But it would obviously be inept to proceed with this without *some* sense of the character of *amour-propre* as such, in its non-inflamed form (indeed non-elaborated either to cruelty *or* to humanity). Lacking this, it would be easy to lose the overall bearings of the discussion. I shall now, therefore, give a very brief sketch of what I take to be the core of the case, simply to serve as a reference point. (See also the discussion in chapter 1, sections 2.5 onwards.)

*Amour-propre* as such is what Rousseau posits as the character, the form, that our innate concern to be well and do well in and for ourselves takes (our *amour-de-soi*; cf. E 4, 212–14; IV, 490–3), as and when we have regard to ourselves in our standing and place with other people engaged in transactions with them. When we become (consider ourselves in respect of being) involved with others in ways that require our concerted, collaborative, activity, we necessarily do not wish to be discounted, as unnecessary to be heeded or heard in such matters. We wish to be located in the founding and progess of such transactions as someone categorically and inviolably of significant moment in determining their scope and limits. If this were not so, we should be being treated as mere conveniences, tools arbitrarily to be employed and disposed of. It is our *amour-propre* that directs us towards ensuring we are not thus treated; towards ensuring that we are met, heeded and honoured as a person of significant standing in our own being as such. I stress that the kinds of transactions we may be involved in with others are very various indeed; we may be lovers, friends, co-workers, citizens of the same state, and so on. In each of these cases, what constitute due standing for us as a fully acknowledged person in the transactions will differ. But in each case there remains the appropriate and necessary desire (demand) to be present in the character and progress of the transactions as duly recognized. *Amour-propre* sets us to seeing that this shall be so for ourselves.

As an unconditionally significant presence to and for others I am claiming to myself the character of a *morally* characterized and potent presence. I claim as mine certain titles (different ones in different cases), such as not to be treated in various ways, and to be received, to be heard, and to contribute to collective determinations and actions in other ways. *Amour-propre* then, in short, is as such due care of, and claim for, our status and proper power as morally significant beings. It is this concern and claim for ourselves that my acquire humane, gentle, secondary elaborations, or may acquire malign and cruel secondary elaborations. With this as background, I turn to consider the latter.[16]

### 4. 'Inflamed' *Amour-propre*

Although the terminology is usually thought to be a later introduction, we may say, in Rousseau's *own* words, that in considering the form our lives take as

shaped by *amour-propre* we are considering the being we have 'for others' (see
E 1, 40–1; IV, 251), our 'being-for-others'. Since it is so widely held that if *any*
of our own self-constitution has come to be constituted as it is 'for others'
then by that fact alone we are self-dispossessed or have lost our own proper
integrity, it is desirable to spend a moment showing that this is not so. It is
when, and only when, our self-constitution is determined in *particular* ways by
(what we feel to be) the requirements that others lay upon us that we become
self-estranged.

What is it to have 'being-for-others', quite generically? As a mere immov-
able physical obstacle in the path of another I have a certain 'being' for him; I
am for him, present in the content of his own deliberations and actions, as
something that must be circumnavigated. The being I have for him, in this
case, is as a 'lump of matter'. (This is the being for others that protesters
sometimes take upon themselves (or reduce themselves to possessing) when
they lie down in the road, though this is not all there is to the case of course). I
would be crazy if I always took myself for, and wished only to be present to,
and in the deliberations of, others as being a lump of matter. I normally take
myself for a moral being, one entitled to be treated and regarded in certain
ways. This immediately entails that I want to hold, to demand if necessary, a
certain decisive being for others. I claim to be present for them as someone
who exerts certain limits and conditions on what they are entitled to do, may
fittingly undertake, etc. I wish to be incorporated into the grounds and direction of their determinations and actions in certain categorical terms.

This means I am to myself someone who wants to enjoy significant being for
other people. My aiming to have this for myself will comprise one of the
self-constituting purposes and concerns integral to my being. This, so far from
constituting self-abandonment to the other, is essential to intact self-
possession in the face of the other. In so far as I do wish this, I will do and feel
things arising from the characterizations they place (explicitly or tacitly) upon
me. I may for example feel indignant or outraged; or if I fall under the pressure
of the reading they place on what I count for, I may feel abject and worth
nothing at all. I may feel acknowledged and potently heard and heeded and
reckon myself well on that account. As we shall see, our *amour-propre* does not
clearly and decisively envisage in advance what our proper titles, fitting to our
duly significant personal weight, should be. We tend to learn what we amount
to from how we are received, and only become slowly and dimly aware that this
may be improper to what we inherently merit. We take as our merit to begin
with the credit we are given, often to our detriment.

The question is not, then, one of our eschewing all forms and kinds of
being-for-others, but of our *properly* owning and holding such. When *amour-
propre* is 'inflamed', however, this becomes improper. What, first, does this
comprise? Second, how does this come about? If and when my *amour-propre* is
'inflamed', I claim to myself a title and significance for others in their

thoughts, feelings, deliberations and actions, which is very great indeed. I wish to be a very 'large' presence for them in their lives (*why* I wish this I shall be discussing later). I arrogate to myself, as my original and categorical title as a potent force in the ordering of our intertwined lives in very many different ways, superordinate claim and position. All of this follows plainly from what *amour-propre* originally is, but now turned to excess, now having the character of a *strident* demand for superior position and title as the terms and conditions of my enjoyment of my due 'moral' being for others, 'Moral' here does not, of course, mean 'morally right' or 'morally acceptable' – far from it. It only means that which pertains to what is fit *or* unfit, due or undue, decent or improper in matters of personal regard, acknowledgement and dealing between people. If I insult you, humiliate you, this is, in these terms, a 'moral' encounter between us, because in so doing I am violating and flouting your proper titles to respect and honourable treatment. If, on the other hand, I am myself outrageously abused and respond to this by reciprocal insult, this is also a 'moral' encounter, but this time with a (possibly) justified response on my part.

It can be seen how this excess of *amour-propre* relates to, but subsumes, the rage for reputation, the craving for singularity, which was so prominent in the first *Discourse*. This is as expected. With this more sophisticated notion to hand, we can make an important distinction between two broadly distinct (but not exclusive) sets of terms in which people contend for superiority over others as meeting the requirements of their excessive, inflamed, *amour-propre*. These are, first, the terms of power and subordination, relations 'figured' as those of master and slave;[17] second, the terms of prestige and humiliated invisibility, ignominy (being without name). The latter requires, as the former does not, (the fantasy of) other's esteem, deferential favour. These two, as I say, are not usually unmixed; but 'power' relations are, in certain ways, less complex for the reason just noted. The desire of reputation is, evidently, the desire for prestigious precedence over others, and thrives in the salon or on the stage just as clearly as in the larger structures of wealth and political influence that shape a whole nation, whereas power relations are crucial in the latter case, and came more to the forefront of Rousseau's thinking. Thus the political and civil disorder of society forms the centre of his argumentation. But we should never lose sight of the underlying unity in these, that they both relate to the over-insistent press of one person upon others as a domineering presence for them.

Suppose someone makes the claim for himself to hold preeminent prestigious place and/or domineering power, and finds people weak or fool enough to afford this to him, how could he be the loser by this?[18] Surely, he enjoys what he wants, and will not suffer or lack anything because of this. We are now in a position to consolidate and extend the reasons Rousseau gave for supposing that enjoyment of singular reputation was only a delusive boon, as discussed before. The ideas we saw at work in that account now gain in richness and intensity.

## 5. 'Dependence' on Others

Rousseau, discussing the sight that 'civilized' man would present to the eyes of one not yet become one of the 'artificial men', writes as follows:

> He [civilized man] pays court to men in power, whom he hates, and to the wealthy, whom he despises; he stops at nothing to have the honour of serving them; he is not ashamed to value himself on his own meanness and their protection; and, proud of his slavery, he speaks with disdain of those who have not the honour of sharing it . . . for him [the 'natural' man, the 'savage'] to see into the motives of all this solicitude the words 'power' and 'reputation' would have to bear some meaning in his mind; he would have to know that there are men who set a value on the opinion of the rest of the world; and who can be made happy and satisfied with themselves rather on the testimony of other people than on their own . . . social man lives constantly outside himself, and only knows how to live in the opinion of others, so that he seems to receive the consciousness of his own existence merely from the judgment of others concerning him . . . everything being reduced to appearances, there is but art and mummery in even honour, friendship, virtue and often vice itself, of which we at length learn the secret of boasting; . . . in short . . . always asking others what we are, and never daring to ask ourselves, . . . we have nothing to show for ourselves but a frivolous and deceitful appearance, honour without virtue, reason without wisdom, and pleasure without happiness (DI 104–5; III, 192)

The rhetoric is fine; but the thought is also very precise. We need to follow the case out.

Although this passage begins by speaking of men in servile and subordinated places, and may seem only to address their condition, it soon generalizes and Rousseau speaks deliberately of all 'social men', whether high or low, powerful or destitute, celebrated or unregarded. How can the generalized criticism he is levelling be made out? When *amour-propre* is in excess, I hold my own importance and significance as a person among persons on the footing of my having masterful domination over others. It is essential to my own self-possessed sense of my significance in my own person that others suffer subordination or ignominy before me. Were they not to do so, my own sense of self-value in my person would be destroyed, for it is constituted by my triumphant standing over others, whose despite *is* my glory. ('. . . if we have a few rich and powerful men on the pinnacle of fortune and grandeur, while the crowd grovels in want and obscurity, it is because the former prize what they enjoy *only in so far as* others are destitute of it; and because, *without changing their condition*, they would cease to be happy the moment the people ceased to be wretched'. DI 101; III, 189 – my italics.)

Those whose self-estimation as significantly counting persons requires them to be 'on the pinnacle' in this fashion are, then, peculiarly tied down by the requirement to gain the conforming submission to them of others. They depend, for the *constitution* of their own sense of their significance to themselves, very intensively on the role and place of others in relation to them. They are obliged, therefore, above all else to be concerned to maintain control over and direction of the ideas, feelings, actions and interests of others; this must be the all-absorbing task. But they can do this only by noting and employing the predelictions and dispositions that others already have, so far as these may be turned to causing them to accept, or be duped into, submission to the person of excessive *amour-propre*. So one becomes, in large part, the puppet creation of their unruly pulling, dancing to their tune even as one tries to lead the band. Note, also, that one will not be the sole contender for invidious preeminence, trying to get the better of all others. Excessive *amour-propre* is not just one person's unique motive. All around one, others will be seeking to usurp what one believes to be one's singular title to leadership. Their submission will be hard won, if at all; they will always be trying to undermine your position by whatever means come to hand.

Three things are at once clear from this. First, the kind and degree of possessed 'large' being-for-others that has come to constitute the centre of the self-constitution of the person of excessive *amour-propre* places him particularly inextricably in the hands of others, dependent on their position and attitude towards him. Secondly, such a person acquires an overriding task of moulding himself into a shape that will terrify or delight those around him, causing them to accede to him. Third, such a person is bound to encounter others as hostile, deceitful, devious and out to denigrate him (as they will encounter him also).

It would be a complete mistake to respond to the first of these points by arguing that, if this is how things stand, we should wish and aim for *no* standing for ourselves at all for others, as part of our self-constitutive value and concern. To wish that would be to wish not to be present in the character and status of a 'person' to others at all, and to hold that one's not being so was of no account to one. That would be absurd. The issue is not that of being nothing to others (and of others being nothing to you, even in respect of the reception they afford you). It is the issue of a benign or a destructive mode of demanding and being 'something' of account for others. The 'dependency' on others – that which rests on their 'opinions', their 'prejudices' – that Rousseau is critical of is that which requires one to be getting the better of others, in order to be 'satisfied with oneself'. Its very constitution as a condition of *well*-being is *comprised* only in the inferiority of others to one, in their being under one's heel, regardless of any intrinsic qualities in one's life or theirs.

The case is quite different when one demands, out of *equable amour-propre*, as one's proper title, standing of oneself for others. Here it is not a question of being preferred before this man, having a larger say and more 'clout' than that one, as a condition of one's feeling established as a person. It is a question of a

kind and level of acknowledgement, of voice and role, which is wholly compatible with (and, in due time, we shall see actually requires) the same level
standing and weight being afforded to others. Of course, if others claim and are
granted altogether dominant titles, one may by this be deprived of one's basic,
categorical, standing. Then it is proper to demand its restoration. But this is
not with a view to doing the others down in their turn – to oppressing the
oppressors. It is done with a view to securing an absolute, non-invidiously
relative, standing and rank as a morally titled person in oneself. This is
consistent with others also holding title. So although one 'depends' on others
to hold and utilize one's 'rank' (for they may deny it to you), it is not a
dependency that requires others to play, or to be forced into, 'supporting-cast'
eclipsed parts in order for you to believe you mean anything. The first
'dependency' is altogether benign, and inevitable; it is what is necessarily
involved in becoming constituted as a man and incorporated with others as an
'integral part of [the] species' (E 4, 220; IV, 501). The second 'dependency' is
not benign and not inevitable; it both perverts the individual and damages
others. From now on, I shall refer to the latter as Dependency, capitalized, to
distinguish it from its benign namesake. Dependency requires the subordination to one of, or the adulation of one by, others as a condition of self-
maintenance as a person; dependency does not, but only respect and
acknowledgment for one in one's basic moral standing. This allows for, indeed
requires, others likewise to hold such standing and receive such respect. (The
respect of those one holds in contempt cannot confer title and dignity on one.
The squeaking of vermin does not glorify a king. If honour is afforded one only
in others' ignominious abjection in comparison, which one precisely seeks,
who is there then to grant one honour?)

This direct, or 'internal', Dependency which is inherent to excessive
*amour-propre*'s construction of what personal good comprises is immediately
compounded by the need to mould and manipulate others to comply with the
subjugated role required from them. One is trapped by *their* hopes and
favours, their vision, of what a saviour should be and do. If, to know one
counts for anything, one needs to feel oneself to be a master, then one needs
someone to be, or to be regardable as, one's slave. The casting of someone in
that role is inherent to the constitution of one's personal construction of what
one is and amounts to. That is the first way one Depends on others. The
second way is that, to get anyone to accept that casting, one must terrorize,
gull, manipulate them into taking it on. But unless their own *amour-propre* has
deserted them – and why should it have? – they will not lie quiet under this
imposition. So one will be Dependent upon their acquiescence in their lowly
standing under one, however retained. Retaining that puts you at their mercy.
For it is not to them, as it is to you, that their significance as real persons
depends on their remaining enslaved. Except in bizarre cases, this could never
be. So the master, who needs his mastery to hold on to his sense of the

significance in his own being, needs his slave more than his slave needs him. Thus the servility of power itself that Rousseau identifies (E 2, 83–4; IV, 308):

> Even domination is servile when it is connected with opinion, for you depend on the prejudices of those you govern by prejudices. To lead them as you please, you must conduct yourself as they please. They have only to change their way of thinking, and you must perforce change your way of acting [and more to the same effect.]

Perhaps one of the most economical instances Rousseau gives of the 'inherent' Dependency in the very constitutive terms of the good for himself that a person of excessive *amour-propre* envisages and covets is this:

> He [Emile] pities these miserable kings, slaves of all that obey them . . . He would pity even the enemy who would do him harm, for he would see his misery in his wickedness. He would say to himself, 'In giving himself the need to hurt me, this man has made his fate dependent on mine'. (E 4, 244; IV, 536)

If I do not weep, he is not happy. Who loses by this?

The good in himself, and the good for himself, that someone of excessive *amour-propre* seeks is always only a 'positional' good.[19] 'Positional' goods correspond to those prestige, caprice, factitious 'merits' or 'excellences' discussed earlier (section 2.3, this chapter). Their character as 'goods' at all comprises *only* their affording their possesser position over others in rendering others servile to or contemptible relative to him. They make no other contribution to the nature and constitution of the life of a person. All that is at issue is marshalling the tides of adulation and esteem so that they flow towards one, and the tides of contempt and disregard so that they flow away. Whatever will deflect the tide in such a way will have to be learned by experience of the moods of the people. It will almost certainly have little to do with what is inherently estimable or disgraceful. As Rousseau said, in the passage quoted at the start of this section, we shall learn the 'secret of boasting' of vice so far as that, we learn, affords us *cachet*.

Everything that is fair and good in itself, apt for yielding sustenance and reward by its proper suitability to our nature, will be despised, denigrated and spoiled by a person of excessive *amour-propre*, because the possession and enjoyment by someone else of such goods will make that someone content with themselves and their lot, giving them immunity from the control of a such a person. They have no need of him, whereas he does of them in order to establish to himself his own potent significance. He must ridicule and revile them and their situation, in the hope that he can force discontent upon them. Then they too will want contentment only on the same terms as he does, and they will then be in the mire with him. Or, if he fails to do this, he can at least assure himself that they have nothing and are nothing, and are only negligible fools in their petty contentment. By this he destroys the possibility of *any* life-sustaining source in life for himself other than that of doing down others (if *that* will sustain life; I have suggested already that it cannot, in section 2.4, above; I will comment further on this). All else he has, by his own project, turned to poison or dust. The crown of his life is this:

> The case is quite different with man in the state of society, for whom first necessaries have to be provided, and then superfluities; delicacies follow next, then immense wealth, then subjects, and then slaves. He enjoys not a moment's relaxation; and what is yet stranger, the less natural and pressing his wants, the more headstrong are his passions . . . so that after a long course of prosperity, after having swallowed up treasures and ruined multitudes, the hero ends up by cutting every throat till he finds himself, at last, sole master of the world. (DI 108: III, 203)

Can 'positional' goods sustain life? Does enforcing servility and contemptible ignominy on others offer sufficient nourishment to yield lasting enrichment to oneself? I do not think this could be held to be so. The indirect consequences of the centrality of these to people, in terms of the character and quality of their interrelations and engagements, will concern me a little later. But what about the inherent sustenance to spirit that is contained in this?

It is clear that not only is there nugatory sustenance; but also, giving centrality to these goods and purposes in actually self-destroying. *Amour-propre* as such directs one to seeking recognition and acknowledgement as the holder for others of a moral position. Such standing is essential to enjoying real presence as one person with others composing the human world, as a fundamentally constitutive member of that 'world'. *Amour-propre* turned to excess, on the other hand, requires in order to establish one's reality as a significant person, that others accept or are forced into positions of subjection directly referential to oneself as dominant over them. But the reality of one's personal being, which one seeks, lies in possessing being-for-others. By one's own project, however, those others are denigrated and nullified in their significance, in their counting import, whilst yet one depends on their submission or adulation. That which is nothing cannot, by its comportment under one, prove to one that one is something. One therefore destroys the ground upon which one needs to stand. The very phenomena which could establish for oneself one's own signification as a person – namely the return to one of the response and recognition of others who are persons – are, by one's own strategies, precluded from existing. It is then inherent to the progress of excessive *amour-propre* that it should defeat itself. It also denies to itself, by its own perverse mechanisms, even some moderate and equable answer to the need for personal standing (which, anyway, would be regarded as too little, too late). For that you have to allow that there are other significant persons as well as yourself, and that the man of excessive *amour-propre* does not and cannot allow. I have mentioned this briefly before, also.

This is most exactly, and terribly, described by Rousseau in his account of the motives of the old lecher given at E 4, 349–50 (IV, 684ff.). Vice, he writes there, is internally inconsistent; it is 'wide of its [own] mark . . . precisely when it gets what it wanted!' The whole passage deserves very careful study.

We are, now, faced with a similar question to that which arose when considering the self-defeatingness of the desire for invidious reputation. If this is how things stand, how can anyone, how can so many, come to be possessed by excessive *amour-propre*? It would seem to be its own disrecommendation. I shall defer looking at Rousseau's answer to this until I look at his account of the deeper psychological roots for excessive *amour-propre*, in section 8, below.

## 6  Social Relations and Inflamed *Amour-propre*

I have already mentioned the character that relations between people must necessarily assume if excessive *amour-propre* is to find its consolidation in the world. It is inherent that other people should be tied to servitude. I want to elaborate certain aspects of this, since they contribute to Rousseau's larger picture and criticism of a 'climate' of social life which discloses and incorporates the demands of excessive *amour-propre*.

There is no question of excessive *amour-propre* being the bent of just one person who is the odd one out among others who are equably secure in their own temperate *amour-propre*. As Rousseau addresses the issues, he is envisaging this excess as widespread, so much so that social strategies, institutions, laws, mirror and reinforce its needs and demands. Each person on entering the 'social world' finds he can make his way only in those terms which draw him into being party to and a sustainer of the goals and strategies that the excesses of *amour-propre* dictate, even if he did not at first reckon things so. (Compare E 4, 236; IV, 525, on the 'spectacle of society'.)

The points I want to stress are those which pertain to figuring the nature and dispositions of others, particularly as these relate to oneself, that are implicit in excessive *amour-propre*; and to the figuring made of the construction *they* place on one's nature and dispositions, particularly as these latter bear on these other people. (It must never be forgotten that these figurations may be entirely erroneous; they comprise only the accountings of what is going on inherently generated by the excess of *amour-propre*.)

As I am moved by excessive *amour-propre* I necessarily construe others as repositories of will and feeling which I am concerned to bend into submission. I will not think, unless I am demented, that their submission will be given freely to me at their own election. Indeed, in some cases I shall need to feel it is not; exemplary proof of my potent being for another may require beating down a (supposedly) contending and resistant will. Cruelty and sadism are inflamed by utterly passive submission; they require vindictive triumph over opposing will for their satisfaction. Where excessive *amour-propre* motivates many, I shall be obliged to suppose that others are deploying their concerns in relation to me as I am deploying mine towards them. We necessarily encounter one another then as mutually hostile, deceitful, subversive and out to undermine and humiliate.

> The philosophers, who have inquired into the foundations of society, have all felt the necessity of going back to a state of nature; but not one of them has got there . . . Every one of them, in short, constantly dwelling on wants, avidity, oppression, desires, and pride, has transferred to the state of nature ideas which were acquired in society; so that, in speaking of the savage, they described the social man. (DI 45; III, 132)

I must suppose also that what they present of themselves to me and to others can only be what they calculate is most likely to win power and prestigious eminence for them over me and others:

> . . . wit, beauty, strength or skill, merit or talents . . . being the only qualities capable of commanding respect, it soon became necessary to possess or to affect them.
> It now became the interest of men to appear what they really were not. To be and to seem became two totally different things . . . Man . . . must have been sly and artful in his behaviour to some, and imperious and cruel to others . . . Insatiable ambition, the thirst of raising their respective fortune, not so much from real want as from the desire to surpass others, inspired all men with a vile propensity to injure one another, and with a secret jealousy, which is the more dangerous, as it puts on the mask of benevolence to carry its point with greater security. (DI 86–7; III, 175. I shall be considering this passage again later. Compare DAS 6–7; III, 8–9).

Others are figured by me as being, as they too figure me to be, envious, jealous, deceitful, malicious, spiteful, aggressive, over-bearing and vindictive. Each of us supposes the other to present to the world a face painted in the colours that custom or fashion dictate as apt to curry favour and precedence. Trust will be foolish gullibility; cooperation an invitation to be exploited; generosity giving an opening to be taken advantage of; and so on.[20]

Such being the reciprocal constitution we represent each other as having, social processes and structures will bear a coordinate meaning for us. Law will be only a device to enforce dispossession; government a means of abusing and impoverishing; public honour a platform from which to demand peremptory privilege. Such, Rousseau contends, is the form and composition of social and political life as we ordinarily find it to be. To this, an important corollary attaches, hinted at before. I do not know for myself clearly in advance what should amount to my enjoyment of title and claim as an acknowledged person. What the content is of holding such a footing is something I can only find out by seeing in what ways and forms people accommodate and receive one another. As explained, I necessarily desire to be received and reckoned with as significant in my own person. If, then, I find that such reckoning is afforded to someone only by his contending maliciously and vengefully for precedence, I shall inevitably take this on as the manner in which I can find and hold a 'place'. Not knowing that there is any other possibility, I become constituted, in my original self-possession as a person, as one set upon the objectives of excessive *amour-propre*. I become an artificial man with factitious passions (DI 104; III, 192) never having known or been myself in any other character at all.

Fortunately, however, the personally constituting possibilities our culture makes available to each of us are not monolithic, and do not all bear the characteristics of excessive *amour-propre*. We know of the possibility, which our culture also sustains, of claiming non-invidious respect for ourselves, and of also affording dignity and honour to others as persons with categorical standing and title. This makes available to us another possible mode in which our *amour-propre* might find concrete articulation and answer. It is Rousseau's argument that it is *only* in this articulation that it will find answer for *each* of us; and that it does so in a way that simultaneously allows *all* of us to find answer to our need. Its allowing this simultaneously to all is in fact the condition on which each of us can find the answer we severally require. However, it is clear that in order that this possibility should gain any foothold in people's thinking and feeling, they must first unlearn whatever else it is they have come to think constitutes holding position as a signifying person. Part of Rousseau's project is to disclose a new meaning for what it is to have standing as a man among men to take the place of the old meaning. It is not that he takes the content of these notions as fixed, but reworks some of their groundings and implications. This reworking is at one and the same time the working out of, or bringing out vividly again, a fresh significance for them.[21]

What could motivate a move towards the alternative conceptions Rousseau is trying to map out? First, there is the obvious waste and pain that attends the way of inflamed *amour-propre*. But more important is the point, which I have tried to explain, that *amour-propre* in excess turns on and destroys itself by its own perverse internal logic. If, therefore, we *are* to find substantial answer to the demands of *amour-propre*, as we necessarily wish to do, we can only do so by forsaking its excess and living its requirements in equableness and moderation. It is only by doing this that it finds its satisfaction. It is only in moderateness that it furthers its own end. This moderation is, therefore, no enforced renunciation of a desirable objective of supremacy and command, yielded only in resentment. It is rather that which alone makes possible the attainment of the objective of *amour-propre* all along, unconditional standing as a person, as a lasting, irrevocable, gain.[22] *Amour-propre*, if moderated, at last can gain its end. And in doing so in you, it does so also in others. Such is Rousseau's insight.

## 7 Inequality

The express topic of *A Discourse on the Origin of Inequality* is, of course, inequality. It may seem that I have oddly neglected this. But this is not so. For it is constitutive of that footing in domination over others demanded in excessive *amour-propre* that power and prestige should be possessed unequally between people. Without this, excessive *amour-propre* would not be manifesting itself at all. Further, that inequality is not a *consequence* of the demands of excessive *amour-propre*; it is the actual character for personal relations that it demands. The better place one requires for oneself simply consists in having the better of, in negating, the others. That is what *comprises* the 'better' of one's place – its being 'putting one over' someone else.

This explains why Rousseau is interested only in one kind of inequality among men, and why he is so critical of it. He distinguishes 'natural or physical' inequality 'which depends on age, health, bodily strength, and the qualities of the mind or of the soul' from another:

> . . . which may be called moral or political inequality, because it depends on a kind of convention, and is established, or at least authorized, by the consent of men. This latter consists in the different privileges which some men enjoy to the prejudice of others; such as that of being more rich, more honoured, more powerful, or even in a position to exact obedience. (DI 44; III, 131)

(Whether there is any 'essential connection between the two inequalities' is, he goes on, 'a question fit perhaps to be discussed by slaves in the hearing of their masters, but highly unbecoming to reasonable and free men in search of the truth' (ibid.).)

It is clear from this that Rousseau did not deny all inequality between humans. It is also clear from elsewhere that he did not take a hostile attitude to all such, even should they be celebrated in convention too. All he requires is that those attributes in which one person exceeds another, for his superiority in which he may be honoured and esteemed, be ones that disclose excellences in the person that are inherently enlarging to the quality and fullness of his substantial life, and/or beneficial to others. This we saw before in his estimate of Bacon, Descartes and Newton, and in his praise of humanity and gentleness. Nor does he censure personal joy in one's own special attainments. He only wishes it to be the case that the attainment is a real one, and does not constitute an invidious displacement of someone else; and that the joy is in it as a real attainment, not in its forming a triumph over others. Rousseau would have revolted from a levelling mediocrity which is more the product of suspicious envious hatred of being done down than of any belief in the equal value of all. (That belief is entirely consistent with recognizing that some people are very much better than others in some things; one hardly shows recognition of the value of people if one denigrates all distinctive achievement.) The equality in personal footing and respect Rousseau believed was right did not require curtailment in personal attainment; Bacon, Descartes and Newton do not diminish us, they enlarge the possibilities of life for each of us.

One aspect of social and political inequality which particularly engages Rousseau in the second *Discourse* is that entrenched in and consolidated by law, which supports property titles, ranks, and authority with the apparatus of sanction, punishment and criminality. Although this part of his account is cast as a genetic story about the 'invention' of law, Rousseau offers this himself very much as a fable (DI 89ff; III, 177ff). We may take it now without disturbing the sequence. Discussion of *serious* genetic claims made by Rousseau will follow.

With everyone contending for the possession of exclusive power, no-one can be sure of retaining this by their own resources; no-one is that potent. Mutual aid will not be readily available, since alliance means compromise of one's individual ambition and no-one will be eager to make such compromise. According to Rousseau's 'just so' story, those temporarily in the ascendant hit upon the ploy of offering to those destitute and subjugated under them terms of apparent peace, security, concord and stability. They stress the benefit to all alike in this, since it offers relief from remoreseless and implacable competition, hostility and predation.[23] Attention is not drawn to the fact that fixing terms of rank, ownership, and enforcing these with comprehensive sanctions, will consolidate and finalize their own ascendancy and the dispossession of others. Thus the law, claiming authority over all and apparently to the benefit of each and every one in offering peace, codifies as positive right the most extreme inequalities of wealth, possession, enfranchisement, and power.

The poor, the 'people', now live under a dual burden. First, the natural burden incurred by anyone living of scratching a living from the environment. But now also, second, the 'conventional' burdens of, say, arbitrary execution, peremptory loss of livelihood and holding on their lords' non-accountable say-so, denial of any entitlement to contribute to or ratify the laws of society which claim authority and power over them, and so on:

> All ran headlong to their chains, in hopes of securing their liberty; for they had just wit enough to perceive the advantages of political institutions, without experience enough to enable them to foresee the dangers . . . Such was, or may well have been, the origin of society and law, which bound new fetters on the poor, and gave new powers to the rich; which irretrievably destroyed natural

liberty, eternally fixed the law of property and inequality, converted clever usurpation into unalterable right, and, for the advantage of a few ambitious individuals, subjected all mankind to perpetual labour, slavery and wretchedness. (DI 89; III, 178)

Law, morality, political status and participation thus codify and, in their turn, reinforce the patterns of domination and subjugation which are the essence of the social project inherent to excessive *amour-propre*. The whole civil and social scene reproduces, in Rousseau's view, that craving for invidious superiority which answers the needs of inflamed *amour-propre*. It is clear, though, from this that Rousseau does not think that the reform of civil institutions will touch the core of the problems he sees in them. For these are, at the last, products and manifestations of a certain disposition in men's souls. It can only be by – in a Socratic fashion – turning men's souls around that we shall secure social restoration, in Rousseau's view. We shall better understand what obstacles lie in the way of effecting such 'conversion' when we understand more fully the psychological roots of excessive *amour-propre*. I shall consider Rousseau's account of these in a moment. But one more aspect of civil and political inequality needs brief mention first.

The Dijon Academy's question was whether inequality was 'authorized by natural law'. Rousseau says little explicitly in answer to this (but see DI 105; III, 193); his implicit view is plain. There is, in his estimation, nothing authorized by *any* legitimate law, 'natural' or not, which assigns men irrevocably and unquestionably to lots or fates of privilege or nullity, wealth or destitution, power or servitude. In Rousseau's view, any order of precedence, of difference in title or possession, that might obtain between men can be legitimate if and only if it receives the properly grounded assent of each and every several person who is to be party to that order's obtaining between them. Working out the precise terms for such legitimacy, explaining why they do establish legitimacy, is a central concern of Rousseau's explicit constructive political theorizing, which will be discussed in its place. Only passing, undeveloped, mention is made of this in the second *Discourse* (88, III, 176–7); but it bulks large in the closing pages of *Emile* (E 5, 458ff; IV, 836ff) and is, of course, at the heart of *The Social Contract*.

In Rousseau's view, the only original legitimate order of standing between men is each and every one holding a position of equal power, honour, title to take part in the common account and to be accounted to, except where there are signal natural differences in wisdom, virtue and foresight of common good. (I shall consider this last point when I examine the nature and role of the Legislator; see chapter 6 section 2.) Any order that departs from this secures legitimacy only by a kind of authorization by every one of those who are to be bound by it. Any other 'conventional' order is usurpation, tyranny and frightful abuse. The bases and modes of expression of such authorization will be considered later on.

But just as it is clear that conventional orders lacking such authorization are tyrannical, another thing is equally clear. That is that each several individual does not hold absolute, non-answerable, sovereign right to demand that the requirements of common order satisfy him on whatever terms he decrees. For this would be to set oneself up as tyrant in place of the tyrant overthrown.[24] In whatever way it must be that law is not legitimate without the authorization of every last individual who is to live under it, this cannot require that every last individual stand as sole exclusive judge on every point. Such would make the idea of common law and rule incoherent. There must be some way in which we yield our title to judge our affairs by our own discretion alone which does not, however, mean that we are reduced to being enslaved by a rule which subjugates us. Rousseau's conception of the 'general will' is intended to disclose what that way is. We hold the key to understanding this on the basis of the comments, made above, that each several one of us holds that title and standing for others, which will answer the demands of each our own *amour-propre*, if and only if we afford like title and standing to those with whom we live in common life. For that shows that it is inherent to the condition on which we each hold our *own* being as persons that we honour the personal standing of others likewise.

The 'general will' is no imposed will, that enforces tyrannical law on us. It is the will each of us has out of our being and rank as 'persons' one to another. Full self-realization as a person for each requires, as the condition of its own attainment, coordinate full self-realization for all. To be obliged to register and reckon with others is not an imposition; it is an obligation which is inherent to each our own possession of full personal standing. It is the 'law' written in the character of our *own* being. Desertion of it is self-estrangement, self-division. Such, at any rate, is Rousseau's view. He did not hold that individual freedom, acquired on the removal of servitude, meant the power and title to tyrannize in one's turn. Some limitations are 'natural'; they are proper to the inner requirements of the character of each of us. (Compare E 4, 235; IV, 522; and E 4, 325; IV, 651–2).

## 8  The Genesis of Inflamed *Amour-propre*

I have argued, following Rousseau, that what excessive *amour-propre* demands for itself it denies to itself by its own procedures and projects. In this way it is, quite strictly, 'perverse'. It also denies to its possessor even (what would be regarded as) a partial answer to its excessive demands, which might have been, if viewed from a different perspective, enough to satisfy the desire for 'standing'.

In view of this, it is obviously an urgent question to consider how such a perverse desire can gain such a dominant foothold in people's minds and feelings. Why expose oneself to such self-violating subjection on the way to a goal which is in its achievement self-subverting? These questions parallel those asked about the 'rage of singularity' in the discussion of the first *Discourse*.

Rousseau offers what seems to me a very profound account of the origin and imperativeness of this perverse project in people's psychology. He stresses the obtrusiveness of the experience of pain in the infant's first introduction to the world, his introduction to what it 'feels like' to be a creature set loose from his mother's womb. (I shall not give specific references for all of these points; they are to be found in *Emile*, Books 1 and 2). An infant does not, however, inertly acquiesce in his distress, in what he will experience as, quite generally, life's having turned bad (for he does not yet know and differentiate his state as a feeling peculiar to him separate from the overall character of the world). He responds, instinctively, with tears and loud rejection. It is the primitive character of these tears and cries to be *protests*, aggrieved remonstrance and rage against at what is inchoately apprehended as an outrage or affront inflicted on him. Cries are not mere yelps of pain; they are expressions of *grievance*, at being ill-used or abused:

> Since the first condition of man is want and weakness, his first voices are complaint and tears . . . From these tears that we might think so little worthy of attention is born man's first relation to all that surrounds him; here is formed the first link in that long chain of which the social order is formed. (E 1, 65; IV, 286)

This primitive character of the first appropriation of pain and want is extremely complex and elaborated, for all that it is original and inarticulate. First, there is in it an inchoate conception of one's fitting desert, that one should not have to endure the affront of being in pain or want. These are aprehended as an outrage of one's due entitlement. (See E 1, 66; IV, 286, on 'the sentiment of the just and unjust [as relates to oneself] . . . innate in the heart of man'.) This of course implies the quite delusive idea that one has the absolute right to be exempted from the common lot of humankind. Second, there is an 'object-relation'[25] implicit in this first reactivity. Pain and want are apprehended as things visited upon one, as indicative of the presence and work upon one of some source external to oneself (as such notions are primitively being fashioned in the infant mind). Thirdly, and as a further aspect of this, that 'external source' is envisaged as malign, hurtful, vindictive and spiteful. For it is visiting upon one unwarranted pain, affronting want, outrageous distress. ('I am sure that a live ember fallen by chance on this child's hand would have made less of an impression than this blow, rather light but given in the manifest intention of offending him'; E 1, 66; IV, 287).

It is crucial that this assessment of the 'external source' as vindictive, persecutory, aggressive is, originally, *the child's own* construction. (In the passage just quoted Rousseau is supposing that the child already has mastery of differentiating the pain wrought by unfortunate chance and that of offensive intent. But this is a slow, and difficult, differentiation to come to make; it *starts* with the assumption that everything is of the latter kind.) Whether his mother

or nurse be well-intentioned or ill-intentioned in actual fact makes little difference to start with (it may make a lot of difference in the end). Our first
apprehension projects a world animated almost through and through by wills
intent upon spiting us. The infant's original world-construction is persecutory
and self-referential (egocentric).

The intensity of the infant's rage constructs proportionately powerful
attacking monsters.[26] The infant then feels himself very vulnerably at the
mercy of an almost implacable will intent upon destroying him. He has created
for himself this predicament (we have complicity in our own fate), upon the
resolution of which his continued life now appears to depend. Either he seeks
to defeat and destroy this attacking presence – to assert his ascendancy over it,
or else he must turn to appeasing and placating it, by taking whatever servility
or assumption of inferiority and disposableness to it that (he speculates) might
be sufficient to cause it to stay its hand.

> A child cries from birth; the first part of his childhood is spent crying. At one time
> we bustle about, we caress him in order to pacify him; at another, we threaten
> him, we strike him in order to make him keep quiet. Either we do what pleases
> him, or we exact from him what pleases us. Either we submit to his whims, or we
> submit him to ours. No middle ground, he must give orders or receive them.
> Thus his first ideas are those of domination and servitude. Before knowing how
> to speak, he commands; before being able to act, he obeys. (E 1, 48; IV, 261; see
> also E 1, 65–6; IV, 286–7; and E 2, 85–8; IV, 311–15)

Rousseau is here bringing in also what *we do* to the child. But it is most
important to see that what we do would not be of so much importance if it did
not so match the child's own preconceptions. Thus this does not contradict the
emphasis I place on the child's own constructive work in fabricating initial
conjectures about the character and working of the world, and of how he is
engaged with it and it engaged with him. (See E 1, 62–6; IV, 282–8, on the
complex achievement that mastery of the notion of a 'representative' sensation
comprises.)

Rousseau's introduction of the actual behaviour of real parents (in contrast,
and frequently in direct opposition to, the infant's phantasies about the intents
of his own constructed 'external sources') into the account draws our attention
to a further step in his account which is vital for his overall purposes. We know
that one of Rousseau's foundational ideas was that man was by nature good,
but corrupted or depraved by society. It may now seem that, if I have represented Rousseau's thoughts correctly, he cannot coherently be employing this
idea. For, on my account, the infant is, by the work of his own inherent
dispositions, plunged into a world in which he either dominates and
subjugates malign wills, or he goes under beneath them, and is servile and
appeasing. So, pretty well regardless of how the actual world comports itself,
the infant creates for himself the dialectic of master and slave, engaged in a

murderous struggle for survival achieved only by domination of, or acceptance of utter servitude to, his persecutor. (Cf. E 2, 84; IV, 310, on slavery and dependence). So it seems that it is not 'society' that depraves and corrupts man, but man who does it to himself.

This is mistaken. First, although this (paranoid) construction comprises a potent predisposition in the infant, it is not unmodifiable by experience of the *actual* conduct of the world towards the infant. Second, it does not constitute the only world-constructing predisposition in the infant's affect and ideation. Other, more benign patterns contend with it for paramount place. Third, this predisposition does not represent something out-and-out damaging, which should therefore be eliminated if possible. Rather it is an exaggerated form of every infant's need to assert itself as a significant force and presence in the world. It is, that is to say, a manifestation of the primitive root of *amour-propre*. ('But the desire to command is not extinguished with the need that gave birth to it. Dominion awakens and flatters *amour-propre*, and habit strengthens it'; E 1, 68; IV, 289.)

I take these points in turn. The infant's predisposition to read the condition of his existence in terms of a passage of warring wills can and will be, in Rousseau's view, very much consolidated if the actual transactions in which he is placed with others really do exhibit this character, or features of it. With the best will in the world, on his carer's part, often they will. Out of well-meaning intent, a parent will hasten to ease his child's distress at the first cry. The child is then caused to think the world is utterly pliable and subservient to his merest beck (what other 'hypothesis' would it be reasonable for him to form – the evidence recommends this one so far. See E 1, 67–8; IV, 289: 'it does not require long experience to sense how pleasant it is to act with the hands of others and to need only to stir one's tongue to make the universe move'.). But the parent is not always on hand; sometimes he will be tired, preoccupied. But the infant, having been flattered to the opinion of his imperious omnipotence, will experience a degree of outraged shock greater than any he might have been inclined to had he not undergone the misleading 'learning experience'. Consider one other plausible scenario. A child's repeated crying tries the nerves of even the most placid adult. Intending to 'teach the child a lesson', one may jolt him, shout at him. By this, the world has exactly fitted the child's angry construction of it; a vengeful will has been visited on him. So he confirmed in the rightness of his phantasy, persuaded that it is reality.

In these, and many other small ways, the dialectic of domination and servitude is established in the child's feelings as the ordinary pattern of human life. Without the need of any conscious design in this, adults around him may consolidate the construction he is predisposed to make of his situation. Thus others produce in him established traits which, although they are given their opening by some of the original dispositions in him, are not engraved in him firmly and irrevocably from the start. So Rousseau can quite correctly say, as he does, that the child is corrupted by the effect on him of others' treatment – by 'society'. This only appeared to be a difficulty because of a false idea of Rousseau's depiction of the child's original nature. It is not a *tabula rasa*; nor does it disclose no predispositions which lend themselves to perverse developments. The point is that it is not originally perverse, nor unalterably bound to assume a perverse development:

> The first tears of children are prayers. If one is not careful, they soon become orders. Children begin by getting themselves assisted; they end by getting themselves served. Thus, from their own weakness, which is in the first place the source of the feeling of dependence, is subsequently born the idea of empire and domination. But since this idea is excited less by their needs than by our services, at this point moral effects whose immediate cause is not in nature begin to make their appearance; and one sees already why it is important from the earliest age to disentangle the secret intention which dictates the gesture or scream. (E 1, 66; IV, 287. See also E 1, 48; IV, 261; E 1, 67–9; IV, 289–90.)

This seems to me certainly a coherent, and actually a very subtle, account of how 'nature' may be perverted by the effect of others on it (without supposing them to be intentionally destructive).

Secondly, this paranoid predisposition is not the only one at work in the neonate's consciousness. For although the earliest days are very full of pain, there is pleasure too, and analogous phantasy elaborates on that. In this case, a benign life-giving, creative and nurturing external source is constructed, which is supposed to care for and be concerned to sustain the child in its need and weakness.[27] This phantasy feeds the confidence of the child in its power to win recognition and heed, its trust in its own security and footing in a world which will support and sustain it. As before, this phantasy can also be reinforced and consolidated to a degree by the actual behaviours and intentions of real people, as the child slowly gains a sense of these (see E 4, 213; IV, 492, on the child's attachment to his 'nurse and governess'). This fosters benevolence, gratitude and willing collaboration, and promises a quite other footing for mutual recognition and engagement from that pointed towards by rage and persecutory fears.

Both this benign development, and the damaging development, require consolidation and confirmation by experience if they are to become predominant personal traits. How, then, can Rousseau hold that the latter is a corruption or perversion of 'nature', the former not? For neither is the 'pure' outcome of untended nature; each requires moulding to establish and lay it down firmly into character. On this score, then, *both* are unnatural or not-natural. But to raise this as an objection to Rousseau is to misunderstand him badly. For him, 'natural' does *not* signify wholly intended, untouched, unshaped in any way at all by the work of people. (I discussed this in chapter 1, section 2.1). What is 'natural' is that which tends to the preservation, growth, amplitude, of secure, rich, being and life for a creature. What is unnatural defeats or destroys such a possibility. We can now make the connection between this conception of the 'natural' and that discussed in chapter 1. There I said that what was 'natural' was that which was not shaped by the effect of a domineering will. Contention with a domineering will (whether real or phantasised) cripples and stultifies human growth and the force of creative life. Therefore, what is not shaped by the impact of such endless contention, but instead is constructive, positive and effective, is 'natural' both in the sense that it 'makes for life' and in the sense that it is free from the impact of domination. The absence of domination marks out a 'space', as it were, for what is natural: it is not *that*. The positive characterization of what is natural is as what conduces to and fosters ample life. The two conceptions are not accidentally related only. For what Rousseau has shown is that what is moulded by domineering force is also that which destroys the amplitude of rewarding life.

It is at once clear that the 'benign' phantasy, which elaborates upon pleasure and nurture, makes for life, and is natural; the 'malign' phantasy, surrounding rage at pain, makes for decrease and destruction of secure, abundant life. Rousseau spells this out precisely at E 4, 212–3; IV, 491:

> But would it be reasoning well to conclude, from the fact that it is in man's nature to have passions, that all the passions that we feel in ourselves and see in others are natural? Their source is natural, it is true. But countless alien streams have swollen it. It is a great river which constantly grows and in which one could hardly find a few drops of its first waters. Our natural passions are very limited. They are the instruments of our freedom; they tend to preserve us. All those which subject us and destroy us come from elsewhere. Nature does not give them to us. We appropriate them to the detriment of nature.
>
> The source of all our passions, the origin and principle of all the others, the only one born with man and which never leaves him so long as he lives is self-love (*amour-de-soi*) – a primitive, innate passion, which is anterior to every other, and of which all others are in a sense only modifications. In this sense, if you wish, all passions are natural. But most of these modifications have alien causes . . . and . . . are harmful. They alter the primary goal and are at odds with their own principle. It is then that man finds himself outside nature and sets himself in contradiction with himself.

Rousseau could hardly speak more plainly. Yet he is so persistently misunderstood. *Amour-de-soi* may undergo 'modifications' which are concordant with its own principle, and such modifications remain 'natural', true to the informing principle inherent to the organism's life itself. Modification *alone* does not prove 'unnaturalness'. Only such modifications as set us about our own defeat and destitution are unnatural. And we have seen what these are. (By 'passion' Rousseau usually – but not universally – means an actuating sentiment in us which is occasioned by and directed to (what we take to be) others' position or attitudes towards us. See E 3, 208; IV, 488; E 5, 416; IV, 778).

There are other constructive and life-sustaining psychological processes that come in 'on the side of' benign phantasy which engender confidence, trust and reciprocity between the infant and his 'external sources'. These arise as he matures. If his rage and persecution fears are not too intense and dominating, a child will come to understand, slowly, that other people not only aid, or sometimes hurt, him, but also are themselves prone to pain and distress as he is. He will be apt to think, in the first instance, that their pain and distress result from his own angry destructive attacks on them. Providing that he does not feel devoid of creative resources in himself, he will be moved to reparative guilt, to restore the person he thinks he has hurt and damaged. His capacity for reparative restoration is proof to himself of his own creative resource and potency, as well as improving and enhancing the quality of others' lives, and cementing the benign bond between himself and others. These processes will be examined closely when I consider Rousseau's account of the nature and role of compassion (pity) in establishing a footing for ourselves with others which is creative and beneficial to us and to them, in chapter 4. (See, in the interim, E 4, 220–1; IV, 502, on the 'shame of displeasing . . . the regret of having offended'.)

The contrast I have been drawing between rage and the persecution phantasy it breeds, on the one hand, and pleasure and the sustaining phantasy it breeds, on the other, may suggest that the former is 'all bad' and represents an inexplicable inherent 'fault' in man's original constitution. This takes me on to my third point. It would be a mistake to assess the matter like this. The fury, and the monsters it breeds, are only exaggerations of an original impulse, an original passion, which is ineliminable and necessary to our survival and good. This original passion is that of asserting our claim on the world, in the world, to have existence, to be recognized and sustained by our surroundings. This is the constitutive press of any animate being in demanding its own survival and claiming it from its environment. By constitutional differences, and by differences in the reception this original impress of being on to the world receives, this demand may become inflamed and strident. But the solution to the problem is not the elimination of its root. For to cut off the root is to cut off the impulse to life itself. ('I would find someone who wanted to prevent the birth of the passions almost as mad as someone who wanted to annihilate them; and those who believed that this was my project up to now would surely have understood me very badly'; E 4, 212; IV, 491).

Rousseau's 'solution', as the quotation just given makes plain, is not to 'annihilate' this press of self into the world, but to order and regulate its unfolding so that it may strengthen and not trap itself in perverse and self-destructive patterns. The problem that the 'paranoid' fantasy presents is that it is a premature and unmanageably intense introducing of oneself into encounter with the wills of others. One's entire life is given over to countering and preserving oneself from these malign wills, by triumph and humiliation of them; or, more likely – because one is actually weak and helpless – in abjection before them. What must be done, in Rousseau's view, is prevent this premature,[28] and deeply damaging, development until such time as sufficient independent strength and confidence in one's own being has been achieved. One does not then encounter others as threats to one's very survival and significant existence. Emile's long seclusion from direct exposure to the attitudes and feelings towards him of others, as he grows in practical competence and power to fend for and sustain himself (as described in E, Books 2 and 3), is intended only to achieve this. As an effective pedagogic strategy it may be called into doubt. But the underlying psychological insights which direct the strategy seem to me of permanent value. Rousseau is throughout perfectly explicit that this is only a waiting or preparatory period to Emile's full assumption of, really his full *re*sumption of, engagement with the attitudes, feelings and positions of others. This is essential to his own fullness of being and to the completion of the proper amplitude of his claim for a footing in the world. (See E 3, 203; IV, 481, on 'completing the man').

What the 'paranoid' fantasy does is place us too soon in too absorbing and invasive a struggle for survival in exposure to the attitudes and wills of others. The task of self-assertion is too great if undertaken on these terms, in this forum of contention. That sort of encounter, which must come and is essential to our established personal being in the world with and for others, must be prepared for and undertaken carefully. Otherwise all life will remain in the character of a trial of mastery. The child's predisposition to exaggerate his status and the potency of his demand and power must never be encouraged. That will only confirm his idea that to make one's way in life one must dominate:

> I have seen imprudent governesses animate the unruliness of a child, incite him to strike, let themselves be struck, and laugh at his feeble blows, without thinking that in the intention of the little enraged one these blows were so many murders and that he who wants to strike when young will want to kill when grown. (E 2, 97 note; IV, 329, note)

It cannot make for our own well-being and established confidence that we make our way under such terms of omnipresent potential hazard. When we do encounter others, and negotiate our place in their lives and dealings, we shall need to be already well-assured of ourselves if we are not to feel the need, once more, to dominate and control in order to guarantee our survival (cf. E 4, 215; IV, 494, on the passions 'born (now) in spite of us').

We see then that there is no question of the elimination of that press of oneself upon the world as a significantly counting existence. The impulse to that is self-constitutive of our character as animate beings. But this 'press' can take several forms (the several 'faces' of *amour-de-soi*). It may take the form of an enraged demand upon the world's absolute service. This animates the world with malign, vindictive wills. This places our life in permanent peril, and our task becomes almost exclusively that of contending for mastery or triumph with these wills. Other routes to self-maintenance and survival are discarded or unknown; the trial for ascendancy alone becomes the total objective. This 'modification' must be, in Rousseau's view, prevented at all costs. He thinks this is best done by artificially concealing the work of others' wills from the circumstances of Emile's life at first. In this way, Emile will be relieved, for many years, from the imperative need to stand in combat with other human wills. He may, instead, learn the way the natural world works and may be turned to his useful service, and acquired self-maintaining competence and assurance of his effective potency and practical competence in ensuring his physical survival and well-being.[29] With this solid ground of self-possessed existence we can have some hopes that when he (re-)enters the human world, encountering and transacting with other beings concerned to impress their significance upon him, he may not feel constrained to meet them as if in a trial of strength for mastery or enslavement, domination or subjection. Thus, upon the assumption (resumption) of his 'moral being', his being as a bearer of titles to be reckoned with by others, he may only require moderated standing for himself which allows like standing to be enjoyed by others also. So, as indicated previously, his own *amour-propre* may receive full acknowledgement and answer which it cannot in its excess. This will be compatible with, indeed also require, the acknowledgement and answer of the like requirement of others for themselves. Chapter 4 will be concerned with these points.

All of this investigation by Rousseau of the original psychological predispositions of the infant is, then preparatory to, and explanatory of, the vicissitudes of *amour-propre*, in its excess and in its equable moderation, which are constitutive of each our incorporated participation in the world of human engagements. I said before that Rousseau introduced nothing *ad hoc* to explain the nature of, and significance to us of, our character in our 'moral being'. I hope to have now shown that this is true. Rousseau offers an account very acute in its penetration and subtlety.

Finally, we can understand how and why the objectives of excessive *amour-propre* should come so easily to assume the status of ends in themselves. Under the influence of rage and aggression at distress and pain, apprehended as affront, the infant phantasizes malign, persecuting external sources, directed against him to eviscerate or devour him. He is then obliged to devote his energy and effort to contending with and warding off these attacks, this now being essential to his survival. This becomes his central concern, since it appears to be the absolute prerequisite of his continued life. Other tasks, which would in reality afford him nourishment, sustaining and vigorous survival, become marginal. The trial for mastery assumes preeminent place. His real need is neglected; he spends his being in a struggle of his own creation.[30] It is, also, a struggle he cannot win, for it is never going to be the case that he can subjugate everyone and everything to his imperious demand. Yet upon doing so, he thinks, his very existence as a significantly forceful being depends. So his own desire of existence takes on a misconceived target; and one which is, anyway, incapable of achievement.

Such a pattern, confirmed, consolidated and entrenched, is the life consumed by the demands of excessive *amour-propre*. It is surely quite clear why Rousseau can justly say that, in this 'modification' of it, *amour-de-soi* has an altered 'primary goal' and is 'at odds with [its] own principle' (E 4, 212–3; IV, 491, quoted above). It should be clear why, also, he can say that excessive *amour-propre* promises, to its possessor, only despair and destitution of life as much as it inflicts pain and damage upon others. This is not empty rhetoric on Rousseau's part, but a closely argued case.

All of this has concerned the account of the genesis of inflamed *amour-propre* in *Emile*, which constitutes Rousseau's definitive account. The treatment he gives to this in the second *Discourse* is, in my view, less satisfactory and – once we have the account from *Emile* before us – less important. I shall, therefore, discuss it only briefly.

Whereas the discussion in *Emile* treats of the psychological dispositions and developments of one (exemplar) individual, the discussion in the second *Discourse* considers the supposed history of the fortunes of humankind at large. This difference already suggests that the latter account will be more general and programmatic, lacking that subtlety and detail which is so impressive in the argument of *Emile*. But there are other differences of importance as well. In the second *Discourse* Rousseau hardly speaks of *amour-propre* in a non-inflamed or moderated form at all; and he has very little to say about its essential significance and importance to us in that form. His attention is almost wholly given over to the genesis of inflamed *amour-propre*. For the emergence of this he conjectures two instigating causes: first, sexual jealousy; second, competition for 'consideration' in the social groups which have formed between men under the impact of changes in their circumstances of life (see DI 81; III, 169).[31]

Under the pressure of the need to secure the means of survival under unfavourable material conditions people form, first, temporary 'mutual undertakings' (DI 78; III, 166), and then establish a more settled life in villages or secure encampments. This gives rise to sustained contact between people in a character additional to that of their being, each to each, merely collaborators in producing an economic good. Rousseau particularly mentions 'young people of opposite sexes' as coming to be reciprocally engaged in modes of relation of other kinds. Although the wording of the passage is obscure through affected coyness, it is clear that Rousseau is speaking of sexual attraction towards particular persons, involving the desire to have exclusive command and possession of the body, feelings and attention of that person, and wanting that person to give privileged exclusive favour to one, disdaining and dismissing all others. Arising from this, the possessive lover becomes susceptible to the estimate his loved one makes of him. On their privileging sexual favour of him comes to depend his joy and delight, and also his self-estimation as being someone who is interesting. The lover seeks to control the one he loves because he has become dependent on the latter's regard of him. This will immediately give rise to jealous vindictiveness and suspicious malice in regard to the behaviour of the loved person and in regard to others. Competition, spite, and hatred come to be dominant themes in human interrelation, out of the desire to achieve invidious precedence in the favouring regard of another, because of the jealous love of them.[32] So although Rousseau does not specifically name (inflamed) *amour-propre* at this point, it is clear that the same processes are going on here as are there involved.

The points Rousseau makes here seem to me well enough taken, and could be developed further. I do not do so for two reasons. First, because this line of argument is superseded in Rousseau's work by the ideas developed in *Emile*, which seem to me deeper. Second because there is, I believe, an explanatory hiatus in Rousseau's discussion here. The disposition towards jealous exclusive sexual possessiveness is introduced by Rousseau without licence or justification, 'out of the blue'. It might be replied that no special justification is called for; surely this is all too well-known. This, perhaps, may be; but Rousseau cannot so easily take it that it is. For if he does, that commits him to supposing that the liability to the development of the attitudes, self-estimations and modes of relation inherent to jealous exclusive sexual possessiveness is intrinsic to humankind. This would, I think, make it very hard for him to maintain consistently that man was, by nature, good – whatever precisely this should be taken to signify. For the inherent character, and extended ramifications, of such sexual development are, on the account Rousseau gives in this place, identified as unequivocally evil. The disposition towards such unsatisfactory attitudes and actions appears to be part of man's natural constitution.

Rousseau could not defend himself against this difficulty by maintaining that since this comprises only a latent disposition, which if the relevant circumstances never obtained would not be actualized, it cannot be regarded as an inherent evil attending man's constitution. For there are other capacities and dispositions which are also latent in man in Rousseau's view, which he *does* regard as part of our 'natural' constitution. He has, therefore, no reason to make an exception of this one. Man's 'perfectibility', his 'free will', even his disposition towards pity are all, in the discussion of the second *Discourse*,

reated by Rousseau as elements of man's natural character, whilst yet waiting
certain external circumstances for their actualization.

It might, I dare say, be just possible to defend Rousseau on this point if one
took enough care and showed enough ingenuity. However, such effort would
be largely wasted, because I do not think he really needs to be defended on this
matter. The account of the second *Discourse* is replaced by the treatment given
in *Emile*. It would increase, and not reduce, the perplexity facing us if the
former account were shown to be wholly cogent. For we should then have two
competing cogent accounts of the same range of issues, and some reconciliation or integration of them would be required. I am, therefore, content to let
the story given in the second *Discourse* go, and to allow the later treatment to
stand as definitive. I have no specific evidence for saying that Rousseau was
himself aware of and troubled by these drawbacks in the views he advanced in
the second *Discourse*. But it is plausible enough to suppose he was, and took
himself to be working through the issues again, on a better footing, in the later
work.

Like difficulties also attended the second conjecture Rousseau offers about
the origin of inflamed *amour-propre* here. Continuing the theme that people
who met and engaged with each other initially only as co-workers would come
in time to develop other modes of mutual encounter and assessment, Rousseau
suggests that: 'They accustomed themselves to assemble before their huts
round a large tree; singing and dancing . . . became the amusement, or rather
the occupation, of men and women thus assembled together with nothing else
to do.' (DI 82; III, 169) In this setting, the following ensues:

> Each one began to consider the rest, and to wish to be considered in turn; and
> thus a value came to be attached to public esteem. Whoever sang or danced best,
> whoever was the handsomest, the strongest, the most dexterous, or the most
> eloquent, came to be of most consideration; and this was the first step towards
> inequality and at the same time towards vice. From these first distinctions arose
> on the one side vanity and contempt and on the other shame and envy . . .
>
> As soon as men began to value one another, and the idea of consideration had
> got a footing in the mind, every one put in his claim to it, and it became
> impossible to refuse it to any with impunity. Hence arose the first obligations of
> civility . . . every intended injury became an affront . . . the party injured was
> certain to find in it a contempt for his person, which was often more
> insupportable than the hurt itself. (DI 81–2; III, 169–70[33])

This is an attractive tale. But, as with the emergence of jealous sexual
possessiveness, little explanation is given of why the wish to consider and be
considered should emerge; nor of why, once it has, it should come to dominate
and shape individual human character and human relations so pervasively.
The appearance of such patterns, and their role in the psychological structures
of the individual in himself and in his address to and engagement with others,

is simply asserted. Even if the assertion were correct, that it stands as mere
assertion would be a defect. It contrasts markedly with the continuity and
interlocking detail of the argument given in *Emile*. Again, although Rousseau
says that the emergence of these wishes constitutes only the 'first step' towards
vice, and not finished and established vice, there is little suggestion that they
portend anything other than vice. Thus he is committed to supposing that
wishes presaging vicious human relations are inherent to man. So it is hard to
see how man could be said to be innately good, that is, possessed by nature of
no attributes which, if not subjected to deforming pressures, would dispose
him towards hurtful and damaging attitudes and actions in his dealings with
others.

I say only that there is 'little suggestion' that such wishes presage anything
other than vice, not that there is no suggestion to this effect at all. For, just
after the passage quoted above, Rousseau appears to suggest that these *first*
assertions of a demand to receive 'consideration', which take us beyond 'the
indolence of the primitive state' but do not yet carry us to a condition wherein
the 'activity of our *amour-propre*' has become petulant, must have established
what was 'the happiest and most stable of epochs . . . the very best [state] man
could experience . . . the real youth of the world' (DI 82–3; III, 170–1). Men
were lifted out of the ignorance and stupidity of their 'savage' character and
circumstances; moral awareness and standing was, in some measure, obtained,
so something of true 'human stature' was possessed and enacted.[34] This does
*hint* at a necessary and good role that the assertion of a demand for consideration might have. My complaint, such as it is, is that nothing is made here of
this hint. No worked-out account is given of the significance and ramifications
of this possibility. It is only with hindsight, possessing what is made of this in
the theory given in *Emile*, that one could really recognize that a telling possibility was being indicated here. The resources do not exist, given the material
of the second *Discourse* alone, to make anything of it.

Barely hinted-at suggestion though it is, it does however mark the introduction of a further step in Rousseau's argument which I want finally to consider.
Rousseau says that only some 'fatal' accident (DI 83; III, 171) could have led
men to depart from this best state. What accident was this; and what crucial
differences did it make? According to Rousseau it was the introduction of
metallurgy and agriculture that was the fatal accident; and it was fatal because
it caused 'one man . . . to stand in need of the help of another', and caused it to
appear 'advantageous to any one man to have enough provisions for two'
(ibid.). What does he have in mind here?

Metallurgy and agriculture exaggerated, in Rousseau's view, differences in
natural power, ability and talent. The strong and enterprising, possessed now
of relevant skills, prospered. Those less strong etc., not only prospered less,
but the strong took over for their use the resources, previously in less intensive
exploitation enough for all, that the less naturally well equipped could also use

adequately enough for their survival. These latter were then reduced to indigence; the weak man could now no longer just 'get by' well enough but 'could hardly support himself' (DI 86; III, 174). Exploitation and appropriation of natural resources proceeding on Lockean principles (DI 85; III, 173) removed his means of support. Men looking in addition to their future well-being proceeded to monopolistic accumulation.

The strong and energetic having made their first advances proceeded to further exploits. To this end they required to secure the collaborative cooperation of others in furthering their appropriative ambitions. But since their advance entailed the destitution of others, those others must be flattered, tricked or constrained to give over their labour to the rich man's projects, and further to weaken their own position. For no-one, knowing the situation and able to evade it, would engage himself to another on these terms. Thus to cause others to think that they would 'find their advantage in promoting his own' (DI 86; III, 174) the strong man 'must have been sly and artful in his behaviour to some, and imperious and cruel to others; being under a kind of necessity to ill-use all the persons of whom he stood in need, when he could not frighten them into compliance, and did not judge it his interest to be useful to them' (ibid.). Indeed not only would the stronger man have been so, the weaker also – so far as it lay in his power – would be. For such now are the terms of relation between people under which one proceeds in the way of trying to have the resources for one's survival. So relations of domination and servitude, mastery and enslavement, exclusive appropriation and enforced dispossession come to be the dominant terms of human engagement.

Rousseau's argument wavers at this point, however, in a very significant way. Rousseau needs to explain why it is that, upon the introduction of metallurgy and agriculture, the stronger and more enterprising will *want* to take advantage of these new possibilities to the detriment of others. That they *can* do so is not enough; there must be some reason why they take full and unremitting advantage of this opportunity for themselves. There are, I believe, two importantly distinct lines of thought he has about this, which become mixed up. First, there is the idea that by taking advantage of these new resources a person's security, provision against hard times, will be increased. The incentive to their use comes from the hope of improving personal well-being, where by 'well-being' we are to understand the flourishing of the body and secure provision for its needs. Second, there is the idea that ample possession and monopolistic appropriation signifies personal importance, is the mark of having great personal significance as a 'man of substance'. These correspond to two aspects or significances in the phenomenon of 'property' or personal ownership, to which idea Rousseau frequently refers at this point as being part of, perhaps indeed at the root of, the decline of the condition of humankind. On the one hand, 'property' can signify securely available resources necessary for survival. On the other hand, it can signify personal excellence, magisterial importance and the tangible mark of prepotence of standing.

My reservation about Rousseau's line of though is this. The argument as he introduces it starts from the idea of men wanting to increase and extend their power to further and conserve their well-being in the first sense outlined just above. But, in mid-progress, it converts into a discussion of the possession of property as one of the constitutive components of well-being, where one's 'being well' requires that one be a 'person of substance', a 'man of property'. And this crucial transition in the significance of what property 'means' to people is not *explained*, though I do not want to dispute that it does, and very largely, come to bear the second significance Rousseau identifies. (Rousseau has the fine comment that: 'the rich have feelings, if I may so express myself, in every part of their possessions . . .', DI 91; III, 179).

It is surely clear that some ancillary principle to that of, say, fear of hunger or hardship is needed here to explain the emergence of the 'meaning' of property as the mark of personal distinction. When Rousseau writes as follows: 'Insatiable ambition, the thirst of raising their respective fortunes, not so much from real want as from the desire to surpass others, inspired all men with a vile propensity to injure one another, and with a secret jealousy . . .' (DI 87; III, 175) he makes the appropriate distinction ('real want' in contrast to 'the desire to surpass'). But he does not tell us how and why the latter comes to operate and predominate. What he is covertly appealing to is the idea of a desire or need to find one's good *in* the destitution or abjection of another. But this idea is needed to account for the peculiar 'magic' and importance of property and cannot be explained by reference to it.

It is, I suggest, the theory we are offered by Rousseau in *Emile* that accounts for this, accounts for why it is (which with the ideas offered in the second *Discourse* alone at our disposal we could not account for) that:

> The wealthy, on their part, had not sooner begun to taste the pleasure of command, than they disdained all others, and, using their old slaves to acquire new, thought of nothing but subduing and enslaving their neighbours; like ravenous wolves, which, having once tasted human flesh, despise every other food and thenceforth seek only men to devour. (DI 87; III, 175)

That subduing and enslaving others should become our *end* needs more of an account than referring to the needs of survival and self-preservation can provide. But such an account is not yet in Rousseau's hands in the second *Discourse*.

I suggest then that, just as with the two earlier arguments of Rousseau's looked at here, which are intended to explain the emergence of the terms of self-constitution and of interrelation characteristic of *amour-propre* in its 'inflamed' character, we find in this third conjecture supplementary notions and processes invoked which are underexplained. I offer this only as a mild criticism. It seems to me reasonable and intelligible that the difficult task, of understanding fully the origin, development and ramifications of the 'desire to surpass', occupied Rousseau for many years and he had to make many attempts properly to fathom its depth.

## 9 An Agenda

I have attempted in this chapter to present and to interpret the nature and basis of Rousseau's account and criticism of 'society' and of 'civilized' or 'social' man. I have argued that, in his most finished assessment of the case, Rousseau assigns to inflamed or excessive *amour-propre* the principal explanatory-interpretative place in his examination of the character of the components and structures which comprise the (deformed) constitution of civilized man, and in his account of the forms that (degenerate) social and civil life characteristically take. I have also argued that it is mistaken to suppose that Rousseau held that man's 'salvation', in his own person and in his social and civil relations, lay in his ceasing to be actuated by *amour-propre* at all, thus ceasing to stand and live in engaged relation to others at all (for with relation to others, of all but the most rudimentary kinds, *amour-propre* also comes; see E 4, 243; IV, 534; E 4, 235; IV, 523). To think this is so is to mistake 'inflamed' *amour-propre* for *amour-propre* as such. It is to fail to understand the absolutely essential role that *amour-propre* as such must play in the constitution and personal good of each one of us. These two mistakes having been made, Rousseau's own constructive attempts to characterize forms of social and civil life beneficial and creative to each of us, and to all of us equally at once, will appear wellnigh incoherent. At best, it will be held that there is the odd nugget of gold to be salvaged from mountains of dross. This is, however, the result not of his ideas, but of a misunderstanding of his ideas.

I have already given firm indications of the line of account which I hold to be Rousseau's. Our *amour-propre* moves us to demand for ourselves recognition from and standing with others as each our own categorical title. To require this for ourselves is no improper demand, it is essential to our full constitution as a person among persons. In requiring it for ourselves we are required, by the inner logic of our own demand, to grant like recognition and standing to others. For it is only from persons that I can receive standing and be afforded the character of a person myself in my own being.

We are thus in a position to derive, from the extended critical examination and diagnosis Rousseau has offered us of depraved man in degenerate society, an 'agenda' of themes and issues which he will need and want to address in order to establish his own position regarding man's best constitution, best life and best social and political situation.

'Civilized' man is a stranger to himself, fashioned into a character dictated by what is requisite to achieve power or invidious precedence over others. He seeks 'goods' which are merely caprice or opinion goods, which do not answer his own proper true need, but intensify his lack even while he pursues them. He hates and despises all those around him upon whom he yet Depends for his own well-being; others hate and despise him equally. The climate of his relations with others is formed by competition, deceit, the craving to humiliate. Trust, mutual support, cooperation, care, true honour are foolishness or cunning disguises put on to disarm, the better to slaughter.

But man who is not an 'integral part of his species' (E 4, 220; IV, 501), not inwardly tied to others of his kind, is only half-human, uncompleted. The full possession of the amplitude of his being requires that he possess and enact his proper character as a moral person. This requires that he have being-for-others. The task must then be to show, first, what form the possession of such being must take, in order that self-estrangement, self-defeating domination, the pursuit of spurious goods, the obsessions of hatred, do not comprise the composition of this footing for oneself with others. Further, second, the task must also be to show how such a form may be articulated in social and civil institutions, processes and structures. Finally, third, it must be shown how the development and entrenchment of 'inflamed' *amour-propre* may be inhibited or precluded altogether, and instead its necessary and proper interests may be cultivated and set firmly. I take it as a confirmation of the accuracy of the account given of the character of Rousseau's inquiry into corrupt man and society that the agenda for personal and social restoration implied by it turns out to name the heads of the constructive projects Rousseau does indeed attempt to follow through.

Most of all I want to repeat that Rousseau is not concerned with blanket, all-or-nothing, repudiations of dependence, of *amour-propre*, of property, of sociality. He always had in view particular, specific, forms of these for the unsatisfactoriness of which he gave very detailed arguments. Rousseau is, I contend, perfectly precise and consistent in his criticisms and constructions. Some may still wish he made the grand, simplistic, iconoclastic gestures he is so renowned (or notorious) for. But his is a more subtle achievement; and is not less but more permanently decisive in its effects for that.

# 3

# A Rejected 'Solution':
# The Self in Isolation

## 1 Introductory Points

I hope I have shown already that Rousseau never had in view, as offering a resolution to the deformations and sufferings that social relations and socialization can inflict on the individual, that men should live and have their being wholly out of contact with, and untouched by, each other (if they ever could manage this anyway). The belief that he did have this in view is the product of deep misunderstanding of his ideas. Furthermore, saddling him with this as his view inflicts two quite unnecessary and inappropriate burdens upon him. First, it convicts him of the most elementary confusions regarding the attributes and accomplishments men might have outside of any social contact. For instance, as mentioned earlier on, language is a social construction and can only be acquired by the assimilation into oneself of social practices. Yet Rousseau never envisaged restored intact man as speechless: his development would be radically truncated without access to the resources of the elaborated conceptual network of linguistically comprised thought. Is Rousseau then, inconsistently, drawing on socially created resources whilst disowning society? Secondly, it represents him as having devised an almost insoluble problem for himself. On the one hand, he is said to believe that only outside of all social contact and influence can men hope to remain true to their own proper needs and nature and to find happiness. But yet, on the other hand, outside the civil state, man is a 'stupid and unimaginative animal', not yet an 'intelligent being and a man' (SC 1, 8; III, 364; see also E 3, 203; IV, 481). So is it our true nature and need to be a stupid and unimaginative animal? Or, if we aspire to be men, do we, in the process, make ourselves and others into monsters?

These are not Rousseau's problems, in the sense that his very terms of account engender these difficulties for him, whilst yet they have no independent reality. Of course, he believed that only too easily man in society became a monster. But this is the product of the real nature of the case, not some spurious suggestion thrown up by Rousseau's theory about it. Rousseau's theory, rather, explains the case and suggests how it may be rectified.

If I am right in my approach it may seem that nothing remains to be discussed under the heading given to this chapter. The 'self in isolation' appears to play no significant role in Rousseau's thinking, let alone to be offered by him as a solution to the individual and social deformations he has been discussing. But these would be hasty conclusions to draw. The nature and activities of the 'self in isolation' do play an important role in Rousseau's argument, though *not* the role assigned to them by the familiar assessments made of his ideas. It is the principal purpose of this chapter to try to give a better account of what Rousseau means by, and what work he wants to do with, the idea of man 'alone' (cf. E 4, 214; IV, 493).

Centrally associated with the idea of man alone, the idea of the self in isolation, are three of the principal notions in Rousseau's system of thought: the idea of man's nature, of what is natural in and to man; the idea of *amour-de-soi*, of proper care for one's self-preservation and well-being; and the idea of natural goodness, of the uncorrupt and potentially creative dispositions of men. I have touched on all of these before; here they will be more fully considered. I emphasize that these ideas are only *associated* with Rousseau's considerations of man alone; they are *not* necessarily connected to such a creature and absent elsewhere. To hold that the connection was a necessary one would be to perpetuate the misunderstandings about man and his social life and character I have exposed. I repeat briefly one previous argument to make my point plain. I argued (in chapter 1, section 2.2) that what was 'unnatural' in Rousseau's view was that which was shaped by the domineering will of another directly or indirectly, whether this be something in the make-up of a person or in his life-circumstances. One signal circumstance in which a person's constitution and situation are unmarked by the will of another at all (whether that be a domineering or a collaborative will in fact) is where others are altogether absent. This is where man is alone, where his self exists and discloses its character in total isolation. So a study of what men would be like in isolation can *contribute* to a study of what is not deformed by the work of a domineering will; it can contribute to a study, that is, of what is not unnatural. But, clearly, the two studies are not equivalent. For it is quite possible for one person to engage and interact with another in a way that does not involve the attempt by either of them to exert mastery and claim invidious precedence over the other. In which case it is perfectly possible for what is 'natural' to man to show itself and disclose its character in such a 'social' situation also. Indeed, unless it were appropriate to man to have no dealings of any kind with others of his species – and Rousseau never maintained any such thing – it will actually be necessary and good that we should meet and interact with others in ways which will extend and enlarge our natural being. So the study of man alone can only ever be *part* of the study of the total constitution and expression of what is 'natural' in man. But it *is* a proper part of that study and cannot be neglected.

Furthermore, as I have also suggested previously, I urge that we consider Rousseau's discussions of man alone only as his using a concrete metaphor for what is the real target of his interest. His real target comprises a study of those among men's needs, interests, values, abilities etc., that make no essential reference to the existence of others; or, more particularly, make no essential reference to the feelings and attitudes of another as these are directed towards the individual under consideration. This distinction is required, and is one Rousseau makes with perfect consistency, because Emile engages in, for instance, relations of work and exchange with others whilst yet being said still to be alone. It is really only when I start to have feelings and attitudes towards myself that incorporate beliefs about others' feelings and attitudes towards me that Rousseau says that 'isolation', in his intended and relevant sense, has been decisively left behind. (See E 3, 187ff; IV, 458ff; E 3, 208; IV, 488; E 4, 233; IV, 520, for instance.) Such needs, interests, values still remain in an adult, fully socially incorporated, person; for not all of our being and activity is directed to and involves relation to others. Why should it be? So we are not really being asked to believe in a time and place where man had no knowledge of or contact with other men. We are being asked to separate from among the many diverse strands in the soul of ordinarily social persons, living ordinarily circumstanced lives, those strands which do not pertain to their emotional and moral footing with others. We look at man in respect of that in him that contributes to his being and self-maintenance without reference to such involvements with others, without supposing for one moment that he actually has no such involvements, nor supposing that we have conducted a comprehensive study of all that his being does and should properly comprise if we have not yet attended to such involvements. We study, in Rousseau's words, in Emile (anyman) 'of virtue . . . all that relates to himself' by himself (E 3, 208; IV, 488); the social virtues, which are our own proper virtues also, will be studied in their turn (in chapter 4, here; and in Book 4 of *Emile*).

To begin this account of the powers and dispositions of a person that contribute to his own inDependent, and also in some part independent, self-maintenance and life I look at Rousseau's notion of *amour-de-soi(-même)*, which he posits as:

> The source of passions, the origin and principle of all the others, the only one born with man and which never leaves him so long as he lives . . . a primitive, innate passion, which is anterior to every other, and of which all others are in a sense only modifications. (E 4, 212–3; IV, 491)

*Amour-de-soi* is, originally and principally, the constitutive principle of animate, active life as such. It directs a creature to lay hold on existence, to strive for its self-preservation, self-maintenance and an amplitude of securely possessed life. It is the instinct for life, for well-being and well-thriving which comprises the urge to the maintenance of its existence that *is* the being of an animate creature.

It is clear from this that *amour-de-soi* is not confined to the human species, but is inherent to all animate species. This accords wholly with Rousseau's view. Second, and most important, what objectives and activities the *amour-de-soi* of a creature will direct it to will change and extend, in some cases quite substantially, depending on changes and extensions in the actual and believed attributes and character that the self (the *soi*) acquires. In every case, *amour-de-soi* moves us towards being well and doing well in the character we have at any time. But, subject to certain deforming pressures, it may be turned 'at odds' with itself – as discussed in the last chapter (cf. E 4, 213; IV, 491). Rousseau offers, as I have tried to show, a clear and incisive account of both what it means to say that, in these manifestations, the 'primary goal' of *amour-de-soi* has become perverted and turned against itself; and of how it can come to be that this occurs. The 'secondary passions' of cruelty, malice, envy and covetousness (E 4, 235; IV, 523) are disclosures of *amour-de-soi* (it is the 'origin and principle of *all* the others'), but disclosures of it in which it has been subjected to modification by 'alien causes' which cause man to 'find(s) himself outside of nature and . . . in contradiction with himself' (E 4, 213; IV, 491, again).

In these passions, men hurt, damage and ruin themselves every bit as much as they inflict hurt upon others. Because this is so they 'contradict' themselves, that is negate the principle which directs them to claim life and well-being. But, Rousseau's point is, this is not because there is alongside *amour-de-soi* some converse innate principle of self-destructiveness and evil despoliation which battles with that for supremacy in the soul.[1] It is rather because, subject to certain vicissitudes, the endeavours in which *amour-de-soi* exhibits itself become self-subverting. *Amour-de-soi* may be turned to its own perversity.

However, just as it may be so turned, it may not be. The will to life is still at work, however perversely, in the self-contradictions (or self-contravolitions) that the person of 'inflamed' *amour-propre* suffers. That will may be turned away from these to embrace true amplitude of enjoyed life; or prevented from falling into its own subversion in the first place. When this is so, *amour-de-soi* claims its own real increase yielding fullness of life. In studying the character, forms and role of *amour-de-soi* we necessarily also study Rousseau's accounts of the character and forms that human good comprises, in the various stages of actualization of full humanity in each of us.

It may be objected that, in commenting on the 'contradictions' that may come to beset us, I have moved from considering *amour-de-soi* to considering *amour-propre*. But, the objection continues, these are radically distinct principles – the former setting us to our well-being and good, the latter to our ill-being and despite. This objection is quite misplaced, as I have argued already. *Amour-propre*, in its equable and moderate form, is the proper disclosure of *amour-de-soi*, when the 'self' that is to be well-cared for has become the 'social' self or 'moral' self, the self in its standing and engagement with others. Even in its 'inflamed' character, *amour-propre* is *still* a disclosure of *amour-de-soi*, but now at odds with its own principle and defeating its own end. There is no substitution or replacement of *amour-de-soi* by *amour-propre*, let alone any necessary conflict or opposition between them. *Amour-propre* is the name given to the continuing unfolding of the intent inherent to *amour-de-soi* as and when we take on our character and titles as one 'person' with standing in relations to other people. Non-inflamed, non-perverse, *amour-propre* is just *amour-de-soi* directing us to see that we are well and do well in and for ourselves in our standing with others (see E 4, 235; IV, 523).

In the next chapter I shall be considering what our well-being and doing in our characters as 'social' or 'moral' beings consists in. The comments just made are only to establish that there is *no* discontinuity in moving from looking at the good of the self-alone and the good of the self-in-relation (see E 4, 214; IV, 493 on 'physical being' and 'moral being', quoted earlier in chapter 1, section 2.4. See also E 1, 41; IV, 251). These are, of course, two different 'selves'; the latter has more, and different, needs, desires, values, etc. than does the former (though it includes those of the former also). But, in each case, it is *amour-de-soi* that directs us in seeking to procure and enjoy the well-being of that 'self', which is our self.

Rousseau's procedure is, it seems to me, clear and orderly in taking matters in this way. Aristotle, to mention only one other case, proceeds in a very similar way.[2] The structure of Rousseau's discussion is obscured only by incomprehension, not by its nature.

## 2 *Amour-de-soi*: Elementary Forms

The concern then is to follow Rousseau's account of the character and proper good that pertain to various phases of the constitution and unfolding of the human body and soul, starting *without* taking into account components and structures that involve response to the feelings and attitudes of other people. As will soon be shown, it is Rousseau's view that these are not all of one uniform character, but exhibit many differences in composition and elaboration. I shall take them in order of increasing complexity. As with the discussion of 'inflamed' *amour-propre* I shall separate analytic from genetic issues (the latter are, in this instance, far less pressing in any event).

In respect of both analysis and genesis there are, in this case, some quite significant differences (though at no time incompatibilities) between Rousseau's treatments in the second *Discourse* and in *Emile*. Because of this, I shall to some degree look at these separately, though to avoid covering similar issues twice over I shall not observe a strict distinction between them.

I start with the most elementary configuration of the mind, of dispositions and activities which comprise a creature's being moved by *amour-de-soi*, as this is characterized by Rousseau in the second *Discourse*. This I shall call 'primordial' *amour-de-soi*, which incorporates no awareness of or responsiveness to (real or phantasized) sentiments or attitudes of other persons at all. Constitutive of this configuration are such features as this. There is an innate, instinctive attraction to things which actually conduce to the creature's survival and physical integrity, and a coordinate aversion to things likewise hurtful. This is wholly non-reflective and non-deliberative, and does not involve conceptualized judgement of things as 'beneficial' or 'hurtful', but only sensational response which is, *de facto*, appropriate. Particular desires will, as they arise, render elements of the environment significant. Upon their being answered quiescent indifference and, in effect, cancellation of that in the composition of the environment will follow. Sleep is, in fact, the norm; it is punctuated merely by the sporadic irruption of need. Foresight – which requires elaborated awareness of oneself as a continuing consciousness with other than immediate needs to be met – is absent. Life is absorbed in present sensation, or immediately felt lack. (For all of this, see DI e.g. 56; III, 144)

Such primordial consciousness and capability is, of course, not unique to human creatures. In respect of this we are altogether one with animals, as Rousseau stresses. Not until greater extension has occurred does anything distinctively human enter into the case. Although, as noted, no relations to others enter, it is clear that this mode of consciousness relates the creature intimately to his environment, places him in engagement and transaction with the 'furniture' of his world. There is no question of original consciousness in this character being solipsistic in the sense of not acquainting us with, and putting us in no active material engagement with, an external reality.

It is true that Rousseau does say one or two things that imply a greater complexity of mind and awareness than is proper to primordial *amour-de-soi*. For instance, he writes that 'the native Caribbean', whose soul, we are told, 'is wholly wrapped up in the feeling of its present existence' will 'improvidently sell you his cotton-bed in the morning, and come crying in the evening to buy it again; not having foreseen he would want it again the next night' (DI 56; III, 144). But it would be foolish to take serious issue over this; the story is charming and does not seriously affect the position.

The *actual* good of the creature directed by primordial *amour-de-soi* (not conceived by him as such; nor, because so conceived, pursued by him) comprises the maintenance of the health and vigour of the body, security from threat and fear, and a cloudless ease of an untroubled, because largely vacant, mind. Rousseau obviously feels attracted as everyone does from time to time by this vision of simple foolishness of soul, protected, by oblivion, from the torments of full humanity. But to maintain, as some have done, that this comprises his vision of 'the best life for man' is mistaken. He makes it quite clear, in fact, that we have yet nothing proper to man at all; this is a mode of being all of a piece with animals. Though we may, from time to time, wish we were not men, it would be out of place to contend that a non-human life was the best human life. Rousseau, at any rate, did not contend this.

## 3 Reflective *Amour-de-soi*

Properly, then, Rousseau does not rest his case with this. We move now to a creature whose configuration of capabilities incorporates more that is distinctive of humankind, when we consider what I call 'reflective', or 'practical', *amour-de-soi*.

In this case, we have in view a creature that has awareness of itself as having an extended life-history, in particular of itself having needs relating to its survival at times other than the present, even though it has no present spontaneous interest in answering such needs. Going along with this is the ability and disposition sometimes to inhibit or defer present desire with a view to assuring future good; sometimes to put in train activities directly on the ground of their importance in assuring future good; sometimes to organize and regulate the environment with a view to future good. (For all of this, see DI e.g. 53–4; III, 141–2) This comprises a much more sophisticated constitution of thought, purpose and agency than that just considered. First, some notion of what personal good and ill constitute must be possessed and employed. Second, some power of general judgement about the related character of elements of the environment must be employed, and also of how its causal structure operates and may be harnessed. Finally, third, some deliberative and regulative power in ordering desire and satisfaction must be available, or all this increasing awareness would be idle.

Let us look a little further at each of these points, starting with the first. It is important that the notion of one's own 'good' that is in use at this point still remains 'physical' in its content, though now also in conception as well as fact (DI 64; III, 152). That is to say, on the one hand, that it is the needs of physical self-maintenance that have primacy above all others. On the other hand, it is also to say that there are no 'moral' components in the constitution of personal good as so far entertained; that is, there are no components relating to one's standing, responsibilities and rights, with others. The absence of these latter components is obvious. In respect of the former, we should further note that although out of his *amour-de-soi* a man pursues his own good, thus conceived, this is not the result of any opinion that it is good or proper that he should thrive or have abundant life. *This* sort of reflective evaluation of the significance of one's pursuing and enjoying one's well-being does not enter the case as so far constructed. When things are held to be good or bad it is always in relation to their promotion or hindrance of personal well-being, the pursuit of that being taken for granted. All evaluations are those of practical efficacy towards, or component contribution in, the enjoyment of 'physical' good for oneself.

Nor, of course, is there evaluation of the good of one's life in terms of the prestige and power one enjoys – but this hardly needs mention. Certain 'relative' estimates of one's quality and abilities will come into the case we have before us, as I shall explain in a while. But it is important to be clear that these estimates in the *first* instance relate only to one's being better or worse equipped for furthering one's own 'physical good', and do not involve a superior estimate of one's importance as a person, or of the superior value of one's enjoying one's well-being. Also, finally, there is the absence from the case we have so far of any estimate of one's virtuous character, where this does not at all involve one's standing for others, and whether or not one's fitness to have life and enjoy well-being is dependent on this or not.

We need, for the later stages of the argument, to make a distinction between someone's 'moral' character and his 'virtuous' character, which there has been no cause to make before now; some clarification of this is required. (Of course, the terminology one uses to make this distinction is, largely, discretionary. The choice I have made, which follows Rousseau's, is not ideal, but nothing of substance hangs on the words, only on the distinction itself.) In these terms, the distinction, in outline, is this. When we consider someone in their 'moral' character, in their 'moral' being, we consider them as bearers of a certain standing or title in their encounters and dealings with others, as bearers, we might say, of human dignity or as persons worthy of respect. I have looked at this in some detail already (in chapter 1, section 2.5, particularly). It may be, and usually is, that a person's own sense of himself as someone worthy of respect is partly comprised in his feeling himself to be a fit recipient of such recognition from others.

It would be an error, however, to suppose that all the bases of self-respect and good self-regard make reference to our standing or fitness to have standing for others. Consciousness of virtue, or of other more generally excellent human abilities (e.g. certain exemplary skills), can and does ground a sense of oneself as a decent and worthy being in oneself without necessary reference to one's actual standing, or claim to standing, for others in their regard towards one. It is not necessary, for this to be so, that the 'virtue' should relate only to one's own well-being and doing (such as 'temperance' does). Justice, kindness, generosity, all pertain to one's regard for and treatment of others. But the significance of these to oneself as meritorious characteristics is not exhausted by their qualifying one to bear oneself in good respect because deserving of others' respect (even if one does, by them, deserve others' respect). They have significance in one, and for one, because they are, in themselves, honest, decent and good dispositions whether or not one through them enjoys moral standing and recognition from others. They are part of what it is to be an intrinsically good person; and someone may want to be such without regard to the footing with others afforded him.[3]

I am not, of course, saying that one should take disdainful pride in oneself for one's virtue. This is, plainly, to preclude the virtue; and, here more significantly, it is to make the merit of the attributes in one's eyes comprise the opportunity they afford one to think oneself better than others, superior over them. That is a perversion of inflamed *amour-propre*. But to think that one is not all bad because one is loyal, truthful, honest for instance is not pride of this kind. It is proper recognition that these are good things, worthy of respect, and one would dishonour them if one paid them no tribute. The fact that one is oneself the bearer of these qualities makes holding them in honour a potentially more dubious attitude, but does not automatically rule it out as tainted. To want to be good, to behave with honesty and generosity (to embody and enact these virtues), is to want to serve others well; it is not to want to make an idol of oneself. It is, then, proper to have such an objective; and achieving it is some ground for a form of self-respect which is distinct from that form which involves having, or the entitlement to have, the respect of others (it may, in fact, enable one to survive when not in receipt the respect of others).[4]

Crudely, in sum, 'moral being' signifies standing as a categorical bearer of rights for recognition and standing in human transactions and engagement. 'Virtuous being' signifies possession of intrinsically excellent dispositions and attributes (standardly the ordinary virtues, but also skills and powers of certain kinds, as we shall see). These two are distinct, but not unrelated nor in opposition. By failures in virtue (e.g. by injustice) one can forfeit (some elements in) one's moral standing. By steadfastness in virtue one can merit (though one does not always receive) certain privileges, certain (proper) precedences in moral standing (such as honours, tributes, office). Where 'moral' being is in view it is more a matter of an absolute incorporation into the body of humanity as a 'person' that is in question (though there are 'grades' of standing, of course, such as citizen or magistrate, common soldier or officer, to take different sorts of case). When 'virtuous' being is in view, it is more a matter of degree, of greater or lesser respect (or esteem or affection[5]). Only a moral being can be *recognized* as a virtuous being (though he may *be* a virtuous being unrecognized, as were the inmates of concentration camps in relation to their guards). 'Moral' being is presumptively possessed in full, unless forfeited by ill-doing. It does not have to be earned by good works, as if one started without it and had to show proper excellence to merit it. 'Virtuous' being of course does have to be won; only by good dispositions and proper actions does one possess this character. One might almost say that, at ground level, moral being is a stipulated or decreed character; virtuous being is a real, material character.

Thus, self-respect can be grounded in one's moral standing or virtuous character (or both). One expresses one's sense of one's undeniable dignity as a human person by claiming standing as a morally counting presence for others. This assertion of claim may, but need not, depend upon any sense of one's 'virtuous' worth (in the narrow or broad[6] sense), although if one is signally vicious it may be improper. Mere 'ordinariness' does not disqualify one from holding oneself in proper self-respect in this manner. And, or alternatively, one's self-respect may be grounded in one's goodness, without reference to one's footing for others, though one may perhaps think one deserves well of others if one has served them well. But this last point is only contingent. The possession and exercise of virtue, the good in a person it comprises, and the good about himself he may properly value in regard to this, are logically not connected to holding standing for others and the meaning and value of that to a person, however naturally they may go together.

This excursus has taken me some way away from elucidating the character of 'reflective' *amour-de-soi*. Its content will be brought into play, however, soon enough in explaining further elaborations of *amour-de-soi* both as these pertain to man-alone but also to man-in-relation to others.

Moving on, now, to consideration of the further characteristics I said were constitutive of the character of 'reflective' *amour-de-soi*, it may generally be objected that the elaborations of awareness and agency involved could only be available to someone through his mastery of language. Language being a social 'institution' it is clear that we are not really any longer dealing with man-alone. (See Rousseau's own subtle discussion of this; DI 58–63; III, 146ff.) I have, I hope, said enough before now to show the misplacedness of this objection, and I will not pause to consider it again.

What, then, more specifically is there to say of such characteristics as knowledge of the causal order of the natural world, and of the power to judge how to turn it to beneficial use (e.g. by planting seeds in damp, not bone-dry, place)? This adaptability and practical sagacity Rousseau attributes to man's 'perfectibility', his capacity for self-improvement (DI 54; III, 142). Rousseau intends nothing sublime or edifying by this notion, only the human power to learn from experience, to modify objectives and patterns of behaviour to suit changing circumstances, and so on. This stands in contrast with the tropistic, 'wired-in', routines that characterize much of the behaviour of the lower animals (compare the nest building of birds with human house building). It is obvious that such plasticity of response confers great survival advantages on humans, enabling them to inhabit great areas of the planet whereas most animals are confined to a particular habitat.

The capability men have to inhibit or defer present impulse, or to set in train courses of action based on beliefs about needs which will come to press in the future, Rousseau attributes to human free will, man's 'character as a free agent' (DI 53; III, 147).[7] At this point, Rousseau again intends no very far-reaching significance for this notion, only the power to regulate the immediate inclinations of instinct. Later on (in chapter 4, section 5 and chapter 5, section 5), I shall examine the full significance Rousseau attributes to human freedom, which is one of his key notions overall.

Perfectibility, free will and reflective *amour-de-soi* (of which the first two are really just components) comprise the three principal characteristics which Rousseau most clearly attributes to 'natural' man in DI. There is, however, also a fourth characteristic he mentions, namely pity, first introduced as a principle 'prior to reason . . . exciting a natural repugnance at seeing any other sensible being, and particularly any of our own species, suffer pain or death' (DI 41; III, 126. See also DI 66; III, 154). I shall defer discussion of the character of this, and of its claim to be regarded as a 'natural' characteristic in men, until the next chapter. It is, however, worth noting in passing that, on the one hand, pity obviously establishes a bond between people; their sentiments and actions are, in complex ways, interrelated. So it clearly involves some kind of social interaction and connection. But, on the other hand, Rousseau is quite emphatic that the possession and expression of the disposition of pity is an element in human nature. So this provides yet further reason for saying that what is 'natural' in man is not, and cannot be, only that which involves no connection or association with others of any kind at all. What is so significant about pity, for Rousseau, is that it promises the possibility of establishing and consolidating social relations in ways that do not involve our encountering each other in contention for mastery, domination, triumph and so on. It opens the possibility, that is to say, of human relations not perverted by the demands of 'inflamed' *amour-propre*, not deformed by the war of vindictive wills. It thus may allow social relatedness to become incorporated into the constitution of each of us in a fashion which is thoroughly natural and good. How Rousseau's arguments about this proceed I shall be considering.

One final point on reflective *amour-de-soi*. Rousseau allows that the development of practical sagacity in each of us will enable us to recognize each other in the character of potential aids in the accomplishing of projects too difficult or arduous for a single person. So it is that a 'loose association, that laid no restraint on its members, and lasted no longer than the transitory occasion that formed it' (DI 78; III, 166) might form between men. Men are as yet to each other only useful 'hands', which may be moved to push all at the same wheel, if each possessor of them sees sufficient good to himself in doing so. No more densely characterized mutual human encounter than this is involved. But these needs requiring collaboration do comprise one of the principal bases for human society, and they will, in due course, be incorporated by Rousseau in his full account of the character of civil communities. When Rousseau, as he does from time to time, recommends economic self-sufficiency on each of our parts, this is not because he thought that social ties established by a need not answerable by our own labour alone were always corrupt or corrupting. It is because he thought that such ties could so very easily *become* corrupt and corrupting that he wished to keep them as minimal and loosely binding as possible. He never seriously envisaged that any human community could survive and thrive without a very great deal of exchange of goods and labour, cooperative and concerted activity – as is obviously true. The issue was, for him, to make this a source for human trust, loyalty and mutual respect rather than a source for what it so standardly becomes, an opportunity for enslavement, dispossession and hatred.

## 4 Self-estimating *Amour-de-soi*

In my treatment of reflective *amour-de-soi* I showed that there were various kinds of self-appraisal, judgements about the character, attributes, qualities of oneself, which were not involved in this, even though certain other forms of self-assessment were. These additional kinds must now be considered; I shall say they form components of 'self-estimating' *amour-de-soi*. Any treatment of those aspects of human being which do not involve being for others would be seriously incomplete without treatment of these.

There is little explicit reference to self-estimating *amour-de-soi* in DI. Rousseau, at one point (DI 66, note 2; III, note xv, 219) says that in the primitive condition 'each man regarded himself as the only observer of his actions, the only being in the universe who took any interest in him, and the sole judge of his deserts . . .'. There are one or two other points, which I shall come to, where allied ideas are suggested. But there is little extended consideration of the matter. It is clear from the passage quoted that something in addition to, and different in character from, that practical sagacity of reflective *amour-de-soi* is involved here. The 'observation' of one's actions is not that of determining whether they were practically successes or failures, efficient or inefficient. It is rather an 'observation' in which we judge our 'deserts', in which we judge whether we have behaved with decency, propriety, acquitted ourselves as good people should. It might be proper to say that it is an exercise of our own conscience in judging ourselves.[8] That is certainly the direction in which Rousseau is moving. But one should not invoke this notion too emphatically here, for two reasons. First, Rousseau makes no mention at all of conscience in this discussion (it is not treated of in any detail until quite late on in *Emile*). Second, the notion of conscience is too narrowly 'moralistic' for Rousseau's purposes. Conscience chides one for one's viciousness, laziness, ingratitude, and leaves one in peace in relation to converse matters. But the good consciousness of oneself which Rousseau has in mind at this moment can rest not only on such points, but also on one's skills and powers if these are of a high order, as I shall show.

The principal points regarding this form of self-estimation are these. It involves a reflective assessment of, broadly put, what manner of person one is, an appraisal of one's dispositions, powers, objectives with a view to establishing whether these make one a decent, creditable, specimen or not. Rousseau's thought is that we do make such appraisals of ourselves, and that being able to come to a satisfactory verdict about oneself in this way is an essential part of feeling happy in and about oneself, and in the overall satisfactoriness of one's life. Our *amour-de-soi* will direct us to acquire and to cherish in ourselves those attributes which do enable us to live in good company with ourselves. The second *Discourse* does not reveal anything very explicitly about what such attributes could be. But we can easily see what they could *not* be.

They could *not* be those attributes to which such signal importance and priority is attached by inflamed *amour-propre*. For these involve us in implacable hostility and competition with others as the condition for our own self-possession of life and a sense of personal value, such that we are inwardly terrorized by the fear of humiliation, servitude, vengance and annihilation. I have tried to explain how this is so. Someone whose good consciousness of himself hinged on the possession of such invidious distinction would not only be self-estranged, subjected to the opinions on him of others (E 1, 104; III, 193). He would also be tormented by fear, and be moving further and further away from the possibilities of true reward. *Amour-de-soi*, not caused to be at odds with its own principle, could not direct anyone to this.

So excluded from the directions of sound, intact, self-estimating *amour-de-soi* is acquiring and valuing any attributes whose 'merit' reposes in their conferring invidious distinction, positional power and prestige, on their bearer. From this we can infer two things about the attributes *sound* self-estimating *amour-de-soi* will guide a person to the election and valuation of. First, all such attributes must not have whatever human significance they may have because of their affording their possesser prestigious precedence before, contemptuous superiority over, other people. Second, such attributes must not be valued in the manner of their giving their possessor the opportunity to gloat over the humilating inferiority or impotence of others as if that were their real meaning and value. These two points are logically independent. For, to take an example of Rousseau's (E 4, 339; IV, 670–1), it is reasonable to think signal excellence in running (athletic prowess) a real and not a factitious human excellence. But it is certainly possible for someone to seek to excel in running only to afford himself the pleasure of deriding and despising those he beats. For him, it is not the excellence in the achievement that is of interest. It is only the fact of its being a way of cornering prestige for himself and thus enabling him to do down others, which is what he wants for himself. (Cases where it works the other way round can also be devised.)

It follows, then, that self-estimating *amour-de-soi* will direct us to intrinsically valuing (seeing and cherishing as good as such, not as power- or prestige-conferring) intrinsic goods (not invidious power or prestige 'invented' factitious 'merits'). As I have said, the second *Discourse* is not very explicit about what attributes, materially, would fit this bill. But we can conjecture – and later on will try to prove – that discharging the 'obligations of humanity' mentioned in DAS (14; III, 17) would be among these. It is no objection that these involve transactions with others, for we should know by now that what is 'naturally good' for us is not taken by Rousseau to exclude all reference of all kinds to others. The only social relations that are excluded are those that involve mastery, tyranny, prestigious precedence over others. These are excluded in this case.

More than this is, in fact, excluded from the case as Rousseau presents it here. It is not only such relations, but also those of proper, equable, moral standing for others that are not yet being considered. This is because Rousseau is still confining his attention to those things that pertain to a man who has only being-for-himself, and is considering nothing that depends on or derives from his being-for-others (whether this be proper, as with equable *amour-propre*, or inappropriate, as when *amour-propre* is inflamed). Rousseau is not at all suggesting that there are no important values for ourselves that derive from our being-for-others. His purpose is rather, for the time being, not yet to consider these, but to look at those which do not relate to one's footing with others at all. The intrinsic value to oneself of a good consciousness of oneself as a valuable being, decent in oneself, is just such a value. This self-possessed sense of oneself as a valuable being in oneself may be necessary to prompt one to claim one's proper due and title as a moral being for others. But even if this were true, the two conceptions of personal value involved are distinct, as I have tried to show by my differentiation of 'moral' and 'virtuous' character, above.

There is one further aspect of the case to be looked at, regarding non-ethical bases for good personal self-estimation; and also regarding certain related forms of self-estimation of one's attributes relative to those of others. In an interesting passage, Rousseau writes as follows (DI 77–8; III, 165):

> [The] repeated relevance of various beings to himself, and to one another, would naturally give rise in the human mind to the perceptions of certain relations between them. Thus the relations which we denote by the terms great, small, strong, weak, swift, slow, fearful, bold . . . must have at length produced in him a kind of reflection . . . which would indicate to him the precautions most necessary to his security.
>
> This new intelligence which resulted from this development increased his superiority over animals, by making him sensible of it . . . Thus, the first time he looked into himself, he felt the first emotion of pride; and, at a time when he scarce knew how to distinguish the different orders of beings, by looking upon his species as of the highest order, he prepared the way for assuming preeminence as an individual. (See also DI 47; III, 135).

The first part of this passage presents no problems. That practical sagacity, characteristic of reflective *amour-de-soi*, causes us to note and make use of information regarding the powers and capabilities of those other creatures who surround us, and may aid or hinder us in our actions for our self-preservation. Equipped with this and other knowledge, and with our ingenuity and adaptability, we find ourselves 'all round, the most advantageously organized of any' animal. By this our security and prosperity increases; but also, Rousseau says, we come to think well of ourselves as having the better of animals. We think of ourselves as, crudely, rather splendid creatures since we can outdo the blundering beasts. And, Rousseau goes on, possessed of this good estimate of ourselves *qua* human, this readies each of us to want, to claim, preeminence among humans, for we have so high a sense of our merit and credit.

Several things are interesting about this. First, obviously something additional to reflective *amour-de-soi* has now come in; what I have called self-estimating *amour-de-soi* is disclosing its character. Second, the bases of the good self-estimate made are clearly not here those of our virtuous or ethical attributes, but our superior powers, skills, aptitudes and so on – our generic species talents and excellences. (Thus *any* one of humankind can think he cannot be just nothing on this sort of basis, almost however ethically limited he may be). This connects immediately with, for instance, the example of athletic prowess, admired among humans, discussed before.

Third, comparisons or relative judgements are being made here. But we need to be very clear that there are *two* aspects of these. First, there is the merely *cognitive* need in order to determine, e.g. that I am very strong, to make comparisons between my attainments and those of others. There is no other basis for arriving at such judgements. But then, secondly, these comparisons are said by Rousseau to meet a *conative* (or affective) need, the need to be able to rate myself as a rather good person because I am strong to this or that extent, or stronger than most, or extraordinarily strong. We know already that this self-approving rating can proceed in two very different ways. First, discovering that I am a certain strength, and that being so is a cut above the ordinary, I may realize that I have a rather special attribute. I may think this makes me specifically excellent in my kind in this respect, a specifically admirable person. But this is not to say that the value to me I see in my signal strength is precisely comprised in the power it gives me to command the admiration of others, to cast them into the shade, and to congratulate myself in my having humiliated them. This is, of course, definitive of the second form of self-approving rating. The constitution of my self-approval in this case *comprises* my ability to look down on others, to think of myself as having the better of them.

Which of these is involved here? Is it pleasure in oneself because one finds oneself to be quite good in some way? Or is it pleasure in oneself because one finds one can humiliate and do down others? Is it excellence, or despotic power, that is the good to one in this? If it is the latter then the first movements of inflamed *amour-propre* are being revealed here. Rousseau's own account is rather problematic. He seems almost to suggest that man, conscious ('sensible') of his practical superiority, would employ it not only to better his security and self-preservation but to 'trick', to 'scourge', animals as if rejoicing in his power to make mock of them (however oblivious to this the animals might be). This argues a vicious delight in vindictive power. But this would be a hostile reading to place on this, I think. There is no real reason to suppose, what for so many other reasons we should not suppose, that Rousseau is here positing the spontaneous emergence of glory in vindictive power. Rather, he is surely thinking that what our ability to 'trick' (to outwit) and to 'master' animals exhibits to us is our force of being as active, ingenious, effective creatures which is something that is, when borne in on us, a source for consciousness of ourselves as creatures with some distinctive merit about us. This does not require, indeed it precludes, gloating contempt in the stupidity of the brutes. Such opinions display a sense of insecurity about one's real potency and effectiveness, demanding insistent testimony by beating down an opposing will, rather than by effectively furthering one's concrete good.

The sense in which this good consciousness of ourselves prepares each of us for assuming 'preeminence as an individual' is that we become used to the idea that we can be, that it is fitting to us to be, the controlling masters of our affairs and environment. Thus when men come together in association, and are required to coordinate their activities, each will bring to this task the supposition that it is fitting to one of his powers and excellences that he should be a director and disposer of the affairs. This is, of course, bound to engender conflict, and quite possibly grievance and hostility when it is found that everyone claims this and no-one accedes to another's claim. But this is not yet to introduce inflamed *amour-propre*. For there is no suggestion that what we take to be our fit right is that others should be subordinate to us, should yield to us in servitude. For not only do such ideas introduce 'moral' terms of relation, which have no place in the case so far, but also the good opinion of one's significance is not, as I have explained, comprised in one's holding power over others. It is just that one's power over the situation discloses that one is a to-be-reckoned-with potent presence. Indeed it is proper that one *should* bring such a sense of oneself to human transactions. For it will cause one to assert one's perfectly proper claim on others to be taken account of, and to be given account to, in common transactions. We shall consider, in chapter 5, how several persons, all used to enjoying unconstrained sovereignty over their affairs, and regarding it as part of their proper good and good self-estimate that they should, can, without serious compromise and loss of this be brought to deliberate and act in concert.

One point emerges very clearly, that it is a bad misreading of Rousseau if we believe that *whenever* he speaks of relative or comparative judgements being made between people he is (consistently, or in self-contradiction) supposing that those kinds of relative and comparative judgement which form part of corrupt inflamed *amour-propre* are in issue. It is when, and only when, the comparison is part of, or a means to, a judgement of invidious superiority in power or prestige that it is corrupt and depraved, and is criticized, therefore, by him. Other comparisons, or comparisons made for other purposes, are regarded by him as not only inevitable, but natural, proper and reasonable. This has not stopped commentators treating it as virtually axiomatic that Rousseau wanted to exclude all comparisons of whatever kind between people, and then accusing him of not being at all consistent in this. This is not Rousseau's problem.[9]

## 5 Man-for-himself: Points from *Emile*

The three modes of disclosure of *amour-de-soi*, actuating 'selves' of differing complexity, that I have isolated in my discussion of the second *Discourse* map very roughly on to periods in the development in the individual life of Emile. Primordial *amour-de-soi* corresponds, more or less, to elements in the first stirrings of infant life, described in *Emile*, Book 1. Reflective *amour-de-soi* is very clearly the topic of Book 2 and most of Book 3; and self-estimating *amour-de-soi* is considered in the later pages of Book 3, and in some parts of Book 4 (particularly E 4, 314ff; IV, 637ff, even although much of this book considers Emile in his 'moral being' and will be discussed in the next chapter).

That there should be these similarities, despite the very different overall character of these works, is not surprising. For, as I have stressed, we are not really being invited either to consider moments in mankind's history (real or conjectured), nor the empirical observation of the nursery, but to consider those aspects of, elements in, the comprehensive character and activity of a completed person which do not, however, depend on features which arise because of his footing and engagement with others, especially other's sentiments and attitudes towards him. The exercise is principally one of selecting a limited range of attributes for consideration first; moving on then, later, to consider further aspects of the finished person. So, despite differences in narrative bedding and general presentation, visibly the same points are under review.

Where, then, there is real overlap of accounts between the second *Discourse* and *Emile* I shall not repeat the material. I want to focus on some of the points of additional elaboration and subtlety which are to be found, as always, in the later account, for some of these are of considerable interest.

We have seen, in chapter 2, that it is Rousseau's view that the earliest stirrings of the infant soul include elements of great complexity. By virtue of these, the infant animates his life-world and may become wholly taken up with the struggle to contend for life with vengeful persecutors. This material, also, I do not wish to touch on again. What Rousseau then does, pretty much from the start of Book 2, is to fashion around Emile a world in which he does not have to make and find his way amidst the challenge of human wills directed onto him, but a world in which (he is caused to think that) he is solely engaged with *things*, whose character and ways he must study, learn and harness if he is to secure and preserve his own life as a creature at large in the world. Rousseau has two purposes in doing this. One is the analytic purpose, described already, to select for consideration only those human powers which do not involve encounter with and response to other human wills challenging or confronting a person. But he has also an actual developmental reason for this. He thinks that if Emile is artificially held back as long as possible from having to make his way in the melée of contending human wills, he may – when he encounters these, as he will and should (cf. E 4, 219; IV, 500; E 4, 215; IV, 494–5) – quietly and securely be assured of his own happiness and well-being, of his power to provide for himself, and of his own inherent value and worth. He need not feel the need to make a large, domineering, claim on others in order to secure proof of his own potency and worth. So, Rousseau thinks, he may be saved from the toils of excessive *amour-propre*. It is not that he will not be actuated by *amour-propre* at all in his later life; it is necessary and good that he should be. But it might be hoped that his demand for standing will be proper and equable. This does not seem an unreasonable conjecture.

In relation to primordial *amour-de-soi* the two most important elaborations *Emile* introduces are these. First, Rousseau does not assume that we spontaneously possess, in an articulate and finished form, a clear grasp of the distinctions between ourselves and the external world, between what is our mood or our feeling and what is a real character of our surroundings. Pain is taken for attack; hunger for famine (if one may so put it). A great deal of the infant's early learning is, in fact, his unlearning constructions and conjectures about his world and his situation in it that his elementary phantasies establish for him. The processes of world-interpretation are at one and the same time processes of determining the character, powers, aptitudes which are constitutive of that particular point in the world which is oneself. So, second, it follows from this that we are not, as we were in the case of the account given in the second *Discourse*, given one finished structure which, then, somehow is elaborated and extended. Rather, we have in the first workings of the infant's principle of life (of his *amour-de-soi*) rudimentary forms of self-characterization and world-characterization which stand in immediate complementarity. What Emile's particular upbringing does is to consolidate and confirm certain among those patterns, establishing them as the secure framework for Emile's knowledge of himself and his surroundings, and for the nature and scope of his action upon it.

One might say that what is being attended to here is the operation of the 'reality principle' in Emile (any man). If an infant's paranoid construction of

his world and his engagement with it is not too intense, he will have the
readiness slowly to learn that, for instance, nourishment comes, possibly at the
'wrong' time, possibly 'too little', but yet predictably enough to him; that his
cries sometimes procure aid, sometimes not; that beaten tables (see E 2, 88; IV,
314–5) are still apt, obdurately, to stand in one's way; and so on. By this he
slowly constructs a conception of what nature, scope and powers the world has;
what coordinate nature, scope and powers he has; and of how he and the world
stand and interact with each other, a conception which corresponds more or
less closely to the actual facts of the case, such actual facts as these: the world
does not bend its knee to command; food is not always available to peremptory
demand; to get something one must walk over to it; one is much weaker and
smaller than many things, and so on. With such truths incorporated by him as
determining the character of the sphere of his action, and his power to operate
within this sphere, his *amour-de-soi* can set him reliably, sensibly and with
some prospect of genuine success about the business of making his way in the
world, and finding support and sustenance from it.[10] So long as he remains
ruled by his paranoid responsiveness, he can only proceed with such business
imperfectly, falteringly, inappropriately.

The qualities of patience, ingenuity, resourcefulness, persistence,
industriousness, fortitude, self-possession, pleasure in effective competence
and in oneself as competent, calm endurance (see E 3, 208; IV, 487–8, and
Book 3, *passim*; E 4, 320; IV, 644), which comprise what is Emile's completion
as a being-for-himself, are, in effect, merely those qualities which someone of
finite powers easily baulked, needing to achieve his own preservation in a
world which must be studied and harnessed if it is to yield fruits to him,
necessarily acquires if he learns and lives according to the *real truth* about his
character and circumstances. Emile learns to incorporate into himself, as the
basic constitution of his understanding and the automatic principle of his
projects and actions, that he lives, moves and acts in the common place and
under the common lot inherent to human kind.

Treat your pupil according to his age. At the outset put him in his place, and
hold him there so well that he no longer tries to leave it. Then, before knowing
what wisdom is, he will practise its most important lesson . . . Let him know
only that he is weak and you are strong, and by his condition and yours he is
necessarily at your mercy. Let him know it, learn it, feel it. Let his haughty head
at an early date feel the harsh yoke which nature imposes on man, the heavy yoke
of necessity under which every finite being must bend. Let him see this necessity
in things, never in the caprice of men. Let the bridle that restrains him be force
and not authority . . . let 'not', once pronounced, be a wall of bronze against
which the child will have to exhaust his strength at most five or six times in order
to abandon any further attempts to overturn it.

It is thus that you will make him patient, steady, resigned, calm, even when he
has not got what he wanted, for it is in the nature of man to endure patiently the

necessity of things but not the ill will of men . . . The worst education is to leave him floating between his will and yours and to dispute endlessly between you and him as to which of the two will be master. (E 2, 91; IV, 320; see also E 2, 88; IV, 315; E 2, 161; IV, 422; and E 5, 446; IV, 820, on living with the knowledge of death.)

This is the 'wisdom' which Emile's life-alone incorporates, and which all Jean-Jacques' pedagogic efforts are directed to instilling into him. Its meaning is to fit Emile, incarnating the truth about his life and situation, to make his way in the world, surely and securely to preserve himself and see that he prospers, freed from all damaging delusions that things should be different and he is ill-used because they are not. *Amour-de-soi* thus directs him to his true good, since it is the good which corresponds to the truth about his nature, powers, needs and circumstances.

Rousseau gives many marvellously engaging and detailed examples of how to instill into Emile the desire to know and to have competent mastery of his powers and the workings of the world, so that he eagerly enjoys his increasing facility and ability in fending for himself, exploring and utilizing his surroundings to his benefit and pleasure. At every point his own present level of comprehension and understood ideas of good and enjoyment are addressed; he is insensibly led to a larger, deeper and sounder understanding of what he is, of what he needs, what he can and cannot expect and do. This is done in such a way that he is not caused to think it is his right, that it is owed, that he should not have to labour to find nourishment, not have to learn the layout of his surroundings to find his way home, as if it were the case that sustenance should always be laid on, as if someone should always be on hand to put him right. Emile learns that problems for oneself caused by one's own over-reaching are practical problems one has, oneself, the responsibility for resolving; he unlearns that they are unjust harms vengefully inflicted on him by an unfair world, which he does not deserve to suffer.

It is not possible to go through Rousseau's engrossing presentation of all these points in their concrete immediacy. Their general intent is clear enough. I stress three further aspects of the matter, only. First, as indicated, Emile's 'education' is as much a process of unlearning, of certain predispositions being muted and their development discouraged, as it is one of positive learning. Tendencies to contend for mastery, to claim obedience, to demand service, are all blocked. Rousseau hopes that by this the interpretations of self, other and world they import may be abandoned. In their place that assured vigour and competence that bespeaks a person firmly and with assurance able to make his own way and provide for himself in quiet self-possession is encouraged, a person at home in the real world (see E 2, 159; IV, 419).

Second, Rousseau makes many subtle observations about the developments of understanding and reason, arguing, rightly, that a child begins from immediate apprehension and response to concrete particulars of his experience, and only slowly comes to grasp the significance of generic ideas and general principles (cf. E 2, 108; IV, 345; E 2, 132; IV, 380). Rousseau therefore argues that it is inappropriate, that it is often a way of controlling and humiliating the child, to instruct him with long explanations and theoretical discourses that he has neither the taste for nor the power to follow and to use (E 2, 102; IV, 336). Instead his studies, which seem to him more entertainments and opportunities to increase his possesed strength and power of action, should be initially concerned with concrete, particular, problems which relate to immediate everyday activities (E 2, 125; IV, 368–9). These ideas of Rousseau's have, of course, had substantial impact on educational practice (not always, in my view, to great benefit in fact). The outcome is, in Rousseau's view, this:

> Emile has little knowledge, but what he has is truly his own. He knows nothing halfway. Among the small number of things he knows and knows well, the most important is that there are many things of which he is ignorant . . . Emile has a mind that is universal not by its learning but by its faculty to acquire learning; a mind that is open, intelligent, ready for everything . . . (E 3, 207; IV, 487)

Thirdly, it is part of Emile's learning to incarnate and act always on the ground of the truth of his condition that he learns the basic realities of human labour and exchange of goods and services. Prefigured in the episode of Robert the gardener and the uprooted bean, Emile acquires a rudimentary, original 'physical' notion of property as 'the right of the first occupant by labour' (E 2, 99; IV, 331; see E 2, 160; IV, 421, also). But Rousseau is most emphatic that the sense Emile attributes to this, and allied notions, is originally largely restricted to physical control and use of resources and to some primitive idea of being not interfered with in this, of being allowed to proceed without check. This is his first introduction to a basis on which men can stand on terms and have a footing with each other, as materially useful one to another, being participants in and contributers to processes of material production and exchange. Rousseau writes:

> The practice of the natural arts, for which a single man suffices, leads to the investigation of the arts of industry, which need the conjunction of many hands . . .
> Your greatest care ought to be to keep away from your pupil's mind all notions of social relations which are not within his reach. But when the chain of knowledge forces you to show him the mutual dependence of men, instead of showing it to him from the moral side, turn all his attention at first towards industry and mechanical arts which make men useful to one another. (E 3, 185–6; IV, 456–7)

Emile's situation is this:

In place of the social laws which he cannot know, we have bound him with the chains of necessity. He is still almost only a physical being. Let us continue to treat him as such.

It is by their palpable relation to his utility, his security, his preservation that he ought to appraise all the bodies of nature and all the works of men . . . the art whose use is the most general and the most indispensable is incontestably the one which merits the most esteem; and the one to which other arts are less necessary also merits esteem ahead of the more subordinate ones, because it is freer and nearest independence. These are the true rules for appraising the arts and manufactures. Anything else is arbitrary and depends on opinion. (E 3, 187–8; IV, 458–9)

So it is that Emile learns the true measures of value and worth in the 'real material relations' (E 3, 190; IV, 462) of collaboration and exchange, which are fundamental to all human society (E 3, 189; IV, 461), in which we are to each other potential providers of beneficial services, on the basis of exchange. Emile knows that to receive from others he must have something to give them in return; that their relations are not those of charity or gift, but practical relations of mutual utility; and that to engage with others on this basis one must have a skill and the power to employ it (E 3, 193; IV, 467). It is the basic principle of this first mode of social relation that one must work, one must have some product to present to others, if one is to be in a position to make use of their product. This is the simple consequence of living in accord with the reality of one's human situation with others likewise situated.

A man and a citizen, whoever he may be, has no property to put into society other than himself . . . Outside of society isolated man, owing nothing to anyone, has a right to live as he pleases. But in society, where he necessarily lives in dependence upon others, he owes them the price of his keep in work. This is without exception. To work is therefore an indispensable duty for social man. (I have amended Bloom's translation here) (E 3, 194–5; IV, 469)

Emile is equipped to work, to have a product to exchange for the products of others he requires (there is no other reasonable ground for them to render these products to him). He will become a carpenter (E 3, 201; IV, 478). He will have a skill that is always useful, always in demand; the product of it is humanly necessary and does not enslave him to 'fashionable' trends to make a living. It can largely be practised on one's own; one does not require many minions, the products of many lands, large markets and the like. It is clean; it allows for invention and taste. It will equip Emile self-possessedly to hold his own in the elementary transactions of civl community. Then whether fortune smiles on him or not, he will be able to make his way, without begging or fawning, without bullying or imposing:

. . . he rises to the station of man, which so few men know how to fill. Then he triumphs over fortune; he braves it. He owes nothing except to himself; and when there remains nothing for him to show except himself, he is not nothing, he is something. (E 3, 194–5; IV, 468–9)

This is Emile's finished state *as man-for-himself*, in his engagements of material practicality with the world and men as producers. It is *not* his completion: 'Emile is not a savage to be relegated to the desert. He is a savage made to inhabit cities. He has to know how to find his necessities in them, to take advantage of their inhabitants, and to live . . . with them' (E 3, 205; IV, 483–4). 'We have made', Rousseau says, 'an active and thinking being. It remains for us, in order to complete the man, only to make a loving and feeling being – that is to say, to perfect reason by sentiment (E 3, 203; IV, 481). What we have considered represents the finality of his self-constitution and modes of activity in respect of powers and dispositions that do *not* involve him in relations to and transactions with others beyond those dictated by the requirements securely to further and foster his happiness as a 'natural man', his health, freedom (absence of command and obligation), and the necessities of life (E 3, 177; IV, 444), living wholly on the basis of the 'truth of things'.

The further elaborations of man's self-estimating *amour-de-soi* that are considered in *Emile* will concern us later. Rousseau largely introduces them after his consideration of the 'moral man', for reasons that will be explained. We shall see that these, too, can be understood as extensions of the same progressive articulation of self in relation to the world which is delineated in *Emile*, without the abrupt transitions worked by extraneous factors which mar the discussion in the second *Discourse*.

## 6 The 'Natural Goodness' of *Amour-de-soi*

Let us set down as an incontestable maxim that the first movements of nature are always right. There is no original perversity in the human heart. There is not a single vice to be found in it of which it cannot be said how and whence it entered. The sole passion natural to man is *amour-de-soi* . . . (E 2, 92; IV, 322).

The love of oneself is always good and always in conformity with order. Since each man is specially entrusted with his own preservation, the first and most important of his cares is and ought to be to watch over it constantly. (E 4, 213; IV, 491)

According to Rousseau, we all possess, innately, a concern which directs us to lay hold on life for ourselves, to seize the means of our own preservation and well-being. This is the principle of ongoing life as such in us; it is *amour-de-soi*. The first movements prompted by it are 'purely mechanical effects, devoid of knowledge and will' (E 1, 61; IV, 280). But knowledge, experience, reason and will enlarge what we are, and what we take ourselves for. *Amour-de-soi* continues to prompt us to the pursuit of our well-being. If it is to hit its mark, we must know what our well-being is composed of. We are multi-faceted creatures, active, sensitive, inquiring, productive, feeling, reasoning, loving – these are our active powers. Our passive powers include vulnerability, weakness, dependence, ignorance, incompetence, and so on. In all these aspects, we seek our well-being, secure and enduring strength of being and amplitude of vigorous rewarding life for ourselves.

What could Rousseau mean by saying that such an innate concern, in time amplified and elaborated in all sorts of ways, is 'always right', 'always good'? He has two things principally in mind, one positive the other negative in emphasis. The positive emphasis is this: it is proper, fitting and reasonable that human beings should seek their own well-being – there is nothing *as such* amiss about such an interest in the well-thriving of oneself. Of course, it may *come to be* sought in activities, and by means, that are 'amiss' (in a sense to be clarified). But, first, this does not show that this concern is as such inappropriate. And, second, it is Rousseau's guiding thought that just as and when the content and means of pursuit of one's well-being come to be, in the relevant sense, questionable, in just those very ways one is in fact precisely harming oneself, not successfully pursuing one's well-being. In these cases, *amour-de-soi* is 'at odds' with its own principle, and one is acting 'in contradiction' with oneself (E 4, 213; IV, 491).

Leaving this second point for a moment, could the first sensibly be denied? I can think of only three possible reasons for saying so, none of which seems to me defensible. First, it might be said that it really makes no sense to say that it is good *or* bad, admirable or offensive, that humans should strive for their own preservation, just as any animate species does. This is simply the way things work, and it is not coherent to judge the case one way or the other. I do not think this is correct. The judgement may be quasi-aesthetic, but it is one we can and do make, to say that it is good that this or that creature should live, move and have being: the panoply of creation is the richer for it, or, at least, not diminished and marred by it. It is intelligible, at least, to hold such a opinion about humanhind.

It may be agreed that the judgement is intelligible, but mistaken. From time to time one is taken by moods in which the sight, or thought, of the swarming mass of humanity fills one with revulsion. One thinks that the world might be a far more beautiful and harmonious place if mankind had never been. Such thoughts are, I believe, readily intelligible; but I think their real root lies in the third point to be considered. It is the sight of greed, avarice, ambition, self-obsession, spoiling depradation that revolts. To hold, then, that humankind's concern for life is, as such, objectionable, one must hold that these – and allied dispositions – are inherent to that concern. But it is Rousseau's argument that they are not; that in these dispositions *amour-de-soi* has been turned aside from, against, its own proper objective. In such dispositions we secure death for ourselves, not amplitude of abundant life. He argues this because it is his view, which I have tried to defend in chapter 2, that such dispositions comprise maladaptions, made under the pressure of self-deforming phantasy, to the real circumstances and parameters of human living.

Greed, for instance, is an angry attack on the world felt to be denying one proper nourishment and life-sustaining good. It discloses the modes of feeling and relation inherent to the paranoid response to one's life situation and footing in the world. It is all of a piece, then, with the dispositions to attack, to injure, harm, humiliate and subjugate others, perceived as vengeful competitors seeking to control and inflict suffering on one. If someone pursues their well-being by such means then, in my words, his pursuit of it has gone 'amiss', is 'questionable'. But, we now see, this is so far from being inherent to *amour-de-soi*, that it is actually in contradiction to its direction. So there is no reason to suppose that such dispositions boding so ill for others are intrinsic to our desire of life for ourselves. I have indeed suggested – and will argue in detail later – that it is dispositions of regard and support to others that are intrinsic to that. Not only are the former excluded, as turning *amour-de-soi* against its own principle; the latter are included, as proper constructive manifestations of that principle.

This leads to the 'negative' emphasis in Rousseau's contention that 'the first movements of nature are always right'. Relieved from the (largely self-engendered) delusion that the constitutive terms under which we make our way in life are those of an unremitting trial for mastery, the 'movements of nature' do *not* direct us at all to hurt, to hate, to enslave, other people. These moral evils are not only not part of these original movements, they are also contradictory to their inherent objective. So one of the senses in which our love of self is good is that, rightly ordered according to its own principle, it excludes moral evil from our objectives and dispositions.

In making some of these points. I have been looking ahead, to the direction rightly ordered *amour-de-soi* will take us in the forum of human transactions as 'moral' beings. I have done so because it is only in connection with that that much of the force of Rousseau's insistence on the 'natural goodness' of *amour-de-soi* can be seen. (Of course, I have yet to make out the cogency of Rousseau's ideas in these regards; I shall soon be doing so.) If we put all such aspects of the case aside, and look only to the attributes and dispositions of man-for-himself then Rousseau's claim that he is, in these, 'good' seems altogether innocuous and hardly worth mention. The real 'bite' of his thought only becomes clear when we look at the extension of the dictates of *amour-de-soi* to our need and good in our being-for-others. That is why I have emphasized this here.

We see then, once more, how mistaken it is to equate 'natural goodness' with the goodness of disposition, and the good in the life, of isolated man, whether 'isolation' be taken literally or metaphorically. The attributes and

dispositions which are unconnected with our 'moral' footing with, and affec
tionate ties to, others comprise only a sub-set of our attributes and disposi
tions. We can, and do, seek our own good not just comprehending these, but
incorporating *all* our attributes and dispositions. We can follow the path o
nature, that is to say the path of our greatest life and abundance, in all ou.
associations and bonds with others. Providing that we, at all points, avoic
coming to be absorbed in the contention for mastery which denatures us, we
can have life for ourselves living with others in society as much as we may
have living for ourselves alone. I consider, in the next chapter, Rousseau's
fundamental account of this.

# 4

# *The Self Completed: Standing with Others*

## 1 The Terms of Rousseau's Argument

Human beings are dependent beings. This is the ineliminable character of their circumstances and nature. Our happiness or despair, our completion or truncation, our fulfilment or impoverishment, decisively hinge, in Rousseau's view, on how we accommodate and manage this permanent feature of our life. We can try to eliminate it; we can pretend to deny it; we can hate it; resent it. But we can only harm ourselves in the process, for we can never eradicate it – it always remains (see, for instance, E 4, 354; IV, 690, on the rich man's self-defeat; and E 2, 84; IV, 310 on changing dependence into slavery (into Dependence). We can, on the other hand, recognize this truth of our nature and condition, and without delusions about it or futile resentment of it, incorporate this principal fact appropriately into the shape and content of our lives. Doing so, we do not end up with some second-best life for ourselves – as if the best life were that from which this central character was absent. It is believing this last that is the origin of most of our pain. Rather, we obtain for ourselves full personal stature and completion, meaning and value in ourselves and our lives, and 'the supreme happiness of life' (which is to love and be loved in return; E 4, 327; IV, 653; E 5, 419; IV, 782; see also E 4, 221; IV, 503, to which I shall return). This is the life proper to man; no other is appropriate to his nature and condition. It is a life which can yield altogether sufficient good to him, which trying to live on denial of its irrevocable character can never yield.

It is the purpose of this chapter to consider Rousseau's account of how we may and should accommodate this ineliminable character of our being and circumstances, in such a way that we shall prosper and grow into full humanity through it, not be defeated and destroyed by it (as, in his view, we normally are). The 'whole of human wisdom in the use of the passions', Rousseau writes, comprises this: '(1) To have a sense of the true relations of man, with respect to the species as well as the individual. (2) To order all the affections of the soul according to these relations. (E 4, 219; IV, 501; see E 4, 214; IV, 493, on 'moral being' and relations with men, quoted in chapter 1, section 2.5). By 'relations' Rousseau means those interdependencies of one person with another I have been indicating. His notion of a 'passion' – which I have discussed briefly before – will be looked at a little later. So the purpose is now to consider the 'wisdom' Rousseau intends to offer us here. Recall Emile's earlier learning of wisdom in respect of his being-for-himself, summarised at E 2, 91; IV, 320, quoted in chapter 3. In that matter, he 'knows himself only in his physical being' and studies and furthers his good 'in his relations with things'. Now we are to consider him in his 'moral being', in his being-for-others, where he must study and further his good 'in his relations with men' (the quotations are from E 4, 214; IV, 493). It is quite clear that Rousseau is not presenting us with a picture of man as irreversibly damaged once exposed to social relations and involvements. I have consistently rejected this conventional reading of Rousseau. He was sharply aware of the *potential* for damage that the coming to prominence, to dominance, in a person's life of his 'relations to men' threatens, of which he gives a highly detailed account (examined in chapter 2). But this is far from saying, and he never said, that 'damage' was unavoidable. On the contrary, only through such relations – provided that they are properly incorporated – can we come to our full individual humanity and taste a happiness which is properly human, which answers our full being. To try to exclude them is to try to turn ourselves into non-humans.

Rousseau's consideration of our 'relations with men' goes through four roughly distinct steps. First, there are the opening parts of his argument concerning human relations established through the sentiment of pity or compassion. In these parts, Rousseau shows how we establish for ourselves our significance potency and active creative force in encounter with others. Second, there are the further parts of that argument. In these parts, Rousseau explains how we find a 'rank' for ourselves in the reciprocal encounters and transactions of men (cf. E 4, 235; IV, 523, discussed at some length in chapter 2, section 3). We come to possess in and to ourselves, and be present to others as, 'moral beings', bearers of certain rights and titles to act, to be received, in various ways. The significance of our footing for others penetrates more deeply into the constitution of our own motives and values as this larger and more complex 'selfhood', constitutive identity, is assumed.

Thirdly, there is full exposure of the need of the self to be met, responded to and valued in the regard of it coming from the sentiments of another; the need to be known and loved, found to be good by someone upon whose judgement on oneself one's self-respect and happiness depend. This is the most formative, and most fateful, of the relations to others that enter into the structure and the composition of our own selfhood (cf. E 5, 416; IV, 778). The potential for self-deformation and dispossession is at its greatest in this matter. But avoidance of it is also defeat for the self. The fate of our need of mutual reciprocal exclusive cherishing intimacy, of mutual love, marks our individual destiny more deeply than virtually any other hazard our lives are necessarily exposed to. This is the principal concern of Book 5 of *Emile*, and comprises the real intent of Rousseau's treatment of the relations between Emile and Sophie (his beloved). Rousseau's general comments on the character, work and status of women, which have attracted so much critical objection, are subsidiary to this other theme.

Finally, Rousseau considers our 'civil' or political standing with others as the constitutive members comprising one politic body; our identity, titles and responsibilities as citizens (cf. E 5, 448; IV, 823). Rousseau gives only brief, schematic, treatment to this in Emile (E 5, 455ff; IV, 833ff). It is, of course, the central concern of *The Social Contract*, and will, therefore, be considered when that is discussed (in chapters 5 and 6).

In taking the matters he is concerned with in these four approximately distinct steps Rousseau is concerned carefully to sort out various aspects of our total constitution and action for the sake of clarity and precise treatment, not eliding crucial distinctions. I have explained this procedure of his before. But he is also making certain seriously meant developmental points as well. First, he thinks, in a way we have considered previously, that as each of these steps involves us inwardly more deeply and inextricably with how we encounter and establish ourselves with others, it is crucial that we come to some assured stability and security in the earlier steps before we take on the more fraught and difficult tasks which lie ahead. He is not supposing that, in actual fact, it goes like this. On the contrary, it is his view that people plunge themselves into, or are thrown into, relations with others of the most potently challenging and affecting kind all at once (compare E 4, 214–19; IV, 494ff.). But this is, in his estimation, to their detriment; they are not ready and equipped to live and thrive on such terms. Instead they drown. I think his views about this are perfectly sensible, but will not consider them in detail. (Relevant points are made at E 5, 416; IV, 778; E 5, 431–2; IV, 799–80.)

Second, we are witnessing here the re-emergence of that panoply of attitudes and feelings about oneself and towards others, the phantasies (and realities) of their attitudes and feelings, which comprised those first responses of the infant to his predicament in the world, discussed in chapter 2, section 8. The terms of life then, and again now, primarily comprised finding oneself in intense encounter with the wills of other animate beings, coming in terms and making one's way with them. Now, as then, one may badly misfigure one's status and claim, the relations to one of others and their readiness to acknowledge and sustain you. These problems were, deliberately, not resolved by Rousseau for the infant; instead they were deferred, put into abeyance. During the 'latency' period in artificial seclusion from affective engagement with the good or ill will of others, Emile finds his footing in his dealings with things.

Equipped with this essential human competence, he may now – Rousseau believes – re-enter the world of negotiation with the wills of others not believing (as he did in the primitive figurations of his infantile construing of the world) that the *whole* footing on which he holds any life at all depends on his making an indelible and undeniable mark on the action towards him of such wills. He will realize that although secure possession of standing is necessary and good, to have that is not the absolute be-all and end-all of his viability and self-conservation altogether. Thus, Rousseau thinks, we may *hope* that this need to achieve for oneself a telling reality-for-others will not take that inflamed and exacerbated form which characterizes excessive 'amour-propre, and which, in fact, damages and defeats our own possibilities for life.

Issues which are absolutely central to the inner nature and inner needs of human beings are, therefore, being returned to centre-stage by Rousseau at this point. He does so suggesting a way which, first, promises an optimally beneficial and creative outcome for each individual as he encounters these issues. And, second, he shows the continuity and integration of these issues into the overall systematic character and development of the individual. This is no small achievement. Thus he writes:

> . . . you will see where our *amour-propre* gets the form we believe natural to it, and how self-love [*amour-de-soi*], ceasing to be an absolute sentiment, becomes pride in great souls, vanity in small ones, and feeds itself constantly in all at the expense of their neighbours. This species of passion, not having its germ in children's hearts, cannot be born in them of itself; it is we alone who put it there, and it never takes root except by our fault. But it is no longer the case with the young man's heart. Whatever we may do, these passions will be born in spite of us. It is, therefore, time to change method. (E 4, 215; IV, 494)

The 'passions' Rousseau is here speaking of are those born of the uprush of the desire to secure another's exclusive, absolute, love which is the insistent objective that is apt to take over at the moment of 'semination' (see Bloom's note to E 4, 214; IV, 493 – Bloom trans. p. 488, referring to IV, LXXX). These breed 'emulation, rivalries, jealousy . . . dissensions, enmity, and hate' and raise 'opinion' on 'an unshakeable throne' thus at once giving *amour-propre* its 'inflamed' deformation. (Rousseau's point is, of course, that we believe *falsely* that this is 'natural to it', to *amour-propre*; it is not.)

What this passage makes clear is that *amour-propre* is the overall generic motive which is throughout operative in directing our concerns and activities in all these four stages of finding and holding a footing for ourselves with others. It is appropriate, therefore, to recall some of the general points made in earlier discussion about the character and significance of *amour-propre*. In our ordinary activity we engage in transactions with the physical world, but also, and more centrally, with other human beings. Our engagement with the latter is very much more complex, in form and content, than with the former. We relate to others not merely as sources of material benefit to us, as producers for instance, but as 'significant others' for whom we wish to have a significant presence. This is not just because if we are disregarded or despised by them we shall be physically neglected or mistreated. It is because to be treated as a nullity by others is an affront to our human character as such. To know and feel ourselves to be potently alive and effective as human beings, we need tangible evidences of our undeniable effectiveness in making others 'sit up and take notice', to put it crudely. If this is not so we are caused to feel we do not exist as human at all, that we have been eliminated from the forum of human interchange as no party to that. And though it is not wholly impossible, it is virtually impossible to survive as an intact, self-possessed and self-respecting individual under such circumstances. To hold one's *own* awareness of oneself as human, as a person, one needs to know that one's being, wishes, feelings, actions have, as such, 'moment' among the desiderata which ground and direct the activities of *others*.

The particular ways in which our being, wishes etc, should undeniably tell in the determinations of others will properly vary from case to case. A wife or husband should count in the determinations of their spouse in ways and with a weight substantially different from that given to a neighbour or casual acquaintance. But there is a rough baseline of acknowledgment and reckoning the denial of which is a denial of humanity, of possessing character as a person as such, under any circumstances. Very approximately, such denial would comprise any or all of the following (the list is not meant to be exhaustive): being treated as if one did not exist at all; being treated as a mere physical, material, presence (or obstacle) to be addressed only as a piece of matter; being deprived of any power or scope of any self-direction or determination at all; being beholden to the whim or absolute discretion of another for one's continued existence or means of survival; being appropriated to compliance with a course of action without any reference to one's wishes, needs or own estimation of the value of that course of action to you, Any of these represents an elimination of a creature from being a participant in the human world, a cancellation of them as humans. (Compare E 4, 220; IV, 501, on Emile being constituted as a man and 'an integral part of his species').

Whatever other footing in the lives and determinations of others we want or demand for ourselves, we both necessarily want and rightly require that we do not suffer such (non-)reception from them. We require and demand, on the contrary, that we hold categorical standing for others as 'moral beings' in our presence to them. Requiring and demanding this is essential to our holding the humanity in our own person, and a necessary part of our proper good as such. Being so, it is *amour-de-soi* which directs us to securing this for ourselves (for *amour-de-soi* directs us to 'love ourselves', to see that we are well and do well in whatever character and in whatever circumstances we find ourselves; E 4, 212–3; IV, 490–1). When our 'character', our self-constitution, incorporates our standing for others as moral beings, then that original self-love is termed *amour-propre*, which, in its orderly and equable form, is a necessary and good concern to see that we receive what is proper to us, from others. *Amour-propre* is, as such, nothing different from, discontinuous with or opposed to, *amour-de-soi*; it comprises the further direction of that as extended to our having and enacting our character as full 'persons' (see E 4, 235; IV, 523).

Studying Emile's (any man's) proper footing with others is, then, at one and the same moment studying what is proper to man's 'moral' standing for others, what his *amour-de-soi* should direct him to in order to have good life, and what his equable and appropriate *amour-propre* requires by way of the reception and regard paid to him by others. These are all aspects of the same phenomenon, the assumption and self-possession of personhood as one's proper being, character, and foothold in activity.

Because of disquiet about the significant purchase of his need on the recognition and regard of others which is experienced by the child, largely owing to his (paranoid) phantasies, he is apt to believe that he contends for a footing for others under the most hostile and intractable conditions. His *amour-propre* is very apt, in a context thus construed, to take an exacerbated, inflamed, form. This was discussed in chapter 2. It is not necessary that it should; and Rousseau intends to show how it may not. We can take from this reminder, however, a point that has been masked by my order of exposition.

For ease of explanation of the significance to each of us of acquiring the character and titles proper to our possession of humanity for others, I have represented the case as if we knew ourselves to be faced with a body of fully charactered persons interacting with each other, and we were trying to obtain entrée to and full participant standing in their dealings. But this is obviously a misrepresentation of the case, in general. For we need to *form* a construction of the nature, dispositions, attitudes, values, etc, of others as part of our project of finding what we shall take for an appropriate recognition of us by them. Unless we have some picture of what others are like, we shall have no picture of what *our* being afforded 'human acknowledgment' by them requires from them. If we think, for example, that others are full of hostility and resentment to each other, and cede standing to someone only if they are reckoned unmasterable, then we shall think that to have human standing we likewise must contend for mastery. If, alternatively, we think that others show categorical acknowledgment of someone by never disregarding their pain, or never imposing on them, then we shall look to hold that sort of place for others for ourselves as comprising acknowledgment of our humanity.

The implication of this is as follows. Self-configuration in the character of a 'person' involves simultaneous configuration of the standing and significance of others for one, and for each other. This has a very important corollary, which has been adverted to previously. If, to consider myself a signifying person, I require mastery, this requires the devaluing and degradation of others under me. But the reception given to me by those I revile and consider nothing cannot confer on me the character of a humanly reckoned and recognized being. I invalidate the very creatures whose acknowledgment I require for my own possession of the character I need to hold. Inflamed *amour-propre* devises a significance for others which directly denies the possibility of achieving its own inherent goal, that of securing categorically recognized standing.

It is if, and only if, I attribute inherent value and moment to the feelings and attitudes of others that my receipt of recognition from them can afford to me potent human signification, as I wish to enjoy. My *amour-propre* can attain *its own purpose* if, and only if, it allows, it grants, to others dignity and weight as counting beings in their own right. My *amour-propre*, therefore, can only receive answer, and it receives full proper answer if, and only if, I meet others on terms which answer the requirements of *their amour-propre* likewise, their demand to be regarded as humanly counting presences *for me*. Thus there is no incompatibility between, no only half-meeting of, the demands of each our own *amour-propre* in answering the demands of the *amour-propre* of others. It is, in fact, only on the condition that we do so that we obtain the standing we each want severally for ourselves. Standing for self and for others mutually entail each other; basic equality of dignity and honour for *all* alike is the implication internal to the wish of *each* to have dignity and honour. The requirement to afford this equality is not an externally imposed demand. It does not inflict a constraint on the demands we each separately need to make for ourselves from others, leaving us baulked and frustrated. It comprises, rather, the fulfilment of the dynamic internal to the proper principle of the desire of each of us for standing.

I shall be returning to this theme – which comprises, I think, Rousseau's deepest discovery in social theory – later in this chapter, and in chapter 5. It is the foundation thought to the great bulk of Rousseau's civil and political principles. Here I want to conclude the preliminaries to considering the opening stages of Rousseau's account of our 'relations to men' with one or two further briefly made points.

The first point concerns some clarification of the sense Rousseau gives to the notion of a 'passion'. Although he does not quite always use the term in the elucidation I am about to give it, I am showing its most central and crucial employment. By a 'passion' Rousseau understands an affective response on our part (with its attendant thoughts, dispositions and objectives) to the feelings, dispositions, attitudes, traits of another person particularly as these are directed towards us and incorporate an estimate our standing, value or worth (in general or for that person), and/or an intent to benefit or harm us. Thus, for instance, resentment or gratitude would be clear cases of 'passions' so understood. Cruelty or friendship are passions too, but more complex and elaborated cases.

Now, of course, Rousseau can elect to attribute to the notion of a passion whatever sense he chooses, providing he does not cause unnecessary confusion. But he is not engaged in gratuitous verbal legislation here, but making an important substantive interpretation of psychological phenomena. For the class of, generically, 'emotional' responses Rousseau is picking out have several significant features for his purposes. First, they are responses in and through which we are directly engaged with and reacting to the feelings and intentions of others bearing on us. The (believed) character of the other is, thus, incorporated into the basis and direction of our own inner life, our own motivation and intent. Some, at any rate, of our own being depends on and derives from what (we believe) we are for others. They are not just external objects we encounter and negotiate a path around, but are carried in us in the immediate substance of our self-comprising desires, fears, feelings and purposes. Self and other are not in a loose, external relation here, which may be severed leaving one's self, in its proper character, untouched. The severance of relation to the other is, in this case, severe hurt to the proper substance comprising one's self. Thus the 'involvement' of self and other is peculiarly deep-going, and the maintenance of the uniting relation is very fateful to the welfare of the self. So there is particular reason to be especially concerned with the character and prosperity of such 'passions' if one is concerned with the fate of the individual's happiness and inner integrity, as Rousseau centrally is.

Secondly, and as an immediate corollary, this that I have called a deep-going 'involvement' of the other in the constitution of one's self is, in substance, a *dependence* of one's self upon the other (whether for good or ill). Some of the constitution of one's own psychology depends upon the disposition of the other towards one. So, in a certain way, one is 'at the mercy' of the other for the possibility of one's (good) life. The term 'passion' come from *patio*, I suffer, I am worked upon, I undergo change exerted upon me by external sources.[1] When I am subject to passion, I am precisely not the sole instigator and director of my purposes and actions, which disclose as much of the other as embedded in me as they do of my own separate self. This is not to argue that my 'self' could or should remain thus 'separate'; passions properly do come to comprise constitutive parts of my self; my self incorporates the other *in* my affect. Rousseau, as I have shown, does not deny this; indeed, he insists upon it. But it is equally the case that the retention of a 'separate' self – in the relevant non-passionally-dependent way – can easily seem to someone a crucial issue. Not only can the loss of self-enclosed individual sufficiency seem an onerous tie or check, but – more deeply – the fact that in one's passion one is 'at the mercy' of others can appear a powerful threat. One may feel impelled to respond to this dependence by counter-attack, by trying to control and dispose of the other. Even if the dependency is always to one's benefit, because the other always bears affection and good care towards one, it is difficult to learn trust and confidence, and a residual resentment of lacking absolute self-possessed sovereign separate completeness remains. Thus, in Rousseau's idea of a 'passion' we are brought again directly to his central concern with the proper accommodation of dependency, and the acute fears and threats to personal well-being and retention of intact selfhood that surround this. His specialized notion of passion is tied immediately to this governing theme.

Finally on this, it might be objected that if this is Rousseau's principal conception of what a passion is, then pity or compassion do not clearly count as passions. For it is not obvious that these involve responses to the personal evaluating of one, or good or ill intentions towards one, of another. Yet it appears to be Rousseau's argument that it is through pity or compassion that we best gain a footing for others, and others gain a footing for us; they comprise Emile's entrée into the world of human engagements. So either the elucidation I have given to Rousseau's thought here is mistaken; or else his thinking is sharply confused.

The objection is misplaced, though it has illuminating implications. It requires two responses. First, it is in fact the case that Rousseau rarely refers to pity as a 'passion', but rather as a 'sentiment' or an aspect of Emile's 'sensibility' towards others, his capacity to be aware of and touched by their feelings, needs, attitudes etc. There are more substantive reasons also for recognizing that a difference of importance is being made. As we shall see in more detail in a while, Rousseau holds that the most acute problems of interpersonal contention and standing arise only when each of us in a relation feels himself to be the object of the appraising verdict on our person made by the other. However, a footing for oneself in the life and needs of another can be acquired prior to, and as a preparation for, engagement with such appraisal of oneself. This can be built on gradually, introducing step-by-step more complex and elaborately self-involving ties to another. One reaches, finally, a position with and for another where one is most completely exposed and sensitive to their feelings and judgements upon one. This is the stage of 'passion' proper. But Rousseau's hope and intention is to see to it that by the time this occurs one will feel no inclination to experience one's exposed vulnerability to the other as a threat to be met in combat for supremacy. Because one has encountered, and come on terms with, others starting and moving on from a basis which does not at all involve the other's presence to one as a threat to one's integrity there is some prospect that when one stands fully exposed in one's need to the verdict of the other, one will not bring anger and resentment of them to this situation, nor will one encounter their vindictive wish to humiliate or annihilate one.

It is the role of the sentiment of pity to provide the means whereby one may be present to other, and other present to one, in a way which does not represent either as threatening, hostile, exploitative or malicious. So it is through this that an 'image' of others may gradually be built up which promises the possibility of constructive, collaborative relations of trust, support and aid. Just as this is the characterization one learns to afford to others, so they learn to afford a like characterization to you, as kind, considerate, helpful and gentle, because of the attention and care you practically give to them. Each becomes to each, then, an object of affection and trust, not of hatred and suspicious wariness. It is central to Rousseau's argument that the human relations constituted through pity do *not*, at the start, involve 'passion'. Those relations provide the ground upon which the development and installation of reciprocal passions may occur, but ones, he reasonably hopes, which will be mutually benign and creative not corrupting and destructive. So there is no confusion in Rousseau's discussion. He is, rather, following a carefully ordered progress.

That pity plays a foundational role for the emergence and consolidation of the 'attractive and sweet passions naturally pleasing to men' (the passions of 'goodness, humanity, commiseration and beneficence') is made quite clear at E 4, 223 (IV, 506) from which these quotations are taken. There he stresses that Emile's 'nascent sensibility' (through which he is aware of and sensitive to the feelings of others, particularly as they bear on him) must be 'expanded' by cultivation of his sensitivity to the pain and suffering of others which he is able to relieve. Usually, he remarks, that sensibility is caused to 'contract and concentrate and tighten the spring of the human $I$' by dwelling on the hostile domineering power of others, and this breeds 'envy, covetousness, hate, and all the repulsive and cruel passions which make sensibility, so to speak, not only nothing but negative and torment the man who experiences them' (ibid.). Pity, then, is a mode of unfolding of sensibility, which allows for the development of loving, beneficial passions (to oneself and to others). It is not a passion itself; but that does not preclude it from having a perculiarly important place in shaping the character of our sensitivity and attachment to others (cf. E 4, 233; IV, 520–1). Rousseau is quite emphatic that Emile's first 'real' passion is his love for Sophie (E 5, 416; IV, 778). By the time he is ready to experience this, he has already found a highly structured and complex footing for himself for others on other terms. This will be made clear.

The second response I want to make to the objection is this. I have been suggesting that what Rousseau is arguing for in his treatment of the sentiment of pity is that there are available to men, within their psychological repertoire, possibilities of apprehension of the character, capacities and dispositions of others, and forms of response to others, which allow for trust, affection and mutual care to relate men. But, as we well know by now, this is not the only possibility of apprehension and relation available. The 'paranoid' structures, which inform 'inflamed' *amour-propre*, are, indeed, more readily present and dominant than those made possible through pity in Rousseau's view. In this case, others are perceived as threats, and vengeful, and are responded to with fear and hatred. It is clear, therefore, that some remission of, or move beyond, the dominance of paranoid apprehension must occur if the modes of life implicit to this are to be displaced.

To some extent Rousseau thinks he has provided for this through Emile's long seclusion from self-exposed human engagement. But Rousseau stresses that this is not by itself enough to provide for the whole of Emile's need and life, for it does not yet directly address the matter of his standing for others. As soon as that issue becomes central, paranoid possibilities of response press forward again. Is there, then, no aspect of Emile's (any man's) psychological constitution which at the same time *does* concern his standing for others but does not involve incipient hostility and anger, which can allow for pity to claim a role, not thoroughly displacing anger and resentment – for these always remain at some level – but at least predominating over them?

There is a plausible account[2] which suggests that there are developmental processes which lead to the formation of a different structure of the self and mode of response to the world from that inherent to the paranoid position. Slowly, and intermittently, the infant beings together into one object those separated representations of the world as containing vengeful tormentors of him, and of it as containing sustaining and nurturing carers for him (corresponding, respectively, to his resentment and envy, and his pleasure and gratitude). This involves the recognition of the possibility of his having attacked and destroyed the very same object (now more recognizedly one person) upon which he depends for nurture and support and towards which he feels grateful affection. And both out of a need to preserve the source of life for himself, and out of concern for the harm he (supposes he) has inflicted, there will occur a reparative or restorative impulse which aims to mend the damaged object, to assuage the hurt or alleviate the harm inflicted. *Compunction* about the damage caused (in phantasy at least, if not in reality) begins to be felt; this can lead to restraint of aggression and to concern to remedy the suffering caused. The infant is pained by the pain he inflicts, and seeks to relieve it. This restorative, reparative, concern contains the germ of the possibility of pity. This is, as one might crudely put it, the beginnings of an awareness of responsibility for his comportment towards others, a sense that he must himself take in hand, and answer for, his dealings with the world. (Note that this is *not* an externally imposed demand that he 'pay for' what he has done. This would only breed resentment. Rather it is an inherent element in the proper structure of the infant's own impulse – it is the 'law' of *his own* being. Of course that impulse is often deformed, and being called to account is experienced as one more inflicted denial imposed on ruthlessness.) This allows for an extension of concern to hurt and suffering persons where there is no (real or phantasy) hurt that one has oneself inflicted on them.[3] With that extension, pity rather than compunction stays one's hand and substitutes care.

It is a significant part of this structure, normally called the depressive-reparative position, that the infant's disposition and power to effect restoration is experienced as tangible proof of his own creative power to effect good. (Those that have no sense of their power to do good are incapable of pity). By his ability to put to rights, to repair, the damage and hurt he has caused, the infant finds palpable confirmation that he is able to work potent effects upon the (his) world and begins to know himself for a centre of constructive force capable of making an impress on the world. This is a source of pleasurable self-confirmation to him. It establishes to him his felt reality as a potent human presence; it answers (some part of) the requirements of his benign (temperate) *amour-propre*. The concerns and acts of compassion are, for Rousseau, indeed precisely that – constructive and creative ways of finding real answers to the needs of our *amour-propre*. That we are in a position to see this suggests that this account I have been sketching illuminates his discussion. But are there more specific evidences that he saw the matter in the sort of terms I have been proposing?

Rousseau speaks, in fact, quite specifically to this very near the start of Book 4 of *Emile* (E 4, 220–1; IV, 502). He writes:

> He is sensitive to the shame of displeasing, to the regret of having offended. If the ardour of his inflamed blood makes him too intense, easily carried away, and angered, a moment later all the goodness of his heart is seen in the effusion of his repentance . . . All of his fury is extinguished, all of his pride humiliated before the sentiment of his wrong . . . Adolescence is not the age of vengeance or of hate; it is that of commiseration, clemency, and generosity.

This passage immediately precedes Rousseau's discussion of pity, and serves as an introduction to it. From this, we can infer that he too saw the roots of the possibility of pity as lying in the compunctious impulse which directs us to feel responsible and to make amends for the wrong our anger has provoked us to. It is immaterial that Rousseau is here speaking of Emile at age twenty. Emile is, at this point, recapitulating on the earliest psychological transformations which his seclusion kept him from undergoing. In any event, this chronological presentation is irrelevant, as I have argued. What is really in view are analytical hypotheses about the structures of human motivation and judgement. It is this psychological possibility (and actuality too, of course) that provides the seed-bed in which human compassion can grow.

Thus, I suggest, pity can be seen as an elaborated extension of transformations which primitive passions undergo (particularly anger) under the impact of changes in the construing of the world and of one's place and involvement in it which are part of human psychological development. So, whilst not itself a 'passion' proper, according to Rousseau's central conception of these, it is not either some wholly separate affect the significance and centrality of which is plucked, by Rousseau, out of thin air simply to satisfy the requirements of his theory. Here, as always, he is operating with an extraordinarily subtle and penetrating insight into the character and interrelations of human psychological propensities.

Two closing notes before proceeding to follow through the steps of Rousseau's discussion are these. First, as briefly noted above, there is no incompatibility, in Rousseau's view, between pity and (temperate, proper) *amour-propre*, but only between pity and 'inflamed' *amour-propre*. These are in violent opposition because the originating dispositions which feed each of these are quite at odds. Pity is rooted in compunction and reparative care; inflamed *amour-propre* in implacable ruthless anger. Pity, in fact, is a mode of satisfaction of the requirements of our orderly *amour-propre*, since it affords to us a place of significant creative effectiveness for others in a way that affords to them, also, significant reality and value, such that their reception of us can indeed confer human meaning on us as we wish for. Thus it is quite particularly through the human bond established in pity that that mutual acknowledgement and recognition of personal significance which is requisite to answering the need of each our *amour-propre* is achieved. The detail of this will be worked out below.

Second, I claimed earlier that the recognition of the fact of our inevitable human dependence did not require us to settle for some 'second best'. Rather, this was the key to our human completion and happiness. It may be protested that I am contradicting Rousseau's express words when I say this. For he writes (E 4, 221; IV, 503): 'Every attachment is a sign of insufficiency . . . A truly happy being is a solitary being. God alone enjoys an absolute happiness'. Does this not say that our happiness ('our frail happiness', ibid.) is a second-best? The proper thing to recall here is a comparable remark made by Aristotle (EN 1177b, 15ff) where, having argued that the 'complete happiness of man' lies in the contemplative activity of reason, he proceeds to say: 'but such a life would be too high for man; for it is not in so far that he is man that he will live so, but in so far as something divine is present in him.' (The precise interpretation of this passage is debatable. I am making here one possible reading which I do not assert to be finally right.) What Aristotle is primarily addressing is the life that is happiest for man 'in so far as he is man'. Even if there is some absolutely happier life, if that is not a life suitable to man 'in so far as he is man', *man* will not be happier leading that life. Such, I suggest, is Rousseau's thought too (and he has no really comparable notion to Aristotle's about man's composite nature, man with a 'spark of the divine' in him as well). God alone is wholly self-sufficient, standing in need of nothing, wholly active and impassible. Men are not so made. Men are, if you will, 'imperfect beings' (E 4, 221; IV, 503, again). But this means that an absolute happiness, which is the happiness enjoyable by a perfect being, would not be congenial to man. Man's happiness is proper to man, and that is the happiness of a creature who is weak, stands in need of others, is not self-sufficient but dependent. It is still a true happiness, even if in some 'abstract scale' of happinesses not the highest of all happinesses – only the highest of all humanly possible happinesses. So nothing I have claimed contradicts Rousseau. In fact, I have followed his sense faithfully (see also, E 3, 193; IV, 467; E 4, 327; IV, 654; and E 5, 419; IV, 781–2).

With these preliminary clarifications made we are now in a position to follow the steps of Rousseau's argument about the proper, constructive, mode of coming to hold being for others plainly and easily. I take, then, the first of these steps.

## 2  Pity and Human Relation: The First Step

I have claimed that Rousseau considers the incorporation of relations to others into the composition and structure of the individual's sentiments, values, actions etc. in a number of more or less distinct steps. (Indeed, certain relations with others, as producers and exchangers in material transactions, are dealt with by Rousseau even before Book 4 of *Emile* opens.) In particular, I have claimed that his discussion of the role of the sentiment of pity in instigating relations between men and establishing them on a mutually significant footing falls into two stages. In the first 'stage', I suggested, we find for ourselves a sense of our significant potency in the arena of human encounters by our capability of effecting creative and beneficial aid to others in their need or distress. In the second stage, a greater complexity and intensity of involvement with another comes in, for one becomes the object of their sentiments and judgements which arise in view of what one has done for them, and one in turn is affected by, responds to, these 'returns' they are making. (There are further stages to come as well, but these are the only two that concern me at present.) By the time Emile has incorporated these modes of encounter of and transaction with others, he has gone a very long way towards amplifying the range and composition of his self-constitutive desires, feelings, powers of judgement etc. such that he is now more fully 'complete' as 'a man and an integral part of his species'. He has become a human person with other human persons, recognized and reckoned with as such, just as he recognizes and reckons with others as such. In the same time, also, he finds for himself a 'rank' or 'position' as an acknowledged person in the web of human dealings, and in so doing the requirements of his *amour-propre* find their answer. (This is part, in fact, of the same process of human 'completion'.) He does so in a way which necessarily affords to others their standing as acknowledged human persons as well. By this, there is a mutual reciprocity of value and significance received and given, which meets the need for personal recognition that each and every person has.

It is clear that Rousseau intended his discussion to be read in two parts.[4] He writes:

So long as his [Emile's] sensibility remains limited to his own individuality, there is nothing moral in his actions. It is only when it begins to extend outside of himself that it takes on, first, the sentiments and, then, the notions of good and evil which truly constitute him as a man and an integral part of his species. It is on this first point, then, that we must initially fix our observations. (E 4, 219-20; IV, 501)

Following the division Rousseau makes here, I shall call the initial part of the discussion the 'sentiment' argument regarding pity; and the latter part the 'notion' argument. The 'sentiment' argument runs through E 4, 220-33, (IV, 502-20); the 'notion' argument begins at E 4, 233 and runs to E 4, 255 (IV, 520-51), although there is much further pertinent material in the pages which follow 'The Profession of Faith of the Savoyard Vicar' which is located in the middle of Book 4. (This 'Profession' will be looked at in chapter 7, below.) Rousseau writes (E 4, 235; IV, 522): 'Finally we enter the moral order. We have just made a second step into manhood' – referring back to the preceding half-dozen paragraphs. He shows, by this, that he is adhering closely to his originally stated plan.

I shall, of course, explain what the materially substantive differences are between the first and second steps which are being distinguished, and show why Rousseau is right to register significant alterations in the case. But for now we look at the first step, the sentiment argument.

In Books 1 and 2 of *Emile* Rousseau stressed the enormous importance to human character and relations of the tyrannical and angry dispositions we have, with their attendant constructions of others' character and our footing with them. At this point, in Book 4, he emphasizes as well the affectionate and grateful propensities we have, preparing to show the importance of these to the formation of benign human interdependencies. He writes:

The love of oneself [*amour-de-soi*] is always good and always in conformity with order . . . we have to love ourselves to preserve ourselves; and it follows immediately from the same sentiment that we love what preserves us. Every child is attached to his nurse . . . At first this attachment is purely mechanical. What fosters the well-being of an individual attracts him; what harms him repels him . . . what transforms this instinct into sentiment, attachment into love, aversion into hate, is the intention manifested to harm us or to be useful to us . . . At first the attachment he has for his nurse and his governess is only habit. He seeks them because he needs them and is well off in having them; it is recognition rather than benevolence. He needs much time to understand that not only are they useful to him but they want to be; and it is then that he begins to love them.

A child is therefore naturally inclined to benevolence, because he sees that everything approaching him is inclined to assist him; and from this observation he gets the habit of a sentiment favourable to his species. (E 4, 213; IV, 492)

Of course, as Rousseau immediately notes himself, benevolence is not the only habit which may become established; imperious and vindictive dispositions also develop. But in Rousseau's strict sense, it is of these two the only 'natural' habit, the one, that is to say, expressive of and furthering our true inherent concern to preserve ourselves and have abundant life. Imperious and vindictive dispositions, as Rousseau explains, are harmful to us and set this principle by which we have our being at odds with itself. Rousseau is, therefore, already suggesting that benevolence is, in this sense, 'natural' to us. That is, our good will towards others comprises a tendency inherent to our own proper nature and need, and is no imposed and self-constraining rule. It is the sentiment implicit to our own constitution and well-being.

What, then, becomes of this 'habit of a sentiment favourable to his species'? What draws men together according to Rousseau is their needs born of their incompleteness and non-self-sufficiency as separate, unattached, beings. The first direction of Emile's attachment to others that is rooted in his response to an awareness of others' intention to benefit him, is to think well of them and to wish them well. We saw, above, that one crucial exhibition of this concern for others will be a compunction at hurting or distressing them, leading to apology, reparation and the acceptance of a subordinate positon in pleading for forgiveness. No-one who wishes others well can rest easy if he has hurt them; one hates to injure what one loves. This provides a pattern for the further extension of this habit of sentiment. It is the distresses, hurts and weaknesses of others that are the first natural target of that benevolent concern which is responsive to the feelings of others. And, as just noted, humankind is peculiarly prone to these mishaps which necessarily attend its limited character and circumstances. Our natural benevolence makes us sensitive, first, to the harm we inflict on others, and then to the sufferings of others more generally.

There are two other reasons Rousseau gives as to why it is the pain and hurt of others that forms the first foothold for our creative and benign attachment to them. The first is that if we encounter people who are well pleased with themselves and their lives, who are thriving and securely assured of their contentment, we tend to feel that they have no need of us at all, that we are rendered superfluous and irrelevant to their lives which show that we count for nothing, cannot contribute anything. Because of this our *'amour-propre* suffers . . . in making us feel that this man has no need of us' (E 4, 221; IV, 503). Moreover, as Rousseau profoundly comments, we are apt to feel envious resentment that this person enjoys a happiness which (we phantastically think) should be ours alone, and that in obtaining his pleasure he is denying to us, or removing from us, what is our rightful good (ibid.). On the other hand, we feel that the unhappy man's suffering 'exempts us from the ills he suffers' and so we more readily open ourselves to the possibility of a response to this predicament. Added to which, in seeing that he suffers and we (at present) do not, we are made better pleased with our present state because we see what we escape. And, a corollary to the above, our *amour-propre* is satisfied in this situation, since we feel we *can* be potently significant and an importantly telling presence for the suffering man.

The second reason Rousseau gives for the central significance of pain and hurt is that Emile (any man) will be very familiar with these states from his own experience, since they are 'what truly belongs to man' (E 4, 222; IV, 504). Thus, in coming to discern and to be able to respond to the feelings and desires of others (as he is through his 'nascent sensibility'), these will be states he will very well recognize as ones he also is intimate with. The recognition alone might provoke a response of contempt or gloating at the abjection of the other person. But we know that these responses are born of anger and hatred; whereas what is now being brought forward is the habit of the sentiment of benevolence, which directs care and affectionate concern for another in his weakness.

There are a number of points about this first step in forming our attachment to others which need amplification and comment.

First, in speaking of Emile's sensitivity to others' hurts, Rousseau uses such language as this:

> In fact, how do we let ourselves be moved by pity if not by transporting ourselves outside of ourselves and identifying with the suffering animal, by leaving, as it were, our own being to take on its being? . . . It is not in ourselves, it is in him that we suffer. (E 4, 223; IV, 505–6; see also DI 68: III, 155–6)

Some of these remarks have caused difficulty. For instance, if, in pity, we 'identify' with another, if we 'take on [his] being', then, it has been argued, we do not have here any real relation between two separate selves, but the (temporary) assimilation into my sole ambit of experience of the distresses undergone by another. Pity, so far from relating distinct persons abolishes the distinction between persons, and therefore cannot establish a relation between them.[5]

There is a mixture of muddle and propriety in this objection. The muddle is this. The notion of 'identification' with another used here in no way implies that I overlook or become unaware of the fact that his and my consciousnesses are perfectly distinct and comprise different persons, in any but a sense to be explained in a moment. How could Rousseau say, as he does, 'it is *in him* that we suffer', if the distinctness of 'him' from 'me' were lost? What 'identification' signifies is that just as when I feel a pain I am *immediately and directly* moved by distress to try to alleviate it, so, in pity, I am moved to try to alleviate the pain of another with that same immediacy and directness. His pain assumes, in my pity for him, the same direct position in my dispositions as something to be relieved; it, as it were, stands as close to me as my own pains do. What this is in contrast to is, for instance, my willingness to relieve his hurt on the ground that I hope or expect some return for this; or because I have promised to help, when I am not in fact 'touched' by his pain. All that the idea of 'identification' imports is intended to clarify what being relevantly 'touched' involves, where there is no mediating ground for my being concerned to assuage his hurt other than the fact that it does hurt (which is how I stand and respond to my own hurts). That is the *only* way in which 'me' and 'him' have diminished our distance. It would not be pity but sympathetic suffering (or possibly even some more elaborate condition *projective* identification[6]) if I truly suffered as he suffered, or thought (behaved as if) I were in pain, not he. The compassionately moved person does not nurse his own leg, but that of the person knocked down by a car.

On the other hand, the protest has an element of propriety, though not one that causes any difficulty for Rousseau – far from it. Just because, in pity, another's pain is as 'close' to me as my own pain is, in the way explained, we may say that the project of relieving that other person's pain is held by me with just as much immediacy and directness as projects which are altogether self-constitutive. Relieving that other's distress is taken into me as concern which is intimately mine. In this way his toil is mine; he and I are not externally linked by trade-off or contract, but turn in immediate unison to the same task (that of removing this hurt, never mind whether it is his or mine, that he writhes and I do not). So, we may say, the distinction of persons is diminished (see, again, Schopenhauer who, in discussing this very sequence of points, called Rousseau 'undoubtedly the greatest moralist of modern times'[7]).

But, as I remarked, there is nothing in this to trouble Rousseau. For it is a central component of his *whole* approach to man in relation to man that we incorporate, as elements in our own self-constitutive feelings, attitudes and purposes, much that depends on and derives from the nature, feelings and attitudes of others. This is essential to each our own self-completion. As I have put it before, the other is present *in* us as part of our own constitution. It is an illusion to suppose we are not made full human persons through interaction with and responsiveness to others. The other is always present in the self; the distinction of self and other is never absolute, but always only relative to certain purposes at certain times. That it should not be absolute in this case, then, is not only what Rousseau would expect, it is just what he would want to reveal.

A second point of note is this. Rousseau says several times that 'pity is sweet' to the compassionate person because when, in pity, we notice the distressed state of another, this causes us to reflect, or to feel, that we ourselves aren't doing so badly after all: 'If the first sight that strikes him is an object of sadness, the first return to himself is a sentiment of pleasure. In seeing how many ills he is exempt from, he feels himself to be happier than he thought he was.' (E 4, 229; IV, 514) And, he goes on, we 'share the suffering of [our] fellows; but this sharing is voluntary . . .', as a change from our own pain which we undergo involuntarily and with dislike. This leads to a further thought, that we are in a 'condition of strength which extends us beyond ourselves and leads us to take elsewhere activity superfluous to our well-being' (ibid.) that is, superfluous to our self-absorbed well-being. 'Commiseration' he concludes, 'ought to be a very sweet sentiment, since it speaks well of us'.

Rousseau's comments may seem at first sight surprising. One is inclined to object that being in the presence of another's hurt is the normal and proper occasion for sorrow, not for pleasure in and at one's own better condition and delight in one's relative strength and free power of action. Again, might not this awareness of his own preferable condition lead someone to suppose he leads a charmed life, invulnerable to the hurts that bring down lesser mortals, and so scorn or dismiss the sufferer? Or might not someone use his own freedom of action, when the other person is debilitated and hampered by pain, to abuse them, or to enforce an obligation on them which they have no power to resist at the time?

Rousseau speaks directly to these two last points, but mostly later on in his discussion. So I shall come to them then. On the first point, however, it is a misunderstanding to suppose that Rousseau has in mind a self-indulgent and self-congratulatory rejoicing in one's own good state which comparison with the sufferer's abject conditon has pointed up to one. His thought is rather the true one that the opportunity and power to help, which pity reveals to us, is pleasurable because it is an exhibiiton of our own present vigorous life and plenitude of possibility – things we may lose sight of if we always enviously look at those 'above' us in health and wealth. We are, in pity, *glad* to help, and find gladness in helping, because we are quick with life in such acts, and such is character of all real human pleasure. We might, in a way, be grateful to the person who suffers for giving us something real and significant to do, in doing which we are potently alive. Rousseau is arguing that there is nearly always a wretchedness greater than one's own, which one can do something about, and, by doing so, find that one is, after all, alert, alive, free, effective and valuable.[8] And what greater source of life-confirming pleasure can there be than that discovery?

This connects also with the point mentioned earlier about the significance of the power to help for one's *amour-propre* (though, for reasons to be explained, *amour-propre* does not feature largely in this first step of Rousseau's argument). Just because we can evidently help the suffering person we receive a sense that we count for something as a forcible presence in human dealings. But this is only the first beginnings of an answer to the need of our *amour-propre*, for there is as yet little conscious recognition and valuing of us by the person we are helping. This is introduced in the second step of the argument. All that transpires so far is that *we* know ourselves for important contributors to human lives; our being recognized, and reckoned with, as such is still to come. Also, this aspect of the case is susceptible to a perverse development. I may take advantage of the weakness of the suffering person to gratify my (relative) power to gain control over him. Rousseau is well aware of this possibility, and takes steps to counter it as we shall see.

A third aspect of this first step is this. Rousseau says – as quoted before – that he is examining here how Emile's sensibility 'takes on . . . the sentiments . . . of good and evil'. We need to be clear what this involves. I think that what Rousseau has in view, bearing in mind that he distinguishes the sentiments from the 'notions' of good and evil, and gives to the former an earlier more basic place, is this. Emile's compassionate concern, his repugnance at inflicting hurt and his desire to relieve it if it does occur, is that *actually* proper to the moral significance of others, their title not to be injured, the duty to help the needy, but without being informed or guided by conscious knowledge and allegiance to these duties and principles. Here again we can make a helpful comparison with Aristotle, who makes a distinction between 'natural' virtue and virtue 'in the strict sense'.[9] The distinction is a complex one, but in the present context we need consider only certain aspects of it. A child, for instance, may show care and concern for the distress of his friend, and be moved to comfort and help him (at least, this may happen on some occasions). At that time, he is showing that his friend's distress is something important to him. But it would be absurd to suggest that a child articulates the thought: my friend's suffering is an evil which I feel obliged to remove. And equally absurd to suggest that relieving his friend's distress (or anyone's) has become a principle for his conduct yet. We all know that a child's sympathy is easily dispelled, and replaced by impatience or indifference, upon which he equally uninhibitedly acts. But, despite these overall differences, the child's sentiments and behaviours are actually proper to the moral requirements of the case. It is from such occasional responses, indeed, that the child may be led to a fuller moral consciousness and ordering of his action to known proper ends.

I suggest, then, that it is these sorts of contrasts Rousseau is employing when he distinguishes the 'sentiments' from the 'notions' of good and evil. (It is not the case, of course, that when the notions are possessed the sentiments are left behind. Coming into possession of the notions is, rather, a matter of extension and consolidation of the base established by the sentiments. Possession of them *incorporates* the sentiments.) There is, as yet, no articulate knowledge that it is fitting, proper and demanded that one relieve others' suffering. Rousseau would insist, in fact, that such knowledge would be useless, indeed inimical, to moral development if there were not already in feeling an actually appropriate direction of concern. Nor, secondly, is there any question of the incorporation of this knowledge into the structure of a person's motivation as an objective of committed principle and intent. Rather, it is a simple(r) question of just being moved as is in fact appropriate to the moral requirements of the case. Emile remains, at this point, governed by the onset and direction of his sentiments as they come, not as yet ordering his conduct by principles of obligation and duty. But the crucial thing is that these sentiments do *de facto* accord with the requirements of such principles, and thus are ready for, and make Emile ready for, the enlargement of understanding and additional regulation of action which will be involved when he acquires the notions of good and evil.[10] Nor is the accord of sentiment just a fortunate external coincidence, having nothing to do with an inner congruence between the informing order pervading them and the notions of good and evil. Such congruence is present in fact. For in pity we are alert and responsive to the claim that another's suffering presents, even if not to it in its character as a 'claim'. So that when we learn the notions of good and evil, come to the knowledge of the 'obligations of humanity' (DAS 14; III, 17), we are coming to the knowledge of the inherent objective of pity now in its character as a claim which requires our steady and committed allegiance. We are, that is to say, simply deepening our understanding of an involvement with an objective we already, more shallowly, have.

Fourthly, I want to stress a point about the present case which has been mentioned in passing already. As Rousseau is unfolding his case, he starts with what are only the most basic elements in a human relation instigated through pity. He concentrates, to begin with, virtually exclusively on the compassionte person's response to another's pain and his actions of care. He does not introduce the responses of the helped person to his helper at this time. This is not because he thinks these are not naturally and properly involved; nor because he thinks that the human relations established by pity come, as it were, in two kinds, one where this consequential response is not involved, one where it is. It is just that he wishes to separate out various strands and elements in the one overall complex interaction between people that is involved, in order to show the various significances and implications that attach to these. The exclusion from consideration of the return from the helped person at this point is made quite deliberately by Rousseau. For this enables him to consider how the helper and the helped stand to each other, before the issue of the helper assuming a certain significance in the feelings and attitudes of the helped person comes into the case.

The helped person is, of course, not insensible. He is suffering, in pain or distress. But these are self-absorbed concerns; or if they do involve awareness of another, as when, for instance, one is distressed by the humiliation one has suffered before someone, it is not awareness of one's helper in his character as such that is involved in the constitution of this distressed consciousness. The helping, compassionate, person responds directly to this pain at the start; he is not responding to, nor are his sentiments and behaviour modified by, feelings or attitudes that the suffering person may have towards him – as he believes. For none such are involved. Thus he cannot be affected by the thought that he is, for instance, regarded by the suffering person as his 'saviour' for the help he has given. Nor can he be helping with a view to winning such accolades, or with an image of himself as deserving such distinctions.

All these things can be, and often enough are, involved when the (real or imagined) response of the helped person is considered. They obviously hugely alter the complexity of the human interchange involved, and increase the potential for vanity, exploitation and conceit to (dis-)colour the relation instituted through pity. It is precisely because of this that Rousseau elects to look at these aspects of the case separately; and it causes him to emphasize that all of these follow on *after* the original movement of care for another's pain which lies as the foundational component of pity. Rousseau argues that most of these added complexities are perversions and corruptions of pity, not inherent to its character as such. Without this firmly marked base line, it would be hard for him to defeat an objection that, for instance, pity always embodies a sense of superiority over the suffering person, or embodies a desire to impose obligations on him, and hence cannot serve, as Rousseau wishes it to, as the source for benign human relations of mutually good care and regard. Because Rousseau has identified the original human bond instigated by pity – a plain and direct reaching out to another in their pain – as he has, he can argue that these are deforming secondary elaborations of that, not of the essence of the case.

Putting the matter as I just have may, however, lead to a different doubt. It may be objected that Rousseau is here dissecting and interpreting the phenomena of pity in a way just to suit his theoretical needs. But the actualities of the case do not sustain his interpretations; the phenomena of pity do not exhibit that character he wishes to impute to them. It might further be claimed that no human psychological phenomena have the character Rousseau needs to find in them to suit his theoretical purposes. Thus his project, at least in the terms in which he has set this up, is vitiated.[11] There can be no human relations that do not involve unremitting contention for invidious power and prestige. Or, if there can be, Rousseau has not shown how this might be.

The second complaint falls if the first is not sustained; so I address that. It seems to me that Rousseau is not at all 'twisting' the facts to suit his case, but in fact reporting clearly on the actual phenomena without distortion from preconceptions. It is the character of pity to comprise a *direct* concern for another's pain and a desire to ameliorate that, after the fashion I have tried to clarify. It is a fact that helping someone out of compassion is a pleasure and confirmation of life to oneself. It is a fact that, in compassion, one's concern is freely given, without conditions or terms, to looking after the welfare of another, this being incorporated as one's own immediate concern. It is a fact that pity comprises a real possibility for human feeling, an exhibition of *our own* inclinations and the direction *we* want for our lives. Concern for others does not always have to be imposed on us by a rule, dragged out of us by threats or manipulation, traded by us in exchange for equivalent goods, and so on. Of course, the disposition to, the impulse of, pity can easily be suppressed and silenced, as Rousseau himself stresses. It can also be deformed into a deceptive snare, as I have indicated and will consider further. But all of these represent the loss of the possibility of pity; they are not features of the phenomenon itself.

It is not Rousseau's theoretical demands which falsify the facts. It is the preconceptions of his critics (often, on this matter, said to be 'the philosophers') that lead them to deny or to distort the case, making pity out to be, for instance, a snare for the unwary. Given Rousseau's own abundant fear that his good nature would be (was often) siezed upon and exploited, it is remarkable that he could, for all that, present the real nature of the case so clearly and without falsifying glosses.

Nor is it an objection[12] that the possibility of pity will need support and encouragement if it is to become a leading element in someone's character. This does not make it 'unnatural' in any relevant sense, as I have explained. All our tendencies of feeling require, or depend on, certain external influences if they are to become consolidated features of our make-up (whether good or bad). Pity stands in no special place in this respect.

My last amplifying point about the 'sentiment' argument is this: Rousseau stresses (E 4, 226; IV, 510) that the 'roads' by taking which Emile will be encouraged in his compassionate concerns should be mixed with 'the least possible personal interest'. This may cause some confusion. Rousseau's point is not that Emile should take no personal interest in the predicament of the suffering person. That would be absurd. Nor is it that he should not be concerned for the particular individuals in whom he has a personal interest and with whom he has a particular connection. Quite to the contrary, Rousseau insists that any general and abstract concern for 'the sufferings of humanity' is something that can be genuinely understood and felt only if one begins from the care felt here and now for this particular person. One loves man only by loving this particular man and that one; otherwise it is empty cant (see E 4, 225. IV, 509; and E 4, 233; IV, 520, for instance). What he means by excluding 'personal interest' from these 'learning episodes' is excluding features of the case which might lead Emile to feel he was on his mettle, that the other person was in contention with him for distinction, that his standing was 'on the line', and such matters. For these aspects in the case would tend to bring to the fore other dispositions in Emile, to see that he was not bested, to see that he had made his mark against the combative posture of the other person, etc. And this would silence pity for, as Rousseau says, none of these matters is 'without some impression of hatred against those who dispute with us for preference', for precedence and centre stage (ibid.). Rousseau does not deny that 'these dangerous passions will . . . be born sooner or later in spite of us'; but he says that they are best kept aside from the source of humanity in us which otherwise they irrevocably taint. So Emile is best introduced to his bond to humankind in situations where there is no blatant competition for power and prestige. Situations where others are, however temporarily, confounded by their suffering or examples drawn from the general lot of man as a weak and hapless creature, provide just such appropriate occasions.

This concludes the treatment of the 'sentiment' argument. I consider, now, the second step, the 'notion' argument, and show the significant additions this brings into the case and why they have the important implications Rousseau attributes to them.

### 3 Pity and Human Relation: The Second Step

In the 'sentiment' argument, the involvement of the other in the content and structure of my desires, feelings and purposes was fairly limited. I 'incorporate' the other only as a suffering creature; and I am directly moved to wish to relieve his suffering. My footing in his soul is as yet even less. I am, to him, simply the agent of relief for his pain. Rousseau has not looked at the attitudes or feelings towards me this might evoke from the person I help; nor at how I might respond to these. But even this first role I have for another is of substantial significance to me. For, as explained, it is a source of pleasure to me, a tangible proof of my strength and vitality. This is a large confirmation of my personal reality already.

In the 'notion' argument, further elements of human connection are introduced, and their significance considered. In particular, Rousseau begins by looking at the response of the helped person to his helper (E 4, 233–5; IV, 520–3). This is an extremely dense and detailed passage in Rousseau's discussion; I want to examine it quite closely.

In so far as I pity another, I am exposed in my feelings to the condition of that other person, even at the level contained in the first step. This first exposed involvement of my own feelings, desires, etc. with those of another prepares for the possibility of wider, more complex, interactions (inter-reactions) between us. As Rousseau says: 'In becoming capable of attachment, he [Emile, any of us] becomes sensitive to that of others and thereby attentive to the signs of this attachment' (E 4, 233; IV, 520). That is to say, being susceptible to another's pain in the first instance leads on to our becoming sensitive about other feelings another person has, and particularly those that comprise their sensitivity towards us. We become sensitized to how others respond to us, and we respond to our responses to them. So for each of us our feelings become multiply mutually interoriginated and connected. Rousseau at once considers, in a very compressed way, some of the possibilities here. (All of the following comes from the passage referred to; I shall not give more specific references).

First, it might be that the helped person feels, or is caused to feel, that in helping him in his need, you were intending to place on him an indebtedness to you 'while feigning to oblige him for nothing'. This breeds resentment. For the helped person feels abused, imposed upon and treated as if bound 'by a contract to which he did not consent'. He did not ask for, contract for, your assistance; you gave it, supposedly voluntarily, spontaneously. Rousseau makes one of his most savagely true remarks about this: 'Ingratitude would be rarer if good deeds were less commonly things lent out at interest' (my translation). We rebel against claims made against us for benefits which were given us as if gifts; we feel tricked and manipulated. Instead of gratitude we feel hatred towards our 'benefactor'; indeed, a double hatred. If he had neglected or hurt us, that would have been plain at least. But he pretended good feeling for us, but only then to claim that we were now obliged to him. We are deceived, and then abused (and in our weakness as well).

Are we then to expect, to want, no recognition, from someone for what we have done for them in their need (albeit that we did this at our own prompting, not their command nor for exchange or contract)? This is, Rousseau says, a natural, proper expectation. The crucial thing is that we shall actually gain this recognition if, and only if, we do not constrain, exploit or demand it from the other. Gratitude is, of necessity, the free response of a person left free to respond as he will, not as you demand. What comes extorted by reproach, or imposed obligation, cannot be gratitude. The deeds of compassion are the free gestures, freely given, of a free soul. The response of gratitude, if it is to exist at all, must be the same.

Why should it not exist? That affection for another which underpins compassion for them finds also direct expression in recognition of another's good intent towards us (if we do not spoil or resent this out of envy or omnipotent greed). I discussed this earlier. This affection is not confined to the helper; it is as ready a possibility for the helped person also. The aid he receives discloses a benign concern for him coming from the world, and evokes grateful pleasure at this. What stifles this can be many things. In the present context, it will be most obviously the discovery (or suspicion) that the concern was not benign at all, but a constraining trick. It can only live as a possibility if it is allowed the room to be what it is, the responsive gesture of a thankful heart. ('The heart receives laws only from itself', as Rousseau says). But, if it is allowed this room, there is no reason why it should not come. And if it does, the helper is receiving that response to him which is the *only* one which truly testifies to his being recognized and valued for what he is and has done for the other. Constrained responses are only semblances; they mask hatred behind the words of thanks.

It is, therefore, only by waiting, without control, for the free response of a person left free that we receive from another testimony to that significance for them which we want and merit – our significance for them as valued, trusted and well loved. Two things are immediate corollaries of this. The first is that a reciprocal mutual relation and recognition of our value to each other as persons is established. For my original response of pity displays the importance of the other's good to me, as much as his response of gratitude displays his good esteem and holding in high value of me (though these are responses on different levels.). Second, this mutual reciprocal valuation and well-regarding can only exist between people who are unconfined, unconstrained, by each other. Their responses are their own direct self-expressions. So, the bond of mutual recognition of value is the disclosure of each our own proper inward desire and disposition. It is a disclosure of the law of our own true being; it is the direction of the unfolding of our nature as it tends towards full expression and completion. Thus to value others is not an imposed law. It is, in fact, a requirement inherent to the nature of our own selfhood, part of the immediate expression of that. The importance of this result for Rousseau's philosophy, and in general, cannot be exaggerated. I have alluded to this idea of Rousseau's once or twice before. We see now (some of) the grounds he has for putting it forward.

We have not yet, however, finished with the complexities of the case. Just as I may impose my 'compassionate' deeds on another as a binding obligation, so I may, alternatively, convey the impression that I am only there to serve, that my place is only to help others. But, by this, the other 'sees only your dependence, and he would have taken you only for his valet'. Yours is, though, not 'a slave's attachment . . . but a friend's affection'. What is given is the deed of a free person of standing and proper weight. Just as one may impose too onerously on another, one may undervalue oneself and degrade oneself in their eyes. It is proper to the transaction that one is to oneself, and presents oneself to the other as, an honourable person of significance. Indeed, without doing so, the meaning of one's deed as testifying to concern for the value and good of the person helped is voided. The attentions of a slave show nothing of this kind. It is only as the deed of a freely caring person that the help given is something of value, something that shows the helped person that *he matters* to his helper. Otherwise the help is of no significance more than e.g. spontaneous remission of toothache (and often it is something quite disagreeable, for all that one's pain is actually alleviated[13]). Thus, just as I must not degrade the other when I offer help if I am not to poison that, I must not degrade myself in offering it otherwise it is poisoned too (in a different way).

The conclusion of this is the same as that arrived at just above, that it is the mutual level encounter and freely given recognition of people valued by each other and valuing themselves that keeps faith with the real character of the deeds and responses which connect them, and makes possible the unconstrained self-expression of each in the relation. We can, furthermore, supplement this conclusion in an important way. We saw, earlier, that my *amour-propre* found some answer in my undertaking compassionate actions. These showed me my potency and significance as a contributor to human affairs (at one level). But now also I am *recognized*, and valued, as a significantly effective and good contributor to the life of another; I have from him aknowledged meaning for him (in his grateful response). Thus I achieve what I want, which is to be received and respected as having significance for another; my *amour-propre* is more amply satisfied. But it is not only my *amour-propre* that receives satisfaction from this interchange; that of the grateful person does too. This may seem puzzling. For is he not in the position of the person whose *amour-propre* suffers because he feels his (happier, stronger) helper 'has no need' of him (see E 4, 221; IV, 503–4, discussed above)? At first this may seem so. But when it is recognized that the assistance of his helper deliberately leaves him free and unobligated, incorporates respect for his intact separateness and title to respond as his own heart directs and does not seek to control him; and when it is also recognized that his helper needs and values the response of gratitude he (the helped) gives precisely as being the recognition that is being afforded by a person of value, dignity (for, otherwise, that response is fraudulent or valueless); then from these two points it is clear that he is for his helper a person of significant weight and deep human meaning. And this will, in turn, satisfy some good measure of the needs of his *amour-propre* as well, and in the same interchange. Thus it is not merely that what we do and are for each other is mutually satisfactory and satisfying at the level of desires met, feelings gratified. It is also that each receives that testimony to his titles, and the respect proper to his standing, as a fully counting person for others. (This is part of the point of another case Rousseau considers where he says it is important to leave place for the *amour-propre* of the actually disadvantageously placed person in an interchange, cf. E 4, 248; IV, 541).

In this more complex interrelation, then, we find the basis for a mutual, reciprocal, *moral* recognition and acknowledgement of persons by persons. Each is to each someone to be respected, honoured, esteemed and valued as having standing in their own right, sovereign commander of their own feelings and behaviours, not the controller of, nor the subservient tool of, the desire or command of another. Without this, the exchanges between them looked at are impossible, or fraudulent or exploitative. This self-possessed, self-directing, sovereignty in one's own person is precisely *not* one which extorts submission or disposal of another, one which disregards others, or sees them as constraining presences. It is something that one can possess in and for *oneself* if, and only if, one acknowledges it in *another*. My own sovereignty in my character as a person contains *in its own constitution* the 'law' of the recognition and acknowledgment of the like ordered sovereignty of others; *mutual respect* is the inner rule of each our own *self-respect*. Self-respect does not require another's subordination; subordination of others in fact destroys the possible grounds of self-respect.

It is in the light of this that we can understand Rousseau's emphatic conclusion to this passage of discussion. He writes:

> Finally we enter the moral order. We have just made a second step into manhood . . . the first notions of good and bad are born of the sentiments of love and hate . . . *justice* and *goodness* are not merely abstract words . . . but are true affections of the soul enlightened by reason, are . . . only an ordered development of our primitive affections . . . the entire right of nature is only a chimera if it is not founded in a natural need of the human heart. (E 4, 235; IV, 522).

(The note to this passage should be looked at also.) We have seen how it is that the 'ordered development of our primitive affections' does give rise to just respect for every several person; and how such respect is 'founded in' a need which is one inherent to our own 'heart', and does not require an alternative origin nor imposition on us. Rousseau mentions the notion of 'conscience' several times at this point as well – I have omitted these remarks from the quotation. I defer my discussion of his account of conscience until chapter 7 (section 3). It must be remembered, however, that what I say here about the character and sources of moral feelings and judgement in an individual in his relations with others remains in need of completion by consideration of 'conscience'. However, as I shall show, bringing in this final element does not require withdrawal of anything said, only its supplementation in certain respects. So the present claims can stand adequately enough on their own terms.

This, then, is the outcome of the acts of pity and the return of gratitude that is proper to the character of each of these, and which is truly 'natural' to man in that it comprises that extension of *amour-de-soi* to cover our involvement with others which is in accord with the proper principle of that, namely to yield creative life to us in greater abundance. This in effect concludes the positive side of Rousseau's argument up to this point. But it is instructive to follow some of the further turns of his discussion, because in these he directly answers some of the objections which might be raised to his thesis.

Emile, now, is 'interested in his brothers; he is equitable' (E 4, 244; IV, 536). He also now knows the harm men do to themselves as much as to others by their 'inflamed' *amour-propre*, and feels glad that his own need for standing and human recognition does not call for answer (which it can in fact never receive) in this way. (This is gone through by Rousseau in this context at E 4, 235–43; IV, 523–33.) But this may lead him to form a highly conceited estimate of himself, as being above other men, not deceived by the follies they expend their being upon (E 4, 245; IV, 536–7). In so doing his *amour-propre* takes on a perverted form; for he now sees his good as comprised in his elevation above contemptible (to him) people. Emile is right, Rousseau says, to *prefer* his way of being; for, in it, he is happier, more composed and self-sustaining than others. But he should not think that he is better than others, who are inferiors in whose desolation he finds the constitution of his own well living. So Rousseau takes great pains to disabuse him of this idea, which is as mistaken as it is damaging. Emile is exposed to the flattery and manipulation of swindlers, and becomes their dupe. And Jean-Jacques does not protect him from this, but thanks these men who have shown Emile his own mortality. By this, Rousseau hopes, Emile will be saved from vanity, and will realize that it is his good fortune and no special merit in him that has allowed him to escape the snares which lay others low. Thus, he will know by vivid, lived, experience that the 'common order' of men and positions is entirely sufficient (it is the only order that in fact suffices) to afford the happiness, station and value to him he requires (E 4, 245; IV, 537).

One more case. I have approached these issues very much from the position of the compassionate man offering help to others, because this is how Rousseau introduces them. But this may cause a real distortion in Emile's (in our) perception of our position in the vicissitudes of human fortune (E 4, 224; IV, 507). He may think he is the one who is immune from the shocks of ill happening, not so easily vulnerable to and weak before pain and suffering. This may lead not only to misplaced conceit in his own supposed superiority to the common lot, as just discussed; it may also lead him to suppose that he is exempt from others' kind of trouble and has no occasion to be over much concerned about their predicament. But, Rousseau insists, this is a complete mistake. Emile is heir to the common fate of all humankind, which is to suffer, to be undone, to die. Thus it is that he will suffer and be helped in his turn every bit as often as he helps others who suffer. So Emile will be tied into the complex web of human interconnection constituted by the reciprocities of pity and gratitude sometimes as he who pities, sometimes as he who is grateful. Thus he values others both in their weakness and in their strength, and is himself similarly valued. So the different kinds and levels of mutual respect and esteem converge together on every several person; there are not those who are valued in one way and on one basis only, and others valued on another.

It is worth, briefly, considering one more possible deformation of the human bond that pity and gratitude establish which, so far as I am aware, Rousseau himself does not consider. For the liability to, indeed the inevitability of, this deformation is one which has been argued for as a consequence of his views,[14] and seeing why this assessment is mistaken will further clarify and reinforce Rousseau's own position. If the person I help responds to me with gratitude, he holds me – for so long as his gratitude lasts – in high estimation. It is therefore *possible* that I may set about giving help to others just in order to win for myself this exceptional esteem and praise. This, of course, would be satisfying to my *inflamed amour-propre*, which conceives my good as comprised in my elevation above others. In so doing, I do not at all value and respect the person I help, but see him only as a tool for advancing my sanctification which requires his inferiority and helplessness under me.

This does, undeniably, constitute a possibility. But it should be plain that it is not a necessity of the case. It can seem so only if a basic mistake is made about the character of *amour-propre*, that it necessarily takes an inflamed form requiring disdainful contempt for others. But, as I have argued, this is not so. The concerns of (proper, temperate) *amour-propre* are involved in the human transactions set in train by compassion; but they receive answer without requiring the degradation and ignoring of others. (This is, in fact, the only way in which they will receive answer.) Emile (anyone) is pleased to be found, and values being found, someone good, helpful, humane, someone who counts, and is known to count, for something in human dealings. But this is not a separate, prior, goal to his being caring and humane towards others. For it is precisely in and through being so that he acquires and holds the footing for others he wishes for himself. As soon as the desire for 'human standing' splits apart from the desire to do well for others then it becomes attached to delusive objectives which render it impossible of satisfaction. Emile is not, and rightly so, indifferent to the praise and significance he acquires from others. But only if it is acquired upon the basis of his doing something good and worthwhile which is appreciated by people who themselves know and value such things, and who are recognized as themselves persons whose assessment is significantly valuable, has the praise and acknowledgment any substance, and can it offer him what he wants. Rousseau explains this matter with complete clarity on E 4, 339 (IV, 670).

So there is nothing here which need trouble Rousseau. And although other objections to his account are no doubt possible, I take the power of his views to accommodate these looked at as sufficient proof of the congency of them.

So far, we have concentrated on the pattern of interconnection, in desire, feeling, valuation etc., established between particular persons. But the mutual reciprocal care and respect of which Rousseau is here concerned to explain the sources and significance, is not intended to be confined to those particular persons into whose company chance throws us, and whose plight touches us. If this were so, we should have advanced only a very little way to showing the place of justice and the duties of humanity in the 'ordered development of our primitive affections' (E 4, 235; IV, 522-3). For these are not confined to those whom we happen across and who stir our feelings; they are virtues which have *anyone* in need, or suffering degradation, as their concern, at least ultimately.[15] How is this extension of scope to take place? In particular, how is it to take place in a way which is not only consonant with, but actually an extension of, each our own inner need, the 'law' proper to our own heart? This is a particularly pressing question since, to put it crudely, the question of the benefit of justice to the just man himself has been, and remains, among the most vexing of all questions of moral theory ever since that study began.[16] If the dictates of justice are not, as such, the dictates of a person's own (enlightened) heart, why should he concern himself with them? Will not their rule over him involve a suppression or distortion of his own personal self-development and expression?

This is, in effect, the issue that Rousseau now begins to address (E 4, 250ff; IV, 544ff). We shall not see his complete answer to it until we have examined his civil and political ideas, for an account of the claims of impersonal, impartial, justice upon the individual are quite central to these. But at this point we can see how Rousseau makes a start on these problems. It is his own view that this ancient question can be resolved in such a way as to show that the directives of justice do comprise the direction of the proper inner need and being of each individual. We need to examine the grounds of his view.

## 4 'Extending' *Amour-propre*

Rousseau's emphasis on the bond between particular people as the starting point for an examination of the claims of justice is not accidental. As I have remarked before, he is most emphatic that the 'love of men' is not the love of some abstract entity, but begins and ends with loving this person, and this one, and then that one . . . and so on.[17] So stressing, he is already making a serious moral and psychological point. First (to pick up a point made in chapter 1, section 1), that 'lóve of one's nearest' is the principle from which a more extended and wider-scoped love grows and necessarily grows (see E 5, 363; IV, 699–70). For it is not in human nature to know or love the abstract and remote from nowhere, but only by knowing and feeling it as an enlargement of the concrete and close with which one is intimate. Second, that justice and humanity are good only because they enrich and improve the lives of people; and people's lives are the lives of particular people, this one and that one. Some may argue that if done so it is being done too slowly, and in the wrong way; some injustices are wholesale and pervasive and demand 'structural' changes. Rousseau would not disagree. But he would disagree if it means that the fate of one is nothing before the fate of many. For him, justice is done when, and only when, each several separate person has justice: 'universal' love is love for each particular person as precious, until it encompasses every one. Despite what has often been argued concerning Rousseau, he did not believe in treating people just as units in a collective and addressing the good of the collective. He believed in the absolute right and good of every unique person. This will be more fully discussed in chapters 5 and 6.

However, even bearing these points in mind, it is clear that the situation so far described is improperly confined. How shall it be extended? The answer is plain. Emile's compassion is a disclosure of his benevolent disposition, finding a particular focus. But there is no reason why it should not make him more widely sensitive and attentive, make him alert and perceptive to pain or need not immediately forced on his attention. Not that he will become a do-gooding busybody (a 'knight errant', E 4, 250; IV, 544). He will not 'meddle in public affairs, play the wise man and defender of the laws . . .' (ibid.). Rather he will be modest, circumspect, and direct, reconciling the estranged, redressing a wrong, alleviating the causes of hatred (E 4, 251; IV, 545; see also E 5, 474; IV, 859). And, gradually, he becomes ready and familiar with the manifold occasions where one human can be helpful and constructive in his dealings with others.

These points culminate in that disputed passage, referred to before (chapter 2, section 3) where Rousseau speaks of extending '*amour-propre* to other beings'. 'We shall transform it into a virtue', he goes on 'and there is no man's heart in which this virtue does not have its root'. I now offer my interpretation of this passage. We know by now that the *amour-propre* in view here is not 'inflamed', that whose pleasure consists in another's unhappiness or destitution. It would be ridiculous, or incoherent, to suppose one could 'extend' such a disposition to others, and to suppose that in so doing it was 'transformed' into a virtue. If we suppose that the 'extension' takes some such form as moving from 'Let me have dominance' to 'Let everyone enjoy dominance' it is absurd to say that 'virtue' would result. Nor is it intelligible how such an extension 'has its root' in each person's heart since, by this extension, he sets others in competition for dominance with him whereas his 'heart' sets him the objective of exclusive possession of this for himself.

The picture alters radically, however, once we bring a different understanding of the nature and requirements of *amour-propre*, such as I have argued for, to the interpretation of Rousseau's thought here. My own *amour-propre* directs me to secure for myself significant, counting, moral being for others. If we 'extend' this expectation for ourselves to others, we are recognizing and acknowledging that they have, should have, these same requirements for themselves as well. We allow that others have their *amour-propre* too, and we determine to respect this in them. (Another possible reading of the meaning of 'extend' might be this: I extend my *amour-propre* to others by taking *their* need for human standing 'on board' as *my own* concern, and thus strive for them to enjoy this just as much as I strive to have it for myself. This would parallel the way in which I take relief of another's pain 'on board' as my immediate pressing concern in my pity of them, as discussed earlier. It does not matter which reading we employ, since the same result ensues.)

If we do this, it is at once clear that a 'virtue' does result, the virtue of just respect and honour for each several person as their due and title, together with clemency and generosity. So that part of Rousseau's thought makes sound sense. But why should we do this; what incentive in, or call upon, each of us is there to make such an extension? Rousseau says that doing so is rooted in every man's heart. How is this? It has been examined closely already, in fact. It is rooted not only in each person's benevolent concerns of pity and gratitude, which are dispositions inherently proper to their own enlarged 'sensitive' being. It is also rooted in each person's own *amour-propre* which requires the recognition and esteem of others, but can only achieve this if it affords to others respect, dignity and value as significant beings in their own right, whose sentiments and judgements count for something as those of a properly standing person (as explained). So it is intrinsic to the direction of our own *amour-propre* to honour the *amour-propre* of others, to honour their need to be respected and esteemed as telling human presences for one in themselves. This is the respective human footing which we necessarily wish to assign to others out of the dictates natural to our own need.

Thus, so far from this passage betraying any confusion or obscurity on Rousseau's part, it encapsulates with great economy and precision some of the most central of his claims. It shows how mutual reciprocal individual respect and care obtaining between all men comprises the completion and fulfilment of the full scope of being of each several person as they constitute an integral member of their species. This gives answer, the only coherent answer, to the *amour-propre* of each person in giving answer to that of every person at the same time. So we have at least the schema for an account of how individual need and good is not only compatible with the need and good of others, and with the requirements of justice for each and all, but actually implies this. I say only the 'schema' of an account, not because Rousseau has not argued intensively and in detail for this conclusion overall, but because the particular concrete ways through which this implication will be realized in the lives and institutions of men remain to be filled out. These need to be spelled out to give specific immediacy to this generic claim. How Rousseau does so in connection with Emile's general involvement in ordinary social affairs will be looked at in a moment. The civil and political concreteness will be examined in the following chapters.

## 5 Taking One's Place in Society

The general principles of the integration of a person's desires, needs, feelings, values etc., with those of others have now been enunciated and defended. But there are two further aspects of this progress into humanity which Rousseau spends some time on in Book 4 of *Emile*, which I want to say a little about.

The first concerns the concrete detail of Emile's presentation of his person to others, the footing and role for them he assumes, when he is set loose in the 'social whirlpool' (E 4, 255; IV, 551). (I defer, for consideration in chapter 7, 'The Profession of Faith of the Savoyard Vicar' which comes in the middle of Book 4.) Rousseau announces this theme on E 4, 327; IV, 654:

> Emile is not made to remain always solitary. As a member of society he ought to fulfil its duties. Since he is made to live with men, he ought to know them. He knows man in general; it remains for him to know individuals. He knows what is done in society; it remains for him to see how one lives in it. It is time to show him the exterior of this great stage, all of whose hidden mechanisms he already knows.

It would be tiresome to look at every aspect of this, concerned, as it must be, with much of the minutiae of social transactions among civilized persons. Also, the general principles in use guiding Emile's swimming in the social pool are clear. But one or two broader aspects of the case deserve note. First, Rousseau introduces Emile to the possibility of love and intimacy with a woman as one aspect of his more specific need. This is followed through in the

Fifth Book of Emile, and will be considered separately below. The portrait of Emile in the midst of society is given from E 4, 335 (IV, 665). He is modest and simple in his manner and speech. He is humane and thoughtful, does not flatter or seek prestige. He is calm and quiet, preferring not to be noticed rather than to compete for distinction. He will be respectful and aim to give real (not 'opinion') pleasure and show true consideration for the well-being of others, not by formal shows of politeness and observance of the punctilios of social nicety, but by being always well disposed and attentive to their best need: 'It is only for the man who does not possess true politeness that one is forced to make an art of its outward forms' (E 4, 338; IV, 669). Emile will 'not be celebrated as a likeable man' – a jolly good fellow, a swell – 'but they will like him without knowing why'; he does not try to assert himself over them, is not knowing, smart, noisy, demanding the stage (E 4, 339; IV, 670). He keeps his own counsel, but if asked answers helpfully, constructively. He is not forward, but neither does he draw attention to himself by affecting weakness or pretending need. He is a thoroughly ordinary, decent, considerate, unobtrusive but kind and helpful presence. So it is that he may swim and not be sucked under as the whirl of life surrounds him.

The second general point I want to consider is much deeper in its significance and ramifications for Rousseau's ideas. Emile is now situated as a moral person in reciprocal standing and interaction with other moral persons, in the fashion I have tried to explain. He interprets his own being and position in the terms appropriate to this, as someone possessed of certain rights, titles to be treated and received in certain ways, and acts in the light of and on the basis of his moral titles. He likewise treats and receives others. Because this is so, it is no longer appropriate for Jean-Jacques to treat him as his 'pupil', and to organize his life and affairs in ways which do not address his new character (which was not present in the form of their earlier transactions). As Rousseau says: 'He is still your disciple, but he is no longer your pupil. He is your friend, he is a man. From now on treat him as such'. (E 4, 316; IV, 639). The general importance of what is going on at this point is this. Emile's representative change in status, in the footing of his relations and dealings with his tutor, is an exemplar for the change in status for others that, e.g., is enjoyed when a child attains 'adult standing' in our society, with the rights (and responsibilities) that go with 'coming of age' – for instance the right to vote, to make hire-purchase contracts for oneself, and the like (though *these* are not the actual titles Rousseau has in mind). Vested with these new entitlements, a person is now capable of entering into a whole extra range of relations with others. He will do so on a different basis from that on which he has entered relations earlier, with different liabilities. It would, therefore, be quite inappropriate to continue to treat him as if he were no longer 'responsible for himself' (at least in terms of his legal position). He has acquired the standing of someone who is answerable for his own actions, which is to give him a new self-directing standing as enjoying sovereign discretion over certain matters which he did not possess before. In short, his freedom is enlarged, in that he is not (legally) answerable to anyone else any longer for what he elects to do over certain matters.

Rousseau is not, at this point, concerned with a legally stipulated, conventional, transformation in standing, but with a real change in Emile's self-possessed and enacted *persona*; the example was only offered to clarify the overall character of what is going on. But, on the other hand, the issue of Emile's increased freedom is crucial, his coming into the possession of the title not to be obliged to answer to his seniors (his father, tutor, guardian, or whoever) for his decisions and actions. I shall be examining Rousseau's account of freedom in full in the next Chapter. But some examination of what transpires in these pages (E 4, 316–26; IV, 639–53) is highly pertinent preparation for that.

These are two different sides to Emile's freedom that are of significance here. First of all there is this. Until Emile has become aware of himself as, has come to articulate to himself his own character in terms of, a bearer of titles fit to be received and treated in certain ways by others, the issue of his own 'sovereignty' over his choices and actions has no sense or significance for him at all. ('Authority and the law of duty were unknown to him'; E 4, 316; IV, 639). For him, the *sole* significance, the only meaning, the issue of his personal freedom had was: have I the natural ability and resources to do what I want to do (see, for instance, E 2, 84; IV, 308–9)? The issue of any duty of obedience, any requirement to submit to an authority or to gain permission from someone who has the right to gainsay, was quite excluded from the ambit of his self-awareness, the desiderata which bore on his actions. This exclusion was, of course, quite deliberate on Rousseau's part; Emile must begin negotiating with the force of things, not the wills of men. His unfreedom, his constraint or confinement consists only in some disproportion between his desire and his ability to satisfy it. The disproportion is removed by moderation in desire by reference to a realistic appraisal of need, possibility and so on; but also by assiduous acquisition of skills, techniques for working effectively in the world (as considered before, chapter 3, section 3). In both these respects, his life is, in fact, guided and structured by Jean-Jacques' virtually absolute control over him. But this control is present to him as if it were just part of the given natural character of his life's environment, and is not encountered and challenged as a controlling will exerted over and against him ('Up to now you got nothing from him except by force or ruse', E 4, 316; IV, 639). I shall call this (with or without the 'masked' ordering of the environment) Emile's possession of 'circumstantial' freedom, his ability to operate without impediment in his actual circumstances where he 'wants only what he can do and does what he pleases' (E 2, 84; IV, 309).

Circumstantial freedom does not cease to be an issue when we turn to the second side of the matter here. But there a new, more prominent, element in the phenomenon of personal freedom comes in. For now Emile not only wants to do something, and knows he can (circumstantially) do it; he also knows that he may, is entitled to, do it; that it is proper and fitting that he shall undertake such a thing without let or hindrance from another, who has no right or title to impede him, challenge him, or to demand account from him. That is to say, his actions now possess for him a moral significance, are present and make their mark in the arena of justifications and challenges; they are open to questions of authority, of 'by what right?', and the like. So the question of personal freedom acquires a further, different, aspect. The question is not only: has he the circumstantial facility of doing it; but: has he the title to do it, and what is the ground or source of that title? Is it his own unregulated say-so that settles the issue decisively? Or must he vindicate himself by the 'moral law'? Or is he answerable to some named other, or to the panel of his peers, or to some civil authority? In this connection, quite different constraints can hedge around a person's scope of action from those established by intractable practical problems presented. There is, on the one hand, the most extreme confinement or deprivation of freedom in this second sense (which I shall call 'elective' or 'discretionary' freedom) which would consist in being not only answerable to the absolute discretionary permission or authorization of someone else to put in hand any project, but being under their direction and instigation in establishing any projects at all in the first place. Here one would be nothing but an appendage to them, their living tool. Certain forms of slavery amount to this, the location of someone as a 'non-person' in the arena of human decisions and actions.

On the other hand there is complete elective and discretionary freedom, not subject to any moral check or ordering of any kind, nor to the assessment or judgement of any other person. Here a person's own immediate say-so is non-accountably and absolutely authoritative and decisive in establishing the legitimacy of his undertaking. The *fiat* of an arbitrary despot or absolute ruler would approximate to this. Now two highly significant questions are raised by *this* conception of what complete discretionary freedom is. Firstly, although this clearly comprises the absolute enjoyment of one sort or form of freedom, is there not, perhaps, another sort of freedom it precludes; or, perhaps, another sort of unfreedom which it masks but in fact incorporates? If this is so, what are the respective importance and value to us of the different forms or sorts of freedom involved? Secondly, and clearly connected, there is the question whether, if this be the character of complete discretionary freedom, we want to enjoy it, whether it is something valuable for us, the possession of which is to our benefit (as we believe, and/or in actual fact)?

Rousseau's answers to these questions should occasion no surprise. I shall only barely indicate them now, since I shall be exploring the case in detail in chapter 5. The person who 'enjoys' complete discretionary freedom, as here outlined, is very like indeed the person who has achieved the satisfaction of the most excessive 'inflamed' *amour-prpre*. And we know very well by now that achieving the satisfaction of that does not at all entail that a person enjoys a high level of (some other forms of) freedom, let alone enjoys a state which is beneficial and agreeable to him. He is enslaved to the opinions of others; the very constitution of his conception of personal good requires constant 'measuring' of himself and his condition with reference to others; etc. The inflammation of his *amour-propre*, indeed, discloses his subjugation to fear of invasion and control by others. So, in many diverse ways and at many levels, his life is one of extremely limited freedom of various kinds indeed. And it is pretty clear that the lack of the various freedoms he does *not* enjoy is far more damaging and hurtful to him than the freedoms he does enjoy are beneficial and constructive for him. In fact, it is doubtful whether his despotic liberty is beneficial to him at all (see, especially, E 2, 86–8; IV, 312–15; E 2, 91; IV, 320).

The convergence between the nature of complete discretionary freedom, and that standing and those imperious titles someone demands for himself out of inflamed *amour-propre*, is altogether intended by Rousseau. It is precisely this effective identity between the two states that leads him to insist that complete elective freedom is, at best, a sham sort of freedom, and is of no value to us (is, in fact, damaging to us). The identification of it is, then, not the identification of some position we should want and demand for ourselves; it is only an illusion to suppose that, deprived of this, we are deprived of anything we should want or be better off having.[18]

Does this, then, mean that we should want, and be better off with some sort of 'slavery'?[19] The question is incoherent. For we cannot be slaves if there are no masters enslaving us. But it has just been shown that being a master is nothing of value. So being a slave cannot be the alternative to that. The alternative is, as Rousseau views it, that circumscription of personal discretionary freedom which inherently and automatically incorporates respect for the titles, needs and standing of others as the in-built inviolable moral limit to the exercise of discretion. By this alone do we enjoy a liberty which is both real and valuable. Real because eliminating all the covert forms of enslavement to others. Valuable because affording to us that value and recognition from significant others which gives us the meaning and dignity as persons we need for ourselves.

I shall call that form and scope of freedom in decision and action, which is regulated by the directive inherent to each person's own moral standing to respect and honour the rights and titles of others in their like character and standing, 'principled' freedom, to distinguish it from that wholly unregulated exercise of elective say-so which comprised complete elective freedom as I described that. It is a form of elective freedom, in that it has to do with the individual's title to elect to do, or not to do, this or that as he sees fit and good. But it is an exercise of that title invariably and ineluctably according to fixed, determinate, principles which fix the limits to proper use of that title to make one's own non-answerable elections. But these are principles which are not, in their nature, externally imposed and constraining of the individual's good scope of self-determining election. They are the principles through conformity to which the individual possesses and realizes a freedom in his person and action which is real and valuable. They are, in Rousseau's strict sense, the 'natural' principles for our freedom. The possession of freedom is the possession of a will which orders itself to the requirements inherently proper to its own need and significant value. It is submission to the laws of its own being and value. (E 4, 325; IV, 651; and E 5, 444–6; IV, 817–19; E 5, 473; IV, 857; and GP ch 6, 186; III, 974).

I choose the name 'principled' freedom, rather than those more commonly used such as 'moral' or 'positive' freedom because these latter terms are likely to awaken prejudices which will hamper an open hearing being given to Rousseau's thoughts here. But I shall not proceed further on this theme at this point; I return to it later on. What is at present material is the precise form of elective freedom to which Emile now accedes. For it is this, some kind of this, form of freedom that he now enjoys, his coming into possession of which marks his decisive break from the position previously occupied with respect to his tutor, and calls for a renegotiation of the terms of their relation. As Rousseau says: 'It is only at this present moment that they [Emile's rights] begin for him' (E 4, 316; IV, 639, my translation).

What use is it proper and good, hence natural, for Emile to make of his newly held right of knowing himself for elective sovereign over his actions? He has this title; what will his (the rightly ordered) disposition be in regard to the use he makes of it? We know the answer to this already. He is disposed to regard his fellows, to regard others in general, as persons of like standing and title to himself whom he respects and honours just as he demands that they respect and honour him (cf. E 4, 316; IV, 639). It is, therefore, immediately apparent that he will not contemplate as a moral possibility for him any decision or course of action which will involve the denial of the respect and honour fitting to another. It will be automatic to him to confine his elective will within the bounds of the duty of humanity and respect of persons. In particular, this will entail that he cannot expect or require that he is not to be called to account by others about anything he does, to explain, justify, vindicate himself, or to gain their consent or compliance to some courses he proposes. It is in the nature of his elective will, then, that he is not, and does not claim to be, an absolute despot. He is from the start an answerable and accountable agent, not sole sovereign of all his determinations, but subject to a sovereignty over him of some kind. The precise kind(s) of legitimate superordinate sovereignty will not detain us just here. The present purpose is only to establish the general necessity and propriety of such superordinate sovereignty over the individual, and to show how this is not a constraint upon his freedom, but a constitutive enabling principle of the possibility and possession of that.

In fact, Rousseau is rather unspecific at this point about Emile's own self-administered self-regulation, for he (Emile) voluntarily resigns to his tutor his governance once more, realizing that he is, as yet, ill-prepared to take himself in hand, as it were (E 4, 325; IV, 651). It would be a mistake, however, to infer that Rousseau took this for an analogy for the highest mode of self-possession and self-utilization of freedom we could attain to – that we *always* require a wise guide and counsellor, and our own wisdom consists only in realizing this and comporting ourselves accordingly. This might be used, for instance, to explain the significance of the 'legislator' in the argument of *The Social Contract*.[20] It is perfectly clear, however, that Rousseau regards Emile's voluntary acceptance of continued discipleship as still only a half-way house to full self-possessed elective self-determination, which is proper to complete human standing. For he returns to the matter in Book 5 (E 5, 444ff; IV, 818), and the stress there is on Emile becoming wholly 'his own master', and no longer (whether by his own choice or not) guarded and guided by the wisdom and care of someone else exercised for his sake (see also E 5, 473; IV, 857). So there is no evidence that Rousseau regards some sort of moral or civil 'sonship' as the best available, or the best as such, form for the use of elective freedom to take. Admittedly, even when Emile becomes himself a real father, he still turns to Jean-Jacques for advice and guidance (E 5, 480; IV, 867–8 – the very last lines of the whole book). But it is plain that this is now the advice of a trusted and valued family friend, heeded and deferred to out of affection and respect, and it does not at all involve some hesitation or reticence on Emile's part in fully taking up for himself *all* the powers and responsibilities that his possession of ordered elective freedom equip him with. He is now, in fact, 'on his own', no longer in any way relieved of (or ceding) any of the burdens of being one who must maintain and uphold the order, and not rely on others to do so and give him the lead. He is, by then, a father, a land-owner, a citizen; and such people must, in effect, *establish* the actual law as it exists concretely in human affairs, even should one suppose there to be some abstractly higher and truer law (e.g. God's law).

As I have said, many of these points will be amplified and scrutinized in detail when the idea of freedom as that plays its part in the arguments of *The Social Contract* is examined. But what Rousseau presents here is an essential lead-in to that; and, in fact, it makes clear much that is abridged or presumed upon in other arguments.

## 6 Intimacy

Although, given the point now reached, the constitution and principles of many elements of Emile's own self-conception, his desires, values, attitudes etc., incorporate, in a deep and inextricable way, the presence of others to him, there are many possibilities of exposed engagement of his feelings and self-assessments to those of others towards him which he has not yet experienced. His *amour-propre*, which requires that he receive the acknowledgement and esteem of others as a significantly valuable person is substantially answered. But it is so very much on the basis of mutual practical care and the reciprocities of justice. For all that this constitutes an inwardly penetrating bond between persons, it is still a fairly remote or 'cold' relation and mutual involvement. Emile's own self-assessment of his worth and value as a person is not so tied up with the reception he receives from any particular person that he cannot survive as an intact self, still well-possessed of a sense of his palpable human potency, if he is, from time to time, ill-used or marginalized (see, for instance, E 4, 250 note; IV, 544 note). No more perilous exposure of his sense of personal value and the good of his life to the 'verdict' on him of another has been undergone.

It may be said that this is all to the good; and that Rousseau would wish it to remain like this. For does Rousseau not continously inveigh against this sort of putting oneself at the mercy of the opinion of another? This retort is misplaced. Rousseau does, indeed, constantly warn of the perils and hurts which this sort of dependence of one's weal upon the assessment made of one by another threatens. But it is mistaken to conclude that he held that we should avoid such dependence at all costs, at least if it carries us beyond what is involved in the pity/gratitude relations looked at above. For if we do, we deny ourselves the possibility of mutual reciprocal intimate personal love, that relation between persons that makes someone 'as happy as [they] can be', which comprises 'the whole value of life' in its felicity (E 5, 419; IV, 782). In such intimate personal love, the lover is skinlessly exposed in all his hopes and fears, his sense of himself and what he means, to the return of his loved one to him and to his love (E 5, 416; IV, 778). His fate (he will think) hangs by a thread. But unless he takes this risk, he cannot taste the greatest felicity of human experience. So the issue is not the avoidance of this dependence, the avoidance of love, but that of attempting to enable the good of love to be possessed and enjoyed.[21] (We can see, now, that 'inflamed' *amour-propre* is rooted in the rejection of the hopes and claims of love.)

In examining the character of love in its significance for Emile's (our) self-estimations and feelings, for the happiness of life, etc., Rousseau is examining the proper place of 'passion' in human need and good – recalling the elucidation given earlier (chapter 4, section 1) of the central sense of this notion for Rousseau. Thus, when Rousseau says, on E 5, 416; (IV, 778), that, for Emile, this is 'his *first* passion of any kind' (my stress), he is being wholly clear and consistent in his articulation of his material. 'Passion' has not established and configured those relations instigated by pity and gratitude. These are 'sentiments' which inform our conduct and tie us together. So there is further ground to be traversed here, and Rousseau is now making the journey across it.

With the onset of passion proper, the likelihood of the sorts of self-deformations and enslavements that mark inflamed *amour-propre* is very great, as Rousseau is well aware (see the discussion of (sexual) jealousy on E 5, 429–31; IV, 796–8; and the comment, quoted in the Introduction, that 'in learning to desire', Emile has made himself 'the slave of [his] desires; E 5, 443; IV, 815–6. The pieces of the jigsaw all fit together, in time). His principal concern is, then, to consider how passion may shape and pervade a persons's life without 'disfiguring' him (E 5, 439; IV, 809). This is, I suggest, the predominant concern of *Emile*, Book 5, and far more significant for Rousseau's overall thematic intentions than are his general comments on the nature and status of women which also feature largely in this book. Rousseau supposes – as how should he not? – that Emile's love will be love for a woman, and the hope of love returned by a woman. This is what causes him to consider at length, in the first part of Book 5 (E 5, 357–406; IV, 692–763), the general character of women before he turns to consider the significance of passion. But the over-riding issue in the Book is this latter one; his comments on the former matter could be very different indeed without affecting the latter. Rousseau's principal interest is in how human (sexually informed) passion may be creative, liberating and beneficial to the passionate person and to the object of their passion and not be, as is so generally the case, a source of the deepest misery and pain to both. I shall, therefore, treat these two matters separately, discussing the possibilities for a creative incorporation of passion first, and Rousseau's assessment of the position of women second.

Rousseau's treatment of this first matter is informed throughout by the idea that there is a constant need to guard against that form of hapless, humiliating, dependence on another in one's passionate feeling for them which is so prominent in inflamed *amour-propre* (it is 'men' not 'monkeys' that can feel, and receive return for, passion; E 5, 404; IV, 761). Rousseau stresses that it is the feeling of a person who is honourable, generous, humane and good that is an expression of something valuable, for it is an expression of a spirit that recognizes and cleaves to what is good and fair. But this entails that the lover, even in the extremity of his passionate feeling, must retain his integrity and allegiance to these goods, or else his own feeling is debased.[22] If it is debased, there can remain little cause for the object of his attachment to receive and respond to his feeling with pleasure, to recognize it as something of value, a mark of the highest real esteem, and a testimony to care for their real good. So the likelihood of any return of love is diminished; why should one be moved with love for a love from someone which discloses only, say, greed, deceit, jealousy and anger? So, not only will the lover damage himself if, in passion, he forsakes all he knows and feels that is good, humane and generous (cf. E 5, 418; IV, 781, on Emile's character); he will also insult the person he loves and reduce the prospect for a meeting of his love. To have other attachments, to justice, mercy, kindness, as well as one's loving attachment, and to retain these throughout one's love, is not to diminish or to preclude the whole-hearted reality and goodness of that love. Rather, doing so is a condition of the reality and goodness of one's love, or so Rousseau argues. Thus he has Emile say:

> 'Sophie, you are the arbiter of my fate. You know it well. You can make me die of pain. But do not hope to make me forget the rights of humanity. They are more sacred to me than yours. I will never give them up for you.' (E 5, 441; IV, 812–13).

Rousseau's hope is that Sophie, or anyone who is the object of someone's love, will recognize that the love they are offered, the lover who offers himself, is of real value, discloses a true honour and recogniton of their value, and is a pledge of constant faith in care to them. He believes that, under those circumstances, the love may well be returned; and, being a love that responds to such love, it too will be of that same character. Emile wins his loved one by all that is natural to his heart: 'esteem of true goods, frugality, simplicity, generous disinterestedness, contempt of show and riches' (E 5, 433; IV, 801). He can have no cause, then, through his love, to lose or forsake these virtues; these enabled him to give love and to receive love, and must,therefore, remain. Thus Sophie, any loved one, does not 'want a lover who knew no law other than hers' (E 5, 439; IV, 809). Because of this, Emile (any lover) will not become the puppet and mock of his loved one (nor, more subtly, want to turn her into his puppeteer and derider, as is done by lovers who can understand no terms for human relations than those of domination and subjection; see E 5, 431; IV, 799, on the five ages of man, and the 'springs of action' characteristic of each). Thus he will be spared (will spare himself) that self-dissolution that inflamed *amour-propre* entails; and he will spare his loved one from becoming entangled in the destructive web of such a relation which would disfigure them equally.

Rousseau is emphatic, then, that one contends creatively with passion, for oneself and for the others one tangles with, by 'fixing' the early habits of mind, feeling and disposition and continuing to hold true to these in one's new situation and involvements (E 5, 431–2; IV, 799–800). They establish the possibility of such passion being a good to oneself and to its object. Requited love may be life's greatest felicity, but it builds on and extends the knowledge and experience of many other goods already felt and cleaved to. Retaining allegiance to these goods is, however, no easy task, so great is the desire to think and do nothing but what concerns one's loved person. Rousseau, therefore, considers two further aspects to this.

First, he enjoins Emile to acquire the capacity to endure the necessary restraints on his passions analogous to his power to 'endure the law of necessity in physical ills' acquired before he was touched by the need of another (E 5, 443; IV, 816-7). He now needs strength to supplement and consolidate his commitment to good, whereas up to now the pursuit of good has been his pleasure and that has been sufficient. His 'natural' virtue must now become virtue 'in the strict sense' (see above, secton 2):

> I have made you good rather than virtuous. But he who is only good remains so only as long as he takes pleasure in being so. Goodness is broken and perishes under the impact of the human passions. The man who is only good is good only for himself.
>   Who, then, is the virtuous man? It is he who knows how to conquer his affections; for then he follows his reason and his conscience. . . Up to now you were only apparently free. You had only the precarious freedom of a slave to whom nothing has been commanded. Now be really free. Learn to become your own master . . . (E 5, 444-5; IV, 818).

Self-sustained virtue which 'conquers' passion is, then, in Rousseau's view one of the final elements which contributes to the full self-possessed freedom of man. I have touched on this before, and shall be returning to it. Here we need only note that the 'principled' freedom Rousseau clearly has in view here is not intended to be a matter of obedience to externally promulgated and enforced principles, even if these should be principles the observance of which preserves us from servitude and lead us to our own complete good. It is rather, in its final form, self-possessed and self-sustained resolution and determination which comprises the freedom proper to man. Whatever role the devising, administration and enforcement of wise positive law may eventually have – in general, or in Rousseau's own theory – it is clear that it cannot, in his estimation, ever fully take the place of the individual's own self-sustained and furthered commitment to the laws of his own freedom. Thus Rousseau writes:

> . . . the eternal laws of nature and order do exist. For the wise man, they take the place of positive law. They are written in the depth of his heart by conscience and reason. It is to these he ought to enslave himself in order to be free. The only slave is the man who does evil, for he always does it in spite of himself. Freedom is found in no form of government; it is in the heart of the free man. (E 5, 473; IV, 857-8[23])

This thought will have considerable importance for a proper understanding and assessment of Rousseau's political theory, in connection with which I shall look at it again.

It is in connection with becoming self-administrator of one's own law that the second further matter Rousseau introduces comes in. He recommends that Emile leave Sophie for a couple of years (E 5, 447; IV, 821). There are many reasons for this, which we may briefly note. First, the discipline that accepting this hurt imposes on him will help to teach him that fortitude and endurance for the sake of a cherished good we have just been considering. Second, it will remove him from the situation which provokes him to heedless impetuosity in his behaviour and feelings and will enable him to learn the real depth and permanence of his loyalty to Sophie (and of hers to him). Third, he is, during this separation, to travel and to learn of the ways of other peoples and countries, with a view not only to broadening his still narrow experience of human ways and matters, but to learning something of the character of civil society and government. This is particularly significant, for as and when Emile and Sophie marry and raise a family they will become members of a state (E 5, 448; IV, 823); and Emile barely knows anything of what that consists in, what it is to bear civil standing and civl responsibility. Rousseau follows this point up with a thumbnail sketch of many of the central ideas to be found in *The Social Contract*, consideration of which I defer until that work is examined (see E 5, 455–67; IV, 833–49).

This concludes Emile's entry into the bond of love for another. His being, his self-possessed and enacted character, has been further extended and elaborated by this additional step, so that the constitution and structure of his desires, values, self-estimations, etc., is even more deeply shaped by what he is for another. But, Rousseau hopes and intends, this shaping will not have involved deformation and disfiguring of him. He will, rather, have incorporated the bond of intimate personal love into the order of his being and life in a way that both conserves and extends the possibilities of his own true well-being and intactness as a person of value, worthy of respect and honour. In conserving this in Emile, the same possibilities also exist for the person he loves (as explained).

Whatever the value of Rousseau's ideas about this may ultimately be, I have made plain that there is little in them that specifically depends on the fact that Rousseau is considering the love of man and woman. His concern is, quite generally, with the character and significance of passionate attachment for another, the gender of those involved being subsidiary. But given that he is examining passion between men and women, and given that the protagonist throughout the book has been first a boy, now a man, Rousseau also spends some while considering the nature and character of girls and women to fill in the so far neglected side of the relation. It is his discussion of this material I now want to look at.

## 7 Rousseau's Account of Women

Rousseau gives his account of women through an account of an exemplar woman, Sophie, just as his account of man is given through the exemplar man Emile. Rousseau has been placed in the catalogue of irredeemably 'sexist' thinkers about women, and his views are the subject of very much adverse criticism. It is impossible at present to discuss the matter in full. I shall, therefore, give only a brief, but I hope just, account of Rousseau's estimate of what 'suits the constitution of Sophie's [a woman's] species and her sex in order to fill her place in the physical and moral order' (E 5, 357; IV, 692), with little amplifying comment. One overall point is worth bearing in mind, however. Rousseau tends to stress those aspects of Sophie's nature, dispositions, aptitudes, etc., which particularly bear on the possibility of her being one participant in a mutual reciprocal relation of passion with a man (though he does not attend to these exclusively). This is not because he thought the only place suitable to a woman was to be a member of such a relation, and that there was nothing else of significance to say regarding her position. It is rather because it is the general issue of the possibility of creative and beneficial relations of mutual love between individuals that is his dominant theme in this part of *Emile*, and his concentration on matters which do not bear on this is circumscribed. This is equally true regarding what he discusses at this point regarding Emile. Were we only to have had the reflections of Book 5 to help us know what Rousseau thought about man, we would receive a very partial impression of his ideas on that, since only that range of ideas respecting man as a potential participant of a loving relation is under review. But in neither case is there *any* assumption that the only things of significance to be said overall come from considering that particular possible human relation.

Two things follow from this. Many of the points made about Sophie's accomplishments, her self-assertion, and so on have more to do with how *either* the one *or* the other person in an intimate relation should act and react towards the other party involved if that relation is to be mutually satisfactory and satisfying, and have less to do with their being peculiarly female attributes. 'Role reversal' is something that could quite well apply in respect to many of the points Rousseau in fact makes as being specifically about a woman's role (although he did not envisage this). Secondly, there is nothing to suggest that Sophie does not, and should not, have a general moral and social standing, which is concerned with her overall position in the human world, which is every bit as significant as Emile's. Her position is not to be confined to hearth and home, and elsewhere count for nothing. Admittedly, her enjoying as great a signficance as Emile does not amount, in Rousseau's eyes, to her enjoying that in just the same terms, in just the same ways, as he. And this may excite objection. But it is not the same objection as complaining that women are denied any general social significance overall, by Rousseau. It is true, too, that Rousseau lays special stress on a woman's significance for others in the home. But this is, again, not an exclusion of her possession of standing at any other time and in any other context, but an emphasis that, *if* certain child-bearing and rearing responsibilities are handled in a certain way, this special position in the home for a woman will be the proper result. It is a conclusion drawn from another ground, not a prior prejudice.

Rousseau in his life, encountered women in many different social stations, with widely various dispositions, expectations and attitudes. However, he endeavours, from this experience and on the basis of general reasonings as well, to distinguish what are 'unjust man-made' inequalities between men and women, and what are inequalities which 'the work not of prejudice but of reason' (E 5, 361; IV, 697). He maintains that, in respect of what they have in common, men and women are equal; where they differ they may be unequal, but not in virtue of the one having more than the other of what is proper to both, but rather in having different titles and powers because having different needs and requirements (E 5, 358; IV, 693). The root difference is sexual, in respect to the character of sexual desire, and role in sexual reproduction. From these physical differences, Rousseau argues, moral differences issue (E 5, 360; IV, 697).

Male sexual desire is easily roused, and when roused is impetuous, assertive, urgent and seeks physical possession. The place of the woman in respect of such male desire, as it relates to the instigation of procreation (cf. E 4, 316; IV, 639, on the importance of reproduction), is not that of putting the process in hand but in putting up little resistance to what male desire has initiated. But the woman has much power to regulate man's desire, a power which is related to the very different consequences sexual intercourse has for man and for woman. No woman can want to accept the insistence of man, willy-nilly, and thus it is:

> . . . an invariable law of nature which gives woman more facility to excite the desires than man to satisfy them. This causes the latter, whether he likes it or not, to depend on the former's wish and constrains him to seek to please her in turn, so that she will consent to let him be the stronger. (E 5, 360; IV, 695-6)

If man's sexual advance is not to become rape (which Rousseau explicitly denounces as 'the most brutal of all acts', E 5, 359; IV, 695), then he depends upon the consent of woman, and thus must please her. Her place in the sexual 'negotiation' consists in resisting in order to yield; she is not obliged to initiate the encounter; man readily does so already.

The difference of place of man and woman in relation to sexual desire and sexual advance does not, then, lead to subordination of the latter, but an equality of power, though power held on different bases. Woman govern while (seemingly) obeying (cf. E 5, 371; IV, 712–3). The consequences of sexual intercourse are, also, very different for men and women. If sexual union is to lead to the union of a whole family, a man must have confidence that he is the father of the children the woman he is united with has borne. This leads to further differences in the moral situation and standing of women; that she not only be faithful, but everywhere and by everyone be known and esteemed as faithful. Thus, there 'are reasons which put even appearances among the duties of woman' (E 5, 361; IV, 697–8) in considerable contrast with men:

> When a man acts well, he depends only on himself and can brave public judgement; but when a woman acts well, she has accomplished only half of her task, and what is thought of her is no less important to her than what she actually is. (E 5, 364; IV, 702; see also E 5, 417–18; IV, 780, on the different basis of Emile's and Sophie's honour.)

So it is that girls are governed by what will be thought of them, whereas the same motive has no such empire over boys (E 5, 365; IV, 704; see also E 5, 396; IV, 750–1). Boys consider what something is good for; girls what pleasing effect it will have (E 5, 376; IV, 719). Woman is 'enslaved by public opinion' (E 5, 377; IV 720) to an extent and in ways in which men are not.

Meshing in with these differences which derive from their role in reproduction and the implications of that for family unity, are differences between men and women in regard to the possession of 'station' (E 5, 364; IV, 702). This is given to women by men. (I presume Rousseau is speaking of economic and social status being acquired by marriage.) Men are more at home and purposeful in the affairs of the world; but women are more immediately practical in getting things done once what is to be done is known. So:

> The social relationship of the sexes is an admirable thing. This partnership produces a moral person of which the woman is the eye and the man is the arm, but they have such a dependence on one another that the woman learns from the man what must be seen and the man learns from the woman what must be done. If woman could ascend to general principles as well as man can, and if man had as good a mind for details as woman does, they would always be independent of one another, they would live in eternal discord, and their partnership could not exist. But in the harmony which reigns between them, everything tends to the common end; they do not know who contributes more. Each follows the prompting of the other; each obeys, and both are masters. (E 5, 377; IV, 720–1)

Rousseau is clearly aiming to describe a complementarity of ability, desire and disposition between men and women which is equally advantageous to each and makes their mutual dependence beneficial and agreeable to them. He nowhere suggests a one-way subordination which, in his view, would be hurtful to both. But neither does he suggest an identity of capability and role.

Some, at any rate, of his suggestions are detachable in principle from the gender assignments he gives to them. If they are so detached then they may, perhaps, be seen as suggestions about 'divison of labour' within a shared enterprise, and, as such, they may be worth entertaining.

Women's differing and greater dependence does not, however, entail that she should become self-estranged and the mere artefact of man's power or caprice. There is a proper integrity of nature in women which must not be violated (E 5, 386; IV, 736). The opinion which governs women must be, at all times, subjected to the 'inflexible' rule (of morality) 'for the whole species' which is 'prior to opinion' and 'judges prejudice itself' (E 5, 382; IV, 730). If this is not so then the esteem women give is degraded. The points made earlier (chapter 4, section 6) regarding the conditioning requirements for the value of Emile's love apply with equal force here. This implies, therefore, that Sophie (woman) can and does embody and enact the same principles of humanity, generosity and justice as the principles proper to her own nature and its development. There is no idea that women are morally 'less developed' creatures and cannot exercise full moral judgement (see E 5, 383; IV, 730[24]). Just as Emile does, Sophie values only that praise and admiration which displays real knowledge of true merit and honest love of that; 'Sophie is not constituted to give exercise to the small talents of a clown' (E 5, 399; IV, 754). So 'women are the natural judges of men's merit as men are of women's merit. That is their reciprocal right . . .' (E 5, 398; IV, 752; see E 5, 390; IV, 742). Even if a woman may have to 'endure' a man's injustice, she is not required to pass no judgement on it, nor has she no other standard than a man's to appeal to.

This is the outline of Rousseau's assessment of the position and manner of life appropriate to the characteristics peculiar to the sex of women. Sophie's particular education and the particular dispositions and accomplishments she is encouraged to are in conformity with these general indications, and I shall not discuss them specially. There is just one concluding point worth remark. When Emile and Sophie first feel their mutual attraction, and love springs up between them, Rousseau makes it quite clear that it is Emile who is the one who is most apt to degrade and debase the relation and to force upon Sophie a character (as his capricious tormenter, as a demon goddess) which is not hers at all but the phantasy creation of his own desire and fear. It is Sophie who firmly retains her proper character and continues to act and react in a true and honourable fashion, refusing the 'invitation' to become party to this destructive folly (E 5, 424ff; IV, 789ff). It is Emile who becomes an enemy to himself and would bring down Sophie with him (E 5, 443; IV, 815–6), forcing her to comply with the insane demands of his jealousy, for instance (we may think of Othello's demands on Desdemona). However much Rousseau may fail to see clear and true about the character and standing of women, he does not attribute to them any complicitous part in the instigation of men's perverse sexual phantasies, and, in that, he may have something right.

## 8 Recapitulation and Prospect

We have behind us, now, all the major substance of Rousseau's account of man in his moral relations with other men' (E 5, 455; IV, 833), which comprises his assessment of the grounds and ways by which man becomes an integral part of his species, gaining his own proper completion thereby. Rousseau has hoped to show how the incorporation into oneself of having being-for-others can be achieved in a way which enriches and enlarges the possessed life and well-being of the individual, and need not issue in the radical deformation and enslavement which so standardly attends to the (mis-)handling of this aspect of our being. It will be useful, at this point, to make a brief review of the arguement since, as I shall suggest in a moment, the results of it are foundational for Emile's (any man's) assumption of 'civil relations with his fellow citizens', which assumption comprises the concluding moment of his possession of his being and situatedness in all departments of human life, which I shall be moving on to consider. One is reminded here of the five cardinal virtues in Greek moral theory: courage, temperance, justice, piety and wisdom. It has been suggested,[25] that one of the underlying thoughts that dictates the drawing up of this 'list' is that, looked at in a certain light and taken fairly broadly, each of these virtues comprehends one of the principal areas of human being and self-activity; and together they comprehend all of them. It is possible to suggest that Rousseau, consciously or unconsciously, was following this same patterning. Thus: 'temperance' comprises right disposition and activity with regard to the things that are good and bad for oneself in one's physical being, properly mindful of one's overall good as a separate individual. 'Justice' is the comparable virtue concerned with one's standing and relations to other people. 'Piety' concerns one's right posture before the gods (this will be considered in chapter 7). 'Courage' is a generic virtue, which concerns one's resolve to hold fast to the right rule in the face of difficulty, and pain, making each several virtue a virtue 'in the strict sense'. Finally, 'wisdom' presides over all, as the source and measure of truth for each and all in coordination. Rousseau, then, may be understood to follow this pattern (in considerable measure at any rate) in his consideration of the phases and aspects of Emile's completion as a person in transaction with all elements in his world.

*The* question of morality is this: what significance should the being and needs of another (of others generally) have for one in moderating, redirecting and supplementing one's desires, feelings, attitudes and behaviour? How should others be incorporated and accommodated into the content and shape of one's soul and one's conduct? This question has an immediate complementary corollary: What significance should my being and needs have for others? These enquiries concern the content of the requirements of morality. There is also a second set of questions of equal importance to morality. What contribution, what addition or subtraction, to the quality of my life – to my felicity, to my sense of personal value, to the meaning of my own existence and the felt import of my life and my projects – would be made if I afforded to others that significance for me it is said (or: morality requires that) I should afford to them? And, complementarily, if they afford to me that significance they should? These enquiries concern the motivational 'hold' or 'claim' on the individual of the directives for dispositions and actions morality proposes.

Both sets of questions urgently require answer, and answers which mesh together. Precise directives proper to morality, proper to the moral importance of others, which, however, do not make any serious, supportable, claim to merit governing the actual choices and motives of individuals are left practically idle. On the other hand, proper motivational stringencies which are do not connect with the requirements of morality also leave morality practically idle (or else the name of 'morality' is given to whatever such stringencies turn out to be). Moral theory and moral practice tend to stand insecurely between these two alternatives: determinate requirements which are motivationally idle; or motivational potency, but without general determinate requirements, only individually relative ones. This is just a more general and abstract statement of the perennial issue mentioned before of the value of justice to the just agent himself.

Rousseau provides a remarkably compelling integrated answer to these problems. He shows that the sentiments of benevolence and compassion lead to an incorporation of concern for the fate of others' weal and woe into the dispositions and actions of the benevolent individual. Such sentiments, if they are genuine and do not seek to constrain or subjugate another, are apt to be met by gratitude which registers a sense of value and esteem for the benevolent person from the person he helps. Generalized and consolidated, this leads to a mutual bond of reciprocal care and kindness, and of justice and respect, for each and all. These comprise the principal requirements of morality in Rousseau's view: to receive and treat every several person with kindness and respect as their undeniable title; and to be received and treated likewise in one's own person. These are the duties of humanity and the dictates of justice.

Rousseau further argues that these requirements are not externally imposed demands which truncate or distort the individual's own proper self-articulation and expression of his vital life. The individual's benevolent sentiments disclose his creative and restorative care and power, are an expression of vigour of positive life and expansive force. They conduce to personal well-being directly, and also establish for the individual a necessary sense of his personal weight and power in human transactions. These aspects of his self-activity are further extended and reinforced both directly and indirectly by the status he affords to others and the return they make to him. The direct extension comes from his vesting others with value as moral persons of dignity, which doing, as it were, puts into his world humans who can reward his iving and involvement with them (one cannot value the company of those one has written down as fools or contemptible). But also, the return from them to him is now a meaningful and valuable return – the honour of honourable people. Thus his *amour-propre* is answered in and through granting answer to the *amour-propre* of others. The indirect extension comes from the reasonable expectation that as he has helped others in their need and difficulty so he will be helped in his. To be just, then, is both an immediate inherent direction of the 'law' of the individual's own true need and heart, and as such is a benefit to him. And it is also an indirect benefit to him, by the help and reward he may consequentially receive. Justice, kindness and the furtherance of personal good are inextricably mutually conditioned; there should be no opposition between them.

The sophistication of Rousseau's response to these issues lies, I think, primarily in two points. First, it lies in a deep and subtle account of the psychological structures and needs of individuals, and of how these involve constructions of the character and dispositions of others. From the start he shows how one's own significant reality to oneself is bound up with one's encounter with and standing for others. Secondly, and closely related to this, it lies in a penetrating assessment of the range and kinds of values, goods, needs that have significance for people and invest them and their lives with significance. No 'maximization of utility' for instance can begin to engage seriously with the depth and ramifications of humanity's desire for meaning. Rousseau does, I think, engage seriously with this desire. Above all, he recognizes that that 'atomism' of individuality and desire which pervades Anglo-Saxon moral and political theory does not constitute an axiom. He recognizes that the alienness of others that this presumes expresses self-alienation. And from self-alienated beginnings one cannot make any better sense of social and political life than one can of the life of the individual, or of the interrelations between these.

This is, then, the finished form of Rousseau's moral theory. It is not the finish of all his theories, for, as noted above, the 'civil' relations of man to his fellow-citizens have not yet been considered. This is the task of the next two chapters. (Emile's relations to the Divinity will need also to be considered.) It will be useful to consider in general terms, as a preliminary to this further material, how Rousseau sees 'moral' standing and relations in connection with 'civil' standing and relations.

I maintained, right at the start (chapter 1, section 1) that the requirements proper to the former, 'moral being', dictate and control the proper character that 'civil being' should have for man – Rousseau's view. I continue to maintain this, and hope to demonstrate the correctness of this assessment of Rousseau's mind in the matter. But there are some powerful counter-indications to this claim, and some of these should be looked at. Specifically, it may be suggested that, in so far as someone becomes a 'citizen' his civil titles and responsibilities must take priority over his moral titles and responsibilities, or else the individual will be 'above the law' – the positive law of the state – which cannot be possible since this would be dissolution of the state. Furthermore, it is inherent to being a 'citizen' that one's position and standing are regulated by the 'general will', which – whatever other obscurities attach to this notion – clearly implies that the individual must forfeit completely independent, self-determining sovereign judgement over what shall or shall not be done. For if it were not so, this would arrogate sovereignty to his 'particular' will, and this too is to imply no state. But, as we saw, it is proper to full individual moral completion that one is self-judging and determining in respect of moral demands. So it would seem the state must deny or limit moral standing. These two points are clearly connected, but not identical. The first implies a necessary subordination of an individual's moral standing to regulation by the state, without, however, specifying anything about the source, content and authority of the state's regulations. This might, for instance, derive from the moral titles of the state-comprising individuals, and this would – schematically considered at any rate – avoid the problem indicated. But the second point seems to imply that this cannot be so; an individual's regulation by the state is his regulation by the 'general will'. This appears to entail that he is necessarily subordinated to a rule which does not depend on his own moral titles alone, so in respect of its content and also its claim to be observed the individual's own moral sovereignty is displaced.

I have expressed these doubts tentatively ('seems to imply', 'appears to entail') because, if we consider the matter further, we see that Rousseau counters them more or less explicitly. His response to them does, in fact, decisively mark his treatment of the question of an individual's relation to the (claimed) authority over him of the state. Recall, first this. It is essential to any one individual's possession of moral standing and title that he acknowledge and respect the like standing and title of others, recognize and receive them as moral persons in their own right as they too recognize and receive him (the whole structure is mutual and reciprocal). But this means that it is 'built into' the moral consciousness of any one individual, and his exercise of it, that he is in transaction with other individuals who possess and employ a moral consciousness too, to which the same dignity and weight attaches as to his own.[26] If this is not so, human transactions are merely those of force, deceit or manipulation, no morally structured relations entering the case at all. We all know what it is like to encounter such terms of transaction, with individuals and with the actual acts of existing states. But it cannot be a topic of enquiry how an individual stands to the state on *this* sort of footing – the answer is too plain; he is merely subjugated by it. The only serious issue is: can there be a *legitimate* relation between the state and the individual? If so, what is its character, and how does its having that character make it legitimate? And in what way do 'moral' titles and claims determine, if they do, the legitimacy of the state's supremacy?

Since moral recognition of others is 'built into' the moral consciousness of any individual this has two crucial implications for his activity. First, the *content* of any proposed course of action which involves more than one individual alone may legitimately embody *not* just the moral assessment of what is to be done made by *one* of the individuals involved, but that of more than one of them. For their assessments may differ, and no one particular member of the transaction may reasonably claim that *his* assessment is and must be the one to determine the course for all. For that would be to deny the moral standing of the others involved. This means that any one individual may be morally obliged to do something which does not strike him, on the basis of his own discrete judgement, as the morally best thing to do. This is not a paradox, but quite obvious on reflection. The right outcome must be the outcome which honours the moral standing of all those whose conduct is to be regulated by the outcome. It can only do so if their moral standing is respected in arriving at that outcome, and in what the outcome requires from them. This, however, entails that any one individual may be required to do what was not, to put it crudely, his 'original choice'. But it is important to realize that this does *not* render him simply at the disposal of the group, perhaps in his turn called on to do what which flouts his deepest moral conviction. For if that were called for from him *his* moral standing would be being negated by the others. This is no more proper than his negating theirs would be.

On the other hand, to make any modification of one's 'original choice', in the light of others' diverging views, a non-negotiable challenge to one's moral integrity, the yielding of which would amount to a negation of one's moral standing is, in substance, to claim non-answerable despotic rule over the others, and that cannot be acceptable. It amounts, in practice, often to a kind of moral bullying. This opens to view the second implication which needs to be considered, which, bluntly put, is this. *Who is to decide* whether or not being required to do such and such, contrary to one's 'original choice', is, or is not, a negation of one's moral standing? What legitimate decision procedure, authoritative for everyone involved, is there for resolving issues of this kind?

The importance of the issue is clear. If the individual has the ultimately authoritative decision over whether being required to do such and such does constitute a denial of his moral standing then the others involved are denied moral standing at the last. If, on the other hand, the individual does not have this ultimately authoritative decision, then it is taken out of his hands and his moral standing may be denied to him, *and* he be denied any standing in objection to this. If the former obtains, the individual is above the state, and hence there is no state. If the latter obtains, the state is not limited in what it may demand of individuals, who are absolutely subjugated.

There can be no 'formal' solution to this dilemma, by which I mean a mechanical procedure for resolving such questions of ultimate authority avoiding either individual despotism or individual subjugation. If a mechanical procedure is employed, then the one or the other must result. The dilemma is avoided, in the sense that confrontation of it need not be forced up if, and only if, certain actual conditions prevail among those who are in transaction with each other looking for common courses of action; or, rather, it actually obtains that every single person *does* respect the moral standing of others and has his standing respected. If this is so, no-one will want to subjugate others to their own individual despotic rule; and others will not want to subjugate any one individual among them. It will, that is to say, in actual practice, be inherent to every person's footing with every one else that they are searching for an agreement to which everyone can give their accord, even if it may represent no-one's 'original choice' (as can easily happen). But is it essential to see that I am looking for the accord of someone who is looking for accord with me; and he is looking for accord with me as someone looking for accord with him. I am not, and cannot be required to, look for accord with someone who insists that their wishes, or moral views, are non-negotiable. Nor can they accord, or be required to accord, with me if I am despotic. In each case someone's moral standing would be being negated.

So the dilemma over the decision procedure is avoided providing that all disagreements over whether someone's standing has been denied are continuosuly addressed as issues to be resolved by a proposal to which every several person can give their accord, are so addressed by everyone who is party to that agreement. If this is not so, force or separation is all that remains. This being the dominant informing principle which directs the resolution of all interpersonal disagreements can be expected if, and only if, everyone holds their own moral 'sovereignty' in the terms Rousseau articulates. For it is inherent to the character of individual moral sovereignty, on his account, that it includes the like moral sovereignty of others. The manifest exhibition of that character will be the search by everyone for proposals for common regulation of action to which everyone can accord. Where things 'go wrong' is where one or the other of us approaches our divergencies without the will to find a solution with which both of us can be in accord. The power of Rousseau's idea is that the will to find such solutions is inherent to each our own possession of moral standing in our own person. One of the weaknesses of the standard 'liberal' solutions to the problem of common rule is that, whilst it insists that no-one subject to that rule must be oppressed (denied their individual rights) by it, there is no adequate account given of (a) why those on the 'winning side' (i.e. the oppressors) should *mind* that others are being oppressed, and limit their actions accordingly; nor any account given of (b) who has the right to decide whether or not oppression is occurring. Rousseau has, as I judge, given a powerful answer to both these questions.

We see from this two things. First, that the 'problem' of the individual's submission to a rule of which he is not the sole, non-answerable, deviser is answered from the core of Rousseau's theory of individual moral sovereignty in an absolutely consistent way. Second, we see the outlines, at any rate, of the conditions any rule must meet, if it is to be a legitimate common rule for many, these conditions also stemming from the core of Rousseau's theory of individual moral sovereignty.

Thus, so far from there being a discontinuity between Rousseau's theories of individual moral standing and sovereignty and civil standing and civil sovereignty, there is complete continuity between them, the 'civil' theory following from and being shaped at every turn by the moral theory. Rousseau's 'ideal' state does not diminish or circumscribe the moral standing of individuals in their own right; it, rather, gives final comprehensive embodiment and consolidation to that. It is only a false view of individual moral sovereignty (as personal despotism) which produced this representation of Rousseau's stance. But it is that view, not Rousseau's stance, which is misplaced.

Rousseau says (E 5, 448; IV, 823) that the question of Emile's 'rank' in the 'civil order', of the character of his civil 'self' (E 5, 455; IV, 833), arises when he contemplates becoming head of a family. The reasons for this are not spelled out, but presumably have to do with Emile's becoming, in that act, also a property owner, a person determining the inheritance of his children, the rights of a family and the like – all of which entail the order of civil society. But these points are not followed up in *The Social Contract*, so I shall not amplify them. I shall in due course, however, be drawing extensively on the precis of the 'science of political right' (E 5, 458; IV, 836) which Rousseau offers Emile at this time (E 5, 458–67; IV, 836–49[27]).

# 5

# The Self Indivisible from the Whole: Politics and Freedom

## 1 Introduction

It would appear that Rousseau first planned a (large) work on political institutions when he was secretary to the French ambassador in Venice (1743–4).[1] The first fruit of this plan, or one of its offshoots, was the 'Discourse on Political Economy', published in 1755 in Volume 5 of Diderot's *Encyclopedia*. (The First and Second *Discourses*, considered already, contain many observations on political power and government, of course. But there is little attempt to consider the problems raised by these in a systematically constructive way.) Rousseau's progress on his ambitious project was slow, however. He was working, from 1755 onwards, not only at that, but on *Emile*, on his novel *Julie* (*La Nouvelle Héloïse*), and on editing and excerpting the works of the Abbé de St. Pierre,[2] together with other smaller undertakings. About 1759, he decided to abandon his original objective and used parts of the material he had to form the basis for the work we now have as *The Social Contract*. This was published in 1762, the same year as *Emile*. There exists an earlier version of *The Social Contract* (usually called the Geneva manuscript) which, though incomplete, contains some additional material of value.[3]

Many books, larger than this one, have been devoted to an assessment of *The Social Contract* on its own. It is clearly out of the question to attempt a comprehensive treatment of it on that scale here. I shall select for consideration only certain issues it raises, but try to give to these a fairly thorough treatment. Naturally, I hope the issues I consider are the most decisive for a just understanding of the whole; but even if I have judged this right, I must acknowledge that certain parts of the book get very little attention here.

*The Social Contract* is Rousseau's best-known work, and the most extensively studied. Two errors of judgment arise because of this, however. First, it gives rise to the idea (looked at before, in chapter 1, section 1) that everything else Rousseau wrote on social and moral topics was written with its relation to issues concerning man's situation in civil society as the dominant guiding concern throughout. And that, furthermore, it is man's civil situation that is the primary circumstance for the whole of his being and situation, all else in which must be explained by reference to his civil conditions (as if being a 'citizen' was the decisive determining condition for all else regarding a person). Neither of these things is true regarding Rousseau's approach to civil and political issues. (It may, as a matter of fact, be that a person's civil condition dictates everything else about him and his life. But Rousseau would regard this as something objectionable, not the proper nature of the case.) Secondly, it gives rise to the idea that the central concerns, arguments and ideas of SC may be well understood and well defended without looking outside the ambit of that work. But this is really not so. Very much in the issues Rousseau sees as central, the desiderata he sees as bearing on them, the outcomes he favours, the material he appeals to defend his assessments, cannot be well taken at all unless seen as arising from and grounded in arguments canvassed in his earlier works, particularly *Emile* (which is, though published in the same year as SC, if not chronologically earlier at least argumentationally more foundational). When they are so seen they are better understandable, and Rousseau's overall thinking about political themes becomes much clearer and more convincing. I shall hope to show this in what follows.

None of these points amounts to saying that the assumption of the status of 'citizen' effects *no* alteration in the character of these more foundational modes of being a person possesses, e.g. as a moral person. A person who lives in a state is subject to the rule of positive law promulgated to him by certain bodies, and is subject to sanction if he fails to observe such law. Whatever else may pertain to his civil position this certainly does, and none of this has entered into the matters so far considered. The obtaining of these elements in a person's life-circumstances cannot fail to affect the position, titles and responsibilities he enjoys in respect of other activities and relations he is involved in (e.g. looking after his own self-preservation, making a livelihood, being a father and so on).

But the question Rousseau is now interested in is not the question of how being a member of an actual state does actually affect the titles, etc., of a person – this he has already considered and assessed in the most critical way. His question now is: what titles, powers, responsibilities, burdens, etc., should a person *fitly* acquire, be protected in or have demanded, as a member of a state? On the consideration of this question it is possible, and in the case of Rousseau's approach to it, certain, that matters regarding a person's *other* titles, etc. should have a bearing, indeed a decisive bearing. What Rousseau is in effect doing, I suggest, is exploring the ramifications and elaborations which these prior titles etc. must undergo if a person's incorporation into a larger community (the state), and his being made subject to state-promulgated law and sanction, is to be fitly, justly and well done. It is with these prior titles as a base and guide that he determines what are the proper claims and proper burdens that attach to someone's becoming a member of a state, a true 'citizen', not just someone who is actually borne down upon by the superior power of the agents of a group he cannot escape from or defy. The picture that will finally issue will not incorprate these prior titles in a form and manner which precisely matches the character they had before looking at their place and significance for a person in a state. But this does not imply that the shape and content of this final picture has not been governed throughout by the implications of these for the new situation now being considered.

Rousseau's principal concern in SC is, then, with the 'science of political right' (E 5, 458; IV, 836); that is, with an investigation of the grounds, procedures and principles according to which a person is rightly (justly, fitly) taken to be subject to an authority which is legitimate, one which is rightly entitled to promulgate rules of conduct to him, to enforce obedience to these and to sanction disobedience. He grounds his treatment of these issues, the central issues of political philosophy, firmly in his conception of the moral standing of persons. His primary contrast is with conditions of life in which a person is merely subjugated by a superior power which tyrannizes over him and which exacts obedience from him only because of inescapable force (compare DPE 132; III, 256). But he also considers, in order to reject, certain models of the relation between citizen and sovereign which depict this as a moral relation but of the wrong kind, in his view; e.g. as being like the relation of father and son (SC 1, 2, 166; III, 352).

My treatment of these problems, and allied ones, will take the following path. I shall concentrate, in this chapter, on what I believe to be the decisive elements in Rousseau's account of the foundation and character of a fitly constituted and regulated state or civil society. These comprise his notions of the sovereign, of the general will, of the citizen, and of individual freedom in the state. In the next chapter I shall consider further more specific and detailed aspects of his political theory, and look at how he envisages his conception of the good and just state being realized in historically conditioned circumstances. I have said already that several matters in SC will receive only passing mention which means that a wholly balanced account is not in view. But, also, this division of the material I am making may be misleading. It may suggest that Rousseau had in view some pure ideal form for satisfactory human communities, one which, however, he recognized would have to be comprised and limited in varying ways when faced with recalcitrant actuality. But this, though frequently asserted about Rousseau, is an unjust stricture. Rousseau throughout recognizes and plans for the fact that the realization, in the concrete particularities of the lives of particular peoples, of the requirements of a fit community would cause the institutions and procedures of such communities to differ. This is no more surprising than that, for instance, sentiments of

welcome, which are common in all peoples, should find differing expressions –
handshakes, embraces, gift exchanges and so on. One would hardly say that
the pure form of welcome was adulterated and deformed because there was no
one single universal mode of expressing it. So, somewhat analogously, is it
with the political requirement that for instance no citizen whatever be dis-
honoured or denied respect (compare DPE 127; III, 251). What the substantive
matter of honour and dishonour of a person is, naturally and properly may be
various whilst still fully comprising honour (or dishonour). It is no compromise
of Rousseau's principles that they take varied material realizations; it is proper
to their character that they should. It should not, then, be inferred that
Rousseau's ideas are 'all very well in theory' but in practice they must be
blunted and twisted. This may be true, but not just on the ground that one rule
suits the Poles another the Corsicans.[4]

My first concern will be to elucidate the character and significance of the
'general will' in Rousseau's political ideas. This is the single most important
idea in his theory of the good body politic and unless sense is made of this most
of the rest will remain dark. But, first, a few merely terminological points (see,
especially, SC 1, 6, 175; III, 360). Rousseau is interested in determining the
principles and procedures of a properly, justly and well ordered human community, every member of which is subject to one common set of rules for their
personal and interpersonal conduct, and in which observance of such rules is
enforceable and non-compliance with which is sanctionable. The ultimate
source of the rightful authority of those common rules, the supreme non-
accountable and non-answerable judge and director of all that transpires or
should transpire in the community, is the Sovereign. The composition, structure, modes of procedure and deliverances of the sovereign are clearly decisive
for everything else and will be what preoccupy me in this chapter. That set of
persons who are under the governance of one common sovereign constitute
the State, or body politic. As these persons contribute to the constitution or
determinations of the sovereign they are Citizens of that state. As they are
ruled by the deliverances of the sovereign they are Subjects of that state. The
exercise of the sovereign in devising, promulgating and delivering common
rules is its legislative authority or power, and its determinations comprise
Law. The administration or application of law to the subjects is the task of
Government (see SC 3, 1 and 2; III, 395–402). The officers of the government
are, taken severally, Magistrates; considered collectively they comprise the
Prince.

Some of these 'definitions' do not correspond exactly to ordinary usage
(which is anyway vague and imprecise); they may be regarded as stipulative.
This need cause no difficulty, since nothing whatever of substance is settled by
these terminological proposals, nor is it meant to be. (The only point worthy of
note is that the sovereign is defined as the *legitimate* supreme authority. I shall
call a supreme power – which may or may not also claim authority but

wrongly – a Tyrant or a tyrannical power.) So far as what has been as yet said goes, there may be no citizens in a properly constituted state. For it could be, for instance, that the persons under the authority of the sovereign should not contribute to its determinations; and those that do contribute to its determinations are not under its authority.

Everyone knows, however, that this last is not Rousseau's view of the matter. He holds that, in a rightly ordered body politic, the sovereign is comprised, in a certain fashion, of *every single person* who is to be properly counted as a member of the state. If someone lives under the direction of a sovereign of which he is not, in the appropriate way, a member then he is merely subjugated by the sovereign, not a subject or citizen and not bound by any *obligation* of obedience to the directives of the sovereign (unless he lives in the state voluntarily as a foreigner; see SC 4, 2; III, 440). As Rousseau says: 'The moment the people is legitimately assembled as a sovereign body . . . the person of the meanest citizen is as sacred and inviolable as that of the first magistrate . . .' (SC 3, 14, 238; III, 427–8). I stress that every several person (who may rightly be considered to be a true 'member' of the State and hence obligated by its requirements) comprises the sovereign *in a certain way*. It will be one of the issues needing careful consideration to determine the precise footing on which, and manner in which, each person goes to make up one 'indivisible part' of the sovereign (SC 1, 6, 175; III, 361). As we shall see, it is only in a particular character – bearing with them, as it were, only some among all their needs, interests, values – that people contribute to the composition and determinations of the sovereign.

For Rousseau, then, the sovereign consists of the whole people (given the rider made above). The sovereign establishes and declares law, and those same people who as members of the sovereign participate in devising and authorizing law also live under their law as subjects. Law, simply considered, consists of a body of directives for conduct, of 'thou shalts' and 'thou shalt nots'. Directives are, naturally considered, the expressions of volition or intent, and thus law may be considered as the declaration of the will of the sovereign. Thus the sovereign must be considered to have a 'will'; and the will of the sovereign in its legitimate and properly authoritative declarations is said to be 'the general will'. This specifies the structural position of the general will in Rousseau's theory. So the general will is the source of the legitimate expression of legislative power, the fount of genuinely binding law which lays an obligation of obedience upon subjects. It is *somehow* the outcome of the wishes of each and every several person who is properly a member of the state as and when they are properly assembled and appropriately determine issues as constituents of the sovereign. In addition to the volition, the will, of each member in their capacity and character as parts of the sovereign (their will *qua* citizen which is the general will), people in a state necessarily have another 'will', and *may* have also a third 'will'. That further will everyone necessarily has is their 'private' will, which, approximately, comprises that which they do looking to their personal advantage (or would resolve upon doing if they considered themselves just as separate, unattached, persons not united with others, not subject to any common rule). That third will which someone may have would be their 'corporate' will, as, for instance, a member of the government, in their character as magistrate. (They only 'may' have this will, since not everyone will be, or need be, a member of this or any sub-group (intermediate association) standing between the individual and the whole social body).

One's will *qua* magistrate, for instance, comprises that which one resolves to pursue in order to maximize the benefit that would accrue to one in respect of those projects that are one's just in virtue of being a magistrate – these projects that attach, constitutively, to the occupancy and discharge of *that* role (and no others). This is all set out at SC 3, 2; III, 400–1. There is nothing mysterious about the possibility of one person having different 'wills'. In one's life one takes many parts, occupies many positions. Some of these positions are partly defined in terms of the pursuit of certain purposes. Thus being a farmer is, in the now relevant sense, a 'part' a person may play. It is an element in the part (role) of being a farmer that one has the purpose of growing crops, for instance. If one considers what would be to one's advantage considering oneself *simply and solely* as a farmer, it would be to produce sound crops with little effort, which are saleable at profit, and so on (the details do not matter). This would be one's will *qua* farmer, which is one's corporate will along with other farmers considered solely as farmers. One's will *qua* farmer is not unique and individual to oneself. That same will is anyone's will in so far as they are (or are considered as nothing else but) farmers. My will *qua* farmer is just *a* farmer's will, the will of the farming profession. But, for most farmers, their being *qua* farmer is not the only being they have. They may also be 'family men' and, as such, have other objectives inherent to being one of those. Their 'will' *qua* family man may be compatible with their will *qua* farmer, or it may not. Also, it is quite likely that there is no one common sheaf of purposes non-controversially attaching to being a 'family man'. So even if you asked someone to disclose their will 'as a family man', it would be injudicious to take it that what he said could be taken as the exemplar for what '*the* family man' as such thinks or wants. (The same problem may in fact occur also for what 'the farmer as such' thinks and wants.)

Both these last points apply to Rousseau's cases too. Firstly, he notes, indeed stresses, that there will appear to be not only differences between a person's 'private' will (his will *qua* separate, unique individual) and his 'civic' will (his will *qua* citizen, his will just as any arbitrary citizen), but also conflicts between these wills. Thus:

> In fact, each individual, as a man, may have a particular will contrary or dissimilar to the general will he has as a citizen. His particular interest may speak

> to him quite differently from the common interest; his absolute and naturally
> independent existence may make him look upon what he owes to the common
> cause as a gratuitous contribution, the loss of which will do less harm to others
> than the payment of it is burdensome to himself . . . (SC 1, 7, 177; III, 363)

So Rousseau must consider, as a matter of urgency, what relations there are
between these differing wills, and also what claim to priority the one or the
other has (likewise for a 'corporate' will, if it comes into the case). Do those
objectives one has from one's 'private' will have authority over those one has
from one's 'civic' will, or *vice versa*? If the latter have priority over the former,
does it not follow that law, as the declaration of civic will, oppresses the
individual, and so forfeits any rightful title to obedience? But if the former
have priority over the latter, does this not make the individual into the sovereign and dissolve the sovereignty of the state? Clearly some harmonization or
reconciliation must be achieved here.

Secondly, although he is not wholly explicit in his defence of this point in
these terms, Rousseau must be holding that the 'civic' will of *any one* member
of the body politic can stand for that of *all* members. That is to say, there is a
non-controversial, determinate and uniform set of objectives which attach as
such to the position of being 'a citizen'. So that if two people, each claiming to
speak 'as a citizen', make different declarations, one of them is mistaken in his
claim and is not speaking 'as a citizen'. For *were* he doing so he would, in the
same moment, be speaking 'for all citizens' all at once. Since another person,
also (claiming to be) speaking as a citizen, dissents, one or the other must be
mistaken. (See, regarding this, SC 4, 2, 250; III, 440–1, about mistaking the
general will.)

There is indeed a prior issue even to this one. For we have little idea yet as to
what are supposed to be the definitive characteristics and purposes which
mark out what 'being a citizen' comprises, what being just any one of 'the
people' amounts to. For instance does it attach as such to being 'a citizen' that
one is concerned for one's own security and well-being – is this a concern
constitutively proper to one *qua* citizen? Or does this attach only to one's
'private' will in one's 'absolute and naturally independent existence'? Is one's
'civil' will as such only to be for one's security and well-being in so far as a like
measure of security and well-being is compossibly attainable by, or provided
for, others? Clearly such questions must be looked at and resolved. Upon their
effective resolution much will hinge concerning the relations and proper
priorities attaching to one's private and civil wills. Rousseau's resolution
proceeds through his account of the basis of the 'general will', in its relation to
the will of every individual who is properly to be taken as a subject of its
declarations (a subject of law). It is, therefore, to the elucidation of this we
must now turn.

## 2 The General Will

My procedure in explaining the idea of the general will will be this. I shall draw on only some of the many remarks and explanations Rousseau offers of this notion, and from these excogitate an account of what he means by the idea, spell out some of its implications and ramifications etc. I shall then try to confirm my account by showing that it makes sense of other things Rousseau says about the general will, of the consequences he draws from it, and so on. Obviously I cannot examine every point that attaches to this notion; there are too many to consider. But I hope to do justice to the principal claims, and to resolve the principal problems. This will not be simply a process of showing the internal coherence of Rousseau's ideas (though this has often enough been denied, in any event). I shall hope to show that the account that emerges is of a powerful position that does not 'float free' of political realities or human possibilities but firmly and clearly engages with these.

I draw on four pointers to Rousseau's meaning in this matter. First, there is his remark that for a will to be in very truth general (and hence legitimate) it must 'both come from all and apply to all' (SC 2, 4, 187; III, 373). (A better translation would be: it must come from all *in order to* apply to all – '*pour s'appliquer à tous*'. This will be taken into account.) Second, there is the more general thought that the general will is intended to issue in rule 'by the people, of the people, for the people' – in some sense of this much used phrase. (Theodore Parker, to whom the first explicit use of this phrase is attributed, attaches such-like rule directly to the possession of freedom. We shall see Rousseau's way of making this connection in due course.) Third, we must always carry in mind that what dictates the formation of 'civil associations' (SC 2, 6, 193; III, 380) is, in Rousseau's view, the individual person's inability to sustain his life unaided (SC 1, 6; III, 360). A primary concern which each and every person therefore necessarily brings to the issue of devising the terms and conditions of their association is the hope of bettering their lot through that association. No-one can be furnished with a reason for participation in an association with others, for submitting to the common rule for the conduct of all associates, if he is not made better off at least in respect of his initial need than he would be left by remaining on his own. Submission to the terms of association alone is an added burden. If there is that burden, and a worsening of a person's lot from what it was previously, he has achieved nothing but a dual burden through his participation. No-one can ever have reason to take that on. No-one can be rightly bound to an arrangement that imposes that on him. This is a *minimum* condition to be met by any association which can claim the legitimate title to order the conduct of its associates:

The security of individuals is so intimately connected with the public confederation that . . . that convention would in point of right be dissolved, if in the
State a single citizen who might have been relieved were allowed to perish . . .
For the fundamental conventions being broken, it is impossible to conceive any
right or interest that could retain the people in the social union; unless they were
restrained by force, which alone causes the dissolution of the state of civil
society. (DPE 131–2; III, 256; see also surrounding comments)

Finally, and connected with the foregoing, there is Rousseau's repeated
point that the terms and conditions which establish and constitute an association of men, which are to be law to the members, must, in the first instance, be
determined *unanimously* (SC 1, 5, 173; III, 359: SC 4, 2, 249; III, 440). This
means that every single several person who can properly be taken to be a
subject of the fundamental law which establishes the being of that association
must give, for sufficient good reason, their assent to the provisions of those
terms and conditions.[5] We have just seen above *one* good reason that must be
provided to every several person if they are sensibly to give their assent; their
material lot must be bettered by their participation in the association. Other
reasons for giving assent will emerge in due course.

Two points arise from this last preliminary which I want to mention before
proceeding with the main argument. First, it must be stressed that the assent
of every several person must be grounded in good and sufficient reasons (and,
come to that, their dissent must also be, if they dissent). This is for the
following reason (among others). People can and do, in actual fact, give their
assent to practically anything, whether or not they profit by it, suffer by it, or
whatever. Confusion, ignorance, blind passion, misguidedness can distort
someone's assent in the most drastic ways. No-one would, or should, want to
take their assent, given under such conditions, as indicative of their advised
acceptance of the terms and conditions of their participation. (See SC 1, 4, 169;
III, 356). The least we must require, if their assent is properly to amount to
their acquisition of an obligation to observe the terms etc., is that they know
what they are doing and elect to do that well appraised of its significance and
good to them. We must require, in short, that they assent on good reasons.
But this gives rise to an acute problem, namely: who is the judge of whether or
not assent on good reason has been given? If the agent himself, then the
requirement that it be on good reason becomes quite empty. If, on the other
hand, someone other than the agent is the judge of the adequacy of the
reasons, then the requirement of actual assent falls as irrelevant. For sometimes assent will be ignored as ill-advised; sometimes dissent will be dismissed
as, in reason, groundless. It is the 'dictates of reason' (however these be known
and embodied) which determine the fitness of the terms and conditions in the
last resort, not the assent of persons.

This is a serious dilemma, to which we shall have to return. Sometimes
Rousseau addresses it from one side, stressing actual assent. Sometimes he

approaches it from the other side, stressing the reasonableness for every single person of what is proposed as sufficient to show its legitimacy, their assent or dissent being immaterial. I think that in the end, greater emphasis falls on this last point (as, in my view, it should). But that Rousseau is of uncertain mind on this matter seems to me quite proper, since it is one of the most difficult and taxing points for political theory in general.

The second issue arising concerns majority decisions. Rousseau argues correctly that the obligation of obedience to a decision reached by a majority can only come from prior reasoned assent to the procedure of resolution of issues on the basis of majority decison (see SC 1, 5, 173; III, 359). This directly entails, however, that certain issues must remain exempt from majority decision, namely the fundamental constitutive principles of association. For it is possible – indeed it happens often enough – that a majority determines to dispossess a minority and render their circumstances worse than they would be were they not party to the association at all. But in that moment the bond of association dissolves, there is no obligation of obedience to the decision, and a relation of mere force and subjugation remains. If majority decisions are legitimately to bind, it can be so if, and only if, they leave certain conditions sacrosanct and operate within the limits of these. Once those limits are breached, the authority of the majority ceases. The state must put certain interests of every single one of its citizens beyond the competence of majority decision or else subvert its own authority, and become a tyrant. This point is not well-observed in many actual states, and other human associations.

I return now to the main argument. The most useful pointer to start from to find the sense of Rousseau's notion of the general will is provided by his idea that for a will to be, in very truth, 'general' it must 'come from all and apply to all'. If we reflect on the meaning this bears, we shall be taken to the heart of Rousseau's conceptions. I start with the 'apply to all' side of the question, and I shall use a simplifying model. I shall suppose that we begin with a hundred several separate persons who have no mutual ties at all; they participate in no cooperative action; they have no moral or affective bonds; and so on (compare E 5, 463; IV, 844). We are to try to understand the basis, procedures and principles, on which such an aggregation of persons shall come to be so interrelated and connected that they comprise 'one body', 'one people' of which each person is a one-hundredth part. In particular, we need to understand how there can be a body of rules determining the standing, titles, duties, conduct, relations of each person which legitimately commands the obedience of each. What basis should such rules have? By what procedures should they be arrived at? What provisions should they embody? Rousseau lays it down as one condition of their legitimacy that they 'apply to all'.

The primary significance of this is obvious: every rule is to bear on the same level terms on each and every single one of those hundred people. No-one, that is to say, is to be 'above' the rule (above the law); i.e. no-one can say: this is not addressed to me, I am not one of those who falls within the scope of application of this. But note that this only refers to the like level of encounter of each and every one with the rule. It does not say or imply that the concrete provisions of the rule lay identical requirements on every one. It may be identical for everyone in being a requirement; but what it specifically requires may not be just the same from everyone. Thus, the rule 'Let anyone over six feet tall have mastery of anyone under six feet tall' is laid as a requirement identically upon everyone. But what it requires from those over six feet is quite different from what it requires from those under six feet. It is quite certain, of course, that Rousseau would think such a rule as this absurd and iniquitous. But we must be clear that his principle that rules must 'apply to all' does not, by itself, exclude it. Nor, indeed, does he want to exclude *all* rules which make differentiations among the titles and burdens which fall upon different kinds of persons in one association (see SC 2, 6, 192; III, 379 on privileges). He did not think that all the rules which applied to all had to contain provisions which were precisely the same in their content and results for every single person. In this sense, at any rate, he is not committed to 'egalitarianism'. But which rules embodying provisions which differentiate 'classes of citizens' would be regard as acceptable, and why? The governing principle here is that they must be rules which 'come from all', and this will be explained when that part of the matter is considered.

Rousseau also wants to exclude rules which, in their provisions, identify named individuals. (The application of the general principles of association to individuals is the function of government or magistracy; the principles themselves do not identify individuals). He seems to think that this exclusion is implied by saying that the rules must 'apply to all'; but it is not. For some such rule as 'Let everyone promote the interests of Queen Elizabeth the Second' can levelly apply to all (including the Queen). And, just because its provisions fall differentially on people (the Queen will be serving her own interests, other people another's interests), that cannot exclude it automatically since, as we have seen, Rousseau lays no absolute embargo on such rules. I suggest that, in the case too, the exclusion of the rule will be procured by the implications of the requirement that legitimate rules must 'come from all'.

All that the requirement that, to be truly general, rules must 'apply to all' dictates, then, is that no-one is to be exempted from the scope of application of the rule – all are to be equal in coming before the law. The *content* of the law may direct different lots for different persons. But the question of which differences are acceptable, which are not, is not determinable by this requirement alone (except, trivially, it will exclude such rules as: Let so and so, or such and such a kind of person, not be covered by this rule at all). The principle that the rule 'come from all' determines this. I now consider what this signifies.

The model I have suggested now requires some elaboration. Let us suppose that each one of the, as yet unassociated, hundred persons endeavours to ensure their own survival and well-being without any collaboration with others at all (cf. SC 1, 6, 173; III, 360). We then further suppose that this proves effectively impossible, alike for each one of them. (The questionableness of this supposition – that each person suffers just like difficulty – will be responded to later). The only remedy that lies to hand is some form of concerted action; the 'sum of forces' then available will make possible a betterment of their material lot, a relief of what I shall call their 'natural burdens'. Each one of the hundred seeks relief of his natural burden; no-one could advisedly add to their natural burden the 'conventional burden' of compliance with the requirements for concerted action without appropriate recompense. Principles for action must then be devised in concert which will, whilst adding a burden, produce a benefit for each greater than that burden *and* the natural burden suffered. Such principles will have to specify: Who does what? Who determines who does what? What discretion remains to individuals regarding what they do, when, how, for how long? Who gets what? Who determines who gets what? And so on. Rousseau's claim then is that principles which 'lay down the law' on such questions are proper and legitimate, do oblige each person to obedience of them, if, and only if, they 'come from all'. What would this then signify? My procedure will be to consider various aspects and ramifications of this notion, one after the other, which will lead to a final statement of the significance of the notion of the general will, given in section 6, below.

### 3 Coming From All and Decision Procedures

Their 'coming from all' naturally suggests the idea of a procedure or process by which the principles are evolved, proposed and agreed to, or ratified, by every person who is going to be party to the system of concerted activity. The principles 'come from all' in that each person, and every person, has been the author, the originator, of the principle in some way. The idea of a procedure for arriving at commonly applicable principles, out of the proposals that each person intended to be subject to those principles puts forward, is prominent in Rousseau's arguments. It has, intuitively, obvious bearing on the question why one should be obliged to obedience to a principle. For if it is one you yourself have proposed as the right, or best, way to proceed, why you should follow the requirements of the principle seems quite plain – it was what you wanted and intended anyway. The idea that you might be under an obligation to follow this course of action seems almost redundant. What need is there of obligation to direct and compel action when desire speaks for it anyway? Also, the idea that there need be enforcement agencies, sanctions, to bring about compliance seems almost redundant. If obligation and sanction had any proper contribution to make it could only be to cause people to keep faith with their own intent, to 'remind' them, as it were, of what they wanted to do when they were beset by, say, temptations or distractions. One might say that obligation and sanction would 'force' them (as and when it might prove necessary) to do what they really wanted to be doing, when distractions and disturbances were not troubling them.

This last point is reminiscent, as it is meant to be, of Rousseau's saying that being compelled to obey the general will is only forcing someone to be free (SC 1, 7, 177; III, 364). This has always struck people as one of his most notorious remarks, as revealing the concealed totalitarianism behind his talk of liberty, equality and fraternity. Obviously, we are not yet in a position to understand fully what he means in saying this, and his reasons for doing so. But the point just made above gives a firm pointer to his sense, and will be drawn on later.

There are three clear reasons why the picture of how decisions are made given above is not sufficient to the case, as it presently stands. First, I have spoken as if the principles and determinations which are intended to regulate the conduct of every one, and establish an obligation of obedience on them, simply issued from *one* person. If this were so, then if he and the others got on with their designated tasks, he would be getting things as he wished them to be. But would the others? Very likely not. And even if they were, could it be said the principles 'came' from them if they did not actually have any hand in devising or ratifying them? (It is only on one apparently very implausible supposition, which I shall return to, that we could expect to avoid conflicts between the proposals for all the people made by different members of that (prospective) 'people'.) If there were conflicts, and one person's idea carried the day, then another person or persons would not be getting what they want. And how could their complying with someone else's proposal really amount to their being 'forced' to do what they 'really' want, to their being forced to be free? Even if a compromise were reached, that would seem to mean neither person was getting (all of) what he wanted. Whilst it is easy to say that it was not reasonable to expect to get that under the circumstnaces, it is equally easy to resent one's having to step down from one's maximum bid to find a lesser, compossible and commonly acceptable way. If it is only unpleasant necessity and ungrateful circumstances that are imposing trade-off, there is no need to continue to make that trade if one can find a way not to. To say that would be 'unfair' is true, but idle. For where is the ground of the claim that what is 'fair' should be the governing principle for one's conduct? (cf GSR 160; III, 286). If a principle of 'fairness' is enforced on each of us, is this not mere imposition, not liberation? And where is the element of 'fraternity' in this? Is there any cause in any of this to see one's accommodating one's co-workers as anything other than an unfortunately necessary demand?

What apparently implausible supposition would avoid (some of) these difficulties? It is this. That each several person will or could devise, on their own instigation, a set of proposals intended to direct the conduct of all (including themselves), and each of these individually conceived sets of proposals (i) gives each person everything they want; (ii) is compossibly realizable without compromise or loss to any one. If this were so, there would be no conflict, no circumscription of desired objectives inflicted by the need to 'make terms' to secure cooperation. And enforcement of the rules on any one would, in every case, be in effect to recall them to doing what – by their own declaration – they really wanted. But that this should occur would appear to be nothing short of a miracle – that there should be this spontaneous compatibility, compossibility, of each person's proposals for everyone. If one founds the possibility of legitimately binding law on the obtaining of this possibility, then the likelihood of there ever being legitimately binding law is very slight indeed. Furthermore, even if this minor miracle did occur, it does not yet give us any basis for supposing that amity or fraternity might pervade the relations of those who compose the body politic. The obtaining of such-like relations might be a *precondition* for there being any real hope of congruent proposals being made. For, in that situation, my desires will, to some extent, incorporate the furtherance of your good as my project already, and *vice versa*. But, so far as we consider the outcome only, we might just as well have a set of wholly self-absorbed and self-concerned people, each about their own self-referring business, but in a way that happens to be compatible and compossible. This could not meet Rousseau's idea of a 'bond of union' in society (SC 4, 8, 273; III, 465); in effect, no 'union' has occurred, only separate lives but along shared paths, or compatible paths.

Despite all of this, Rousseau believes in, and argues for, a version of this 'minor miracle' as I shall show. It should be clear, however, that whatever version of it he espouses, it cannot take the simple form just outlined – that would be too unconvincing. But it will be a little while before we can see what version Rousseau does argue for, and whether it can bear scrutiny.

The second reason why the initial picture of the relation of an individual to social proposals for all which 'come' from him is not satisfactory is this. We saw earlier that if someone's assent to a proposal is to signify anything, is to establish that he has an obligation of obedience, for instance, it must be sensible, well-advised, rational assent. Now we can take it as evident, still given only the elementary model invoked so far, that each person making proposals to and for everyone's conduct will be trying to devise proposals which do actually succeed in bettering their material lot – to aim otherwise would be senseless (compare DPE 148; III, 273). But, even with the best will in the world, they can make mistakes about this. It is possible, indeed, that such proposals might be assented to by each one and be 'put into effect', so to say. But, by this, one person – or even many people – may have devised for themselves a seriously damaging outcome (See SC 2, 3, and 2, 7; III, 371 and 381). This possibility cannot be denied; it has very important implications, parallel to those considered regarding assent looked at earlier. For it needs to be determined that someone is making a sensible, well-advised, rational proposal that will actually bring benefit to them. And it needs to be stated who has the right to, or who is in a position to, make this determination.

The individual by himself and for himself cannot be this person; if he could, the present issue would not arise. We could evade the issue and say that it really is up to the individual, to make whatever he makes of it. But that is to allow individuals in effect to consign themselves to serfdom. Rousseau certainly does not take this view; nor, I think, should we. But if it is taken out of the hands of the individual, into whose hands can it properly be taken, and what protection or defence could the individual have against things done in the name of his own good but which he does not at all recognize as containing any good for him? In any event, if this second line is taken, the idea of there being any actual procedure for actual individuals devising and proposing rules drops away. At best there is in view some 'ideal' procedure, of purely rational beings making wholly well-advised proposals. But, then, talk of a 'procedure' is only figurative. All that need be said is: these are the proposals that right reason recommends. Assemblies, voting, secret ballots, and so on cease to have any material relevance at all. The *whole* weight of the issue becomes: what *is* 'right reason' in these matters? Who determines what 'right reason' consists in and requires? If, then, any one individual, (or, perhaps, every one of them?) does not recognize the principles devised as incorporating and furthering what they can recognize as their good, then they are merely wrong, deluded, irrational and need not be heeded (on this score at least).

People view this consequence with reasonable enough alarm. But how is it to be avoided? Before responding to this question, I want to mention the third problem with the initial picture. It is closely related to that just presented, so does not require much additional comment. Whatever procedure may be employed to disclose a rule that comes from all, it can happen that the rule which is hit upon and ratified does, in its actual provisions, dispossess and oppress some members of the association – that is, some of those people who count as 'members' of the association. Are they obligated to obedience? In terms of participation and assent, yes. In terms of following courses of conduct hurtful and depersonalizing to them, no – or not obviously. For no one can 'give himself gratuitously' (SC 1, 4, 169; III, 356). It follows, then, that not only in terms of the *procedure* for arriving at and ratifying the terms of association, but also in terms of the actual *content* and provisions of the terms arrived at, the interest, needs, values, etc., of all (of every one) must, in some appropriate way, be accommodated and reckoned with. If this is not so, there is a conflict in relation to obligation that the supposed subject incurs. In fact, I think, the latter condition (concerning content) takes precedence over the former. For an act of assent to be 'devoured' by the association is 'null and illegitimate' being, in effect, the act of one 'out of his mind' (SC 1, 4; III, 356, again). This is one further reason for supposing that participation in some form of procedure for arriving at rules applicable to all is not the crux of their legitimacy, is not the decisive mark of their 'coming from all' and being the declarations of a truly 'general will'.

But how can the 'alarm' mentioned above be quieted? If we consider the basis for the anxiety carefully, we can see some very important ways in which it can be allayed, which have significant implications for the question of legitimacy of the rule of the association (the laws of the state). The source of the anxiety is this: we cannot take an individual's having initiated a proposal for the terms of conduct of every one in the association as finally settling the question of his 'will' in the matter.[6] For he may be muddled, have unsettled judgment, etc., and make a proposal actually hurtful to himself (and, quite possibly, to others too). Nor can the individual be the final judge of whether he has done so or not. For that would empty the first point of any real content. It follows then that some other person or persons, or some 'abstract standard', must be appealed to determine someone's 'true will' in the case. Those same persons, or that same standard, stand or stands as final judge. (Appeal to an 'abstract standard' is, in fact, largely spurious. For the meaning and implications of any standard need to be mediated and interpreted by the minds and judgement of people. Therefore, other people inevitably must determine and stand as final judges on these matters.) But the result of all this is that the individual is now 'at the mercy' of those others who tell him what his real interest is. If he protests, his remonstrances are dismissed as being misguided and ill-founded. So he loses any real grip on devising or checking the principles by which his life is, none the less, regulated and to observance of which he is supposed to be obligated. How can this be tolerable?

The first thing to observe in response to this difficulty is that every state does, as it must, utilize some normative standard of practical reasonableness (of more or less determinateness) by which to judge, and sometimes find against, the reasonableness some individual may *claim* for his behaviour or proposals. 'The man on the Clapham omnibus' plays such a role in many cases. Every state must utilize some such standard(s), because no state can accommodate, nor need it accommodate, the proposals of, say, a true paranoiac suffering from acute delusions. Nor can it be obliged to answer the paranoiac, on his own terms, to show him that – as *he* will see it – what he is required to do is for his good. The key question is: *how far* can a state move away from such cases before it starts illegitimately denying rationality to individuals, and improperly overriding their avowed intentions and assessments of their own good? I do not see how to provide an abstract, general, answer to this question. The closer an association, in devising the principles of its life, sticks to the 'raw' declared proposals of its potential members the less the likelihood anyone will feel (and be) not taken into account, at the point of 'drafting' so to say. But, equally, the greater is the likelihood that some people will actually suffer unduly under the proposals, unless we suppose an exceptionally far-sighted and carefully collected participating membership. Further, if we suppose even a moderate diversity of ambitions, hopes, preferences among these clear-sighted participants, the number of points on which each and every one will be able, on their own estimation, to agree that they would be advantaged by an arrangement which included that component, would be quite small. It would relate only to pretty pervasive, basic, aspects of each person's life, aspects which affected them just as much as they affected anyone else, despite 'higher-level' divergencies of intent and ambition in regard to what each thought was their good.

With very rare exceptions, each person has an interest (an actual interest as well as a normatively rational interest) in their physical preservation and in having the necessities of life. Also, each person has an interest in enjoying scope for proceeding about their own elected life-project (perhaps, also, in having resources available for furthering this). On these very basic matters we may expect a fair amount of actual instantiated rationality – people who reliably enough foresee, and turn down, proposals which preclude these possibilities to them. So, if a proposal is going to be able to gain the like assent of every one it had better legislate only for such basic things, in such a clear way that virtually everyone can see that they would be better off than they would be if they remained outside the association. If a proposal is more specific, some will feel that they are being required to do what is not to their advantage (as they estimate that) or prevented from doing what is to their advantage (as they estimate that). And they will deeply resent any suggestion that their own estimations are misguided, irrational, and need not be taken into account. The scope of legitimate legislation is, thus, fairly restricted; it touches only the very basic, very widely shared, features of every several person's life – the rest must be left to individual discretion. (Note that all of this still sets aside the issue why I should settle for less than all I want for myself just because I cannot win the agreement of others to my doing so. We shall, of course, return to it).

Rousseau, in fact, speaks as if a legitimate state will tend towards the 'minimal', in so far as that notion indicates what I have just outlined. He writes: 'Each man alienates . . . only such part of his powers, goods, and liberty as it is important for the community to control . . .' (SC 2, 4; III, 373). Admittedly, the sentence goes on: 'but it must also be granted that the sovereign is sole judge of what is important', which seems to void the earlier remark of serious force. But I think we should take the first part seriously. What Rousseau is looking for is not a state which will, or should, legislate for every single minute particular of every person's conduct. Except with a rare, largely preselected and self-selecting, potential membership any such sovereign would be a tyrant. The legitimate scope of sovereign legislation will be confined within certain limits – confined, crudely, to the basics for the life of each person. The reason the sovereign must judge what 'it is important for the community to control' is that we are now familiar with. If the individual judges, no limit on the individual is established. But, by the same principles I have just been sketching, the sovereign's judgement about this can adhere more or less closely to the consensus of the actual verdicts of its constitutive members. The closer it sticks to these generally the less it will judge to be important that the individual should cede control over to the state. For the wider it extends its claims, the less likely it is to command the assent of every one. But, on the other hand, the closer actual assent is taken as the rule, the more likely it is (with ordinary, muddled, people) that harms and mistaken judgments will occur.

The pointers that emerge from considering the sources of the 'anxiety' noted are, then, these. If the actual assent of everyone is the initial baseline for proof of general acceptability, then the fewer the exclusions of people's proposals (as misguided, irrational etc.), but also the fewer will be the matters on which agreement to legislate will be achieved (given ordinary human diversity in 'life-plans'). These matters will be largely issues of basic human need. The likelihood of mistaken provision is increased (given ordinary limitations of judgement), so that people harm themselves, and/or others. But the likelihood of resentment and denial of any obligation to obedience (however misguided these responses may be) is lessened. So a high level of compliance may be hoped for. All of this is, I should judge, fairly commonsensical.

Where does Rousseau stand on this? I have already quoted a passage in which he suggests that the scope of sovereign legislation will be limited, and not control every aspect of each person's 'powers, goods, and liberty'. Also, when he formulates (in SC 1, 6; III, 361) the problem which, he says, he is principally addressing in the work, he mentions only the protection of 'the person and goods of each associate' as the primary task of the association. These, and other comments, suggest he does have in view legislation which will regulate as little as possible compatible with effectively furthering these objectives; and that therefore, in terms of the provisions enacted, his vision of the state tends towards the 'minimal'.

On the other hand, there are many places in *The Social Contract* and in his other explicitly political writings where Rousseau lays great stress on the 'bond of union' between the associates who comprise the community, the need for them to come to 'love' their duty to their fellows and their community. He extols patriotism as necessary and good for the vital life and well-being of a community, and argues for the need to have a 'civil religion' (see SC 4, 8; III, 460) to add extra force to the claim of the law upon the people;[7] and so on. Some of these matters will be considered in more detail in the next chapter. Here I want only to consider their general bearing on Rousseau's ideas about the scope and detail of provision of the laws bearing upon the lives of the community-constituting associates.

It is clear that they all point away from the impression that Rousseau had only a 'minimal' state in view. All that the associates of a minimal state are envisaged as having in common is that each of them alike encounters the same basic problems with meeting their needs for self-preservation and security of life. Beyond that, their loyalties, allegiances, loves and hates may be widely divergent. To put the matter only weakly and informally, the interest and commitment any one person can bring to the project of giving aid or relief to another person when he finds very little indeed to sympathize with, feel shared love and loyalty to, in the life projects of the other is bound to be very weak and limited. It is not in human nature to want to give of oneself, or to limit oneself, greatly for the sake of the well-being of others if one feels no common cause, common destiny, common allegiance with them.

We should recall here that passage from *Emile* (E 5, 362–3; IV, 699–700, quoted above in chapter 1, section 1) where Rousseau says that 'the love of one's nearest' is 'the principle of the love one owes the state', and that it is 'by means of the small fatherland which is the family that the heart attaches itself to the large one' – that is, to the state or one's community at large. Now, the model I have been using, effectively the one which Rousseau himself uses in the opening chapters of *The Social Contract*, makes no special use of the idea of family affections and ties when characterizing those who are prospective associates together in one community. So we cannot make a literal application of this point from *Emile* to the case in hand. However, the broad import of it for the present matter is clear enough. Unless there is some unity of mind, feeling, loyalty pervasive among those who are prospective associates together making up a community *prior to* their endeavour to form themselves into one body politic, the 'conventional' tie of common citizenship which subsists between them will have little vital meaning for them. Its requirements will seem imposed burdens not invitations to pursue a personally cherished end, an end which incorporates the well-being of others as part of one's own. This is in effect to say that not just any miscellaneous random aggregate of men constitutes, in Rousseau's estimate, apt material for state-making. If, in every matter beyond their having the same basic needs, they are quite strange and alien to each other, it will seem to none of them a worthwhile or desirable objective to attend to others' need alongside attending to their own. The laws of the community will require them to do so in varying ways and measures. But, to repeat the point just made, this will appear no more than an imposed demand which, merely in default of there being any alternative, must be submitted to. It will not constitute a project to which they would willingly give their attention and labour.

As an issue in practical statecraft Rousseau seems to me right in what he says. (These points will be taken up again when studying his proposed constitutions for Poland and for Corsica, in the next chapter.) However, there is more at issue here than that alone. If we uncover the additional matters which are also involved, we shall finally see the full basis and full force of Rousseau's theory of the nature and significance of the general will which comes from all.

## 4 The Obligation of Obedience

The first point to recollect is that the concern is to find terms of association to which each and every associate will have a genuine, well-founded, *obligation* of obedience. We need to be very clear about the basis for any obligation here. It is crucial to distinguish this from merely being 'obliged' to do something, as, for instance, when a fall of rock on the road 'obliges' you to take another way.[8] I shall call these 'natural constraints'. The question is: have any of the points so far considered regarding the individual's need to associate with others, and his need in the light of this to establish and comply with terms of association with others, formed the basis for any obligation? Or have they simply comprised natural constraints?

It is clear that they have only comprised the latter. The need an individual has to act in concert with others is a mere practical necessity imposed on him by his inability to provide for his own self-preservation unaided. Likewise, if those from whom he seeks help are not willing to give it him without return (and why should they be?), then he will be obliged to give aid to others in return for the aid they give to him.[9] But this, too, is as yet only a natural constraint. He cannot get away with taking all the time and giving nothing. Nothing so far established shows that someone has any obligation not to try to take advantage of others if the opportunity exists for him.[10] He may be unable to get away with this; but there is no ground as yet to suggest he is under an obligation not to try to do so when he can. Finally, even if terms are settled upon to regularize the gives and takes of the association, terms compliance with which is backed up by sanctions, the individual is still only naturally constrained to compliance, so far as what is so far contended for goes.

It may at once be objected that saying this misses out something quite crucial to these latter two aspects of the case. For surely, it will be said, the requirement to give in return for what is given is not only a natural constraint, but also an obligation: it is a requirement of justice (or, perhaps, of gratitude) that one incurs an obligation to make return for services (voluntarily) received which are not given as a gift. Not to do so is to be a cheat, or free-rider, or whatever.

All of this is quite true, at an ordinary level. But, in the present context, it introduces several further aspects to the case which need to be made plain. First, it presumes that the potential associates putatively comprising the civil body relate one to another not just as 'hands' in the meeting of material needs, but also as moral persons. That is, each presents himself to the others as having certain titles, the right in justice to receive in return for what he gives, for instance. Each demands that he be recognized by the others as possessing such titles and received and treated accordingly. So each expects others to accept certain duties towards him; and each must realize that others will expect him to accept certain duties towards them. Thus both certain entitlements and duties of justice as well as the desire to meet basic material needs are brought by each potential associate to the issue of devising and acceding to any proposed terms and conditions for their association with others.

Again, it will be objected that the terms and conditions which determine the relations of associates in any 'finished' association will not only be *de facto* constraints and strategies of mutual accommodation which cannot, under normal circumstances, be evaded. They will be *de jure* principles of conduct for each associate because each has, in some fashion, pledged himself to abiding by them, has made some kind of undertaking to observe them. The assent made to the terms and conditions is some sort of morally obligating commitment or quasi-promise made to the other associates (as they make also to you, and so on round) to do things in the way arrived at.

This, too, is a pretty familiar picture of the case. But, as with the point just looked at, it adds additional dimensions to the situation. For it requires, first of all, that the potential associates are capable of and willing to enter into morally binding undertakings with one another, i.e. that they are possessed of moral powers and are capable of assuming moral responsibilities. It also suggests, second, that the form that their mutual reciprocal moral responsibility of obedience takes is some form of contract or quasi-promise. It is importnt to note that it *need* not take this form. Thus, for instance, the moral responsibility I incur to help someone injured in the street is not incurred by a promise or contract of mine to them. Nor, again, do the obligations of children to parents have a promise-originated grounding. But perhaps Rousseau thought the obligation of obedience to the terms of association in any legitimate state was grounded in some sort of contract or quasi-promise. For, after all, the book is called: *The Social Contract*. I shall, however, soon suggest – as I have in several places implied already – that Rousseau does *not* consistently represent the ground of the associates' obligation as contractual. In fact, I believe that in his deepest thoughts he did not consider the matter in these terms. Thus the title of the book misleads as to its principal contentions. Other matters need to be resolved, however, before this can clearly be seen.

From the preceding points it can be inferred that we must regard the associates potentially comprising any body politic not merely as bearers of natural needs, but also as bearers of moral titles and moral capabilities. The terms of their association must, therefore, take the latter into account, in some appropriate fashion, just as much as the former. It is certain that Rousseau saw the matter in these terms. The frequently made assertion that Rousseau did not, or could not coherently, believe in the existence of individual moral rights prior to and independent of positively established civil positions is the result of several mistakes. First, it arises from an error regarding the character and circumstances of 'natural man', that he is a savage, merely physical being, with little understanding and even less moral awareness. I have, I hope, thoroughly disposed of this misconception in earlier chapters. Second, it arises from an error about the significance of rights held prior to civil association. Such rights are, of course, usually referred to as 'natural rights'. But the 'natural rights' tradition has one prominent strand in it from which Rousseau dissents, namely that the individual, even when in community with others and a subject, reserves certain of his rights to himself, in particular the right to judge the actions of the sovereign; and, on the authority of his own inherent powers and titles, to dissent from these and declare them illegitimate, hence having no force of obligation for him. In Rousseau's view, if such a right were reserved, this would place the individual above the sovereign of the state, and the sovereign of the state would have authority only by the pleasure and permission of the individual. The individual would, in effect, claim sovereignty to himself. But that would completely deny the reality of the state. It is a mistake to infer that because Rousseau denies this strand in 'natural rights' thinking, he denies natural rights altogether. He does not. Each potential associate brings to the issue of devising legitimate terms for his association with others natural moral titles and claims, which must be fitly accommodated if the conditions of association are not to be tyrannical. But it is a necessary part of the way in which they *can* be appropriately accommodated that no one associate reserves the right of judgement to himself in the matter just outlined. For, if he did, each other associate would, in effect, be placing himself as subject to that one. Therefore, it is a necessary condition of legitimate terms of association that no associate reserves such right of judgment to himself. That is why Rousseau says that the 'clauses' of the 'social contract' reduce to: '. . . the total alienation of each associate, together with all his rights, to the whole community . . .' (SC 1, 6, 174; III, 360). Note that this remark evidently states that each associate *does* have 'rights' before membership of the community, which he cedes ('alienates') to the community. Here, as in many other places, Rousseau is quite explicit about the existence of pre-civic individual rights.

This idea of 'total alienation'[11] arouses dismay. For surely if I wholly transfer my rights of judgement, rights of self-determination and action away to some other holder of these do I not make myself wholly helpless and defenceless against their control and judgment of me? Is this not to give myself into slavery? Rousseau himself denounces slavery emphatically (SC 1, 4; III, 355). So what is going on here? There are three points to make which should resolve this perplexity.

First, the 'holder' of my totally ceded rights is *not* some other particular person. The holder of my totally ceded rights is the sovereign, and the sovereign comprises nothing other than every single member of the association (related one to another in certain determinate ways, still to be specified). While

I wholly transfer away all my rights, so also does every other one of my potential associates. Our ceded rights are given over to possession and direction of a 'public person', the character, powers and scope of which the associates themselves devise, 'create', in their proposals for their terms of association, precisely to be the secure repository of these rights. This 'public person' will redeploy them now as rights (re-)invested in the individuals as their *positive* rights as citizens (SC 1, 6, 175; III, 361). It has no prior character and powers at all. The composition, organization and procedures of this 'public person' consist in certain modes of relation and transaction between the community-constituting individuals, serving in their positions as members of the sovereign. No other party is involved.

The second point is this. Each potential associate may propose a different constitution for the sovereign body to which all associates are totally to cede all their rights. Some such proposals will, in Rousseau's estimate, quite evidently not be for a conceivably legitimate sovereign body. Thus, for instance, I might propose that I be established in the state as absolute, non-accountable, despot, and everyone else be my chattel slave. No-one else could have reason, on the ground of their material need and original moral titles, to accede to such a proposal. The only proposal regarding the to-be-established position of 'citizen', to which each and every potential associate could have just the same weight of reason for acceding, would be one in which each had an absolute guarantee that he would not be worse off than he would be by remaining outside the association; worse off in terms of (a) the amelioration of his material lot; and (b) his possession of an effective power to utilize his pre-civic moral titles and standing. If any potential associate has good reason for supposing either (a) or (b) to be false then he has no reason to accede to the proposal. If he is, none the less, taken under the control of the sovereign he is merely subjugated. (Note: 'has good reason' to suppose this, not just thinks this, however confusedly or irrationally.)

Thus there is a very stringent control on what could be a legitimate constitution for the sovereign, in establishing the office of a 'citizen'. No setting down of the powers and responsibilities that shall comprise the office of 'citizen' can be legitimate unless each several potential associate has good reason to wish to become a 'citizen' as so defined, in terms of the conditions (a) and (b) sketched above. (There may be several equally legitimate possible constitutions of 'citizenship'; there is no reason to suppose a unique solution meeting these requirements). Thus, each potential associate has very good reason not only to suppose that his pre-civic material lot and moral titles will be *matched* by his positively established material lot and civil titles, but to suppose that these will actually be improved upon. For instance, he will have more economic resources to draw upon; and he may have, say, public force to call on to help him in the defence of his person against violation of his rights, not having to rely only on his own self-protective efforts.[12] If this were not so, the claim of the civil order upon him would be illegitimate and establish no obligation. This is one more reason for supposing that ceding one's right will not issue in one's enslavement. For one is entitled to withold relinquishing them until clear good reason exists for one to do so when the terms proposed improve one's natural lot and possession of one's moral position.

Despite this, each person will be powerfully struck that the terms on which he holds an improved natural lot and a strengthened moral standing are said to be legitimate if, and only if, these terms are compatible with, or imply, also a bettered natural lot and strengthened moral standing for each other associate too. (The improvement each enjoys need not be identical. The minimum condition to be met is that no-one be worse off. This is consistent with some being better off than others, providing they are not so in a way that enables or entitles them to reduce others to destitution and ignominy; see SC 2, 6, 192; III, 379, again. But it does require the sure meeting of the minimum condition, and this entails a base-line of improvement which each person must enjoy alike.) So each potential associate is likely to think that whilst in some ways his moral standing and effective possession of his moral titles are strengthened, in other ways they are weakened. For he is abandoning his title to be, for instance, 'sole judge of the proper means of preserving himself' (SC 1, 2; III, 352) and becoming governed and ordered by a rule which has to be satisfactory in the judgement of many, and not just him alone. And this does appear to mark a severe loss of personal sovereignty, of title to self-direction and personal right to judge.

This leads to the third point which needs to be considered. I have shown, in chapter 4, that it is Rousseau's view that the conception of 'personal sovereignty' which grounds this supposed difficulty is a mistaken one. For it is the conception of the individual's possession of his moral standing in terms of his having the titles of a despot, not called upon to recognize and reckon with anyone else as also a morally titled being. But, as we saw, this conception of the moral titles of the individual vitiates its own coherence. It is a condition of my own full, secure, self-possession of my moral personhood that I acknowledge and meet others as morally titled persons also. This entails, as explained, that it is inherent to the proper constitution of my own moral standing that I cannot rightly require or demand that I decide and act without reference at all to the being and needs of others. It is an inseparable element in the constitution of my own moral consciousness that I respect and negotiate with the needs, requirements, titles etc. of others, to find a course that wins common assent between us, or does justice to the needs and titles of all affected by it. It is not just that if I arbitrarily dismiss or override you I violate your moral status and rights, though of course I do. The crucial point is that, in doing this, I violate my own moral standing and vitiate the basis my own position. The law of respect for others as moral persons is the law of my character and need in my own moral personality.

It thus follows that if I am required to follow a rule which has the common assent of all, not just my own isolated assent, I am *not* automatically being denied my proper sovereignty. On the contrary, the requirement to follow rules of that character is a requirement inherent to my full possession and exercise of own moral sovereignty, properly understood. Thus Rousseau can say, as he does in different ways in different places, that the law which is law only because it has the assent of *every* person subject to it is the law appropriate to the moral claims of *each* single person who is subject to it.

Thus, for Rousseau, there is no radical and problematic discontinuity between the individual's sovereignty over himself and his being subject to a common rule which is not devised and authorized by him alone without any reference to the needs or titles of others, but is one devised and authorized by as many as are to live by that rule, in a certain appropriate fashion.

In order to show how these three points, particularly the last one, reinforce Rousseau's insistence that for legitimate and effective sovereignty the prospective associates in the sovereign and as subjects need some measure of unity in loyalty, sentiment, common attachment prior to the formation of themselves into a civil body, we need to recall further points discussed in chapter 4. There I considered Rousseau's assessment of the grounds and motivational source for each of us of the claims upon us of the needs and titles of others, that is of the claims, ultimately, of impartial justice upon each individual. In Rousseau's account the principal mode of incorporation of the need of another as an active and valued component in my own concerns and desires, in a fashion that will not arouse anger, resentment, domineeringness, etc., on my part, is through the sentiment of compassion. The benign elaboration of the human relation instigated through compassion includes the return of gratitude; and there is, as we may say, role-reversal between the pitier and the pitied person on many different occasions. In this mutual reciprocal interchange is established the accepted significance of each person to the other, as being a person worthy of respect and an object of active concern (see, once more, E 4, 227; IV, 514, for instance). This yields to each that knowledge and feeling that he is recognized and reckoned with as an ineliminably tellilng human presence for others which he requires for his own sense of his own reality and value and for his happiness.

The requirements of justice, which require us to respect and honour those who are in no special relation to us, do not move our immediate feelings and so on, are an elaboration and extension of the dictates of respect for the humanity of another which are inherent to this foundational situation. If these more extensive requirements are to draw our understanding and feeling assent, they must never be severed from their root. Continuity must never be lost with the vividly experienced circumstance of finding your own significance in affording significant actuality to the need and standing of another in the relation of pity and gratitude. If it is, the abstract claim of the right of another may receive notional assent. But the real importance for my own moral standing as a human person of acknowledging that right will not be appreciated. As soon as I feel another to be alien to me, to have nothing to do with me, to be a creature whose sufferings do not touch my own weal or woe because his enjoying well-being is no component of what I also need to have for myself to be well, then the requirement to accommodate such a person will be to me only a chafe, an imposition.

Rousseau summarizes these points in the footnote to E 4, 235 (IV, 523). There Rousseau clearly says that 'it is not true that the precepts of natural law [here, the precept to do unto others as we would have them do unto us] are founded on reason alone'; their 'true foundation' is 'conscience and sentiment'. The application of this to the formation of a legitimate civil community is that the terms and conditions of that community cannot enjoy legitimacy and the willing assent of the associates unless they are known and felt to direct them to objectives for each other the good of which they can sensibly experience. We can only do so if others are for each of us not remote, unknown, strange. They must be, in some tangible enough way, close, known, familiar and recognizable fellows. It thus follows that, in Rousseau's view, the only suitable sorts of potential associates to make up a legitimate civil community will be those who share already some measure of fellow-feeling and a sense of a common, intertwined, fate and destiny. The legitimacy of law will become more problematic the more remote and alien to each other are the persons comprehended under that one law.

Of course it is a principal object of the terms and conditions of association also to foster and confirm sentiments of mutual loyalty and mutual care as part of the pervasive climate of the continuing life of the community. But, Rousseau's point is, this cannot begin from nothing, grow up where there is nothing ready in the 'human soil' for such growth. The absurdity of public ceremonials of communal identity and communal life which follow on, say, the triumph of one side after a long and bitter civil war bear out his point. It is equally obvious, however, that many relatively stable actual states are far from containing, in their basic material, the sorts of shared sentiments Rousseau thinks are necessary to legitimate sovereignty. It is possible to believe that this is not a fault in his views, but in fact a fair diagnosis of some of the problems that beset cosmopolitan societies.

## 5 Freedom and Obedience

It is a direct implication of Rousseau's view that the full possession and use of personal moral sovereignty does not preclude, but in fact requires, following rules which take others into account, and receive their assent, is that there is no loss of personal freedom in the very fact of not being the sole, non-answerable, arbiter of all my projects and actions. The dictates of one's own moral character direct one to following a 'common' rule – if I may loosely call it that. So in following such a rule one is doing precisely what one is disposed to do as one is disposed to do it in that character. The unimpeded expression in action of one's own character and disposition comprises free action. Therefore freedom and living by a common rule imply each other, and are not incompatible. Providing, then, that the laws of one's state stand in a proper relation to the moral dictates of one's own character, being subject to those laws is in fact one's own fully free self-expression. Deviation from the law will be a constriction or distortion of free self-expression. So, the obligation to comply with the requirements of law will be an obligaton to refrain from placing oneself in bondage. One will, in short, be being forced to be free, by the imposition of the requirement of law upon one (SC 1, 7, 177: III, 364).

This is a brief exhibition of what Rousseau intends in his famous comment that 'whoever refuses to obey the general will shall be compelled to do so . . . This means nothing less than that he will be forced to be free' (ibid.). In order to engender conviction that he has here a serious view it is however necessary to expand the argument a bit. The nerve of the issue lies in the point that the laws of one's state must stand in a 'proper relation' to the moral dictates of one's own character. I have not yet said what this relation must be like in order for it to be appropriate in the relevant sense. I am still engaged in the process of working this out. We shall, however, finally be ready to see what it must be like if we work out quite carefully what significant notions of freedom are involved here. If we do so, we shall see how personal freedom and even imposed compliance with a common rule are not only not incompatible, but the former may require the latter.

Behind these surface concerns there is another issue which is worth bringing out. It is a particularly striking feature of the activities of states that they deliberately, out of policy, inflict sufferings and deprivations on (some of) their members which they call 'punishments'. States regard themselves as acting legitimately in inflicting these hurts; indeed, they may regard themselves as obliged to do so. Furthermore, the state claims if not a monopoly on the infliction of such hurts, at least ultimate authority and control over their infliction. Thus a state does not (normally) deny a father the right to punish his child; but, if the father does so in a way or to an extent the state judges improper it will take itself to be entitled to intervene, to check the father or even to punish him in his turn. For some infliction of hurt to be a punishment, and not mere violence, it must not only be deserved, but brought about by some person or agency who has proper authority to record, and treat people according to, their (relevant) deserts. It therefore is an urgent question how the state acquires the authority to appoint agents entitled to do this, whom we should not perceive as agents of violence or brigandage, but authorized officers meting out punishment.[13] How on earth can someone be appointed by me to visit hurt on me? I would seem to be insane to make any such appointment. It would seem, roughly, that this can only be sensible if his visiting hurt on me is something I am committed to willing on myself in some way. How could I be committed to this? A possible suggestion is: I am committed to it by my own principles of action. Thus, for instance, my own principles of action may commit me to the following. If I violate the rights of another he is entitled to demand from me some acknowledgment that I have wronged him, and stand in a supplicant position to him. I can supplicate for restoration of my rightful standing if, and only if, I take some penalty, accept some burden in recogniton of the burden I have inflicted on him. However, he is not alone the sole judge and executioner of the penalty; this would give him despotic rule and power over me. Thus, some person or agency must take charge of the restoration of the ruptured relation between us, if he and I are ever to recover a legitimate mutual footing. The acts of that agency constitute punishments, hurts I am, in this fashion, committed to authorizing. Furthermore, if it is true that in wronging another I am equally acting contrary to the dictates of my own moral character, then it is my own moral character which is restored to intactness by punishment. I am returned to oneness with my own true intent – I am caused to do my own bidding, and thus am caused to be free.

Thus, I suggest, alongside Rousseau's more general concerns with citizenship as opposed to servitude, sovereignty as opposed to tranny, there is also a convergent concern with what makes the regulatory actions of a state proper punishments and not just public violence. The discovery of the grounds of the former distinctions promises a ground also for making the latter distinction.

As I suggested in chapter 4, we need to distinguish three effective notions of freedom in Rousseau's work. I called these circumstantial freedom, elective or discretionary freedom, and principled freedom. The first of these requires little additional comment. A person's physical circumstances, the hardship of his environment, his lack of tools and other means, can preclude him from carrying out his wishes, can severely circumscribe his opportunities of action. Hunger and illness may weaken the agent too, so that his abilities are reduced. All of these comprise impediments to his action, limit his freedom of action. As Rousseau represents the circumstances which impel people to association in civil community, they are severely hampered in providing for their own survival. Their material insufficiency is at the same time a circumscription of their circumstantial freedom. The improvement in their material situation each hopes for from association with others is at the same time a hope to increase their circumstantial freedom.

Elective or discretionary freedom has two aspects. The first, less significant here, comprises the power to regulate the dictation of present impulse or desire, in view of some believed future good or harm which present action on desire would affect. This was discussed before (chapter 3, section 3). The second aspect is the important one here. This concerns the individual's (supposed) right, title to be called to answer to no-one but himself for what he proposes to do and does. The individual who enjoys maximal discretionary freedom decides all matters according to his own lights (on his own preferred basis), following his own modes of appraisal, reaching his own decision upon which he acts unchecked and unquestioned. At no point is he required, because the proper subject of another or of any abstract rule, to justify, vindicate or otherwise explain his choices and conduct. The individual is accountable solely to himself for himself.

Should we accept that, in a pre-civic condition, each individual enjoys maximal discretionary freedom? If this were so, then any terms of agreement for concerted action between such individuals would, if they are to continue to allow to each individual his maximal discretionary freedom, be such as the individual can, at any time, reconsider his involvement with and acceptance of these. If, when he does so, it seems best to him to sever his relation, he has an absolute title to do so, for if this were denied him his discretionary freedom would be denied him. If, on the other hand, each potential associate believes that the association will be in permanent danger of collapse because of individually determined secession, then each may utilize their discretionary freedom to cede it to some person or body to serve as the final authorized judge above them. This is not an incoherent choice, although it is one which someone who values his maximal discretionary freedom will want to be very careful in making. He will want the most stringent and powerful safeguards built into the terms of his association to try to ensure that whilst having abandoned his title as absolute judge he will not, thereupon, be abused as titleless slave. But he cannot retain the right to judge whether those safeguards have been properly observed whilst, at the same time ceding his discretionary freedom. For, at the last, he is still reserving that to himself if he claims the title to pass such judgment. If this be so, the individual still places himself above the law. No other individual can be willing that just one of his associates does this, for that would involve his acceptance of servitude to that person as being the arbiter of the terms between them. If one demands this, all have the same reason to. But then the state has no existence. It has existence only if none do, and all alike put their faith, as it were, in the safeguards within the state, which are in the custody and under the judgement of the state, working effectively – that is in fact producing a mode of life congenial to them.

It follows, therefore, that if there is to be any genuine sovereignty of the state, and the state is not just to be the agent of an individual under revocable licence at his discretion, the association-constituting individuals cannot enjoy maximal discretionary liberty. Such discretion as they retain, for instance over their manner of dress perhaps, is retained by the judgement and allowance of the sovereign (cf, SC , 2, 4, 186; III, 373).

To this it might be objected that surely the legitimacy of the actions of the sovereign are capable of being authoritatively judged. If the whole body of the people object then sovereignty is revoked. But this is confused. First, there is no such 'entity' as 'the whole body of the people' until we have determined the terms and conditions of the constitution into one 'body' of the numerous several bodies of different individual people. If one person breaches the law he is a criminal; if a sub-group of the members of a state do they are bandits. If the 'whole body of the people' do, then, indeed, the law is dissolved. But we only have such a thing as the 'will of the whole body of the people' if we resolve the very issue for which this is supposed to present a difficulty. For *precisely* what is being determined is how several persons become 'one person' with its own proper will. Secondly, and obviously, the sovereign, for Rousseau, *is* 'the whole body of the people'. So, taken in one way, the sovereign cannot be revoked, since one cannot revoke oneself. But, taken in another way, the sovereign can, at any time, revoke itself – for the whole body of the people *is* the final arbiter, answerable to none, so can modify its will as it pleases. For Rousseau, it is the *government* which is the licensed agent of the sovereign; the sovereign can at any time revoke the rule of government at its own discretion, as he explicitly says (SC 3, 10; III, 421; SC 3, 18; III, 434). But that is quite a different matter.

We need now to look a bit more closely at the internal workings, so to say, of the exercise of discretionary freedom. The individual is, in this case, the sole arbiter of his choices and conduct. But we can distinguish different terms and ways in which he utilizes this title of sovereign self-judgement. First, he may elect to follow his every whim, mood or fancy as it strikes him; such is his right if he so determines. I shall call the individual's governing principle of action in this case his 'fancy'. Second, note that if he acts like this he often enough hurts himself, does things which obstruct other inclinations he has, and so on. Thus he forms the idea of his own best interest (according to *his own* notions and estimates of what this might consist in), and seeks to regulate and direct his conduct to the achievement of this. I shall call the governing principle of his actions here his 'actual will' – actual because it is his actual avowed preferences and avowed conceptions which inform his conduct. But third, we have also the idea that someone's own notions of what will serve him well and bring him lasting reward and a sense of fulfilment and personal completion may be muddled or misleading.

It would be improper to anticipate any political 'misuse' which might perhaps be made of the idea that there could be a mismatch between a person's own estimate of what will see him well and what will in actual truth do so, in order to deny the reality of any such distinction. The reality of the distinction is undeniable: it is commonplace that we place our hopes for happiness or a sense of personal achievement in things which on attainment yield us nothing but dust and ashes. It may, I grant, be undesirable to make anything of this when devising social or political procedures. For it is by no means obvious that anyone else, or any agency, is less liable to mistakes of this kind than the individual himself. And if other hazards attach to taking the matter out of the judgement and control of the individual agent, for instance the hazard of his being imposed upon by a superior power, then a dual suffering may supervene. On the other hand I think this is always only presumptively better left to the agent. If sufficiently clear evidences and reasons exist for believing the agent will be doing himself no good at all by continuing as he is, we can be justified in intervening in one way or another; we may even be under an obligation to do so. I shall say that someone's actual will derives from his 'envisaged good' – that which he envisages, by his own lights, as good. I want to contrast with this (and the contrast need not amount to a total discontinuity between the two) his 'proper good' which I shall say forms the basis for the determinations of his 'enlightened' will.

Does someone's posssession and employment of discretionary freedom ally with the impulses of his fancy, the decisions of his actual will, or the (possibly hypothetical) determinations of his enlightened will? Or perhaps with some further alternative? Maximal discretionary freedom over the inclinations of fancy would be of little significant value to the agent, so we may put this aside. Is such freedom of permanent value to the agent in relation to his actual will? If we accept anything of what Rousseau has argued so intensively – that our actual will may be dependent on beliefs, attitudes, feelings, interpretations of ourselves and others which are very self-destructive and damaging in their effects upon us – then we can only be very tentative in replying 'yes' to this question. It will all depend on *what* desires, attitudes etc. informs and govern the decisions of the actual will. If inflamed *amour-propre* directs these, then maximal discretionary freedom would be a bane not a blessing. If our desires and beliefs are 'natural' and true, in Rousseau's sense, then it would be a great good to us. If our will is guided by, or embodies, 'practical wisdom', as Aristotle would use that notion,[14] then discretionary freedom is a good to us. If it is not, then it can be at best a mixed good. Using the familiar, if slippery, distinction between 'liberty' (good) and 'licence' (bad), we may say discretionary freedom allied to an enlightened will is liberty; allied to the actual will it may be only licence.

We know, from earlier argument, that it is part of each our own proper good to enjoy secure possession and use of our standing as moral persons among other moral persons. This requires us to afford to others honour and respect in as much as we want honour and respect for ourselves from them. Our enlightened will must, then, direct us to the achievement of this situation for ourselves with others. But this entails that we employ our discretionary freedom as allied to our enlightened will, to move to a situation where we forgo maximal discretionary freedom, and place ourselves under authoritative arbitration that has sovereignty over us (and over others). The outcome of the use of discretionary freedom grounded in knowledge of our proper good leads to our coming to rest in 'principled' freedom as our real asset and need. 'Principled' freedom is the unfettered scope to utilize one's power of choice and action to the pursuit of objectives, courses of conduct, that have the endorsement of right reason, as that is judged not just by oneself alone but by whatever person or agency is the custodial interpreter and arbitrator of what the requirements of 'right reason' actually amount to.

'Principled' freedom is not, therefore, any *diminution* of discretionary freedom and its replacement by some alternative. It is what discretionary freedom *itself* comprises when it presides over the pursuit of one's proper good under the direction of one's enlightened will. What suffers diminution is discretion over one's 'actual' will. But since, by the exercise of one's actual will, one can, and does, lead oneself into bondage, the bondage inherent to inflamed *amour-propre* primarily, being circumscribed in one's discretion over this is no diminution in one's actually enjoyed scope of freedom in oneself and one's actions. One may resent this circumscription, and believe one is being fettered. But one is not, in actuality, being fettered; one is being prevented from placing fetters upon oneself, and being caused to retain one's liberty. This is what it is to be 'forced' to be free. To continue to insist that one has absolute, non-answerable, final decisive authority without regard to anything beyond one's own say-so is not the zenith of personal liberty. It is to mistake despotism for liberty; and Rousseau has thoroughly explored the roots and ramifications of that mistake.

The issue comes to this. If we rest with maximal discretionary freedom allied to the actual will, then any need to come to terms with others will amount to submission to force, or a *faute-de-mieux*, or just unavoidable practical necessity. On any view, there will be, in this case, an unwelcome diminution of freedom. But maximal freedom on these terms is, at best, a dubious personal advantage. We may, instead, suggest a basis for coming to terms with others which involves no imposition of force, and no mere acceptance of no better. This is where there is mutual reciprocal moral recognition, respect and honour. If we follow these terms the authority of our own unquestionable say-so is withdrawn. But the freedom we enjoy within these limits is, first, freedom limited by the requirements proper to our own human need and good; and is, second, an unequivocal personal advantage. If the coherence of this second suggestion is denied; the first remains as the only alternative. If it is, then all social regulation involves, at the last, mere constraining force at times, of no value or good to the constrained person. Can this be the only possible basis for social relation?

It *may* perhaps be the only possible basis for social and civic relations. What is striking, however, is that those who are often most hostile to Rousseau's conceptions of 'principled' freedom, and to his talk of 'forcing' people to be free, are at the same time those who hold out hopes for social and civil relations to be grounded not in mere force and power alone but in ties of mutual moral respect and acknowledgment of common material need. What is, I think, not usually properly recognized is that Rousseau's conceptions are expressly and specifically designed to capture that latter possibility. He sees a great deal more clearly than most that if individuals are left to hold unanswerable final discretionary authority on their own terms this possibility is more, not less, difficult of attainment. And if people are denied such personal authority this does not demean or constrain them unwarrantably, but puts them in a position to possess and enact a form of personal standing as a morally titled and recognized person that is a greater liberty for them.

It appears to be widely believed that as soon as the idea of 'principled'[15] freedom is introduced then the floodgates are opened to all forms of intensely repressive political control in the name of the 'true' good of persons, a good unrecognizable to themselves. This is, however, not a careful judgment. There are clear, articulated principles informing Rousseau's ideas about the scope for and limits of the enforcement of principled freedom. It must be clearly and defendedly made out that the requirements are necessary to ensure that the material lot of each and every citizen is bettered; and also to ensure that each and every citizen irrevocably receives that standing and recognition in the community which matches his moral titles as a person worthy of respect. Any enforced provision which cannot be shown to be necessary to these is tyranny.

What must surely be obvious is that the requirements Rousseau is articulating are those that define someone's fundamental position as an incorporated member of a civil association, such that if he is denied this he is rendered merely a slave. *We* do not regard it as a matter of our individual discretion whether or not to allow other people that standing in the community; we enforce on each person the requirement to grant others that standing. Nor do *we* think that when we enforce this on each individual we are depriving him of powers and titles which were properly his, i.e. the power and title to subjugate and deny the humanity of others. So we also think we are not limiting him in any respect where he ought to have been at liberty. So we are not confining him, we are leaving him free. Rousseau is saying no more than this.

## 6 The General Will Again

We are now in a position to give a statement of the grounds, character, authority and implications of the general will, putting all the foregoing points together.

We started with the point that the directives of a properly general will must 'apply to all'. The significance of this was plain enough. I then looked at the requirement that such directives must also 'come from all'. It is now possible to say what this entails.

First, for a proposal or directive to 'come from all' it is neither necessary nor sufficient that it be the actual proposal arrived at, after some ordered procedure or other, to which every potential subject of the proposal has actually

contributed. The reason for this, as explained, is that the actual contribution
or actual agreement of the people involved may very well be misguided,
muddled, hasty or irrational. We can only take their contribution or agreement
seriously if it is rationally made, on good grounds, clearly understood. But this
means that the whole weight of the issue in determining what shall count as
'coming from all' must fall on establishing what is a good ground and what it
dictates. The actual participation of people in an actual procedure is altogether
secondary.

What then, second, are the good grounds for proposing some set of terms
and conditions applicable to all, or for agreeing to a proposal about these?
They comprise two primary matters. First, that the terms and conditions will
markedly and securely improve each several person's material lot beyond what
it was (or would be) if they were not to be associates one with another on these
terms and conditions. Second, that the terms and conditions will securely and
permanently afford to each associate that recognition and honour of their
being and standing as morally titled persons which is appropriate to their
dignity and proper position as counting human persons. If, and only if, the
terms and conditions provide these benefits for each and every single associate
can each and every associate have sufficient reason to propose, or agree to,
these terms and conditions. If there is even one single person living under the
imposition of terms and conditions who lacks these reasons for acceptance of
them, they are illegitimate in relation to him, bind him only in servitude but do
not establish any obligation of obedience for him (cf. SC 3, 14, 238; III, 428). In
effect, he is no proper part of that civil body which comprises those legitimately subject to those terms and conditions (the laws of the association).

Therefore, a proposal can rightly be said to 'come from all' if, and only if, it
supplies these reasons for assent to it for each and every single person to whom
that proposal is intended to apply. The 'general will' then comprises precisely
this; a will which proposes principles of conduct applicable to all in like
stringency without exception, the content of which proposals is such as to
afford to every single one of those to whom they apply good reason for
acceptance of and compliance with them on the two grounds cited. No will
which lacks this character and basis is general; it is sectional, factional or
individual. If such a will holds place as sovereign authority and power over an
association of persons this is tyranny.

Will the proposals of a properly general will tend to 'equality' (cf. SC 2, 11;
II, 391)? In two major respects they clearly will. First, it will require that each
one alike and without exception enjoys a secured baseline of provision and
protection with respect to their material needs. Above this baseline there may
be legitimate variations (as discussed before); but there is an identical entitlement of everyone not to be allowed (let alone required) to fall below it.
Second, it will require that everyone alike and without exception enjoys
secured recognition and respect as a morally titled person who must not be

disregarded, violated or rendered ignominious. This entails, at the very least, that no-one at all be excluded from account as having any less title to have his needs and being taken into consideration in devising and regulating the order and actions of the civil body; each member is an 'indivisible part of the whole' (SC 1, 6, 175; III, 361). Beyond this irrevocable incorporation as a person of standing, a citizen, there may be differential titles and privileges (again as discussed before). But none of these can destroy or overtake this basic level of recognized standing, and still be legitimate.

Will these proposals tend to 'liberty' (see, again, SC 2, 11; III, 391)? I have discussed this in the preceding section, and do not want to add materially to that now. The liberty each citizen enjoys is their 'principled' freedom, which comprises that individually valuable extent of discretionary freedom that is allied to their enlightened will governed by knowledge of each their own proper good.

This account does, I suggest, make pretty good sense of every part of the 'problem' which Rousseau says he is out to solve, and solves by his notion of the general will. He writes:

> 'The problem is to find a form of association which will defend and protect with the whole common force the person and goods of each associate, and in which each, while uniting himself with all, may still obey himself alone, and remain as free as before.' This is the fundamental problem of which the social contract provides the solution. (SC 1, 6; III, 360).

I have not attempted to treat of every remark Rousseau makes about the general will, but I believe that they all do line up with the account I have presented. There are, however, four particular points which arise that I should like briefly to note.

## 7 The General Will: Supplementary Notes

First, despite all I have said about Rousseau's differing, though related notions of freedom, it is still apt to cause puzzlement how he can say that, in a 'finished' civil association in which each member is subject to law, each associate still 'obey(s) himself alone, and remain(s) as free as before'. To clarify this point finally we need to ask what we should understand by 'obeying oneself alone'; and just how free, in what ways, each associate was 'before'.

The liberties which Rousseau stresses as being those proper to 'the nature of man' before his membership of a civil association, in the context of the argument of *The Social Contract*, are principally two. First, the title (the duty) to 'provide for his own preservation' and to be 'the sole judge of the proper means of preserving himself' (SC 1, 2, 166; III, 352). Second, the rights and titles to act, and be treated, as a moral being deserving of respect and recognition from others; one cannot be rightfully dispossessed of one's humanity, by enslavement for instance (SC 1, 4; III, 356). If we take these points in turn we shall see the propriety of Rousseau's statement.

Within the terms of legitimate association each and every associate has to have sufficient reason for assent in view of his material lot being improved. So, just as before, he is providing (all the better for) his own preservation by acceptance of those terms. If it be objected that he does not remain 'sole judge' of the proper means then the reply is that in so far as he was ever to light on the 'proper' means (i.e. the actually effective, productive means) his being 'sole judge' was never the end of the matter, since he could make mistakes. Rousseau's point is that by saying he should be 'sole judge' he should not be obliged or forced to follow the dictates or instructions of another in relation to so essential a matter as this. And this remains; for he receives his material provision by right under law – no dependence or beholdeness to a master has entered into it.

So far as his moral standing goes, this has been exhaustively treated before. It always was implicit in that that the individual was, in being appropriately obedient to the true law of his moral position, subject to an authoritative rule. The precise form of the embodiment of that rule changes when civil association is instigated. But this involves no change in the general character of the individual's previous situation. I conclude, then, that Rousseau's point is clear and appropriate.

Secondly, there is a passage in SC 2, 3 (III, 371) where Rousseau sets out the relations between the general will and the 'will of all', which is of some obscurity. I am not certain that I have got his meaning here. But, equally, nothing beyond the interpretation of this particular passage alone depends on it, so the matter is of no great consequence. Rousseau says that the 'will of all' is 'a sum of particular wills'. What could this mean? Given previous explanation, a person's 'particular' will comprises what he wants for himself alone, and from others in their relations and dealings with him, which is to serve as the rule for his and their lives without reference at all to the question of whether it is a rule which could or would win the (rational) assent and compliance of others. It may or may not win their rational assent; but it is no ground or part of its recommending itself to you as an individual as the rule you would wish to follow that it should do so.

What might we envisage as the objective of someone's particular will? Rousseau gives us little idea. But we might conjecture something along the following lines. I might wish for myself as my wholly self-referential vision of the best life: ample material means possessed with minimal effort on my part; the esteem and favour of all around me as someone they admire and value to an exceptional extent; long life and happiness all my days. We might also suppose that others, too, want similar things for themselves. Given shortage of material goods, and the need of labour to procure them; given each person's desire to enjoy exemplary favour for themselves alone, it is clear that these visions are not as they stand capable of compossible realization. Now, Rousseau says, we must 'take away from these same wills the pluses and minuses that cancel each other out'. What does this signify? Possibly this. My wishing ample material resources with minimal investment of my labour is a plus for me; but the prospect of this is cancelled out by others also wishing material plenty with minimal investment of their labour, on the obvious condition that material plenty is not a simply natural occurence. The plus is my having this; the minus is that, given others' like attitude, the prospect of it for me is deleted: my optimistic extravagant wish is cancelled out, brought to nothing (as theirs also is). Is there any remainder at all? We each wish material well-being; we each are prepared and able to invest some labour. This is a compossibly achievable scheme we each might adopt which is feasible once we have got rid of the incompossible, because conflicting, extravagant projects of each of us. And it corresponds to the direction the general will recommends, as Rousseau suggests. For, he concludes, once we have done the cancelling, 'the general will remains as the sum of the differences', i.e. the sum of the residual, surviving, components in each of our original projects which *are* compatible, once the incompatible elements between each are excluded.

This is, I suggest, a possible interpretation. I insist, however, that nothing of general overall significance hangs on getting this right. Nothing decisive to the character and claim of the general will derives solely or crucially from what Rousseau contends here. One particular point may confirm this. If I am right that the 'sum of the differences' signifies the sum of those parts of each of our original individual proposals which do not fall into direct conflict with parts of others' individual proposals, and hence do not suffer extinction of possible accomplishment because of this incompossibility, this does nothing at all to show how or why we might want to, or be under an obligation to, follow the provisions of this 'lowest common denominator', common possibility. We might, for instance, still want to fight for personal ascendancy and a larger slice of our original project. Why not? It is clear, I suggest, that whatever Rousseau is contending here, it will only take us a very little way into grasping the deeper ramifications of the general will, as I have attempted to explain these starting from quite other points in Rousseau's discussion.

Rousseau's remarks about the 'will of all' just discussed come as part of his considering whether the general will can be 'fallible' (SC 2, 3; III, 371). I shall discuss, in a moment, what the fallibility of the general will could consist in, and how in Rousseau's view it might be saved from error. But my first concern is somewhat different. In approaching this question Rousseau gives one of his very explicit statements of procedures it would be good and appropriate to follow to ascertain what the will of the general is. The people, he says, should be 'furnished with adequate information'; they should have 'no communication with one another'; and so on (ibid). He thinks, for instance, that if this is so (particularly if the latter condition is satisfied), this will prevent the formation of factions and cliques whose extravagant projects for themselves cannot be adequately counterposed by the fragmentary and divided projects of others, and so could not be 'cancelled out' by this incompatibility. Were this not to happen the 'sum of the differences' would not after all be the general will, but a factional interest subjugating the rest.

Here, then, he talks very explicitly of deliberative procedures, and decision-making processes undertaken by the associates in a civil body in order to arrive at their general will. Also, as indicated before, the very title of his book suggests that the authority of the sovereign body in any civil association, and hence the obligation of obedience of any subject of that sovereign, depends on or derives from some contract, some mutual quasi-promise, between one associate and another. In each case it is the actual voluntary undertakings of the associates that seem to be made central to the case. Yet I have consistently argued that this is not, and could not be, Rousseau's real intention. For people's actual undertakings are, in his estimation, very often ill-grounded, muddled, self-and other-damaging, and so on. We must, therefore, go by what it would be rational, sensible, well-advised for them to undertake, pledge themselves to. But this then is a norm or measure by which to validate or invalidate some of some people's actual undertakings, actual pledges. We have to move to hypothetical 'idealized' deliberations and decisions; hypothetical idealized mutual undertakings – what a well-advised person *would* agree to, not what actual, short-sighted, confused, ill-intentioned people *do* agree to.

It is clear, in fact, that Rousseau himself is moving in this direction already when he speaks of being furnished with 'adequate information'. For the standard for the adequacy of the information cannot be the say-so of some ignorant, blind individual unaware of his own limitations. There must be some body or agency that determines this question beyond the say-so of any one individual. The implication of this, and all other related matters, is that actual deliberations, actual procedures, actual contractings have no serious role to play and drop out of the picture. It is the dictates of reason, as these are interpreted and worked out by some authoritative agency, that are in fact carrying the burden here.

My whole approach has suggested this conclusion. But it is as well to make it explicit. I think, also, that it is Rousseau's own conclusion, one he reaches willingly enough, even recognizing that there are comments, such as those noted just above, which suggest that he does allocate a necessary place to actual deliberations and procedures. This is made particularly clear by the role Rousseau comes to assign to 'the legislator' (SC 2, 7; III, 381). I shall defer my fuller discussion of the significance of this idea for Rousseau's political theory until the next chapter. It is sufficient to say here that one role of the legislator is to be the living incarnation of the dictates of (genuinely) right reason and so serve as the agent who has the title to rectify and order the confused and hurtful proposals that even the best-intended of associates might propose to themselves for law. For that is how the 'general will' might be in error.

Strictly speaking an erroneous 'general will' is erroneous in not succeeding in fact in being the will of the general at all – but some factional will, or a mere confusion of wills. So, by the letter, the general will cannot be erroneous. The point has no substance, however. One can simply say the error is in thinking that this will – this proposal – is a proposal of the general will, when it is not. One can err, a whole people can err, in taking for the general will what is not, in truth, the general will. It comes to the same thing. The error, it is to be noted, is not that of supposing that a procedure had been followed fully when it had not been, for instance. It is the error that may remain even if deliberation has been exhausive, procedures impeccably carried through. For, whilst there may be no 'formal' malpractice, the material drawn on, the judgements, feelings, assessments of the participants, are confused, ill-advised, irrational. No procedure of any kind can preclude this. Rousseau thinks it needs to be precluded: 'this makes a legislator necessary' (SC 2, 6, 193; III, 380). Whether a legislator is sufficient, necessary, or even advisable to resolve this issue I shall discuss in the next chapter.

The final supplementary note I want to make relates to my contention that one of the decisive factors which each potential associate brings to the issue of the legitimacy of any proposed terms and conditions for his association with others is his possession of certain moral titles as properly his in virtue of his humanity as such. No legitimate association can, I said, deprive him of these; indeed it must strengthen his possession of them. It might be objected to this that Rousseau says very clearly, in SC 1, 8 (III, 364–5) that it is only in the civil state that man acquires 'moral liberty', which enables him to transcend the 'mere impulse of appetite' and to become 'truly master of himself' (ibid). This surely implies that I am attributing to man in his pre-civic character qualities which Rousseau claims he only acquires in (or after) acquiring his civic character and standing. I must, therefore, have mistaken Rousseau's argument.

My answer to this objection falls into two parts. First, Rousseau really has no reason, even on his own terms, to represent the character of pre-civic man as if he were simply actuated by the 'impulse of appetite', an unthinking 'slave' of his inclinations. For it is perfectly clear that pre-civic man, taking only what is said of him in this context and not drawing on what we know of him from *Emile* for instance, is capable of some envisaging of his longer term interest and adjusting his present behaviour accordingly. Were this not so, the very idea of associating with others, even when in the most extreme need, would be wholly outside his command. So, I suggest, Rousseau must have had some other point in view.

The other point forms the second part of my reply. Rousseau says that what membership of the civil association, being a subject of its laws, does for the individual is 'force' him to 'consult his reason before listening to his inclinations'. This places his emphasis in a very different place. The issue is not, now, that our civil condition vests us with moral attributes, titles and responsibilities, we did not possess before. What it rather does is bring home to us, by giving these the force of law, the need actually to live by them, not to let ourselves ignore them because of the heedless press of inclination and passion. This is not to equip us with a range of characteristics we did not possess before. What it does is make us effective followers of our own reason, creatures who actually enact the law of reason which is within us. This is quite a different point from that put forward in the objection, but still a perfectly serious point. However, it presents no difficulty for what I have been saying.

We should note, also, that Rousseau's talk of 'the mere impulse of appetite' being 'slavery', while 'obedience to law' is 'liberty' is not just free use of metaphor. For, as we have seen at length in earlier discussion, Rousseau has a very full, careful and rigorous argument explaining how and why if we do unthinkingly follow our 'appetites' we involve ourselves in quite non-metaphorical relations of domination and slavery, dependence and impotence and so on. Furthermore he argues that it is very hard indeed to free oneself from this way of living and acting despite the misfortunes it may hold in store. Only exemplary virtue will save one from this, and that is a character hard won and even when won hard to retain.[16] It is then, in fact, an aid to our own faltering intent and power to have the immediate, visible, sanctions of law attached to avoiding this path dangerous to oneself. This is not a deep or original point in Rousseau, but it is a consistent and clear one.

Obviously there is much more that could be said to clarify the idea of the general will. But I leave it here (though I shall be discussing the legislator later). The final issue I want to confront poses a radical challenge to the cogency of Rousseau's whole frame of ideas about this, not just a query about details. I shall therefore spend time on that.

## 8 The Grounds of Association: A Reconsideration

In approaching the question of the nature and significance of the general will I have been employing an informal 'model' of the pre-civic circumstances of each and every associate. The model corresponds very closely to that Rousseau puts forward at the very start of SC (1, 6; III, 360), as his own lead-in to posing the main issues he wishes to discuss.

A central feature of the model was this. Each potential associate was in a more or less identical material predicament, each one of them having the same amount of trouble as the others in providing for their own self-preservation by their own unaided efforts. Similarly, each one of them was supposed to enjoy the same original moral standing as a titled person worthy of respect and restraint. There were supposed to be no differences in authority and privilege, such as for instance between a feudal lord and his servants.

These were not idle features of the model, but played a material part in grounding the idea of legitimate law. For, as I argued, any rule for the governance of all associates could be legitimate if, and only if, it improved the material lot of each associate and protected each associate in the possession of his moral standing. The possibility of finding rules which satisfy these two conditions is enormously facilitated if we suppose that each one of them starts from the same level, so to speak. Bettering the lot of one is not, for instance, bound to involve taking away from another, as it would if that other's excessive possession was responsible for the present deprivation of the first. For everyone is alike in having insufficient possession brought on by the hardship of nature alone, not the greed of other men. Bettering the lot of some might still involve increasing still further the hardship of others. But this is not inevitable in a way in which it would be if the hardship of some were directly due to the domination over them of others.

If we assume a starting point like this, the task of finding legitimate law, on the principles proposed, is then easier, in certain obvious respects. No-one is bound to be dispossessed of what they at present hold to be their own (justly or unjustly, let us not inquire). No-one is bound to see others asking, demanding, an improvement of their material lot as a threat to their own present material abundance.

If we assume the starting point posited in the model we avoid these problems, but only by precluding their arising, not by having an answer to them. But a political theory which does not address the issues of *re*distribution, of the *abolition* of privilege, on the way to recommending a society of equals, is seriously incomplete. Those who start on a level will perhaps hardly mind ending on a level, especially an overall better level. But those who start not at all on a level, particularly those who are very much better off in terms of material abundance and authoritative privilege, are likely to mind very much finding themselves on a level with everyone else. Is there any reason for them not to mind, not to have good cause for resisting the proposals put to them? Rousseau's claim that they will be resisting legitimate law will not just fall on deaf ears but actually be *groundless* if, to prove its legitimacy, a false assumption has to be made, viz, the assumption of a 'level' starting point – for there may be no such initial level standing.

To put the matter another way. To be legitimate, a law, I said, must be such that each person who follows it will be materially better off. Will a feudal lord be materially better off if he cedes his lands to the peasants so that *their* lot is improved? Surely not. So a law that imposes this requirement on him will be illegitimate for he is not better off under it. It begs the question to say: he never was entitled to his greater abundance in the first place. For this claim needs defence by reference to a principle of legitimate extent of ownership. But principles of legitimate extent of ownership must satisfy the above condition. In his case that condition is *not* satisfied. Therefore there is no legitimate law by reference to which to challenge his standing possession. Therefore no legitimate law entailing redistribution can be established; all redistribution is merely violence.

It may be objected that this difficulty trades on there existing already inequalities of ownership and privilege. These, however, presuppose a civil and political order. Rousseau is concerned with founding a civil and political order, on sound principles, from scratch. He cannot, therefore, be required to contend with this problem. The objection is inappropriate. We never are actually confronted with a scratch situation. If the cogency of all we have to say depends on this being so, we have nothing cogent to say. It is a very severe limit indeed on any theory if it has cogent application only in circumstances which never obtain. We should at least hold out some hope that it has cogent application in some really obtaining circumstances. Yet how could Rousseau's theory? No feudal lord conceivably will be better off, let alone think himself better off, for the redistribution of his lands to the poor. So no law requiring this of him can have his rational consent. His living under such a law is merely his subjugation.

*Is* it the implication of Rousseau's views that the overthrow of the old order can, in the nature of the case and not just as a matter of practicality, never be anything other than the infliction of violence and not the assertion of a legitimate rule upon the scions of the old order? I shall suggest that this is not so. Rousseau's arguments, rightly understood, entail that such a rule is legitimate because, rightly understood, the scions of the old order will be advantaged under the new order beyond the supposed advantages they took themselves to be enjoying under the old. Rousseau is not so naive as to suppose they will readily see this to be so. But he believe it is so, and that their not seeing is their blindness. The overthrow of the old order is, then, in his view legitimate through and through, not just for those who will evidently profit from the overthrow (the previously oppressed). The overthrow, he maintains, is to the profit of the 'lords' too and thus has a legitimate claim on them. If this proves to be so, Rousseau's argument is not confined to a hypothetical starting situation which never in fact obtains. It has cogent hold on actual human civil realities as we find these.

It would take too long to go through the case in great detail. I shall confine myself to a schematic presentation. Let us change our model from that of equal encounter of a similar predicament to one where there are very different sorts and conditions of men. Let there be lords and peasants of a fairly stereotyped kind. Lords have fine houses, extensive lands, the authority to hear and resolve disputes among the peasantry, and power to enforce their decisions. They have the right to appropriate part or all of a peasant's produce; can demand labour from him for their benefit. He is entitled to dispossess a peasant of his home if he is displeased; the peasant dwells there only at his master's absolute discretion. Perhaps he has and uses his *droit de seigneur* also; it was common enough. The complementary lot and standing of the peasant needs no additional comment.

Let us now suppose that some modification in a peasant's standing is proposed. He is to have sovereign ownership of his house and some land, under the protection of law, subject only to certain requirements regarding use, etc., his meeting of which is to be tested (if necessary) in open court, before his peers, according to a process which gives no special authority to any lord. The peasant's home is to become his 'castle' now. It is evident that peasants will be better off, both materially and in terms of their recognized standing, because of this. They have every reason to assent to this proposal. It seems equally evident that lords will not be better but worse off if this provision is enacted. They have, it would appear, no reason for assent on the principles enunciated. Their being made subject to such a law would, then, be tyranny over them. It is idle to argue that the peasants are at present suffering tyranny. For it is not obvious that the replacement of one tyranny by another is any improvement. But is one tyranny being replaced by another? Or is there some reason for thinking the new law does not inflict tyranny on the lords?

We may divide the elements in the advantages of the lords into two kinds; first, their ascendancy in privileges, authority etc. Second, their material affluence. Can we canvass any argument for saying that these advantages are merely apparent? Or that they are less than the advantages they would enjoy under laws which do not dispossess and oppress the peasantry but give them 'level' standing and basic economic security? These questions should, by now, have a familiar look about them. Rousseau's suggestion in answer to them will be along the following lines. First, their ascendancy in privilege, etc., is meaningful and valuable to them only in so far as it flatters their 'inflamed' *amour-propre*. That, we have reason to think, is a delusive good which brings not benefit but harm to its possessor.

Second, in their material affluence we must distinguish that about it which comprises only conspicuous consumption, designed to try to exhibit the invidious superiority of themselves over other. This falls under the character of inflamed *amour-propre* also, and is thus covered by the above (compare E 4, 351–4; IV, 686–91). But there is also the side which has more genuinely to do with not having to exert oneself, expose oneself to cold, strained backs, cuts and bruises and the like in order to amass the wherewithal to live. It is, however, not obvious that the gain they would secure by putting aside the barriers erected by their sneering disdain and contempt of others, and instead working alongside them in amity and mutually recognized cooperation for a shared purpose, would not outweigh the loss of having to exert themselves. Not having to exert oneself is a largely delusive good anyway, as we saw when we examined Rousseau's arguments in the first *Discourse*. Indolence arising from having no purpose sufficiently real and palpably good to command action one can find intelligible and rewarding is a threat to one's sense of one's own reality. Working for one's living along with others whom one respects and who respect one is a palpably intelligible activity and a worthwhile exchange for indolence.

I have made these points only very sketchily, but their general intent should be clear. They may, I am well aware, be found quite ridiculous: Levin's feeble-minded longings for community of sentiment and activity with his peasants are very unconvincing.[17] It is worth repeating, however, that unless some such case as this can be made, the expropriation of the expropriators is an act of violence against them without legitimacy. This entails that they have not just every incentive, but every proper reason, to oppose by violence any proposal which lessens their privileges or wealth. (*Cet animal est très méchant. Quand on l'attaque, il se defend.*) If their opposition fails, they are under the new law only as enslaved by it and have no more obligation of obedience to it than did those who overthrew the old law and replaced it by the new. Rousseau is concerned to find a new order which is legitimate, which may, possibly, require violence in its instigation but is not, when established, nothing better than a continuing rule of violence only with different victims. He may have failed to do so, but I cannot believe his project is a negligible one which we have any right not to take seriously.

# 6

# The Ideal State:
# Problems and Practicalities

## 1 The Purpose of This Chapter

I have tried, in chapter 5, to explain Rousseau's account of the fundamental terms and conditions for any human association which can count as a civil association ordered by legitimate law, to the observance of which each member (each 'citizen') is bound by a genuine obligation. In doing so I offered interpretations of several of the central notions in Rousseau's account, of the 'general will', of the various significant senses of freedom, and the like. Certain issues raised by the consideration of these topics were left hanging; and several parts of the discussion of *The Social Contract* were touched on only very lightly or not at all. The first thing I want to do here is to follow up some of these hanging issues, and to say something more about some of the parts of Rousseau's discussion heretofore put to one side. This will give a more complete idea of his achievement. It remains true, however, that I do not intend to consider every interesting point or angle, which would be effectively impossible. But I hope not to have omitted anything in such a way as to have produced a very unbalanced account.

I want also to consider Rousseau's own concrete engagement with actual political realities as found in his proposals for constitutions and governments for Poland and Corsica.[1] Rousseau is quite often mocked for the supposed remoteness of his specific proposals for historically situated peoples and nations from his abstract vision of the best human civil order. It is said that this demonstrates that his ideal vision lacks serious application; at every turn it is compromised, tenets yielded, *ad hoc* remedies patched up. And since, in politics, practical application is not something to be tacked on after the 'theoretical' problems have been straightened out, but part of the theoretical problem itself (since no law can be good which is inoperable), this shows that Rousseau's theoretical proposals are misfounded. Rousseau's claim that he takes men 'as they are' (SC 1, Preface; III, 351) is shown up as a delusion. Being deluded on this score, much else that follows must be inapposite. It may be added that, in politics, there both should not be, and cannot be, an abstract blueprint good for all peoples, places and times. Necessarily, political theory, as political practice, must incorporate as an ineliminable fact the varieties of history, culture, geography and the like that decisively mark the character of people and peoples.[2] No one universal true order of society can emerge from this, as Rousseau appears to have believed.

I shall try to show that all these charges are misplaced. It never was part of Rousseau's plan that there should be an identical civil order for all peoples at all times and all places. I have indicated already, in previous discussion, some places where Rousseau quite clearly not only allows for (as if it were a regrettable necessity), but constructively incorporates the appropriateness of, differences of sentiment, culture and habit between peoples. I shall, among other things, extend these comments and try to show that Rousseau nowhere deserts his principles; but rather he shows their fuller significance and force in proper consistency with themselves in his concrete and specific proposals.

The first topic picks up a matter left in abeyance in the previous argument (chapter 5, section 7), concerning the nature and significance of 'the legislator' in Rousseau's discussion (SC 2, 6; SC 2, 7; III, 380–4). Proposals may be put forward as comprising the intent of the general will when, in fact, they are not. This can be for a variety of reasons. One could be that some sectional or factional will knowingly and deliberately masquerades as the will of the general, in order to dupe and oppress those not of that faction. But this is not the sort of case with which Rousseau is concerned at this juncture. He is concerned, rather, with the case where each and every associate, with the best intentioned effort that they can muster, none the less devises or assents to proposals which actually do *not* secure their material need and moral standing in the appropriate way. This could be because of deciding on the basis of (blameless) misinformation; inadvertent and unrecognized confusions about consequences or ramifications of some proposal; and so on. No-one is ill-intentioned, acting with knowing malicious scheming. But, for all that, some may end up dispossessed or unregarded. Can this possibility be circumvented? The invocation of a legislator appears to be intended to achieve this. How is it supposed to work; and could it work? I want also to consider some of the further ramifications of the issue that gives rise to this suggestion of Rousseau's.

## 2 The Legislator

The problem towards the resolution of which the 'invocation' of a legislator is intended to help appears clear enough. Rousseau sets it out in detail in SC 2, 6, 193 (III, 380). It comes to this: we may be well-intentioned, determined to legislate appropriately, to establish legitimate law. But we may, by ignorance,

by seductive influence, mistake what will successfully embody our intent.
Can this be guarded against? Here, Rousseau says, we have need of a
legislator – someone of 'superior intelligence', aware of 'all the passions of
men without experiencing them'; independent of need of men for his happiness, but yet interested in ours; and so on (see SC 2, 7; III, 381, *passim*). He it is
who could devise the basic principles, the basic terms of association, to make
of a multitude one body which is both sovereign and state. The legislator is not
sovereign; rather, he constructs the principles which make possible the coming
into being of the sovereign, that is the whole body of the people joined together
by appropriate law. Nor is the legislator a magistrate, or officer of the government. For there is no government save on the authorization of the sovereign
power, and that is not yet in existence. The legislator's purpose is to bring it
into existence.

The legislator therefore requires superhuman capabilities; and the influence
to have his conceptions embraced whilst yet lacking real power or constituted
authority. How can he carry the day? Furthermore, he cannot appeal to the
multitude in terms they will readily understand and see the justness of. For it is
precisely their inability to see matters through for themselves that necessitates
his efforts. So, as Rousseau says, the legislator is 'unable to appeal to either force
or reason' (SC 2, 7, 196; III, 383). Neither can he appeal to 'the social spirit'
(ibid.). The pervasiveness and strength of such a spirit, making a multitude one
commonly loyal body, is the effect, not the cause, of the introduction and governance of the 'fundamental rules of statecraft'. What recourse is left?

The answer Rousseau suggests is the appeal to 'divine intervention' – the
appeal to the authority of god (God) which is an 'authority of a different order
capable of constraining without violence and persuading without convincing'
(Rousseau means, without producing clear and evident rational conviction, for
the reason given just above concerning the multitude's inability to understand).
Each several man, Rousseau suggests, will already believe that as an individual
he lives under the power and authority of the divine – this being the 'law' of his
nature. (We shall discuss this in chapter 7.) If, then, the laws of the State are
represented also as having the power and authority of the divine, those laws will
appear to have the same claim to be obeyed. In this way, each man will 'bear with
docility the yoke of public happiness'. However, what is to prevent deceitful
legislators making spurious appeals to fraudulent oracles? Rousseau in effect
appeals to the maxim: by their works shall ye know them. The fraudulence of
some imposter will be shown up by the impermanence of what he establishes.
'Idle tricks form a passing tie; only wisdom can make it lasting' (SC 2, 7, 197; III,
384). But the proof that it was wisdom, not idle tricks, lies in the enduring as one
body of that which is established; there is no independent route to determining
that wisdom guided the instigation of the law.

This apparently gives rise to a first problem for Rousseau's account. The
genius of the legislator is appealed to avoid the errors that the ignorant multitude

tude might inflict on themselves. But it now seems that we have no assurance that he who puts himself forward as legislator has genius and is no pretender, until we find our whether the community his vision has brought into existence will last, will endure for centuries, or not. There can be no assurance in advance that this will be so. But why, then, could not the multitude devise for themselves a mode of association with at least as much chance of success as they have the chance of being the guinea-pigs of a 'great soul' and not an imposter?

This apparent difficulty should teach us more clearly what Rousseau's concern was, not that he was muddled. What Rousseau saw as probably *the* major difficulty in making a 'multitude' into a 'people' (an 'aggregation' into an 'association', cf. SC 1, 5, 173; III, 359) was that of causing members of the multitude not just to know, but to feel, to breathe, the need they have for one another so that in living and working in concert with and for others they felt they were living and working for themselves as well. Familiar as they are with their isolated, independent existence, they will find quite unfamiliar and uncompelling the sentiments and commitments that might attach to them in any social relation and connection (SC 2, 7, 194; III, 381-2). But it is only by such sentiments and commitments becoming second nature to them that they will find their own being and constitution extended and strengthened. The difficulty is that it seems we need to appeal to something in people, to initiate 'association', which can only be there if association already exists and is their familiar mode of life. What, therefore, Rousseau sees as the primary issue is, so to say, to cause people (as members of an 'aggregate' only to begin with) to expose themselves to the possibility of acquiring those sentiments, loyalties, attachments which will make it possible for an enduring association between them to be established and survive. This, he suggests, might be done by drawing on the existing authority of the divine over them, and suggesting that this authorizes the ways and terms for them to associate one with another. (This is not the only suggestion he makes; I shall look at some others below, in section 5.) By this means they may be persuaded to try a way of doing things which, when once tried, elicits the very sentiments and loyalties that provide for the maintenance of that way. Or it may fail to elicit such self-sustaining sentiments – in which case it was imposture not genius that was persuading. ·

The role of the legislator is, then, not exactly that of taking the general will of the people and seeing to it that it does not make mistaken provisions. It is rather that of trying to bring it about that there is 'a people' and hence that there can be a general will at all. The reason why one of the multitude cannot do this, nor the multitude do it for themselves, is that, as a mere aggregate, they are not possessed of that scope of vision and awareness of the possibility and vitalness to them of the social tie. They are 'sunk' within the confines of the vision and sentiments of their 'physical and independent existence'. In effect, the major 'mistake' that can be made about the provisions of the general will is that of defeating or not creating the possibility of there being an enduring, effective general will at all, i.e. not eliciting and sustaining senti- ments and loyalties which establish the aggregate together as a people. The true generality of the will is proven only by its enabling there to be an enduring association. If a state survives and thrives (Rousseau stresses population growth as a central mark of this, SC 3, 9; III, 420, rather questionably perhaps) then it is viably and coherently a 'people'. Otherwise it is not.

We know, from the discussion in chapter 5, what generally speaking are the conditions which must be met if law is to be legitimate. Each several individ- ual's material need and moral personality must be recognized and strength- ened. If this is done in such a way that each several individual not only sees but feels that the only condition on which he enjoys these things is that everyone else also enjoys them, then these several individuals are, and know and feel themselves to be, one people. But, ultimately, it is the actually sustained inward recognition of this condition which is the objective of statecraft. The state exists and survives if, and only if, this sentiment survives vigorously in each person (cf. DPE 127; III, 251).

If this is the primary purpose of the legislator then, it may be said, he cannot – in this role – secure the individual from dispossession that would result from erroneous legislation, which was the problem we began from. For surely it can be the case that there is a sufficient sentiment of common life and common dependence to make an aggregate an association, whilst yet certain persons are excluded from concern, or do not share such sentiments. To say, as Rousseau does, that no law is legitimate unless it 'indivisibly' incorporates each person into the whole which is the association of us (SC 1, 6, 175; III, 361) appears empty. For as and when an individual protests that he is not so incorporated he will be told that he is self-estranged and in self-imposed servitude. His compliance is the condition of his freedom. We have considered this before (SC 1, 7, 177; III, 33–4; see above, chapter 5, section 4). Within the state he has no other appeal than to the state; all that remains to him is to leave it. But where should he go? And why should not the laws be modified to meet his complaint?

If entering and leaving states were wholly voluntary, and if, outside any state (ordered civil association) one could survive and thrive as well as within one, then, perhaps, these questions would not be so pressing. But neither of these things is true; the questions therefore press. However, in the end, it seems that Rousseau – in his conception of the role of the legislator at any rate – is getting no further in effectively meeting them.

I believe Rousseau's thought here is this. Meeting the material need, and honouring the moral personality of each and every associate, are in actual fact the (only) two conditions on which the sentiments that unite men one with another in one body can survive and endure. They are the (only) two condi- tions on which a multitude will become a people which prospers, becomes strong and lasts. Therefore the legislator who forms a real people will also be one who establishes terms that do in actual fact meet these requirements. If just one or two included under the power and authority of these terms do not feel themselves united with the others as members of the people too, there can be no legitimate footing for them to demand that the terms must be altered to meet their demands. But if their estrangement, their disenchantment finds sufficient echo in the sentiments of others, then there is no bond of union, no association, no one people any more (if there ever was). Aggregation has taken the place of association, and there can be no general will. But what is a 'sufficient number'? How shall their disaffection be made known, and not be put down as rebellion? I do not think Rousseau gives a decisive answer to these questions; but neither is it clear that any decisive answer to them can be given. Such clues as Rousseau gives to the signs that there is no 'death of the heart' (of the legislative authority) of the body politic are in SC 3, 11; III, 424. They are that people do, as a matter of fact, live comfortably enough in the established ways of their community; they are sure of their footing in their community, act and work without perennial suspicion and mistrust. Where this is not so 'the State is dead' (ibid); at most it survives, in form only, by factional force.

It may still be objected that, in the absence of a clear method by which the sovereign can revoke law, or discover that there is no common law which can be arrived at, the body politic may be dead for many years before its death is discovered. Rousseau appears not to envisage, in the discussion in *The Social Contract*, any constitutionally established and sustained right of appeal by a person or persons living under law against the acts of the legislative power, whereby dissent might find its ordered and recognized expression, avoiding (to some extent) either rebellion or repression. This is, perhaps, because he supposed that the proceedings of the sovereign assembly, as he envisaged these, provided sufficiently for this. I do believe that there is a lacuna in Rousseau's account here, though not, I think, an unfillable one. It would, however, take us too far afield to look into this fully. We shall, however, see, when considering Rousseau's constitutional proposals for Poland particularly (below, section 5), that he was far from unconcerned with this issue, and makes some detailed provisions relevant to it. Also, in the full discussion of the Roman system of legislation and government (SC 4, 4–6; III, 444ff.) much that bears on this point is discussed in favourable terms by Rousseau. But this is one area of this argument I shall not go into.

One final point bearing on the significance and role of the legislator is this. It may be surprising that, when Rousseau sets out the issue which the invocation of a legislator is intended to resolve, he speaks of each member of the multitude having a 'physical and independent existence' (SC 2, 7, 194; III, 381), without seeming to take into account the moral relations and standing of persons that precede law. This may suggest that I am mistaken in supposing that these matters are involved at all; or even – contrary to what I have throughout argued – suggest that men have no 'moral existence' prior to civil association at all. But Rousseau makes his point perfectly clear a few pages. earlier (SC 2, 6, 191; III, 378) in an important passage concerning the role of law.

There Rousseau argues that 'doubtless' there exist rules of 'universal justice' which come from reason or from God. However, in order for these rules to oblige one person, the rules of justice must be mutually observed. If this is not so, the just man's justice leads to his undoing. No-one is obliged, by justice, to place himself in the hands of, at the mercy of, the unjust. Therefore 'conventions and laws' are required to join the rights I hold against others to the duties I owe to them. The very *ineffectiveness* of the rule of (God-given, or rational) justice in being a universally heeded law in the absence of conventional sanctions, means that it ceases to establish a practical obligation on me. It is, then, a primary function of sanctioning law that it provides good grounds for actual compliance to the 'pure' rules of justice – as we may call them. There is, then, no question at all that Rousseau saw men, not living under civil law, as devoid of moral titles and moral duties. What they are (or may be) devoid of is any reasonable expectation that these titles will effectively be respected by others. This entails they have no real duty to abide by these laws for themselves.[3] The 'physical and independent existence' Rousseau has in mind, then, is not a character of existence devoid of moral characteristics altogether. It is a character of existence in which there is no effective reason to enact the moral responsibilities which attach to one (as they, in fact, also attach to everyone).

## 3 Government

I do not intend to do more, here, than 'block out' the position and function Rousseau assigns to government as an element in a legitimate civil association. He discusses various possible forms of government at some length in Book 3 of *The Social Contract*; but I shall not at all go into the detail of his account. I gave a very brief outline of Rousseau's conception of government in general in the previous chapter. I propose to extend that account only a little. The issues raised are not, in my view, particularly problematic.

The legislative power declares its will (the 'general' will) only in rules (laws) which come from all and apply to all, in a way I have tried to explain. However, there is the need, in the course of life of a body politic, to bring the provisions of law to bear upon particular persons, particular situations, to determine for instance who in particular should receive a certain office, or suffer a certain penalty. These 'particular acts' are undertaken by a distinct body of persons (or, possibly, by one person only) within the State. The powers and functions they discharge are said to be of 'government', or supreme administration; they are the exercise of executive power (SC 3, 1; III, 395). Those in whom these powers and duties are vested are governors, or magistrates, or kings; the whole body that bears this function is the prince or magistrate.

Rousseau is very emphatic that the prince is not the sovereign. That function which is government is a derived function from the sovereign, and exists for the sake of the good of the sovereign. Those in whom administrative power and authority are vested hold them on commission from the sovereign; they are depositaries of the sovereign's pleasure, and their commission may be revoked at the sovereign's pleasure.

However, once governors are commissioned, 'intermediate forces' exist in the State, lying between the sovereign and each several citizen. Being vested with power and authority, it is possible, indeed it is likely, that governors may tend to usurp the sovereign's authority, or exceed their appointed powers. Furthermore, the governors are likely to perceive themselves as having a joint interest common to themselves, but different from the general interest of the whole body, and the particular interest they may have as individuals (SC 3, 2, 213; III, 400). They may in effect constitute themselves a factional or sectional interest, opposed to the general interest, and opposed to the particular interests of many (if not their own). This sectional will Rousseau calls a 'corporate' will. It becomes an urgent question, then, how to check the potential dominance of the corporate will of the magistrates and to prevent its illegitimate usurpations or excesses. On the other hand, these checks must not be so great as to preclude that function which is government being carried out (SC 3, 1, 212; III, 399–400). That would render the sovereign power impotent to apply its rule to the citizen body.

Rousseau's primary reflections on particular forms for the prince to take are intended to show the considerations and principles which bear upon achieving this balance in a way that is appropriate to the size, dispersion, material circumstances, of an association. He principally considers, in a familiar fashion, the merits and demerits attaching to democracy, to aristocracy and to monarchy (SC 3, 3; III, 402–3). I do not intend to follow through the detail of this discussion. It should be noted, however, that Rousseau does not at all recommend in any straightforward fashion democratic government (either direct or representative). The supposition, which is not uncommon, that he does is due to a failure to distinguish the basis of the legitimate acts of sovereign legislation from the character of the prince, as executive power. Although we have seen very many necessary reasons for modifying the claim, it would be a more or less appropriate claim to make that for Rousseau the legitimate acts of sovereignty are those arrived at by the unanimous assent of all in a directly democratic procedure. But it does not at all follow from this that the only legitimate acts of government are arrived at in the same way. The points are, in fact, wholly independent (see SC 3, 4; III, 404–6).

There is, however, one curious point where 'directly democratic' sovereignty and 'directly democratic' government do have a natural relation. Rousseau discusses this at SC 3, 17, 244 (III, 433–4). Given Rousseau's account of the character of the legitimate acts of sovereignty – that these cannot name particular persons – it seems impossible, not so much that the function of government should be established, but that any governors should be appointed to discharge that function. For that is a particular act; particular acts are legitimate only as acts of government; but we need such acts to have a government. This paradox is resolved 'by a sudden conversion of sovereignty into democracy', such that 'the citizens become magistrates and pass from general to particular acts, from legislation to the execution of the law' (ibid.). Rousseau draws the analogy of the House of Commons converting itself into Grand Committee, and reporting the results of its particular determinations to itself when reconstituted as sovereign – which determinations are then debated once more now as sovereign commissions. Rousseau goes on that it is 'the peculiar advantage of democratic government that it can be established in actuality by a simple act of the general will'. Strictly then, if subsequently the form of government commissioned is aristocratic or monarchical, this, being a particular act, must be the act of the sovereign as democratic 'grand committee'. So democratic government does have a necessary primacy – at least in this one act – before other forms, on Rousseau's assessment. What does not follow is that it needs to have, or should have, priority in relation to any other legitimate governmental acts. Rousseau does not argue for this latter conclusion.

## 4 The Bond of Union

In many different contexts, on many different occasions, I have referred to the importance Rousseau attaches to the creation and sustaining of a bond of union between persons, both on a 'local' level, and also in their civil standing and relations. (I shall also be returning to this topic in the next chapter when I consider Rousseau's account of 'civil religion'; chapter 7 section 2.) This theme is so central in his thought that it is worthwhile drawing together some of the several aspects of this idea as Rousseau employs it. Nothing I shall say really goes beyond points already made. But it is useful to see some scattered points brought together.

As I have explained, Rousseau holds that it is not only that we shall feel an *incentive* to keep to the requirements of basic human, natural, justice in our dealings with others only if we feel some sense of common life and common experience and fate with them. It is also that the very *intelligibility*, and grounded reasonableness, of the idea that we owe each other duties of justice is rooted not in any abstract, rational principle alone but arises from mutual bonds of sentiment. The movement of pity, with its natural return of grati-tude, is the originative kernel for the meaning to us of the very idea that we owe others, and others owe us, respect, honour and care as each our human title. It is only out of, and in continuity with, this basic mode of human relation that the larger, more abstract, notions of justice, rights, responsibility, acquire their proper sense and significance for us. Rousseau does not 'reduce' the obligations of human justice to nothing but structures of sentiment; reason and conscience also come into the case (E 4, 235, 253; IV, 523, 548; the role of 'conscience' remains still to be considered, of course). But it is his central view – his central insight – that these find their proper place in relation to the bonds of sentiment and not *vice versa*.

This entails that the union of men one with another has an ineliminable role in giving sense to, as well as making sensible the force of requirement in, all duties of justice one person bears towards others, however different in scope and character some of these may turn out to be in the end in comparison with the claims and responsibilities inherent in this first relation. For in this first relation, the 'union' of the persons involved is very close and very detailed. Not only is there a shared sense of common predicament, as weak, vulnerable creatures. There is also the 'identification' the compassionate person has with the need of the other, suffering, person for relief. And so on. There is, and need be, no question of a unity of mind and feeling of this density remaining when we are considering men in their civil relations with mutual responsibilities. But it is Rousseau's thought that we cannot ever sever the connection between these latter and the kind of unity involved in the 'first relation' (as I have called it), and still retain a proper meaning and force in the idea of each of us having civil responsibilities one to another. It is this thought which shapes, at a deep level, his contentions about the kind of people who are possible subjects for legislation, possible subjects to come together in one civil body; and also about the primary purpose a legislator, or legislation, must have in view if he or it is to be good and legitimate.

In each case Rousseau stresses that no mere random aggregate of people, who are altogether strange to each other, unfamiliar and unused to one another in respective ways, will constitute suitable 'material' for statecraft, in prospect or in action. Where there is not already obtaining some inwardly constituting feel of a common way of approaching things, of reconciling oneself to things; a shared sense of a common predicament, a common challenge in living; there one cannot make an enduring civil association. There just is no sufficient sense of unity – no sense that we are to each other companions and fellows in arms (as it were). Even if each member of the aggregate comes to realize that he cannot survive and prosper without the help of others, and that he cannot count on that help unless he offers a return in kind, this is apt only to breed resentment at what will be seen as a tie and constraint if there is no idea of the other as a familiar, of him as a person one is reasonably 'at home' with.

Without this 'idea' – really a felt comfortableness with the other as at one with you in many matters of outlook and sentiment – any association will always be ready to fragment, to dissolve. Each member will be ready to withdraw his contribution, if he can get away with it, since he has no loyalty towards others, no wish for their good as persons he cares for (albeit in a 'watery' way only, sometimes[4]). The primary experience of the requirements of common justice can only be, under those circumstances, as imposed commands, submitted to but not loved. For the requirements of common justice to be experienced as, in effect, setting out what one wishes to achieve and holds dear, one must perceive the recipients of one's justice as objects of care and affection. The latter is the primary phenomenon, and needs its prepared ground of shared experience, shared outlook and the like.

I have quoted Rousseau before as saying, in effect, that without the experience of caring for and acknowledging others in, say, family life the possibility of civil association will not exist (E 5, 362; IV, 700). The deep reason for this, in his assessment, is that without this first experience of encountering others as people with whom one shares a life of mutual care and acknowledgement, the possibility of a larger association, which in order to nurture and sustain its members must embody such-like relations also, will not exist.

It is this that causes Rousseau to contend that the best state will be small, culturally integrated, as far as possible self-sufficient, not obliged to other states for economic needs. For, in those circumstances, the scope and rigour of civil obligation will not greatly exceed the scope and dispositions of sentiments of common loyalty. Where the former start to exceed the latter greatly, then the grounds of civil obligation will become more externally apprehended, felt more and more as thankless impositions. Rousseau's political thought is often criticized because of its apparent inapplicability to large, culturally diverse states. However, it is possible to think that some of the problems that such states encounter are (partly) due to their not meeting the kinds of conditions Rousseau stresses. It does not follow, of course, that the dissolution of these larger states would be the 'right solution' (though, of course, many, in theory and practice, contend for this). But it does follow that Rousseau may have in fact identified one of the conditions for satisfactory civil association, and suggested that we do not, for that if for no other reason, satisfyingly participate in satisfactory civil associations. The conclusion is hardly striking; the reason for it is more so.

In SC 2, 10, 203 (III, 390), Rousseau writes:

> What people, then, is a fit subject for legislation? One which, already bound by some unity of origin, interest, or convention, has never yet felt the real yoke of law; . . . one in which every member may be known to every other, and there is no need to lay on any man burdens too heavy for a man to bear; one which can do without other peoples, and without which all others can do . . .

All of this confirms that has been said. But Rousseau goes on (ibid.):

There is still in Europe one country capable of being given laws – Corsica.

With this preamble, I turn now to my final topic in this chapter, a consideration of Rousseau's (unfinished) 'Constitutional Project for Corsica', and also his later 'Considerations on the Government of Poland'. In these works, we can see how Rousseau – taking on himself, in effect, some aspects of the role of legislator – envisaged the work of statecraft for historically and economically conditioned and circumstanced peoples. We shall see that there is, in these, no desertion or compromise of the fundamental driving concerns and beliefs which order the discussion of *The Social Contract*. Rather, we can gather a fuller sense of some of the more abstractly and generically presented ideas of that by seeing what they amount to in concrete specificity and particularity.

## 5 Poland and Corsica

Neither the 'Considerations on the Government of Poland' (GP) nor the 'Constitutional Project for Corsica' (CPC) was published in Rousseau's lifetime. GP was completed in 1772, in response to an approach from Count Wielhorski, a member of the Confederation of Bar, a body dedicated to the preservation of Polish integrity and identity against Russian imperialism and absorption. The work was probably only ever intended for circulation among the members of the Confederation. CPC appears to have also originated in a request for help from a country in crisis. Possibly in response to the remark made in *The Social Contract* about Corsica, quoted above, Rousseau was approached by one Buttafuoco, who may have been an agent of the leader of the Corsican resistance to Genoese rule, Pasquale Paoli. He was asked to make proposals for a new constitution for the restored independence of Corsica. However, Rousseau was, at this time, severely weakened and disturbed because of the attacks on him that followed the publication of SC, and never made more than a start on the project, in 1765. In 1768, France bought Corsica from Genoa, and suppressed the rebellion. Such occasion as there might ever have been for Rousseau's intervention was then past, and the work was abandoned. What we have is, however, still of considerable interest.[5]

Although there are considerable differences between these works, rendered necessary by the very different conditions and circumstances of the peoples to whose predicaments they are addressed, I shall consider them together. There is sufficient in common in them for the purposes in view here to make this possible.[6]

I have argued that there are (at least) five points upon which Rousseau places great weight in his account of the character and good order of an 'ideal' state. These are, first, that each community-constituting member shall enjoy enhanced protected means of self-preservation, of material resource. Second, he shall enjoy level standing as an incorporated, respected and recognized member of the sovereignty. Third, he shall possess and enact 'principled' freedom in that the law of the state is at one and the same time that law which is proper to his moral standing as a person with other persons. Fourth, each citizen shall have the 'space' to put in hand his personal development and projects for self-fulfilment. But this shall be done, fifthly, in a way that does not conflict with but allows for the importance and claim of that 'watery' kind of friendship which comprises that bond of common life and common fellow-ship that is essential to achieve the due incorporation of care of one's co-citizens by each citizen as one of his own cherished concerns.

Each of these points has been explained and argued for in general terms at length already. The purpose now is to show how Rousseau moves from the general to the particular in a way which 'keeps faith' with these salient emphases in his account. I shall try to display that he does so in an effective and illuminating way, so that we better understand, because of his general ideas, why he approaches the particular matter as he does; and also better understand his general ideas because he sees them as having just this import in this particular matter. We shall see, in particular, how much stress Rousseau places on the fifth point mentioned, as providing the basis of a willingness for a set of persons to continue to work together to find a solution to their mutual difficulties rather than dissolving any association they might presently enjoy and proceeding in wholly independent ways thereafter. (Somewhat as a marital difficulty jointly addressed shows the continuing hold of the marital bond.) It is by drawing on that 'friendship' (in whatever form it has vivid hold in people) in general, and by stressing particular components in the matter of the friendly transactions, that Rousseau believes significant social and political change can be put on foot with some real prospect of success. As we shall see, Rousseau insists that social and political proposals must engage with what presently obtains, and work with and through the creative possibilities in that. He did not envisage, and nothing in his general theory implies, the imposition of a 'blueprint' on a set of persons who are viewed as originally only ciphers. This means the extension and modification of present 'national identity', not the abolition or weakening of it. Rousseau thought the cosmopolitan state, the cosmopolitan spirit, was inimical to the well-being of the state-comprising individuals. He held that we are happier and more fulfilled as individuals if we possess a more determinate character and identity, rooted in particular places, particular histories, particular cultures, and find that character in our fellows who support and share it with us.

Thus, Rousseau argues (e.g. GP 13; III, 1020ff) that what he saw (or those who approached him for his ideas saw) as abuses within the social and political order should be ameliorated slowly, with constant attention to existing habits, sentiments and practices. He comments in detail, for instance, on the manumission of serfs and assigning property to them (ibid.), in a way which might seem surprising if he is construed as an exponent of violent revolutions. But once it is recognized that whilst, for him, it is a moral outrage that there should be serfs, he is concerned that the removal of this outrage should lead to their membership of a living community of persons, of the character I have outlined, then we at once understand that this could not be his approach to the issue. For revolution would, even if successful in abolishing serfdom, lead to rule by fear and terror if the owners of serfs are not persuaded. This, as we know, is not for Rousseau any possible basis for a humanly creative social and political body. The existing ideas of honour, power and prestige must be addressed, but turned, little by little, to new objects, new achievements. Inequalities of rank and standing are not to be swept away; the desire of these is to be turned to accomplishments of service to all, not to those which necessitate the destitution of some. Given that such inequalities may be, in this way, ineliminable from the spirit of a people, Rousseau argues that there should be many of these inequalities so that they will counterbalance each other, and no one of them become a dominant factional interest (GP 7, 203; III, 987).

Rousseau devotes much consideration to the corruption by money, employed as a measure of merit and prestige. He argues, in what should be by now a familiar fashion, that money holdings are largely valued because of excessive *amour-propre* (GP 3, 170, 174; III, 962, 964; CPC 1, 325–6; III, 937). Without, however, trying to eradicate the motivations of excessive *amour-propre*, he suggests that the rage for distinction can be met by honours for public service and conspicuous dedication to the common weal. Going along with criticism of money as the measure of men, Rousseau argues that its having a paramount place leads to the economic dependence of one nation upon another. Thus, one nation cannot direct its own affairs by its own sole best judgement, but is bound to comply with the economic stringencies its dependence on another enforces. He would, therefore, like to see nations strive for material self-sufficiency, with agriculture an honoured occupation. As much commerce as possible should proceed by barter; and the performance of duties necessary to the common good should be made by personal labour not by money payments. Money is, in Rousseau's view, devious and secret in its workings, concealed from public view and public accountability. He has this savage remark about the Russians:

> They will always regard free men as they themselves must be regarded, namely as human ciphers moved only by the twin instruments of money and the knout. (GP 15, 270; III, 1039).

As I have stressed, Rousseau attempts to speak throughout to the living feel for place and country which actuates men much more than do abstract principles or claims of right made *in vacuo*. He writes (GP 3, 168; III, 960).

> It is the national institutions which shape the genius, the character, the tastes and the manner of a people; which give it an individuality of its own; which inspire it with that ardent love of country, based on ineradicable habits, which make its members, while living among other peoples, die of boredom, though surrounded by delights denied them in their own land.

And he goes on to say, with scorn, that 'Today . . . there are no longer any Frenchmen, Germans, Spaniards, or even Englishmen; there are only Europeans' (ibid.). Does it follow from this, however, that he valued only the individuality of 'a people' and not that of particular persons within that people? Did he envisage, that is, that we should give the whole, or the major part, of our life to things we do in common with others for the sake of what we have in common with others, so that we become, so to speak, wholly 'public persons'?

A good deal in what he says here seems to point to this conclusion. Rousseau speaks, in apparent admiration, of Lycurgus imposing on a 'degraded' people an iron yoke, which however he caused them to identify themselves with by 'making it the object of their constant preoccupation': 'He kept the fatherland constantly before their eyes in their laws, in their games, in their homes, in their loves, in their festivals; he never left them an instant for solitary relaxation.' (GP 2, 164; III, 957)

And there is much else to this effect (e.g. 'Every true republican has drunk in love of country, that is to say love of law and liberty, along with his mother's milk. This love is his whole existence . . . when he has ceased to have a fatherland, he no longer exists; and if he is not dead, he is worse than dead' (GP 4, 176, III, 966). The disappearance of particular personal individuality seems undeniable in this.

On the other hand, Rousseau speaks elsewhere of Lycurgus, and says that he did not 'purify' the heart of man, he 'denatured' it (E 1, 40; IV, 150). In the comments he makes at that place, Rousseau makes it clear that he thinks that, as things stand, we are faced with either being a 'numerical unity', being 'for ourselves' alone; or being 'a fractional unity dependent on the denominator', with our 'absolute existence' taken away, feeling only 'within the whole' (E 1, 39–40; IV, 249). However, he makes it clear that his object in *Emile* is to unite 'man' and 'citizen' in such a way that they are not in contradiction, but the 'double object', of being for oneself and being for others, can be united in harmony (E 1, 41; IV, 251). It would be surprising, therefore, if he showed no concern with accomplishing this 'double object' in his concrete political suggestions, but abolished the man and created only the citizen.

Are there then, despite the remarks I have quoted, and many others, signs that Rousseau did indeed seek this 'double object' in his discussions of Polish government or a constitution for Corsica? I think it is plain that he did. At GP 3, 174 (III, 964), for instance, Rousseau makes it clear that 'love of country' is only ever to become the dominant, not the exclusive, passion of citizens, and that passion is to be peculiarly stressed only when divisiveness, mutual estrangement or hostility is widespread among the people being considered for alternative legislation and government.[7] The objective is, of course, to cause people to recognize and to feel that their own prosperity and moral standing entail the like prosperity and moral standing of others in mutual reciprocity. But that being so does not entail that there should be nothing else that contributes to the good of, comprises a value to, one individual differently from another individual. When speaking of private property, for instance, at CPC 1, 317 (III, 931), Rousseau says he does not want to 'destroy private property absolutely, since this is impossible', even when he is in the course of an argument for reducing it within very limited bounds.

We must not be misled by the exigences imposed by being faced with a disparate, diverse, people riven by conflict and predation, yet still not dissolved altogether, which may require the elevation of public action to a very high demand. It does not follow that this must, or should fitly, command the whole of a person's being and life and make him only one who enjoys a 'relative' existence exclusively. I do not think there is any compelling evidence that Rousseau thought otherwise.

Indeed, we can find even stronger reasons for supposing he cannot have done. Rousseau considers, in GP 9 (III, 994ff), the right of the individual to veto proposed legislation (and also, in Poland at that time, acts of administration). Whilst he thinks it susceptible of abuse, that it has in fact been abused, he thinks it should be retained for cases of 'truly fundamental laws' (GP 9, 216; III, 997). The intelligibility of the retention and use of the title of veto would come altogether into question if we were to take really seriously the idea that in a well-ordered state the individual had no identity and good peculiar to himself which might be opposed to that of others. He would necessarily think and desire in unison with the rest, and there would be no occasion for the employment of the veto. It is quite certain, though, that Rousseau intended no such thing and should not be encumbered with what is, under any circumstances, a radically unrealistic political objective. The whole of this chapter of GP is, in fact, very interesting for the light it throws on, and amplification it offers for, the very cursory remarks Rousseau makes on voting procedures in *The Social Contract* (SC 2, 3; III, 371; compare SC 4, 2; III, 439). The remark made, almost in passing, in Book 2 chapter 3 that if there must be 'partial societies' there should be 'as many as possible' which are as equal (in numbers and effective power) as possible, becomes, in the context of the argument of GP, Rousseau's vigorous defence of the desirability of a confederative constitution for Poland: 'This federative form of action', he writes, 'although it may have arisen by accident, strikes me as a political masterpiece' (GP 9, 218; III, 998). Here we indisputably see that even an identity in the *public* character of a people is not uniquely valued by Rousseau, even though he would not wish the localized loyalty to one element in a federation to lead to secession.

Rousseau, for both theoretical and very practical reasons, characteristically takes himself to be faced with people who are apt to be divided and antagonistic, and who sometimes need others only because the good in what they have and are only makes sense to them in terms of others' non-possession and non-enjoyment (compare CPC 325–6; III, 937), as I indicated above. In such circumstances, it is natural and necessary that he should lay paramount stress on that which still residually unites them, gives them a constructive mutual concern, enables them to have a common care and loyalty. For without this, no association, no nation, can endure very long at all. But it really would be wrong to infer from his placing such stress on this in these circumstances that he envisaged the disappearance of the 'absolute' self as the desirable objective. His final, best, thought is – as I have tried to explain in earlier chapters – that the full achievement and possession of that 'absolute' selfhood requires, as an ineliminable component, reciprocal acknowledgment, respect and care between persons. Community is not a diminution of individuality; it is a condition and component of it. But to say this is not to say that there cannot be a kind and level of civil requirements which 'denature'. For Rousseau it is not so much a question of getting a proper balance between separateness and unity, private and public, as a question of showing how the best possibilities for each of these are mutually conditioned and implicated. I see him trying, shrewdly and soberly, to work out the concrete forms for the articulation of this reciprocal implication in the specific social, cultural and civil matters presented to him in relation to Poland and to Corsica. I do not see him forgetting, or underplaying, one side of the 'equation'. Rousseau does not envisage the commitment to citizenship as one's dominant principle as being the commitment to becoming a 'worker bee'. Priority attaching to one's civil responsibilities does not entail their claim to exhaust all legitimate human commitments.

What I have tried to do in this brief discussion of Rousseau's consideration of the social and political predicaments of Poland and Corsica is to show how he does put to close use the general principles which are discussed in a theoretical context in the *Social Contract*. I highlighted five of the themes prominent in that, and showed how these are to be found structuring the assessments Rousseau makes of the historically conditioned material he is dealing with. From this we can, as I have suggested, learn more precisely and fully what Rousseau's general themes meant to him. I do not believe we should regard these other works as showing any desertion or compromise of them.

# 7

# *Public and Private Religion*

## 1 The Purpose of the Discussion

The purpose of this chapter is limited. I do not intend to explore in any great depth Rousseau's conception of the divine, his notion of God, as a topic of interest in its own right (although it is). What I propose to do is to concentrate on his conceptions of the content of religious belief, of the character of religious conviction, of the nature and significance of religious practices, *in so far as* these have an immediate bearing on the psychological, social and political ideas that have been discussed in earlier chapters. His religious ideas, and ideas about religion, as these extend and amplify these other themes are my concern. So my treatment of this area in Rousseau's work is very limited.

The particular points for attention are these. First, Rousseau includes, in *The Social Contract*, a long discussion of Civil Religion which has attracted much adverse comment (SC 4, 8; III, 460; he considers some related points in his letter to M. d'Alembert on the Theatre,[1] also). I want to consider carefully what Rousseau's concerns were in that discussion, and how these relate to his overall intentions in his political theory. Secondly, and as noted from time to time in earlier argument, Rousseau employs the notion of 'conscience' quite often in explaining the source and nature of moral precepts and moral convictions. Rousseau clearly held that there was a close connection between conscience and 'the voice of God within us'. So I want to consider his ideas about this connection; and how he sees conscience as contributing to the character and hold on us of moral convictions. In a passage I made much of before Rousseau writes:

If this were the place for it, I would try to show how the first voices of conscience arise out of the first movements of the heart, and how the first notions of good and bad are born of the sentiments of love and hate. I would show that *justice* and *goodness* are not merely abstract words . . . but are true affections of the soul enlightened by reason . . . that by reason alone, independent of conscience, no natural law can be established . . . (E 4, 235; IV, 522-3)

It is therefore clear that we cannot have fully understood the significance Rousseau saw in our acquisition and possession of 'moral being' unless we understand the role of conscience in his view of this.

As for the connection between conscience and the voice of God we may consider this expostulation:

> Conscience, conscience, divine instinct, celestial and immortal voice, the certain guide of a being who though limited and ignorant is intelligent and free, infallible judge of good and evil, sublime emanation from the everlasting substance, which makes man resemble God; it is you alone that makes whatever is fine in my nature. (*Lettres Morales*, 5; IV, 1111)

The final matter for consideration will be aspects of that long section in the fourth Book of *Emile*, known as 'the Creed of the Savoyard Vicar' (E 4, 266ff; IV, 565ff). I say 'aspects' of this because out of that I want again to stress only those points which bear principally on man's moral standing and moral commitments and not to follow out all its ideas.[2]

Rousseau's own religious 'career' was somewhat varied. Born into a Geneva still very marked by its Calvinist heritage (though it is argued that some of the rigours of this were much relaxed in Rousseau's time), he was converted to Roman Catholicism in 1728 when he was sixteen. It is doubtful whether this amounted to any very deep spiritual redirection, and his adherence to Catholic doctrine seems never to have been very exacting. As he became more intimate with 'enlightened' thought in the years after 1742, he gave voice to many anti-clerical sentiments, and seems to have conceived an enduring hostility towards the officers, institutions and practices of established churches. On the other hand, he was never at ease with the mockery and disdain of religious sentiments and convictions which he thought he found in the talk and work of 'intellectuals'. Rousseau felt that there was something ineliminable and very important finding expression in such sentiments, which must be acknowledged and cannot be argued into non-existence without grave loss. In 1754, he was re-admitted into the Genevan Church, though again this does not appear to have signified the discovery of his spiritual identity in the doctrines of that Church. Much would seem to have to do with his need to achieve, to recover, a sense of civic and personal belonging; and his desire to participate in the ordered life of a human community. (There are many who are bulwarks of the Church of England for no more (though also no less) reason than that it is an embodiment of English culture and practices). He never formally adopted any other religious allegiance, although, in renouncing his Genevan citizenship in 1763, he also renounced his membership of the Genevan Church. In his later years he found the scrutable face of God in his love of and attention to plants; botany became his absorbing interest. God's inscrutable nature appears to have filled him with terror; his efforts to place his *Dialogues* on the high altar of Notre Dame seem to have been some obscure gesture of supplication. But alongside his own sense of his disjoint position in the world (especially the world of men), he always retained a conviction in providential harmony and order pervading the world and human affairs, which conviction offered him moments of detachment and peace.

We may, perhaps, see Rousseau's rejoining the Genevan Church as his finding, in himself, and acting upon, the need for 'belonging' in a human community – as suggested just above. That need is one which is intended to be met by devising a civil religion, among other needs towards meeting which this institution is also directed. I turn now to a close examination of Rousseau's conception of a 'civil religion'.

## 2 Civil Religion[3]

Critics are apt to see, in Rousseau's ideas about the need for a civil religion, the emergence into plain view of what they consider to be totalitarian elements in his political theories. Those who do not believe the articles of the 'civil profession of faith' are to be banished. Or if someone has made a public act of recognition of these dogmas, but then behaves 'as if he does not believe them', then he may be put to death. (All quotations are from SC 4, 8; III, 460ff; I shall not give specific references.) This appears to imply that there shall be an enforced religion, and that people's religious observance will be sanctioned. The obtrusiveness of state control seems very great. On the other hand, Rousseau is quite explicit that there will be one 'negative dogma' of the civil religion, namely intolerance. And this suggests that the religious yoke may not be so burdensome. What, then, are Rousseau's guiding thoughts in this area?

His principal concern throughout the consideration of this issue is one which has been considered many times before, namely the formation, consolidation and perpetuation of the bonds of unity which integrate the several citizens of one community together in mutual respect, care and common support. Rousseau thinks that religious sentiment and loyalty constitute one of the greates sources of active commitment and willingness to give of oneself to a 'cause' in people. Where such sentiment and loyalty exist at all, this is undoubtedly true. The issue then necessarily arises as to how this object of allegiance shall be accommodated within the terms of the civil association. Rousseau's argument is that there are four possibilities here. First, religious allegiance could remain unregulated and undirected by the civil association. Second, it could be, as far as possible, marginalized, treated as being an insignificant personal or social phenomenon in respect of the efficacy of the terms of association. Whether this represents a serious possibility will depend on the actual depth and pervasiveness of religious allegiance obtaining. Third, it could be regulated by the terms of the civil association. Finally, religious allegiance could actually be united with certain of the requirements of the terms of civil association (though there could remain elements in that allegiance not so united, and perhaps not substantially regulated either).

It will be clear that Rousseau favours the fourth alternative. He does so for two kinds of reasons, concerned, first, with the hazards presented to the body politic in any other case; and, second, with the positive benefits this alternative will bring to the body politic. I consider these, briefly, in reverse order.

If, associated with the fundamental civil requirements of mutual level respect and care to be afforded by each citizen to each citizen, there are religious sentiments, then breach of these requirements will be experienced as impiety, as being the kind of act which brings down divine retribution as well as civil sanction. Compliance with these requirements, on the other hand, will be felt to find the favour and blessing of the divinity, and will afford the agent the assurance that he will be doing what is pleasing to him who controls the destiny of his spirit. Such sentiments, in short, invest civil obedience with a deeper significance so that such obedience becomes more complete and dedicated. But Rousseau is not saying that, without this, the laws would not have their proper force. It is not a question of turning something which is, in itself, arbitrary and groundless into an unavoidable demand just because hedged around with obscure terrors. It is rather a question, as Rousseau puts it, of making an 'addition' to 'the force [the laws] have in themselves' already. For we have seen, principally in chapter 5, that, without religious connection, the terms (laws) of civil association *do* have cogent force and authority 'in themselves'. This equally marks out the proper scope and limit of that which should become connected with religious sentiment and commitment. Rousseau writes:

> Now, it matters very much to the community that each citizen should have a religion. That will make him love his duty; but the dogmas of that religion concern the State and its members only so far as they have reference to morality and to the duties which he who professes them is bound to do to others. Each man may have, over and above, what opinions he pleases, without its being the sovereign's business to take cognizance of them . . .

What should be plain from this is that 'morality' and the 'duties [we are] bound to do to others' are established first, on grounds the cogency of which owe nothing initially to 'religion'. These comprise the fundamental constitutive terms of civil association, as considered previously. Religious sentiments are then to be added to these, but do not contribute to the original establishment. So it is not, as Rousseau himself explains, that he who disobeys the dogmas of civil religion is banished for *impiety*, but is banished, 'as an anti-social being, incapable of loving the laws and justice'. We may still, of course, take exception to this. But it should now be clear that the exception must be to Rousseau's possibly over-zealous scrutiny of what might contribute to lawlessness, not to his enforcement of religious conformity. If civil dogmas attach to the basic terms of law, then rejection of those dogmas signals a person's intent to override, or ignore the law. No civil association, concerned only with its civil tasks, can remain indifferent to that.

I consider now the hazards associated with the other alternatives Rousseau envisages, but rejects as unsatisfactory. Doing so, we shall also be able to see why he proscribes intolerance, this being the 'negative dogma' of civil religion. Rousseau's first point is that if religious allegiance is unregulated by, or unconnected with, observance of and allegiance to the basic civil requirements of the community, it will comprise an object of loyalty which will be socially subversive or disruptive. A person may, for example, contend that his religious commitments preclude him from, or exempt him from, civil obedience. This, if unregulated, constitutes his setting himself above the law, and his severance of himself from the body politic. But, as we have seen, this cannot be a civilly admissible possibility. Rousseau stresses other points as well. Even if there is no serious conflict between religious and civil allegiance, it may well be the case that the division of loyalty produces a tepid and unconvinced commitment to the maintenance and prosperity of the civil body which, he thinks, cannot be acceptable. He further argues that religious zeal divides the world into the saved and the damned, and thus encourages the zealots either to disregard or to persecute the damned, to redeem them or to rid the world of their noxious presence. This, evidently, breeds social division and hostility and spells the end of the civil association.

Thus, Rousseau distinguishes three 'kinds of religion'. The first is 'confined to the purely internal cult of the supreme God and the eternal obligations of morality'. The second is 'codified in a single country, [and] gives it its gods, its own tutelary patrons.' The third Rousseau calls 'the religion of the priest', in which there is a 'theological system' separate from the 'political system'. Here, the clergy of some religious denomination comprise a corporate body, with a corporate will, distinct from, but claiming authority at least equal to (aided by the power of eternal damnation), the sovereign in the body politic. To each of these Rousseau makes objection. To the third, that it destroys social unity and makes men subject to contradictory duties so that they cannot be 'faithful both to religion and to citizenship'. To the second, that, although it 'teaches . . . that service done to the State is service done to its tutelary god' (which is a good), it also deceives men and becomes tyrannous and exclusive. It 'makes a people bloodthirsty and intolerant . . . and regards as a sacred act the killing of every one who does not believe in its gods'.

To the first kind of religion, Rousseau objects that it leads to indifference to the earthly prosperity and safety of the citizens and the body politic as a whole. The state is open to usurpation of public authority, since 'in this vale of sorrows, what does it matter whether we are free men or serfs?' Finally, it leads to the state being easy prey in war; for 'what does it matter whether they win or lose? Does not providence know better than they what is meet for them?'[4]

Some of these points Rousseau makes in objection are disputable. But his overriding intent in making them should be plain enough. He is concerned to ensure that paramount place in the civil community be occupied by the requirement that each citizen pay to each that equal level respect and care which, as he has argued, comprises the constitutive civil (and moral) bond uniting people together in one common body. Rousseau says, quite explicitly, that 'the sovereign has no authority in the other world, [so] whatever the lot of its subjects may be in the life to come, that is not its business, provided they are good citizens in this life'. That proviso dictates the extent, and the limits, of the regulation of religious loyalty and action by, and of its ordering to, civil purposes. Any further constraint, but equally any less regulation, is contrary to the proper ends of law.

We are, perhaps, less inclined to take the issue of the civil regulation of religious allegiance as seriously as Rousseau. For it is, in the United Kingdom at any rate, no longer any very powerful centre of alternative loyalty. But elsewhere in the world this is not so. And were it not so in the UK, Rousseau's suggestions for the ordered incorporation of such allegiances into the life of the civil body do not seem unreasonable. It should be evident, at least, that his suggestions are designed to exclude religious division and intolerance and to turn religious allegiance to the sustaining and strengthening of common mutual respect. So far from its being the case, then, that Rousseau intends to reinforce religious exclusion and hostility by the sanction of law, he intends to reinforce civil tolerance and equal humane concern with the sanctions of religion. (On this subject, see also E 4, 309; IV, 628; E 5, 381; IV, 728.)

### 3 Conscience and the Voice of God

Rousseau considers the character and personal significance of conscience at length in works which fall outside the ambit of this discussion, in *La Nouvelle Héloïse* for instance.[5] My examination of his views about conscience will not attempt to appraise this additional material. It will, therefore, be very selective. But it remains useful to consider what importance Rousseau attaches to conscience within the context of the arguments I have been looking at. For, at several crucial points, he makes reference to it as contributing to moral standing and understanding, and to moral relations between people. Our grasp of his meaning at these points will, therefore, be incomplete if we do not consider what he had in mind. It is, however, only with a view to securing a fuller grasp of these points that I direct my discussion, and no further.

As mentioned above and elsewhere previously, Rousseau discusses the notion of conscience in this passage in *Emile*:

> I would show that *justice* and *goodness* are not merely abstract words – pure moral beings formed by the understanding – but are true affections of the soul enlightened by reason, are hence only an ordered development of our primitive affections; that by reason alone, independent of conscience, no natural law can be established; and that the entire right of nature is only a chimera if it is not founded on a natural need in the human heart. (E 4, 235; IV, 522. See also the footnote to this paragraph in Rousseau's text.)

I have tried to show, in earlier argument, how central a statement this is to Rousseau's theories. It is obvious, then, that to grasp its full force we need to understand the place, and contribution, of conscience to the 'ordered development of our . . . affections' and to the power of reason to establish 'natural law' and to secure our compliance with that.

Most of Rousseau's assessments of the nature and significance of conscience made in *Emile* come in that long, more or less self-contained, section of Book 4 called 'The Creed (or: Profession of Faith) of the Savoyard Vicar' (E 4, 266–313; IV, 565–635). During the time Rousseau was working on the main text of *Emile* he was also thinking extremely intensively about his conceptions of God and about man's relation to God. This passage in *Emile* contains his fullest statement of his ideas about these matters at this period. Rousseau introduces the discussion somewhat awkwardly in relation to his overall progress, by way of addressing Emile's need at this point to come to have knowledge of God. The main body of the material is presented in the form of a conversation between a young man who has 'struggled against his destiny without success' (really Rousseau himself) and a 'decent ecclesiastic . . . whom a youthful adventure had put in disfavour with his bishop' (E 4, 262; IV, 559). The details of the genesis of this setting will not detain us.

At E 4, 289 (IV, 598) Rousseau gives the following 'definition' of conscience:

> There is in the depths of souls, then, an innate principle of justice and virtue according to which, in spite of our own maxims, we judge our actions and those of others as good or bad. It is to this principle that I give the name *conscience*.

Later on, he says also this (E 5, 473; IV, 857):

> But the eternal laws of nature and order do exist. For the wise man, they take the place of positive law. They are written in the depth of his heart by conscience and reason. It is to these that he ought to enslave himself in order to be free.

Most of what Rousseau finds significant about conscience can be excogitated from these remarks.

In the 'Creed' Rousseau argues that man cannot be understood wholly in terms of his material composition, his sensations, instincts. We are obliged to recognize, he says, a separate principle at work in man, powers and dispositions which cannot be attributed to us solely on the basis of our material constitution and reflexes. The bearer of these additional capacities and dispositions he calls the soul. The primary attribute of man's soul is conscience; and it is principally in view of becoming aware of the feelings and judgments of conscience that we know we have souls (compare E 4, 286; IV, 594[6]). Conscience stands to the soul as instinct to the body. But not only are body and soul distinct, they can be opposed, in conflict, in their promptings. It is conscience that can check us in yielding to the importunate press of sensual desire and pleasure, to resist the urges of inflamed passion, and it can direct us to choosing to do what is right and just instead.

So, in the first instance, conscience is that attribute through which we love the good and hate the bad. Rousseau holds that our having such an attribute is 'innate'; I shall return to this. He adds, however, that we require reason to know good and bad; so although conscience is 'independent of reason, [it] cannot therefore be developed without it' (E 1, 67; IV, 288). Rousseau then encounters the objection that what 'instructs' the dispositions of conscience is not right reason, but only 'prejudices' (E 4, 267, 289; IV, 566, 598). But he argues in reply to this objection that, if we listen to the promptings of our soul with sincerity and candour, it will speak to us in authentic and truthful ways undeformed by the prejudices of men. It would thus appear that Rousseau believes that even if conscience is not, *ab initio*, a cognitive source in addition to being a source of motivation, it comes to bear the marks of right reason in regard to conduct and to be the continuing repository of this in each of us.

What is the ultimate characterization of 'right' reason as that is contained in the judgements and regrets of conscience? These judgements relate to the good order which pervades man, nature and all things, which is placed and sustained there by God. (I shall look at this further in the next section.) So, in the sentiments and judgements of unclouded conscience God's design and purpose for us, which is encoded in our natural constitution and dispositions, is made known to us. In keeping faith with conscience we are keeping faith with the deepest principles of our own integrity as well-made beings ordered to our proper good. Conscience, in sometimes opposing sensual desire and headlong passion, is not thwarting us in securing proper satifations. It is, rather, directing us to continue to hold true and to act for the sake of our enduring well-being, and to eschew pleasures which would only ruin or damage us, however exciting and gratifying they may appear in prospect.

Many of these points appear to be no more than fairly conventional platitudes, at least in respect of a 'protestant' conception of the individual possession of, and sovereignty in, judgements of conscience. However, I suggest that there is a deep core of thought to which Rousseau is giving articulation in these ideas.

We know, from earlier discussion, that Rousseau's primary conception of what is 'natural' to each of us is that which conduces to each our amplitude of rewarding life and the full liberation of our powers and capacities. He has also a profound argument that vicious traits, such as cruelty, malice, envy, greed and the like are, in this same sense, 'unnatural' or contrary to our nature. This is because, in possessing and enacting these traits, we are governed at root by aggression and hatred, and these motives cripple and diminish our own lives quite as much as they can wreak havoc in the lives of others. Rousseau shows, in short, that we benefit from being good, and suffer in doing wrong or evil, through his complex and subtle diagnosis of the psychological significance of the relevantly related human dispositions.

For all that this may be true (and let us here now take it that it is) there are very powerful feelings and desires in humans which prompt them to embrace objectives and actions which are evil and unnatural. This, again, I discussed at length earlier. The knowledge that we harm ourselves by yielding to such feelings may be, and often is, quite insufficient to check their prompting and our action on them. I suggest, then, that what Rousseau sees as the role of conscience is to serve as a motivationally potent alternative source for adherence to what is natural in us, and to what is, being so, both beneficial to us and also the root of morally good dispositions and actions. Of course, conscience though potent is not omnipotent in securing this adherence. But it plays a role in the economy of human motives in addition to the uncertain, and often dim, light of long-term prudence.

The 'eternal laws of nature and order' which find voice in the promptings of conscience come to this. It is Rousseau's fundamental conviction, backed up by detailed argument, that human nature is well-ordered, in that its undeformed expression will lead to personal well-being and to harmonious, constructive human relations. We can, then, 'trust' to our nature for our own good and the good order of human society. Rousseau sees in this fundamental beneficial tendency in integrated nature the hand of a benevolent deity who has 'designed' us in such a way that, if we do not turn against our own proper principles, we shall find individual satisfaction and mutual harmony. So, in keeping faith with our own nature we are keeping faith with the laws that that benevolent deity has inscribed into the workings of his creatures, and at the same time keeping faith with our own deepest need and good and that of those around us as well.

Placing this sort of interpretation on Rousseau's meaning is not just speculative. The passage I quoted above (from E 5, 473; IV, 857) continues by saying that: 'The only slave is the man who does evil, for he always does it in spite of himself.' We know that this is not idle rhetoric on Rousseau's part, since – as I have recalled just above – he has powerful arguments explaining how and why the evil man, in his cruelty, malice etc, is at odds with himself. So it is that, in serving conscience – understood as the repository of the voice of the requirements of intact nature – we are at one with ourselves, free and unimpeded in complete self-disclosure. Again, when Rousseau counters the objection that conscience may be just the work of prejudices (E 4, 289ff; IV, 498ff) he says that the 'sentiments' which evaluate the 'ideas' which 'come to us from outside' lie within us, and: 'it is by them alone that we know the compatibility or incompatibility between us and the things we ought to seek or flee.' These evaluations are the acts of conscience, and by these we know that what we ought to seek is what is 'compatible' to us, and what we ought to flee is 'incompatible' to us.

If we take away the theological implications Rousseau ascribes to these disclosures of conscience, the issue becomes, in effect, one of why anger and hatred should not be incorporated by us as the permanent governing motives of our lives (compare E 4, 287; IV, 595). Why is it that constructive care and good affections should be supposed to be the authentic voice of nature which we are heeding if, out of love, we withhold aggression or envy? I want very briefly to look at what Wollheim says about this sort of issue, working in a context of ideas which, as I have tried earlier to show, have close application to Rousseau's work.[7] Wollheim asks – in a way that recalls the earlier discussion here of the place of compassion in Rousseau's psychological and moral theory – the following question:[8]

> Granted that with the onset of depressive anxiety the child recognizes that it loves and hates the same figure, why does this provide any kind of motivation for it to control hate and to cultivate love? Why shouldn't the child prefer hate to love?

Wollheim suggests two reasons in answer to this as to why love tends to be preferred to hate. First, hate requires an antecedent characterization of its object in order to appear justified. And this characterization is provided by the projection of aggression on to the object. Love, on the other hand, does not require this, or any, characterization, and can 'dissolve' that produced by hate. Secondly, and more important here, is the fact that we have 'a native incapacity' to tolerate aggression, which is shown in the fact that it is projected on to another who is then found hateful. I take this fact, in the context now under discussion, to show that aggression is found to be inimical to the continued viable and abundant life of the individual, and is thus, in Rousseau's notion, 'unnatural'. In so far as morally evil traits, such as cruelty, envy, malice and the like, are rooted in manifestations of aggression and hatred these will also, and likewise, require projection to sustain them, and will be experienced as inimical to the life of the individual. Thus we being to see how what 'we ought to seek or flee' (which I am taking to signify that which is morally speaking good or evil) can be shown to be compatible or incompatible with the possibilities of happy and rewarding life for us.

Although it would take too long to trace the connections out, this line of argument in Wollheim is connected to an account of what he calls 'the pre-history of the superego'. Thus it stands in immediate relation to Rousseau's conception of conscience, and, in particular, to Rousseau's idea that conscience need not be a self-punitive and persecutory attribute but an endorsement and reinforcement of creativity and that which makes for life. If we utilize that approximate and somewhat misleading distinction between the 'superego' and the 'ego-ideal', and say the former is coercive and defensive against fear, the latter intent upon perpetuating love,[9] we can say that Rousseau's notion of conscience approximates to that of an 'ego-ideal'. His awareness of the deep difference, of the opposition, between persecution-induced compliance and love-engendered collaboration has been explored and documented at length already. Command, obedience, duty and obligation are to be 'proscribed' from Emile's 'lexicon' in his early days. (E 2, 89; IV, 316). We now see, yet more fully, why this should be so.

## 4 Man's Place in God's Order

> As for me – I who have no system to maintain, I, a simple and true man who is carried away by the fury of no party and does not aspire to the honour of being chief of a sect, I who am content with the place in which God has put me, I see nothing, except for Him, that is better than my species. And if I had to choose my place in the order of beings, what more could I choose than to be a man . . . Can I see myself thus distinguished without congratulating myself on filling this honourable post and without blessing the hand which placed me in it? (E 4, 278; IV, 582–3)

As early as DI (47; III, 135) Rousseau argued that man was 'taking him all round, the most advantageously organized of any of the animals'. Later, we are told, men became aware of their greater advantages (mainly practical) over other animals, and 'felt the first emotion of pride'. So man looked 'upon his species as of the highest order' (DI 77–8; III, 165–6). We find the same theme being maintained again in Rousseau's mature reflections.

As I indicated, I do not intent to consider in any detail the edifice of religious belief Rousseau believes proper to a 'simple and true man', who is not absorbed by party or sect. I propose only to try to explain the significance of Rousseu's idea that being a man is, as such, an 'honourable post', and the connection between that idea and his psychological and moral themes.

Rousseau stresses the harmonious, interlocking and coordinated order obtaining between all the elements in the world that he believes we find (until disrupted by the perverse will of man). Such order, he claims; testifies to the work of an intelligence, of a supreme intelligence (E 4, 275; IV, 578). The merely fortuitous concurrence of elements could not have produced the 'ordered relations' that we find. There is, then, will which moves things, and intelligence which orders their movement in concert. This concerted action and interaction tends to the preservation and well-being of all that participates in it. This supremely intelligent will is, thus, also good. So, Rousseau concludes (E 4, 277; IV, 581):

> This Being which wills and is powerful, this Being active in itself, this Being, whatever it may be, which moves the Universe and orders all things, I call *God*. I join to this name the ideas of intelligence, power, and will which I have brought together, and that of goodness which is their necessary consequence.

We need then to consider what 'rank' man occupies in this order of things. Rousseau argues that man is of the first rank, because of the scope and ingenuity of his action; because of his industry and practical intelligence; because of his capacity to understand the whole and his own position in that. In all these ways we are distanced from, and elevated above, the brutes. And these reflections conclude with the passage quoted at the start of this section.

What moral lesson is to be drawn from this realization that standing as a man in the order God gave the world is holding an honourable post? There are two immediate points arising from it. First, Rousseau contends that upon the realization that we enjoy this good, enjoy it as an unmerited, unearned blessing, we are moved to gratitude to the 'Author of [our] species'. The structure of this mode of response to a freely given good has been considered at length in chapter 4, above. Although Rousseau does not make the point again in the course of this present argument, we can infer – drawing on earlier discussion – that this gratitude strengthens generally the individual's sense of his own good and hence creative and beneficent potency. This will naturally tend to reinforce his tendency to morally good and sustaining dispositions and actions.

The second point concerns the provocations to inflamed *amour-propre*. I considered, in chapter 2, Rousseau's claim that a person's necessary and proper desire to find established counting standing for himself in the transactions of men will engender humane (secondary) passions or cruel (secondary) passions depending upon the position 'he will feel he has among men' and upon 'what kinds of obstacles he may believes he has to overcome to reach the position he wants to occupy' (E 4, 235; IV, 523–4). If the position contended for is dominating and exclusive, and the obstacles believed placed in the way are thought to be malign and unremitting, then *amour-propre* will take an exacerbated form and breed cruel passion and traits. But we now see that we have the possibility of regarding ourselves as having been elevated, by the free generosity of our Author, to the first rank among all the species and elements of the world. By this alone we can find ourselves well honoured and well reckoned with, and have the demands of our *amour-propre* met. Contention for exclusive, invidious, mastery over other men, perceived as the only condition on which we can find testimony to our telling import as counting presences,

will become unnecessary. Such ambitions will be bred of a delusion of insigni-
ficance which attention to the gift and blessing afforded to us by the good will
of the Deity can expel. The painful fear of insignifance is removed, and with
that is also removed the insistent imposing demand for dominating force in and
over the lives of other men. The consolations of belief in a benevolent Deity are
not that it causes one to put aside the concerns of this life, concerns with happiness, significant status and the like, to turn away 'from all earthly things'
(cf. SC 4, 8, 273–4; III, 465). It is rather that it provides an assured and immut-
able answer to these 'earthly' needs, an assurance of the possibility that all
manner of things shall be well, and that one's being and well-being is ineliminably reckoned with and honoured. Indeed, the certainty gained by this that one
should not be regarded as negligible may form the basis of a not-to-be-gainsaid
demand that other *men* receive and acknowledge one as of the same, honourable,
rank as themselves when, as a result of their own excessive *amour-propre*, they
are apt to enforce ignomiy or dispossession upon one.

In the argument of 'The Creed', Rousseau presents a dualism of motivation
and concern, which divides the 'love of justice and moral beauty' from 'the
empire of the senses and . . . the passions' (E 4, 278; IV, 583). I noted this in
section 3, above. To the first 'principle' he attaches love of God and the
workings of conscience; to the second, sensuality and the demands of inflamed
*amour-propre*. Given his earlier, very subtle and highly detailed, discussion of
the different possible forms of development of *amour-propre*, this dualism
seems unnecessary and misleading. There appears to be no need to conjecture
two disparate principles of action and concern, when we have been offered a
full and careful explanation of how the love or justice and goodness may be
seen to be 'an ordered development of our primitive affections', born of love
and hate (E 4, 235; IV, 523, again). How that development is in accord with our
nature, and bears testimony to the benevolence of our Creator, has been
considered, and seems sufficiently accounted for without introducing psychological hypotheses which are both implausible and under-grounded.

Finally, and again drawing on earlier discussion, we may recall that the
grateful response of a person to his benefactor naturally directs him to make
return, to collaborate and further the needs and designs of that person. So it is
with the gratitude which recognition of our Author's gift to us gives rise to. We
find it natural, in the light of this, not only to carry further his purposes in
preserving the good order of the world, and honouring other people as each of
them is honoured by Him, but to give time to laud and extol His name. So,
when he concludes this passage of his discussion, Rousseau is able to give this
statement of what Emile will now know and feel to be his 'true interest':

> . . . he finds his true interest in being good, in doing good far from the sight of
> men and without being forced by the laws, in being just between God and
> himself, in fulfilling his duty, even at the expense of his life, and in carrying

virtue in his heart. He does this not only for the love of order, to which each of us always prefers love of self, but for the love of the Author of his being – a love which is confounded with that same love of self – and, finally, for the enjoyment of that durable happiness which the repose of a good conscience and the contemplation of this Supreme Being promise him in the other life after he has spent this one well. (E 4, 314; IV, 636)

Although we may be apt to regard such passages as more inspirational and devotional than clear-headed and firmly cogent, I have tried to show how, in fact, many of Rousseau's most pervasive ideas are knit together in a tight and precise way in this treatment of the moral significance of religious conviction. I should maintain that nothing in the significance and force of Rousseau's most enduring moral ideas is lost if we subtract the religious elaborations he gives to them. But I should also maintain that these elaborations are thoroughly continuous with those ideas, and do not muddy or contradict them. I conclude, as I began, by agreeing with Rousseau that he has 'written on diverse subjects, but always from the same principles, always the same morality, the same faith, the same maxims, and, if you like, the same opinions' (LCB IV, 928). This is not because he imposed a unitary theory which he forced everything to fit in with. It is because he discerned, in depth and detail, the recurrent patterns which pervade and shape so many aspects of human nature and human action.

# Notes

Full details of works referred to are given in the Bibliography.

## Introduction

1 Details of the texts used, and of the relation between Rousseau's works considered and the chapters here, are set out on pp. x–xi, xiv
2 The system of referencing employed is explained on p. x
3 There are useful summaries of a great body of interpretative work on Rousseau given in Gay: ch. 8; and Horowitz: ch. 1, Introduction.
4 Rousseau expresses this thought on very many occasions, in slightly different formulations. The most succinct, though I doubt the best known, formulation is in *Rousseau juge de Jean-Jacques*; 1, 934.
5 Canovan, p. 90.
6 Watkins, p. x; p. xxxiv.
7 Plamenatz, pp. 392–3.
8 Charvet, p. 146.
9 The mistake of taking inflamed or excessive *amour-propre* for *amour-propre* as such is one I have also inclined to in the past. See Dent (4).
10 Appeal has been made to the idea of paranoia to explain Rousseau, Rousseau's work, or other political events, by, for example, Hofstader; title essay; Solomon, ch. 3. Starobinski refers in his book to Lacan: *De la psychose paranoîaque*, but I have not read this.
11 See, in general, Klein (1); Segal, especially chs. 3–5.
12 Freud's ideas are employed extensively by Starobinski and Horowitz, for instance.

## Chapter 1 Themes and Issues

1 Compare Geach (2), pp. 94–5; Augustine, Book 2, ch. 4
2 See Butler, Preface; Sermons 1–3, ll, 12.
3 These points will be considered at length in ch. 2.
4 Weil: p. 28 and *passim*.
5 See E 2, 92 (IV, 322); and E 4, 212–3 (IV, 490–91).
6 Compare E 2, 89(IV, 316).
7 See, in this connection, E 1, 66–8 (IV, 287–91), especially p. 68. And compare Bloom's note 2 to E Book 4.
8 A child has, of course, no *prior* possesion of any account of the character and

operations of the physical world nor of human beings. The 'world' is characterized as the complement to the affective and volitional processes of the child. Compare E 1, 66 (IV, 287).

9 For this sort of framework of account, see Segal, Introduction and *passim*; Wollheim (1).

10 Compare E 4, 230 (IV, 515): 'The man of the world is whole in his mask. Almost never being in himself, he is always alien and ill at ease when forced to go back there.'

11 Compare Klein (2), p. 190.

12 See, on this, DI 70 (III, 157–8); E 4, 214–15 (IV, 493–4); E 5, 429ff (IV, 796ff).

## Chapter 2 Self-Estrangement and Subservience to Others

1 See Rousseau's 'replies to his critics', in Gourevitch, Part 2. Especially the *Letter to Grimm*, pp. 56–7 (III, 62–3).

2 The notion of 'invidious' prestige, consumption etc., is explained, and employed to great effect, by Veblen.

3 See E 4, 339 (IV, 671); and compare Gilbert, *passim*.

4 Think of Cassio's fearful outburst (*Othello*, Act 2, Scene 3): 'Reputation, reputation, reputation! O! I have lost my reputation. I have lost the immortal part of myself, and what remains is bestial. My reputation, Iago, my reputation!'

5 How theories of social explanation should be made is, of course, very controversial. For some now classic discussions see Winch; Cioffi; and articles in Wilson (ed.).

6 A very simple, but perfectly convincing, case is given by Foot, p. 87, of being dismayed by something thought good which is 'the prelude to a hunt for the adverse aspect of the thing, thought of as lurking behind the pleasant façade'.

7 See Geach's discussion of this; Geach (1): pp. 90ff.

8 Consider Shakespeare's Sonnet 29; and compare Rousseau's savage discussion of the 'old satyr', E 4, 349–50 (IV, 684–6).

9 These include the *Observations* (to the King of Poland); the *Letter to Grimm*, the *Last Reply* and other pieces. See note 1, above (and III, 31–107).

10 For Rousseau's account of this, see *Confessions*, Book 8, pp. 350ff (I, 375ff).

11 See Bloom's discussion of this in his translation of *Emile*; note 17 to Book 2 (pp. 483–4).

12 Barbara Foxley's translation was first printed in 1911, and has remained in print ever since (Dent: Everymans; Library).

13 Anyone who is inclined to think that the distinction of pride and vanity is clear and effective should consider: Plamenatz, I, pp. 421–2; Smith, Part IV, section iii, para. 35ff (pp. 255ff); Rousseau, CPC 325–6 (III, 937–8). These passages should banish that thought.

14 Charvet, p. 85.

15 Horowitz, p. 237.

16 The nearest approach to Rousseau's idea of proper, temperate *amour-propre* is, I suggest, to be found in Plato's conception of the nature and role of *thumos* in the tripartite soul as described in the *Republic*. But since Plato's idea is as little understood as Rousseau's, making the connection is probably of little help. See Gosling, ch. 3, pp. 45–6.

17 See E 2, 85 (IV, 311): '. . . master and slave are mutually corrupted.' Rousseau's insight into the character and implications of this symbiosis is very deep, as I hope to show.

18  We are obviously intended to think of Thrasymachus' theory of justice as presented in *Republic*, Book 1, when Rousseau raises such questions as these.

19  I have not been able to find the origin of the notion of a 'positional' good. I came across the term in an occasional piece by A.H. Halsey.

20  The *locus classicus* for a discussion of this sort of change in language is in Thucydides, Book 3, para. 82. 'Faces' prepared to meet other 'faces' are found in Eliot's 'Prufrock'.

21  Compare E 4, 278 (IV, 582–3) on the 'honourable post' of being a man. This passage is discussed also in ch. 7, sect. 4.

22  Compare Plato's argument (*Republic*, 581d–586d) to the effect that the desire of pleasure ordered by reason's rule is ordered to *its own* maximal satisfaction, and not circumscribed in its possible 'returns' by that rule. I discuss this in Dent (3), pp. 104–6.

23  Think again of Thrasymachus' theory of justice (note 18, above); and of the Hobbesian account of the 'time of war': Hobbes, ch. 13.

24  S.R.L. Clark gives the following quotation from Mao Tse-Tung: 'It should be pointed out that the source of ultra-democracy consists in the petty bourgeoisie's individualistic aversion to discipline'. Clark, p. 7.

25  On the notion of an 'object-relation' being inherent to the primordial reactivity of an infant, see, for instance, Klein (3), pp. 248-9; Segal, ch. 2. This approach promises, I believe, by far the best account of our formation of the idea of ourselves in our world. But it is out of the question to consider the matter further here.

26  A very clear and telling depiction of the phenomena being considered here is given by Rousseau in his account of the 'two young men' (E 4, 227ff; IV, 512ff). The young man possessed by 'inflamed' *amour-propre* is tormented by ideas of others' mockery, contempt, their plotting to humiliate him. See also *Emile* (Manuscrit Favre) IV, 231: 'The monsters of imagination are forged in the disproportion between desires and power' (to satisfy them).

27  It is important to remember however that envy and greed can (and very often do) spoil these very goods they purport to seek (because these goods are hated for being too little, too late, to put it crudely).

28  Rousseau checks Emile's 'premature' sexual interest; see E 4, 214–9 (IV, 494ff).

29  '. . . the words *obey* and *command* will be proscribed from his lexicon' (E 2, 89; IV, 316).

30  Plamenatz (I, p. 377, note 1) seems to me to articulate this point very clearly and precisely, but professes himself still unable to make sense of it. This testifies to his good nature more than, at this moment, his acumen.

31  Rousseau returns to the sexual element in Emile's character in *Emile* Book 4 and in Book 5. For Rousseau, our sexuality was always central to certain very important kinds of 'being for others' we may come to (want to) have. See also Scruton, chs.2–4.

32  See also the discussion of sexual jealousy at E 5, 429–31 (IV, 796–9). See ch. 1, note 12.

33  Rousseau has a very sensitive discussion of this last sort of point in the *Reveries*, 8th Walk, p. 128 (I, 1078); 9th Walk, p. 148 (I, 1094), for instance. Compare Strawson.

34  Compare also DI, 86 (III, 174).

## Chapter 3 *A Rejected 'Solution': The Self in Isolation*

1 Contrast Klein here, who, of course, affords ineliminable place to the 'death instinct'. See Klein (4), pp. 236–8, for instance.

2 For an account of Aristotle's procedure, see Joachim, pp. 114–5; and Dent (1), p. 335.

3 I discuss this point in Dent (2), pp. 177–8.

4 Adam Smith has a very penetrating discussion of different forms of and bases for self-respect. See, for instance, Smith, Part 1, sect. III, ch. 3; Part VI, sect. III.

5 Compare Mill, pp. 283–4, on the 'three aspects' of 'every human action' – its 'moral', 'aesthetic' and 'sympathetic' aspects. See also Hume on the different sentiments attaching to different species of virtue: Appendix IV, pp. 316–17.

6 See Hume, again, insisting that moral sentiments are not to be 'fettered' by 'narrow systems'. Hume, Appendix IV, pp. 318–20.

7 Compare Schopenhauer's discussion of 'that relative and comparative' freedom of humans. Schopenhauer (1), pp. 32–42.

8 Compare Butler's notion of conscience; Butler: Preface, Sermons 1–3.

9 A very clear example of failing to distinguish these very different kinds of, and roles for, 'comparison' is to be found in Charvet's discussion of Rousseau's arguments about human relations established through pity (Charvet, pp. 84–9). The absence of such distinctions fuels Charvet's critical assessment of Rousseau.

10 Compare Rousseau's 'summary of the whole of human wisdom in the use of the passions', at E 4, 219 (IV, 501). See also *Emile et Sophie* (IV, 883): '. . . the foremost wisdom is to wish what is, and to order one's heart to its destiny'.

## Chapter 4 *The Self Completed: Standing with Others*

1 On the significance of the idea of 'passion', see Dent (2), p. 72. See also Spinoza: Parts 3 and 4.

2 See, for instance, Segal ch. 6.

3 Compare Klein (5), p. 269; Klein (6), p. 293, for instance.

4 I have been very much helped, in making out the structure of Rousseau's ideas here, by Charvet's discussion (especially ch. 3). But I disagree with nearly every substantive conclusion Charvet draws about the material.

5 On this, see Charvet, pp. 92–3. See also Schopenhauer (2), 516ff.

6 On 'projective identification', see Segal pp. 27–8; Klein (7), passim.

7 Schopenhauer (2), p. 183. Schopenhauer's entire discussion is highly pertinent to this whole matter.

8 Compare Cavell's discussion of Mark Tapley's sea-sickness; Cavell (2), p. 361.

9 Aristotle, EN, Book 6, ch. 13. See also Dent (2): pp. 182–4.

10 On this point, see Aristotle again, for instance at EN 1144a, 30–5.

11 This is very much Charvet's conclusion, at least with regard to the way Rousseau has 'set up' the issues as Charvet assesses this. But I do not accept Charvet's assessment; nor do I think that Rousseau has set up the issues in any special, idiosyncratic, way. Rousseau has the nature of the case right.

12 Compare Charvet's objection that since Emile's 'benign' motives require 'education', that throws doubt on their being 'natural'. Charvet, pp. 89–90.

13 I discuss this briefly in Dent (2), p. 29, for instance.

14 See Charvet, pp. 88–9, who argues that the compassionate person's motive is to acquire a value in the eyes of the person he helps.

15 I give brief consideration to this in Dent (2), ch. 6, sect. vi.

16 The *locus classicus* for a presentation of these issues is, of course, Plato's *Republic*. See also Foot, *passim*.

17 Compare Kant (1), p. 423, with his scornful remarks about everybody who 'prates about sympathy and goodwill', but still 'traffics in human rights'.

18 See, again, the remark of Mao's quoted in note 24, ch. 2.

19 Watkins appears to think that the alternatives we are confronted with are either the despotism of the individual or the despotism of the group (with the enslavement of the individual). Watkins, *passim*.

20 SC Book 2, ch. 7 (III, 381ff).

21 See Cavell (1) for a sensitive discussion of aspects of such a matter as this.

22 The unavoidable reference is to Lovelace: 'Yet this Inconstancy is such, As you too shall adore; I could not love thee (Deare) so much, Lov'd I not Honour more.'

23 Compare the late (and often overlooked) passage in Plato (*Republic* 590d), where he says that the control of 'divine wisdom' should 'if possible come from within; failing that it must be imposed from without, in order that, being under the same guidance, we may all be friends and equals'.

24 Contrast Aristotle's comments on the 'deliberative faculty' of women; *Politics* 1260a, 1ff.

25 See Sparshott's very interesting discussion of this; and see also note 2 to ch. 3 above.

26 Compare Cavell (2), p. 326 on how 'moral relationship' is required before moral argument can begin (whether it succeeds or fails as argument).

27 The passages from Emile Book 5 pp. 458ff, IV, 836ff) concerning the 'science of political right' are substantially excerpted in the Cole/Brumfitt/Hall edition of SC (pp. 300ff).

## Chapter 5  The Self Indivisible from the Whole: Politics and Freedom

1 See Rousseau's own account of this, in *The Confessions*, Book 9 (and Book 10).

2 *Julie, ou La Nouvelle Héloïse* was published in 1761 and was an enormous success. See Introduction to McDowell's (abridged) translation. Rousseau's work on the materials of L'Abbe de Saint-Pierre is printed in OC III, 563ff.

3 Some passages from the first version of SC (known as the Geneva manuscript) are printed in Cole/Brumfitt/Hall. See pp. 155–62 ('The General Society of the Human Race'); and pp. 280ff. The whole is printed in OC III, pp. 281ff.

4 I refer to the differing proposals Rousseau makes for Poland and for Corsica (discussed in ch. 6, below). See also SC Book 3 for Rousseau's general reflections on the diverse forms of government and the considerations which bear on assessing the suitability of these.

5 On the individual Veto, see GP ch. 7 (III, 975ff).

6 See Plato's *Gorgias*, 466a–469c, for the classic discussion of the difference(s) between doing as one wants and doing (thereby) what one wills. Rousseau undoubtedly knew and was influenced by Plato's discussion.

7 See Dent (4), and ch. 7, below.

8 See White for clarification of this distinction.

9 Rousseau's discussion bears here, again, very close likeness to Plato's. Consider, in

particular, the challenges of Glaucon and Adeimantus made to Socrates in *Republic*, Book 2, about the source of the need to behave justly.

10  Think, in this context, of the story of the Ring of Gyges which Glaucon tells to illustrate just this point to Socrates. *Republic*, 359c ff.

11  Of course, 'alienation' here does not signify self-estrangement, loss of possession of one's proper being and good. It means ceding to another (to others) the right of judgment or direction over one. Of course, the latter alienation often causes the former, in Rousseau's – or anyone's – view.

12  Compare Locke, §7ff on the 'executive' right of nature which is in 'every man's hand'. Part of the objective of civil association is, in Locke's view, to aid men in the exercise of the executive right while preventing abuses of it.

13  A clear statement of this is given by Anscombe, *passim*.

14  Aristotle gives his 'definition' of 'practical wisdom' at EN 1140 b 20; see also Book 6, ch. 9.

15  I have preferred to call this 'principled' freedom only to deflect, for a moment, the prejudicial preconceptions which the notions of 'moral' or 'positive' freedom are so apt to arouse at once. I noted this in ch. 4. But I dare say those preconceptions will not be dislodged. For an excellent discussion of 'positive' freedom see Taylor.

16˙ This, once more, draws on Platonic material. Compare the discussion of Simonides' poem in the *Protagoras*, 339a–347b, about how hard (difficult) it is to become, and to remain, good.

17  For this, see Tolstoy, Book 8, ch. 11ff.

### Chapter 6  The Ideal State: Problems and Practicalities

1  'Considerations on the Government of Poland, and on its proposed reformation', was completed in 1772. The 'Constitutional project for Corsica' was begun in 1765, but never completed. These works are printed in OC III, 901–50 (Corsica); 953–1041 (Poland).

2  For criticism of this sort of idea, see Oakeshott, the title essay and *passim*.

3  Hobbes, in making his distinction between laws obliging '*in foro interno*' but not necessarily '*in foro externo*' is making just the same point. Hobbes, Part 1, ch. 15.

4  Compare Aristotle, EN 1155a 15–30 for the rightly famous remark that justice is a 'watery' kind of friendship. Aristotle's entire discussion of the relations between justice and friendship is highly pertinent. EN Books 8 and 9.

5  This summary of the historical circumstances surrounding the production of these two works is taken from Watkins (ed.), pp. xxxv–xxxviii.

6  I shall only give limited specific references to these works. They are short, and it should be easy to find the sources for the points made.

7  See Dent (3) for a discussion of a very closely related issue in the interpretation of Plato's *Republic*.

### Chapter 7  Public and Private Religion

1  Rousseau's 'Letter to d'Alembert on the Theatre' is, unfortunately, not yet included in OC., since vol. 5 of that has still not appeared. Bloom's translation should be consulted.

2  This more or less self-contained section from *Emile* has often been published separately, as a statement of Rousseau's religious ideas. The views expressed in it seem to have been primarily responsible for the whole book's being banned by the

Archbishop of Paris. See Rousseau's 'Letter to de Beaumont' on this (OC IV, 927ff).

3 I have discussed some of the issues here also in Dent (4).

4 The content of the previous two paragraphs is taken pretty well verbatim from Dent (4).

5 Horowitz gives a Freudian interpretation of the 'pathology of conscience' in *Julie* in ch. 6 of his book.

6 Compare Kant (2) p. 88, note 1 on the consciousness of the moral law being the *ratio cognoscendi* of (transcendental) freedom. See also Beck, p. 73.

7 These ideas are drawn from Wollheim (2) ch. 7 (who draws on Klein's notions).

8 Wollheim (2), p. 211.

9 Wollheim (2), p. 216.

# Bibliography

The bibliography is composed as follows. Section A comprises further works of Rousseau's, and some additional translations, not already mentioned in 'Works Cited in the Text' at the start. Section B comprises largely biographical works about Rousseau. Section C comprises some commentaries, and collections of essays, on Rousseau, in English and French. Section D comprises some articles on those aspects of Rousseau's work central to this book. Section E comprises books and articles otherwise referred to in this book.

The volume of material written on Rousseau's life and work is enormous. I have made a very small selection from this.

### Section A: Further Works of Rousseau, and Translations (put as far as possible in order of writing)

*Lettre à M. Grimm*, OC III, 59–70. (tr. in Gourevitch).
*Essai sur l'Origine des Langues*, ed. C. Porset (Bordeaux, 1970).
Écrits sur L'Abbé de Saint-Pierre:
  *Le Projet de Paix Perpétuelle*, OC III, 563–600.
  *Polysynodie*, OC III, 617–45.
*Lettre à M. d'Alembert*, ed. M. Fuchs (Geneva, 1948).
*Julie, ou La Nouvelle Héloîse*, OC vol. II.
*Julie, or the New Eloise*, tr. and abr., Judith H. McDowell (Pennsylvania State Univ. Press., 1968).
*Lettres Morales*, OC IV, 1081–118.
*Emile*, Ms. Favre, OC IV, 55–238.
*Emile et Sophie, ou Les Solitaires*, OC IV. 881–924.
*La Profession de foi du Vicaire Savoyard*, ed. P-M. Masson (Paris-Fribourg 1914).
*Du Contract Social*, ou Essai sur la Forme de la République (1st version), OC III, 281–346.
*Oeuvres Complètes de J.-J. Rousseau*, Hachette (Paris 1865–   ).
*Oeuvres Complètes de J.-J Rousseau*, ed. M. Launay (Paris 1967–   ).
*Correspondence Général de J.-J. Rousseau*, ed. T. Dufour and P. Plan (Paris, 1924–   ).
*Correspondence Complète de J.-J. Rousseau*, ed. R.A. Leigh (Geneva, 1965–   ).
*The Political Writings of J.-J. Rousseau*, (2 vols), ed. C.E. Vaughan (Cambridge, 1915).
*Du Contrat Social*, ed. R. Grimsley (Oxford, 1972).

*Rousseau: Religious Writings*, ed. R. Grimsley (Oxford, 1970).
*The Indispensable Rousseau*, ed. J.H. Mason (London, 1979).
*A Discourse on Inequality*, tr. M. Cranston (Harmondsworth, 1984).
*Discourse on the Origin of Inequality*, in *The Social Contract and Discourse on the Origin of Inequality*, ed. L.G. Crocker (New York, 1967).
*The First and Second Discourses*, tr. R. and J. Masters (New York, 1964).
*Politics and the Arts*: Rousseau's Letter to d'Alembert, tr. and intro. Allan Bloom (Glencoe, 1960).
*Essay on the Origin of Languages*, in J.H. Moran and A. Gode: *On the Origin of Languages* (New York, 1966).
*The Government of Poland*, tr. W. Kendall (New York, 1972).
*The Social Contract*, tr. M. Cranston (Harmondsworth, 1968).
*On The Social Contract*, tr. and ed. R. and J. Masters (New York, 1978).
*Emile*, tr. B. Foxley (London 1911).
*Botany – A Study of Pure Curiosity*, tr. K. Ottevanger (illus.P.J.Redouté) (London, 1979).

## Section B: Biographical Works

Cranston M., *Jean-Jacques: The Early Life and Works of J.-J. Rousseau* (London, 1983).
Crocker L.G., *J.-J. Rousseau* (2 vols) (New York, 1968; 1973).
Green, F.C., *J.-J. Rousseau* (Cambridge, 1955).
Grimsley, R., *J.-J. Rousseau* (Brighton, 1983).
Guéhenno, J., *J.-J. Rousseau* (2 vols) (London, 1966).
Huizinga, J.H., *The Making of a Saint* (London, 1975).
Miller, J., *Rousseau: The Dreamer of Democracy* (New Haven 1984).

## Section C: Commentaries and Collections of Articles

### Commentaries:

Babbitt, I., *Rousseau and Romanticism* (Boston, 1919).
Becker, C., *The Heavenly City of the Eighteenth Century Philosophers* (New Haven, 1932).
Berman, M., *The Politics of Authenticity* (New York, 1973).
Broome, J.H., *Rousseau: A Study of His Thought* (London 1962).
Burgelin, P., *La Philosophie de l'Existence de J.-J. Rousseau* (Paris, 1952).
Cassirer, E., *The Question of J.-J. Rousseau* (Bloomington, 1963).
Cassirer, E., *Roussau, Kant, Goethe* (Princeton, 1963).
Chapman, J.W., *Rousseau, Totalitarian or Liberal?* (New York 1956).
Charvet, J., *The Social Problem in the Philosophy of Rousseau* (Cambridge, 1974).
Cobban, A., *Rousseau and the Modern State* (London, 1964).
Colletti, L., *From Rousseau to Lenin* (London, 1972).
Crocker, L.G., *Rousseau's Social Contract* (Cleveland, 1968).
Derathé, R., *Le Rationalisme de Rousseau* (Paris, 1948).
Derathé, R., *Rousseau et la Science Politique de son Temps* (Paris, 1950).

Durkheim, E., *Montesquieu and Rousseau* (Michegan, 1960).
Einaudi, M., *The Early Rousseau* (Ithaca, 1967).
Ellenburg, S., *Rousseau's Political Philosophy* (Ithaca, 1976).
Gildin, H., *Rousseau's Social Contract* (Chicago, 1983).
Grimsley, R., *J.-J.Rousseau: A Study in Self-Awareness* (Cardiff, 1961).
Grimsley, R., *Rousseau and the Religious Quest* (Oxford, 1973).
Grimsley, R., *The Philosophy of Rousseau* (Oxford, 1973).
Hall, J.C., *Rousseau: An Introduction to his Political Philosophy* (London, 1973).
Hendel, C.W., *J.-J. Rousseau, Moralist* (New York, 1934).
Horowitz, A., *Rousseau, Nature, and History* (Toronto, 1987).
Levine, A., *The Politics of Autonomy* (Massachusetts 1976).
Masters, R.D., *The Political Philosophy of J.-J. Rousseau* (Princeton, 1968).
Noone, J.B., *Rousseau's Social Contract* (London, 1980).
Raymond, M., *J.-J. Rousseau, la quête de soi et la Reverie* (Paris, 1962).
Riley, P., *The General Will Before Rousseau* (Princeton, 1986).
Roche, K.F., *Rousseau: Stoic and Romantic* (London, 1974).
Schwartz, J., *The Sexual Politics of Jean-Jacques Rousseau* (Chicago, 1984).
Shklar, J.N., *Men and Citizens*: A Study of Rousseau's Social Theory (Cambridge, 1969).
Starobinski, J., *J.-J. Rousseau: la transparence et l'obstacle* (Paris, 1970).
Talmon, J.F., *The Origins of Totalitarian Democracy* (London, 1961).
Trilling, L., *Sincerity and Authenticity* (London, 1972).
Volpe, G. della, *Rousseau and Marx* (London, 1978).
Wright, E.H., *The Meaning of Rousseau* (London, 1929).

## Collections of Articles:

Cranston, M. and Peters, R.S. (eds), *Hobbes and Rousseau* (New York, 1972).
*Daedalus* No. 3, Summer 1978, *Rousseau for our Time.*
Harvey, S., Hobson M., Kelley, D. and Taylor, S.S.B. (eds), *Reappraisals of Rousseau* (Manchester 1980).
Leigh, R.A. (ed.), *Rousseau after Two Hundred Years* (Cambridge, 1982).
MacAdam, J., Neumann, M. and La France, G. (eds), *Trent Rousseau Papers* (Ottawa, 1980).
*Yale French Studies*, XXVIII (Winter 1961-62), *Jean Jacques Rousseau.*

More generally, *Studies on Voltaire and the Eighteenth Century* has numerous articles on Rousseau, as do the *Annales de la Société Jean-Jacques Rousseau.*

### Section D: Articles on Rousseau (a very small selection)

Bloom, A., 'The Education of Democratic Man: Emile'; in *Daedalus*, Summer 1978 (revised version printed as Introduction to Bloom's translation of *Emile*).
Bloom, A., 'Jean-Jacques Rousseau', in L. Strauss and J. Cropsey (eds): *History of Political Philosophy* (Chicago, 1963).
Canovan, M., 'Rousseau's Two Concepts of Citizenship,' in E. Kennedy and S. Mendus: *Women in Western Political Philosophy* (Brighton, 1987).
de Man, P., 'The Rhetoric of Blindness', in P. de Man: *Blindness and Insight* (London, 1983).

Dent, N.J.H. (4), 'Rousseau and Respect for Others', in S. Mendus (ed.): *Justifying Toleration* (Cambridge, forthcoming).

Gay, P., 'Reading about Rousseau', in P. Gay: *The Party of Humanity* (London, 1964).

Gourevitch, V., 'Rousseau on the Arts and Sciences'; *Journal of Philosophy*, 1972.

Hall, R.W., 'Plato and Rousseau'; *Aperion*, 1982.

Hill, T., 'Servility and Self-Respect'; *Monist*, 1973.

Lloyd, G., 'Rousseau on Reason, Nature and Women'; *Metaphilosophy*, 1983.

Lovejoy, A., 'The Supposed Primitivism of Rousseau's Discourse on Inequality', in A. Lovejoy: *Essays in the History of Ideas* (Baltimore, 1948).

MacAdam, J.I., 'Rousseau and the Friends of Despotism'; *Ethics*, 1963.

MacAdam, J.I., 'The Discourse on Inequality and the Social Contract', *Philosophy*, 1972.

Plamenatz, J., 'On Le Forcera d'Etre Libre', in M. Cranston and R.S. Peters (eds).

Shklar, J., 'Rousseau's Images of Authority', in M. Cranston and R.S. Peters (eds.)

Skillen, A., 'Rousseau and the Fall of Social Man'; *Philosophy*, 1975.

Winch, P., 'Man and Society in Hobbes and Rousseau', in M. Cranston and R.S. Peters (eds,); in P. Winch: *Ethics and Action* (London, 1972).

Winch, P., 'Human Nature', in P. Winch: *Ethics and Action* (London, 1972).

Wokler, R., 'The Influence of Diderot on the Political Theory of Rousseau'; *Studies in Voltaire and the Eighteenth Century*, CXXXII, 1975.

Wokler, R., 'Perfectible Apes in Decadent Culture'; *Daedalus*, Summer 1978.

Wokler R., 'Rousseau's Perfectibilian Libertarianism', in A. Ryan (ed.): *The Idea of Freedom* (Oxford, 1979).

Wokler, R., 'The Discourse sur les Sciences et les Arts and its offspring', in Harvey, Hobson, Kelley, Taylor (eds).

Wokler, R., 'Rousseau and Marx', in D. Miller and L. Siedentop (eds): *The Nature of Political Theory* (Oxford, 1983).

## Section E: Books and Articles Otherwise Referred to

Anscombe, G.E.M., 'On the Source of the Authority of the State', in G.E.M. Anscombe: *Ethics, Religion and Politics*, Collected Papers III, (Blackwell, 1981).

Aristotle, *Politics*, tr. J. Warrington (London, 1961).

Augustine, St, *Confessions*, tr. R.S. Pine-Coffin (Harmondsworth, 1961).

Beck, L.W., *A Commentary on Kant's Critique of Practical Reason* (Chicago, 1963).

Butler, J., *Fifteen Sermons*, ed. W.R. Matthews (London, 1969).

Cavell, S. (1), 'The Avoidance of Love', in S. Cavell: *Must We Mean What We Say?* (New York, 1969).

Cavell, S. (2), *The Claim of Reason* (Oxford, 1979).

Cioffi, F., 'Information, Contemplation and Social Life', in Royal Institute of Philosophy Lectures, vol. 4: *The Proper Study* (London, 1971).

Clark, S.R.L., *From Athens to Jerusalem* (Oxford, 1984).

Dent, N.J.H. (1), 'Virtues and Actions', *Philosophical Quarterly*, 1975.

Dent, N.J.H. (2), *The Moral Psychology of the Virtues* (Cambridge, 1984).

Dent, N.J.H. (3), 'Plato and Social Justice', *Polis*, 1987.

Eliot, T.S., 'The Love Song of J. Alfred Prufrock', in T.S. Eliot: *Collected Poems 1909-1962* (London, 1963).

Foot, P.R., 'Moral Beliefs', *Proceedings of the Aristotelian Society*, 1958-9; reprinted in P.R. Foot (ed.): *Theories of Ethics* (Oxford, 1967).

Geach, P. (1), 'Aquinas', in G.E.M. Anscombe and P.T. Geach: *Three Philosophers* (Blackwell, 1967).

Geach, P. (2), *Providence and Evil* (Cambridge, 1977).

Gilbert, A., 'Democracy and Individuality'; in E.F. Paul, F.D. Miller, J. Paul and J. Ahrens: *Marxism and Liberalism* (Blackwell, 1986).

Gosling, J., *Plato*, (London 1973).

Hobbes, T., *Leviathan*, ed. M. Oakeshott (Blackwell n.d.).

Hofstader, R., *The Paranoid Style in American Politics*, and other essays (London, 1966).

Hume, D., *An Enquiry Concerning the Principles of Morals*, ed. L.A. Selby-Bigge (Oxford, 1963).

Joachim, H.H., *Aristotle, The Nicomachean Ethics*, ed. D.A. Rees (Oxford, 1955).

Kant, I. (1), *The Groundwork of the Metaphysic of Morals*, in:*The Moral Law*, tr. H.J. Paton (London 1961). Page references are given as to the Prussian Academy Edition.

Kant, I. (2), *Critique of Practical Reason*, tr. T.K. Abbott (London, 1963).

Klein, M. (1), *Envy and Gratitude and Other Works* 1946–1963 (Collected Papers Vol. III) (London, 1975).

Klein, M. (2), 'Envy and Gratitude'; in Klein (1).

Klein, M. (3), 'Our Adult World and Its Roots in Infancy', in Klein (1).

Klein, M. (4), 'On the Development of Mental Functioning', in Klein (1).

Klein, M. (5), 'On Mental Health'; in Klein (1).

Klein, M. (6), 'Some Reflections on *The Orestia*', in Klein (1).

Klein, M. (7), 'On Identification', in Klein (1).

Locke, J., *Second Treatise of Government*, ed. P. Laslett (Cambridge, 1963).

Lovelace, R., 'To Lucasta, Going to the Warres'. In: *The Penguin Book of English Verse*, ed. J. Hayward (Harmondsworth, 1956).

Mill, J.S., 'Essay on Bentham'; in:*Mill's Essays on Literature and Society*, ed. J.B. Schneewind (New York, 1965).

Oakeshott, M., 'Rationalism in Politics', in M. Oakeshott: *Rationalism in Politics and Other Essays* (London, 1962).

Okin, S.M., *Women in Western Political Thought* (Princeton, 1979).

Plamenatz, J., *Man and Society*, vol. 1 (London, 1963).

Plato, *Gorgias*, tr. W. Hamilton (Harmondsworth, 1971).

Plato, *Republic*, tr. H.D.P. Lee (Harmondsworth, 1974).

Schopenhauer, A. (1), *Essay on the Freedom of the Will*, tr. K. Kolenda (Indianapolis, 1960).

Schopenhauer, A. (2), *On The Basis of Morality*, tr. E.F. Payne (Indianapolis, 1965).

Scruton, R., *Sexual Desire* (London, 1986).

Segal, H., *An Introduction to the Work of Melanie Klein* (London, 1973).

Smith, A., *The Theory of the Moral Sentiments*, ed. D.D. Raphael and A.L. Macfie (Oxford, 1976).

Solomon, R., *History and Human Nature*, (University Press of America, 1979).

Sparshott, F., 'Five Virtues in Plato and Aristotle'; *The Monist*, 54 (1970).

Spinoza, B., *Ethics*, ed. J. Wild (New York, 1958).

Strawson, P.F., 'Freedom and Resentment', *Proceedings of the British Academy*, 48 (1962).

Taylor, C., 'What's Wrong with Negative Liberty', in A. Ryan (ed.): *The Idea of Freedom* (Oxford, 1979).

Thucydides, *The Peloponnesian War*, tr. R. Warner (Harmondsworth, 1972).

Tolstoy, L., *Anna Karenina* (any edition).

Veblen, T., *The Theory of the Leisure Class* (London, 1970).

Watkins, F., 'Introduction' to: *Rousseau: Political Writings* (Edinburgh, 1953).

Weil, S., '*The Iliad*, Poem of Might', in S. Weil: *Intimations of Christianity Among the Ancient Greeks* (London, 1957).

White, A.R., 'On Being Obliged'; in: *The Human Agent*, Royal Institute of Philosophy Lectures, 1, 1966–7 (London, 1968).

Wilson, B. (ed.), *Rationality* (Blackwell, 1970).

Winch, P., *The Idea of a Social Science* (London, 1963).

Wollheim, R. (1), 'The Moral Psychology of British Idealism and the English School of Psychoanalysis Compared', *Proceedings of the British Academy*, 61 (1975).

Wollheim, R. (2), *The Thread of Life* (Cambridge, 1984).

# Index